Population Education

J.C. Aggarwal

SHIPRA

Rs. 1450

ISBN: 978-81-7541-663-5

2013 Revised Edition
(2010, 2009, 3rd Revised & Enlarged Edition)

Population Education

Published by:
SHIPRA PUBLICATIONS
LG 18-19, Pankaj Central Market,
I.P. Ext., Patparganj, Delhi 110092, India
Ph.: +91 11 22235152/6152
Email: info@shiprapublication.com
Website: www.shiprapublication.com

Preface to the Revised Edition

The author is grateful to the readers for their encouraging response to the publication.

Two chapters added in this Third edition are— 1. Main Features of World Population 2. Demographic Statistics of India vis-a-vis the World, while following six chapters were added in Second enlarged and revised edition— 1. Population Dynamics: Distribution and Density; 2. Population Composition: Age, Sex, Rural and Urban; 3. Fertility Morality and Migration (Mobility); 4. World Population: Trends and its Economic, Social, Political and Educational Implications; Malthusian Theory of Population; Mass Media and Audio-Visual Aids (AVS) in Population Education.

The material has been adapted and computed from the Census of India 2011 and 2001, Economic Surveys, The State of World's Children, UN Wall Charts and several other UN publications. Author is pleased acknowledge and thank all the publishers and their authors

It is hoped that this revised and enlarged edition would prove more useful.

Preface

The book attempts to provide a comprehensive and meaningful account of population education—its concepts, need and objectives for introduction at different levels of the educational structure. It also analyses the strategies for the formulation and implementation of curriculum contents and activities suiting each level. Population growth and economic-cum human development of a country act and react on each other this race, the former is mostly winner in a developing country like India and latter is a loser. This phenomenon has been explained with a comprehensive study of several developing and developed countries.

Population education seems to be the only potent instrument to generate the necessary energy and enthusiasm among the people and especially the students to stabilise population so that people of India may enjoy a reasonable quality of life.

Every possible effort is made to illustrate the text with boxes, charts, diagrams, graphs, maps and tables, etc. The publication incorporated population, demographic and human development data on a number of developing and developed countries.

The material included here has been adopted/adapted and computed from the *Census of India 2001: Provisional Tables, Series-I, India, Paper I of 2001,* Annual Reports of Several Ministries of Government of India, *Indian Economy Survey 2000-2001,* Ministry of Finance Government of India, *The State of World's Children 2001 (UNICEF), Long-Range World Population Projections: Based on 1988 Revision (2000), UN Population, Environment and Development 2001*, UN and several other United Nations Publications.

The publication, though designed as a textbook, should also serve as a handy reference tool for several sections of people interested in population dynamics and human development of nations.

The author extends his grateful thanks to all the authors and the publishers whose publications he has made use of in the preparation of this book.

J.C. Aggarwal

Contents

The theory of Malthus still holds good to a great ... of least developed and slow developing countries ... literal meaning of what he said, the picture presented ... without significance. Message is very clear. Growing po... under control for enjoying a reasonable standard of ...

1

Concept of Population Education

1.1 PROBLEM OF 3PS

There is no doubt that population explosion in India has been eroding its natural resources and diluting all economic and social gains. The Three population, poverty and pollution (environmental degradation – brushing aside moral degradation or moral pollution) have close linkages. In fact, population explosion is the 'mother' of poverty and environmental pollution. Our quest for adequate food, shelter, clothing, health and work for all will remain an illusion unless success is achieved in bringing under control the galloping growth of our population. It is, therefore, very essential to understand the meaning, concept and significance of population education.

Thomas Robert Malthus (1766–1834), an English economist was the first thinker to discuss the impact of growing population on the progress and prosperity of the nations. He is usually called the 'Father of modern population study.' He brought population study within the orbit of social science. In his 'Essay on population' he stated that *populations when unchecked reproduce at a geometric rate (2, 4, 8, 16, 32, ...) while food increases at an arithmetic rate (1, 2, 3, 4, 5, ...). The ultimate result would be lack of enough food to support such a huge population and hence individuals would face death due to starvation and malnutrition... The natural disasters would then control the size of population.*

The theory of Malthus still holds good to a considerable extent in the case of least developed and slow developing countries. If we do not go by the literal meaning of what he said, the picture presented by him is not entirely without significance. Moral is very clear. Growing population must be brought under control for enjoying a reasonable standard of life.

1.2 CONCEPT OF POPULATION EDUCATION AND ITS MEANING

The credit for introducing the concept of population goes to Dr. Sloan Wayland of Teachers College, Columbia University. He visited India in 1965 at the invitation of the Government of India and conducted seminars and workshops on population education.

Several attempts have been made to define population education but no commonly accepted concept has emerged. Perhaps this difficulty has arisen on account of three reasons.

First, the concept of population education is of recent origin.

Second, population issues are not totally similar in all countries.

Third, the traditional and cultural values of different countries are not the same.

Here, some important definitions of population education are given to have its clear perception.

1. According to Harol Howe, population education is 'the educational process by which a revision of attitudes towards family size is to be brought about. The process draws on the resources of a number of fields at all levels of education.' This definition of population education tends to equate population education with family size. It is, therefore, very limited in its scope.
2. In the words of Chauls, "A population education programme should within the context of the student's culture, his society's population situation, and his individual perception of that situation, assist the student to arrive at a more rational comprehension of his population situation, plus the effective prerequisites to act' on his increased rationality. (*Journal of Family Welfare,* December 1970, March 1971, 1973, Family Planning Association of India, Bombay)
3. Intensive Training Programme on Population Education conducted by the Department of Education Philippines in 1972 defined population education as, "Population education is the process of developing awareness and understanding population situation as well as a rational attitude and behaviour towards this situation for the attainment of quality of life for the individual, the family, the community, the nation and the world."
4. According to Massials, "Population is the teaching and learning of reliable knowledge about the ways of inquiring into the nature of human population and the natural and human consequences of population change." (Mehta, T.S. and Chandra, R. (Eds.) *Population Education – Selected Readings*, NCERT, New Delhi, 1972.)
5. Population Education Bureau, Washington (1971) stated, "Population education is an attempt to create a deep, universal, action-guiding perception of the consequences of demographic change. It seeks to bring about a realisation of the individual, family, social and environmental efforts of the explosive increase in human population, the rapid shifts in the concentration and distribution of people, the implications of changing age and other demographic patterns and the conceivable options that may be open to mankind to cope with the consequent problems. It is focused primarily on students who will become the principal child bearers within one two decades."
6. Thomas Poffenberger regards population as, "the communication of those aspects of population dynamics which indicate the significance of population growth in terms of its social, economic and political consequences for a given area: ('*Population Education and the School Curriculum*'. UNESCO Regional Office for Education in Asia, and the Pacific, Bangkok, 1972)

7. A UNESCO Conference on Population Education and Family Planning organised at the Principal Regional Office for Asia and the Pacific (PROAP), Bangkok in September-October 1970 defined population in these words, "Population education is an educational programme which provides for a study of the population situation in the family, community, nation and world, with the purpose of developing in the students rational and responsible attitudes and behaviour towards that situation."
8. Viederman defines population education as, "Population education is a process by which the student investigates and explores the nature and meaning of population processes, population characteristics, the causes of population change and the consequences of these processes, characteristics and changes for himself and his family, for society and for the world." ('*Population Education: Selected Readings*' NCERT, 1972).

   Two most important and comprehensive definitions which explain the concept of population education more clearly and comprehensively are discussed below.
9. Prof. Sloan Wayland explains the concept and meaning of population education in these words, "Regardless the terms used, we are concerned about the situation in the formal system of instructional settings in which young people will come to understand the circumstances which led to the adoption of family planning as public policy and to understand that for the family and the nation, family planning is possible and desirable. This would include an understanding of the relationship of population dynamics to economic and social development of the country and the implications of family size for the quality of life of the individual family. The particular instructional activities at any given school level and in any particular subject field, would of course, be devised in a manner which would be pedagogically sound and appropriate for the particular society." (*Report of the National Seminar on Population Education,* Bombay, NCERT, 1969)

   The definition given by Prof. Sloan appears to be a complete and detailed exposition of the concept and meaning of population education. It also indicates its scope which is quite relevant to the present situation. The main strain of this definition is on better quality of life for the individual, family and the nation.
10. Smt. Avabai B. Wadia, President Family Planning Association of India explains the concept of population education in these words, "Population education is primarily an education programme dealing with the influence of population trends on society and the individual. Education is not population dynamics, is not propaganda, or promoting a set of ideas but a way of conveying knowledge and creating awareness which will help, in course of time, to bring about, new attitudes and behaviour patterns." ('*Report of the Proceedings of Seventh All India Conference*, F.P.A.I., Manipal 1971)

1.3 DEFINING POPULATION AS A FORMIDABLE TASK

It is a very challenging task to give a universally accepted definition of population education. In simple language, population education may be defined as a process of bringing about a change in the attitudes and behaviour patterns of the individual which may enable him to make rational decisions on population issues and implementing them so that it helps him to achieve better quality of life not only for himself but also for the family and the nation. Smt. Avabai B. Wadia, in this context has very aptly observed, "One has strong feeling that population education seems to be one of those areas of knowledge where definitions will probably follow the empirical programmes evolved rather than the other way round. It, is therefore, quite possible to move on the action programmes without spending too much time on perfecting theories."

1.4 POPULATION EDUCATION AND SEX EDUCATION

In the words of D. Gopal Rao, the difference is shown as, "The need for population education mainly arose because of the consequences of the imbalance between the population and world resources. Family life education in the west grew out of the growing evidence of the disintegration of the family, whereas sex education developed as a reaction to an increase in general diseases and out of wedlock pregnancies."

In sex education, the stress is on the individual whereas in population education, it is the interaction between the individual, family and society.

1.5 POPULATION EDUCATION AND FAMILY PLANNING

Taylor Daniel in his book *Developing a Foundation for Population Education* (1968) stresses the motivational relationship between a population education programme and the practice of family planning.

Population has a two-fold task : it is both motivational (encouraging people to adopt family planning) and instructional (teaching students in particular and people in general).

Burbson considers it relevant to include both sex education and family life education within the scope of education.

(Family Planning is discussed separately).

1.6 POPULATION EDUCATION AS AN INNOVATION

Some thinkers regard population as an innovation. It is argued in this respect that it attempts to provide a significant dimension to educational goals.

In the first instance, we may consider the meaning and characteristics of an innovation and then apply these to population education.

The concept of innovation has been described by the Third Regional UNESCO Conference 1991 in these words, "Innovation is the introduction of a new idea, a process or technique. It is not a change for the sake of change. It implies an awareness of the inadequacy of an existing practice or technique, an attitude of searching for new ideas, and put them to use."

According to H.S. Bhola, "An innovation is a concept, an attitude, a tool with accompanying skills introduced to a system or culture which had not been functionally incorporated before."

An innovation has the following characteristics:

1. It is a new idea.
2. It is considered qualitatively superior to the present situation.
3. It is a planned effort.
4. It has an element of specificity.
5. It has functional utility.
6. It is a configuration of ideas.
7. It results in new resources of learning.
8. It is universally applicable with local modification.

Population education fulfils all the above-mentioned characteristics of an innovation.

In due course, when population education becomes an integral part of the educational programme, it will lose the status of an innovation.

1.7 IMPORTANT CHARACTERISTICS OF POPULATION EDUCATION

1. Population education is essentially an educational response to a felt need for a problem – a major national as well as global concern of a great magnitude.
2. Population education is a long term and a continuing process.
3. Population is not an isolate educational programme. It is an integral part of all school activities.
4. Population education is needed for all sections of people.
5. Schools have a special responsibility for imparting population education to the future citizens.
6. Population education can be imparted through formal, informal and non-formal methods of teaching-learning.
7. Like any other innovation, its introduction in an effective manner is beset with several problems. A strong political will and educational commitment are needed for getting the desired results.
8. Population education is needed for all sections of the society.
9. Population education is needed for the developed, developing and least developed countries.
10. Population education is not confined to classroom. It must go beyond it.

1.8 SCOPE OF POPULATION EDUCATION

Prof. Sloan R. Wayland of the Columbia University includes the following elements in population education:

1. *Basic Instruction in Population Dynamics*: Students can be instructed in the pattern of population growth with particular attention to birth and death rates and rates of population increase in their own countries. As the students progress through the schools, the world-wide picture of population growth

can be examined. In classes in national, regional or world history, in geography, and in civics, the significance of population growth can be studied. Routine problems in arithmetic exercises using population data can provide incidental learning.

2. *Development of Basic Understanding of the Process of Human Reproduction*: This can be achieved progressively at different grade levels as the interests and maturity of students permit. Specific facts of contraception need not be presented but factors which facilitate or impede reproduction in various forms of life can be identified. The science curriculum is a natural setting for such instruction. For some age levels and in some schools, health education or domestic science classes may be appropriate. It is assumed that both boys and girls would be reached in instructional settings where the materials that are introduced will seem to fit naturally into the sequence of study.

3. *Understanding of Health Problems Associated with Child-bearing:* Several well-established clinical findings could be examined here concerning the health risks of morbidity and mortality of the mother associated with

(a) pregnancy of the young mother and the older mother;
(b) short intervals between pregnancies;
(c) high parity.

The health problems of children born under the same three conditions should also be considered. From such an examination the health values for mother and their offspring involved in marriage at a mature age in spacing of births and in limitation in the size of the family could be shown. The propositions here are sufficiently simple to be considered in health education classes in the lower grades but also should be examined in more detail in high level health education and science classes. Both boys and girls should be equally concerned since the future father's stake in the health of his wife and children is no less important than that of the future mother.

4. *Appreciation of the Relationship between Quality of Life for a Family and its Size*: In addition to the health values noted earlier, consideration needs to be given to the economic and social consequences for a family of the presence of a number of children. With a given level of resources and earning power, the larger the family, the smaller the share per child. The consequences are felt not only for housing and food but also in terms of the family's ability to provide for the education, health and other needs of children. The analysis of these problems can be viewed both in terms of the individual family and in terms of a community or total society.

5. *Appreciation of the Significance of Population Characteristics and Policies for Social and Economic Development*: In the secondary schools where national history and current development problems are considered, one could expect that adequate treatment of population could be included. Similarly in geography, more serious attention to population is possible. In the lower schools, a selected set of basic ideas could be included with emphasis on the local community, particularly in the social studies classes.

6. *Familiarity with the Population Policies and Family Planning Programme of One's Own Country*: In the context of becoming socialised for adult citizenship roles, each student can be made familiar with the implicit or explicit natural population policies and programmes in family planning. In the lower grades, the presence of family planning facilities and symbols can be treated along with other community resources. A fuller explanation of the factors which have led to the development of current policies and programmes can be handled in increasing depth at the upper school levels.

Students should know enough about the purpose and resources of local family planning clinics, public and private, so that they will be in a position to take advantage of these facilities if they should want to when they are married. Knowledge of the purpose and availability of clinics can be transmitted without teaching about specific contraception methods, particularly in view of the rapidly changing role of contraceptives.

Dr. S.C. Cool (1969) has observed, "Population education must go beyond the classrooms into the homes, the temples, the bazaars, the firms, the factories and, indeed, into every aspect of human existence."

In brief, scope of population education includes the following elements:

1. Basic instruction in population dynamics – pattern of population growth.
2. Development of basic understanding of the process of human reproduction.
3. Understanding of health problems associated with child bearing.
4. Appreciation of the relationship between the quality of life of a family and its size.
5. Appreciation of the significance of population characteristics and policies for social and economic development.
6. Familiarity with the population policies and family planning programmes of one's own country.

1.9 WHY DO WE START POPULATION EDUCATION PROGRAMME IN SCHOOLS?

Population education is given in schools because of the following reasons:

1. School is a social institution started by the society for serving the changing needs of the society.
2. Schools are the appropriate places for laying the foundations of a well ordered life.
3. In the plastic period of their life, students (future parents) can acquire, develop and strengthen knowledge, attitudes and skills regarding population education.
4. Schools have a tradition of being future oriented.
5. Schools are engaged in adopting new inventions and changes.

1.10 PROBLEMS AND SUGGESTIONS FOR INTRODUCING POPULATION EDUCATION

The concept of population education is very new. There are manifold problems for its introduction and its smooth conduct. These problems along with feasible suggestions are discussed below:

Problems Regarding Concept of Population Education: Aims and objectives of population education are not yet clear. The parents and teachers have some misunderstanding regarding objectives of population education. Seminars and symposia should be organised to explain the aims and objectives of population education to the parents and teachers from time to time.

Education of Teachers in Population Education: Our teachers in primary as well secondary schools are not adequately equipped with the right type of subject matter to be dealt within the area of population education and their information is not up to the mark. NCERT should produce suitable literature for teachers in this connection.

Curriculum Planning: The most important and fundamental problem regarding this area is the problem of curriculum, i.e., how it should be integrated with various subjects at the school stage and determination of the quality and quantity of this area at various stages of education. The NCERT and SCERTs and allied organisations have taken up this problem and have prepared guidelines for the use of teachers at various stages.

Education of Parents: Parents should be educated about the necessity of introduction of population education in schools. Common man tends to attribute all the socio-economic ills of poverty; spiralling prices, shortage of food and consumer goods etc. to mismanagement and inefficiency on the part of the government little realising that these are but some of the effects of rapid population growth. Moreover, he links population education with birth control devices. Thus, there is an urgent need that parents should be enlightened about the real objectives and contents of population education.

Co-ordination Among Various Agencies and Use of Technology: At present there is a shortage of suitable instructional material in this area. In order to teach this subject successfully and efficiently, ample use of Audio-Visual Aids is required. Radio, television, the newspapers, films and filmstrips can be utilised to overcome the shortage of needed instructional material. The Central Institute of Educational Technology, NCERT, New Delhi and State Institutes of Educational Technology should take up this challenge.

Need for Sustained Efforts: History bears witness to the fact that man, when threatened, is capable of extraordinary endeavour. Now, that man's very survival is at stake let us hope, he will control his numbers, stop polluting his environment and finally learn to live at peace with his fellow-beings.

1.11 WHAT, WHOM, WHO, WHERE, WHEN AND HOW OF POPULATION

Various dimensions of population education are illustrated in the Box

Why population education	Population education for enabling the students to understand the relationship between population and human development.
What of population education	Curriculum/Contents of population education.
Whom of population education (for whom population education)	For students in educational institutions and out of school youth.
Who of population education (Who is to impart population education)	Teachers and non-governmental organisations.
Where of population education (place or institution)	In educational institutions, in the families, in the adult education centres.
When of population education	Stages or levels or classes in which population education is to be included.
How of population education	Teaching-learning methodology of education. Motivational element.

2

Need and Importance of Population Education

2.1 INTRODUCTION

Charles Robert Darwin, (1809-82), a noted naturalist of England, in his famous book *The Origin of Species* made these observations, "Even slow-breeding man has doubled in twenty-five years, and at this rate, in less than a thousand years there would literally not be standing room for progeny." Alas! These words of wisdom have, by and large, not been given due attention by the people of the developing countries and especially of India. We ignored the significance of population education. The population scenario is very depressing and disturbing. Population of India has been increasing at an alarming rate. The result is there is a substantial population of India that is underfed, under-nourished, under-clothed, under-sheltered and without any reasonable facilities for education, health, sanitation, transport etc.

The situation may be stated as: In 1951, nearly 31 crore people of India lived on an area of 32,87,263 sq km. In 2011, on the same area, lived 121 crore people.

In other words more than three times the number of people shared the same area. The growing numbers present a very gloomy picture.

2.2 SELECTED OPINIONS ON THE NEED AND IMPORTANCE OF POPULATION EDUCATION

Basically school is an important agency of a society. It is expected to address itself to the various problems faced by the society. The Education Commission 1964-66, very aptly observed that the destiny of a nation is being shaped in its classroom. Appropriate knowledge, attitudes and skills regarding various dimensions of population would go a long way in determining and moulding the destiny of a nation in the right direction. Here some selected opinions of experts and thinkers are given on the need and importance of population education in the school programme.

1. *V.K.R.V. Rao*: In his inaugural address at the National Seminar on Population Education held in Bombay in 1969, the then Education Minister Dr. V.K.R.V. Rao highlighted the need and significance of population education as an important factor of human resource development. He said, "Population education is a subject by itself

and should essentially be treated as a part of the much large subject of human resource development, and be included in the educational framework in the light of this opinion."

2. *D. Gopal's Views*: At the Bombay Seminar, Kamala Rao and D. Gopal Rao said, "The investments and efforts will cost less but prove more effective and the learning quicker and more permanent if learners are exposed to those ideas (population concerns) in their young age through the usual channels of formal education."
3. *Edlefsen's View*: On the need and importance of population education for the young, Edlefsen S. in *Population Education : A New Role for the Regional Schools* (Bangkok, 1971), stated, "The young people will constitute the major portion of the adult population of the world in the next crucial decades, i.e. 1970-2000, and their respective behaviour will be of central importance to the efforts to control the rate of population growth. Yet in most countries throughout the world this group has received no attention in population limitation programmes."
4. *Asian Regional Workshop*: The Report of the Asian Regional Workshop on Population and Family Planning held at Bangkok in 1970 pinpointed the need for population education for the young in these words, "Over 40 per cent of the people in this region are still under fifteen years of age. This group will strongly influence the demographic situation in Asian countries in the next few decades. If their future population behaviour resembles that of our parents, today's population problems will be viewed, by comparison, as only minor disturbances. If, on the other hand, these young people become cognisant of the factors of their population, situation, and recognise that they necessitate more rational behaviour on their part, some of the worst consequences may be avoided."
5. *Prof. Jayasuriya's Views*: Prof. Jayasuriya (1972) highlighted the urgency of the introduction of a programme of population education in these words, "As needs can be postulated with varying degrees of seriousness, it is important to emphasise that population education is a matter of the greatest urgency in that the risks to the conduct of civilised life involved in the complex of problems associated with the growth of population are of such magnitude that every single day's delay intensifies them and increases the efforts that has to be made to cope with them."
6. *Noel David's View*: Prof. Noel David Burleson of the Harward University (1969) coined the term 'Population Awareness' which implies 'factual knowledge about population dynamics required to understand the nature and magnitude of the burden imposed by rapid population growth'. He strongly advocates population education and warns us against delay in introducing this in school programme. "Time is now .... Awareness after the impact impresses me as the essence of all tragedy."

7. *Smt. Avabai's Views*: Population education is essential for ensuring safe environment. Smt. Avabai Wadia (1973) strengthens this view in the following words, "What is most significant is that the developed countries with low birth rates who have hitherto felt that population planning was a necessity only in the poorer countries which had fast growing populations, are also coming round to this view point now, impelled by the need to prevent further destruction of the environment and to preserve an ecological balance."
8. *Viederaman's Views*: Viederaman (1972), justifies the need for population education for all countries, developing and developed ones, as the characteristics of a population and the changes that occur in a population touch upon all our lives, whether we believe our country to be overpopulated or under-populated. He further observes, "Population education is as valid for countries such as Argentina and Japan, where there is an assumption that more rather than fewer people may be necessary for reasons of achieving an adequate labour supply or economic growth, or other national goals as it is for countries such as India and the United States that acknowledge in varying degrees their population problems."
9. *Bombay Seminar on the Need for Population Education*: On this issue, Harold Howe stated, "Population education is a moulder of attitudes and a creator of predispositions favourable to the planned families of reduced size. Once the groundwork of receptive attitudes has been created, the direct means of birth control and family planning become more relevant to the individual and more likely to be used by them." (*Report of the National Seminar on Population Education*. NCERT, 1969).
10. *Asian Regional Workshop on the Need for Population Education*: The Bangkok Report of a Regional Workshop on Population and Family Education (1971) observed, "If educational systems are to be relevant to the needs of their societies, they must address themselves to the problems faced by their societies. In every country of the region (South-East Asia), population is one of the most important problems."
11. *Parekh's Views*: B.S. Parekh in his book *Population Education – Inception to Institutionalisation* (NCERT, 1985) advocated the introduction of population education in India on the following grounds:
    1. Better quality of life.
    2. Frontal attack on blind faith.
    3. Dignity of individual freedom.
    4. Establishing equality of sexes.
    5. Understanding the society.
    6. Increase in the national wealth.
    7. Comparison of the styles.
    8. Value-orientation.
    9. Planning a way of life.

2.3 FACTORS LEADING TO THE NEED AND IMPORTANCE OF POPULATION EDUCATION

From the above views of the great thinkers, we derive the following factors which highlight the need and importance of population education.

1. *Controlling Population Explosion*: There is an unprecedented population explosion which poses great challenges to the welfare of mankind. Population education can serve as a 'Safety Valve'.
2. *Ensuring Quality of Life*: Growing population is a great hindrance in enjoying a satisfying life. Over-population puts several checks on getting necessary commodities needed in life.
3. *Optimum use of Natural Resources*: Increasing population has led to an indiscriminate use of natural resources. Several problems have come up on account of this factor.
4. *Better Health*: On account of large number of births, health of women receives a great set back. Several diseases take a heavy toll of life.
5. *Solving Food Problem*: Developing countries find it very difficult to make adequate provision of food for their teeming millions.
6. *Checking Under-Nourishment*: Crores of people in the world and especially in the under–developed countries do not get the proper food.
7. *Well-rounded System of Education*: It is now universally accepted that education in population dynamics is quite necessary for a well-rounded system of education which aims at preparing young people for adult roles in future.
8. *Creation of Healthy Attitudes*: With a view to making a lasting impression on the minds of the children, it is necessary to make them aware of the population issues so that they develop healthy attitudes towards family limitations and act accordingly when the time for such decisions comes on their part.
9. *Impetus to Family Planning Programmes*: It is observed that family planning programmes have not made much headway primarily on account of lack of awareness and appreciation of these. Schools can play an active role in making the parents and the community feel the need for involvement.
10. *Appropriate Reproductive Behaviour*: It is estimated that nearly 45 per cent of our population is under 15 years of age. In the next few years, this group is likely to strongly influence the demographic scene. The reproductive behaviour of this section is very important. Therefore, this group must be properly informed of the harmful consequences arising out of population growth.
11. *Establishing Equality of Sexes*: Implementation of family planning programmes tends to create an impression that it is the female section that has the sole responsibility of using contraceptives. Males need to be impressed upon to accept family planning measures.
12. *Increasing National Wealth*: Population education enables us to look at the population not in terms of its number or consumers of goods and services but also producers of national wealth. It highlights the need for skilled population.

13. *Eradication of Blind Faith*: Population education acts as a spearhead of a frontal attack on blind faith, dogmas, fatalism and superstition.

14. *Value Orientation*: Population education helps us to develop socially desirable values in our children. It assists us to develop a sense of gender equality. It has great potential to develop healthy attitudes and imbibe the spirit of human off affiliation. It indicates how to develop discipline in sexual matters.

Summing Up

Population education is needed for developing, developed and least developed countries. Population education to be effective must be all pervasive. Its importance is not limited to any particular section of population. As observed by Smt. Avabai Wadia, "This new philosophy of living, based on the ideal of planned families, where there is concern not only for individual well-being but for the welfare of a society as a whole, is becoming essential."

3

Objectives of Population Education

3.1 THE NEED AND IMPORTANCE OF CLEAR-CUT OBJECTIVES OF POPULATION EDUCATION

The need and importance of formulating clear-cut objectives of any programme including an educational programme has been recognised by all planners and implementers. No definite programme can be planned and implemented unless the objectives are explicit and practicable. Unguided educational programmes cannot yield the desired results.

The objectives of population education set the directions which are to be followed to make the programme effective, efficient and inspirational. They provide the needed motivation to take up any programme.

Objectives of population education may be different in different countries in accordance with their special situations. Nevertheless the essence of objectives i.e. the improvement in the quality of life is the same.

The objectives of population education have been defined in different ways by experts and thinkers on the issue. Here an attempt is made to consider some of the main objectives of population formulated by prominent educators and national and international organisations.

3.2 CONSIDERATIONS IN THE FORMULATION OF POPULATION EDUCATION OBJECTIVES

Dr. V.K.R.V. Rao, the then Minister of Education and a leading economist, while inaugurating the first National Seminar on Population Education in India in Bombay in 1969, cautioned the participants to be very careful in formulating the objectives, "We must see that the objective of population education is of a long-term character as far as its relation to family planning is concerned and nothing should be done to the children themselves or their relation to the individual families of which they are a part."

According to S.R. Wayland, "The programme of population education should develop an appreciation by the individual of the consequences for his family and society of his own actions and attitudes, and on the other hand it should develop an appreciation of the consequences for the individual of the population changes that are occurring in his own community and nation." (*Issues and Problems in Introducing Population Education*, UNESCO Regional Office, Bangkok, 1972).

Prof. T.S. Mehta suggests two steps in the formulation of objectives of population education :

(i) To make a critical survey of the existing school curriculum.

(ii) To clarify the concept of population education.

3.3 WHAT THEY SAY ON OBJECTIVES OF POPULATION EDUCATION

National Seminar: The National Seminar on Population Education held at Bombay in August 1969 formulated the following objectives of population. These are applicable to all levels including elementary stage of education.

1. To enable the students to understand that family size is controllable.
2. To enable the students to understand that population limitation can facilitate the development of a higher quality of life in the nation.
3. To enable the students to understand that a small family size can contribute materially to the quality of living for the individual family.
4. To enable the students to understand and appreciate that small size of the family in good for preserving the health and welfare of the members of the family.
5. To enable the students to understand that economic stability of the family depends upon population control.
6. To ensure good prospects for the younger generation.
7. To enable the students to appreciate that the Indian family of to day and tomorrow should be small with only two or three children.

Smt. Avabai: Smt. Avabai B. Wadia (1969) suggested the following objectives of population education:

1. Creating among the younger generation an understanding of one of the most important phenomena in the modern world, namely, rapid growth of population, its causes, trends, some of the factors affecting it and ways of regulating it.
2. Studying the influence of population trends on various aspects of life – social, cultural, economic and political – and in particular, the close interaction of population growth and development process, with particular reference to the national programme to raise the standard of living.
3. Recognising the fact that scientific developments are enabling us to get increased control over famine, disease and ultimately death, and similarly control over unplanned births also. Their body of knowledge has to be utilised to correct violent imbalances between the two, and to create stability.
4. Realising the significance of population growth on individual and family life, and encouraging attitudes of responsibility and mutual help and co-operation in all aspects of personal and family living.
5. Appreciating the fact that for preserving the health of the mother, the welfare of the children, the economic stability of the family, and the future prospects of the younger generation, Indian families to day and in the future should be small and compact with not more than two or three children.

Dr. John Edlefsen: Scholars like Dr. John Edlefsen have suggested the following primary objectives of population education:

1. To enable the students to appreciate the need for a small family in which a high quality of life for each person can be attained.
2. To enable the students to realise that large families are not necessary in the present day.
3. To enable the students to realise that the size of the family can be easily planned for the benefit of individual families.
4. To enable the students to understand the health risks involved for the mother and the child.
5. To enable the students to understand the significance of the population characteristics for the present and future quality of life including economic development and the attainment of higher level of health, education, housing, diet and other amenities of life.
6. To enable the students to understand the Government Family Planning Programme and the Population Policy.

Kamala Rao and D. Gopal Rao: Kamala Rao and D. Gopal Rao are of the view that objectives of population education could be spelled out at three different levels:

(a) Policy level objectives.
(b) Implementation levels.
(c) Instructional objectives.

According to them, the policy level objectives are:

1. To develop a methodology of influencing the young through schools and adults through other educational agencies to appreciate the population goals as laid down by the Government.
2. To develop in school and college students and teachers an appreciation of the magnitude of population growth as a national problem and its implication for the nation, society, family and the individual.
3. To stabilise the efforts and achievements of the present population programme through a systematic process of the small family norm among the younger generation (the future parents).
4. To involve the formal educational system – its traditions, curricular techniques, teacher training, programmes etc. in imparting a systematic content on population education at the different stages of school and college education.
5. To assess the broader implications of the introduction of population education for parents, teachers, schools' pupils and society.

Objectives of Population Education Formulated at the Asian Regional Workshop on Population and Family Education held at Bangkok in 1970:

1. Assisting the pupils to acquire knowledge of basic demographic concept, process and methodologies.
2. Assisting the pupils to acquire knowledge of static and dynamic description of the population situation at the micro-macro levels.
3. Assisting the pupils to acquire knowledge of the determinants of population growth.

4. Assisting the pupils to acquire knowledge of the consequences of population growth.
5. Assisting the pupils to acquire knowledge of the human reproductive process as a basis for understanding human fertility.
6. Assisting the pupils to acquire knowledge of the national and international population policies and programmes.
7. Assisting the pupils to develop rational and responsible attitudes and behaviour toward family size and national programmes.

3.4 FOUR-FOLD DIVISION OF OBJECTIVES OF POPULATION EDUCATION (NCERT)

Objectives of population may be classified under four broad heads:

I. Objectives relating to population dynamics (Pattern of change or growth of population).
II. Objectives relating to the impact of growing numbers and our struggle for better living.
III. Objectives relating to the race between population on march and environment on retreat.
IV. Objectives relating to the battle to be fought and won in every family.

I. Objectives of Population Relating to Population Dynamics. These include as under:

1. To enable the students to understand that population becomes stable when there is little difference between the birth rate and the death rate.
2. To create an awareness among the students that the present population explosion in developing countries, especially India is on account of the comparatively steady birth rate as against rapidly falling death rate over the past few decades.
3. To impress the students that the use of science and technology has helped us in bringing down the death rate, and that the same can help us in bringing down the birth rate as well.
4. To develop among students a healthy, rational and scientific attitude towards the natural phenomena of births and deaths.
5. To assist the students realise the socio-economic burden involved in bringing up large families usually resulting in deterioration in quality of living.
6. To develop among the students a realisation that the natural growth in population is due to the a between the number of births and deaths taking place in a given period over a specified area.
7. To help the students develop an idea that populations by their nature are dynamic and never static.

II. Objectives of Population Relating to the Impact of Growing Numbers and our Struggle for Better Living. This includes the following objectives:

1. To develop among the students an awareness of difficulties faced by large families in making both ends meet.

2. To help the students understand why there is not enough improvement in the living conditions of an average person in spite of considerable progress that the developing countries, especially India, have made since independence.
3. To assist the students realise the demands made by the young and dependent population on their families, local communities and the society as a whole.
4. To create an urge among students to see that their country is able to catch up with developed countries and even go ahead of them in respect of living conditions of the people.
5. To impress upon the students the importance of hard work and critical thinking with a view to improve the living conditions of our people.
6. To bring home the students the need for providing equal opportunities to women in every walk of life at the individual, family and social level.
7. To inculcate among the students, a healthy attitude towards women so that the status of women can be raised both in family and social life.

III. Objectives of Population Relating to the Race between Population on March and Environment on Retreat. Following are the objectives in this regard:

1. To assist the students understand the special quality of man that distinguishes him from any other species on earth.
2. To assist the students realise that man's ability to think, to communicate, to work with tools and to co-operate with others and adapt himself to varying environment has been responsible for his tremendous progress.
3. To assist the students understand that man's advance in science and technology has enabled him to husband his environment including resources to his betterment.
4. To impress upon the students that man's scientific and technical skills may endanger his future if not judiciously used.
5. To impress upon the students to appreciate that short–sidedness on the part of man and his growing concern for immediate gains, quick returns and short-cuts to (temporary) prosperity may bring unforeseen calamities to man and his very existence on this planet.
6. To assist the students develop an attitude that would promote living in peace and harmony with nature.
7. To develop an attitude in the students that would promote conservation of nature, environment and natural resources, avoid waste and encourage increasing use of renewable resources in place of those that are exhaustible.
8. To assist children appreciate the significance of economy based on recycling of resources and thereby keeping the wastage of resources to the minimum.

IV. Objectives of Population Relating to the Battle to be Fought and Won in Every Family. Important objectives are given below:

1. To help the students realise that the solution to the entire population problems lies in acceptance of a small family norm by each and every family in the country.
2. To impress upon the students that the happiness of the family lies in fulfilling its basic needs and minimum requirements of food, clothing, shelter, medicines, education, recreation and savings for a rainy day.
3. To help the students realise that other things being equal, a small family is in a much better position to meet the basic necessities and minimum requirements of every member of the family.
4. To impress upon the students that the small family norm is not only desirable but because of modern science and technology it is also now obtainable.
5. To help the students realise that acceptance of a small family norm in actual practice is to be preceded by a conviction and courage of action on the part of the parents.

(Source: Adapted from *Population Education—A Conceptual Framework*. NCERT, 1979)

3.5 LONG-TERM OBJECTIVES OF POPULATION EDUCATION

1. To develop among the students a keen insight into the inter-relationship between population change and the process of socio-economic development vis-à-vis the individual, the family, the society, the nation and the world.
2. To create among the students and the teachers an awareness about the population situation in the country and the strategies adopted to meet this critical situation.
3. To create an awareness among children that the present population explosion in our country is due to steady birth rate as against rapidly falling death rate over the past few decades.
4. To develop desirable attitudes and behaviour in the students and the teachers as well as in the community at large towards the population issues so as to enable them to arrive at rational decision about the quality of life that suits them best.
5. To impress upon the children that the use of the science and technology has helped us in bringing down the death rate and that the same can help us in bringing down the birth rate as well.
6. To help children realise the socio-economic burden involved in bringing up large families usually resulting in deterioration in quality of living.
7. To provide population education its rightful place in the curriculum of the formal as well as the non-formal programme of education.
8. To make curriculum renewal a continuous and on-going process to met the emerging challenges that confront society from time to time.
9. To reorient the system of education to be helpful in the developmental efforts of the country and forge it as an active agent for social transformation.

3.6 SPECIFIC OBJECTIVES OF POPULATION EDUCATION AT THE ELEMENTARY LEVEL

1. To enable the students to understand the basic principles of population growth.
2. To enable the students to learn about the causative factors of population growth.
3. To enable the students to understand the impact of rapid population growth.
4. To enable the students to understand the merits of a small family.
5. To enable the students to understand the close relationship between family income and family welfare.
6. To enable the students to understand the close relationship between people's well-being and socio-economic development.
7. To enable the students to understand that the quality of population is more important than the quantity of population.
8. To enable the students to understand the significance of small family norm and its relation to the quality of living.
9. To enable the students to understand the meaning and significance of environmental harmony.
10. To enable the students to understand that the family size can be controlled as opposed to fatalism and superstition.
11. To enable the students to understand the far-reaching consequences of population density and rapid growth to one's self and one's environment.
12. To enable the students to understand the meaning of key words used in population education programmes.
13. To enable the students to understand the salient features of population scenario of the country.
14. To enable the students to understand the main characteristics of the national population policy.
15. To enable the students to develop proper attitudes and skills relating to welfare of the family, the community and the nation.
16. To enable the individual student to understand that he has a double role to play. He must understand that his own actions have an influence on others as well as that population changes deeply affect his well being.

(For national objectives of population education in operational forms, *see Chapter* 'National Population and Plan of Action)

3.7 INSTRUCTIONAL OBJECTIVES OF POPULATION EDUCATION IN TERMS OF KNOWLEDGE, SKILLS, ATTITUDES AND INTERESTS

Instructional objectives of population education may be categorised under three heads.

1. Knowledge objectives.
2. Skill objectives.
3. Attitude and interest objectives.

Knowledge Objectives of Population Education

1. To enable the students to identify major concepts and terms like migration, emigration, immigration and density of population etc.
2. To enable the students to understand the reasons for uneven distribution of population in different regions of the world.
3. To enable the students to acquaint themselves with the growth trend in population.
4. To enable the students to understand the relation between population and environment.
5. To enable the students to understand the impact of the changing needs of man on environment.
6. To enable the students to understand the impact of Industrial Revolution on environment.
7. To enable the students to compare ecological balance and efficiency in the past with that of the present.
9. To enable the students to distinguish between birth rate and growth rate of population.
10. To enable the students to understand the different ways of making optimum use of food resources.
11. To enable the students to understand the significance of having better understanding among the nations of the world for meeting food shortage.
12. To enable the students to understand energy crisis.
13. To enable the students to understand the reasons for the depletion of resources.
14. To enable the students to classify resources between renewal and non-renewal.
15. To enable the students to understand the inter-relationship between population and environment.

Skills

1. To develop the skill of the students to read population maps.
2. To develop the skill of the students to prepare the map showing areas of uneven population.
3. To develop the skill of preparing posters indicating the harmful effects of environmental pollution.

Attitude and Interest

1. To develop positive interests regarding environmental issues in students.
2. To enable the students to appreciate that growing population is likely to pose severe threats to the standard of life and living.

4

Population Situation in India

4.1 POPULATION OF INDIA AT A GLANCE – TWENTY FIVE INDICATORS

Box 4.1: Main Features of India's Population

1. *Population Position in the World*	Every sixth person is an Indian. 16.87% population with 2.4% area
2. *Rank in Population*	Second in the World. India
3. *Future Position*	First in 2025 A.D. China Second
4. *Annual Growth Rate*	1.76 per cent as against world's 1.4 per cent
5. *Annual Increase*	1.81 crore i.e. more than double the total population of Austria
6. *High Birth Rate and Low Death Rate (2009)*	Death rate 6.4; Birth rate 22.4
7. *Density of Population (2011)*	382
8. *Sex Ratio : Low Female Ratio (2011)*	940 per 1000 males. Kerala with highest sex ratio
9. *Life Expectancy (2009)*	69.89 years
10 *Infant Mortality Rate (2009)*	30 per 1000
11. *Under 5-year Mortality Rate (2010)*	63 per 1000 births
12. *Statewise Distribution of Population (2011)*	Highest – U.P. (19.96 crores); Lowest—Sikkim (6.07 lakhs)
13. *Total Fertility Rate (2010)*	2.6 %
14. *Percentage of Population using Adequate Sanitary Facilities (1999)*	31 %
15. *Percentage of Population without Shelter (2001)*	17 %
16. *Percentage of Population Using Contraceptives (2010)*	54 %

17. *Age Composition 0-6 years (2011)*	13.12 %
18. *Urban-Rural Population (2001)*	72 % Rural, 28 % Urban
19. *Literacy (2011)*	74.04 per cent. Kerala with highest literacy rate
20. *Low Female Literacy (2011)*	Female 65.46 %, Male 82.14 %
21. *Occupational Distribution (2011)*	Mainly agricultural
22. *Family Planning (2011)*	Slow progress
23. *Languages Recognised in the Constitution*	18

4.2 BOOMING POPULATION : WORLD COMPARISON

India's population as on March 1, 2011, according to provisional results of the Census of India 2001 stood at 1,210,193,422 (121 crore). Thus, India became only the second country in the world after China to officially cross the one billion mark.

The estimated world population according to United Nations in 2001 was 6134 million (613.4 crore). The population of the ten most populous countries of the world is given in Table 4.1. Their relative share in the global population is shown in Fig. 4.1.

Table 4.1 Population of Select Countries (2011)

Sl. No.	*Country*	*Population (in Millions)*
1.	China	1352.46
2.	India	1210.19
3.	United States	314.13
4.	Indonesia	238.40
5.	Brazil	196.82
6.	Pakistan	180.35
7.	Nigeria	170.12
8.	Bangladesh	161.08
9.	Russia	141.93
10.	Japan	127.61

Note : Population of India as reflected in the 2011 Census of India and US Estimates (*Population Environment and Development 2001*. UN Population Division, 2001)

India accounts for a meagre 2.4 per cent of the world surface area of 135.79 million square km. yet it supports and sustains a whopping 16.8 per cent of the world population. In 1950, China with 22 per cent share of the world population led the scene followed by India, which had a share of 14.2 per cent. According to UN Population Division estimates, by 2025 India will most likely overtake China

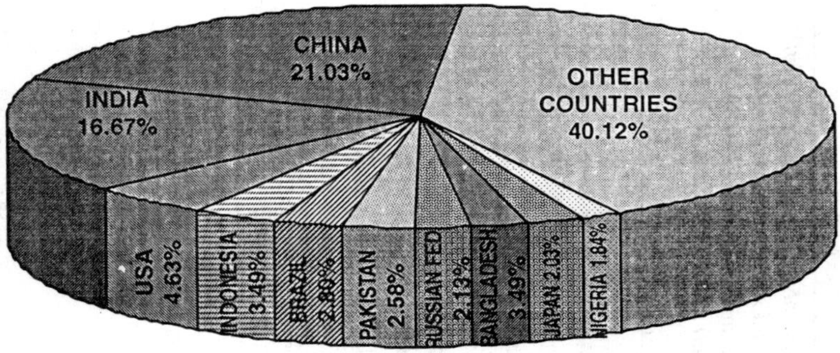

Fig. 4.1: India's share in world population

Sources:

1. Population figures for India as per Census 2001 (Provisional)
2. Population figures for U.S.A. and Japan are as per census 2000
3. Other figures are based on World Population prospects, 1998 Revisions (Vol. II), United Nations.

Table 4.2 Global Population and India's Share

Rank	*Country / Territory*	*Population*	*Date*	*% of world* population
1.	China	1352.46	August 10, 2012	19.20%
2.	India	1210.19	Mar-11	17%
3.	United States	314.13	August 10, 2012	4.47%
4.	Indonesia	238.40	May-10	3.33%
5.	Brazil	196.82	August 10, 2012	2.80%
6.	Pakistan	180.35	August 10, 2012	2.56%
7.	Nigeria	170.12	Jul-12	2.42%
8.	Bangladesh	161.08	Jul-12	2.29%
9.	Russia	141.93	January 1, 2010	2.02%
10.	Japan	127.61	May 1, 2012	1.81%

Source: Wikipedia.org

to become the most populous country on earth with 19.2 per cent population.

India's population exceeds the combined population of 6 most populous countries of the world namely, USA, Brazil, Pakistan, Russia Federation, Bangladesh and Japan (excluding only China, Indonesia and Nigeria).

India's population is equal to the total population of Europe comprising 47 countries and Northern America (five countries including USA).

India adds every ten years to its population the equivalent of 6 Canada's, or 3 Francs or 3 UKs or 2.3 Germanys.

Table 4.3 : Decadal Growth of Population in India (1901 to 2011)

Census Years	Population	Decadal Growth		Change in Decadal Growth		Average Annual Exponential Growth Rate (Percent)	Progressive Growth Rate Over 1901 (Percent)
		Absolute	Percent	Absolute	Percent		
1	2	3	4	5	6	7	8
1901	238,396,327			-	-	-	-
1911	252,093,390	13,697,063	5.75	-	-	0.56	5.75
1921	251,321,213	-772177	-0.31	-14,469,240	-6.05	-0.03	5.42
1931	278,977,238	27,656,025	11.00	28,428,202	11.31	1.04	17.02
1941	318,660,580	39,683,342	14.22	12,027,317	3.22	1.33	33.67
1951	361,088,090	42,427,510	13.31	2,744,168	-0.91	1.25	51.47
1961	439,234,771	78,146,681	21.64	35,719,171	8.33	1.96	84.25
1971	548,159,652	108,924,881	24.80	30,778,200	3.16	2.20	129.94
1981	683,329,097	135,169,445	24.66	26,244,564	0.14	2.22	186.64
1991	843,387,888	163,058,791	23.86	27,889,346	-0.80	2.14	255.03
2001	1,027,015,247	180,627,359	21.34	17,568,568	-2.52	1.93	330.80
2011	1,210,193,422	181,455,986	17.64				

Source: Census of India, 2001 and 2011.

Table 4.4: Phases of Population Growth (1901 to 2011)

Sl. No.	*Decade*	*Trend*
1.	1901-1921	Stagnant population
2.	1921-1951	Steady growth
3.	1951-1981	Rapid high growth
4.	1991-2011	High growth with definite signs of slowing down

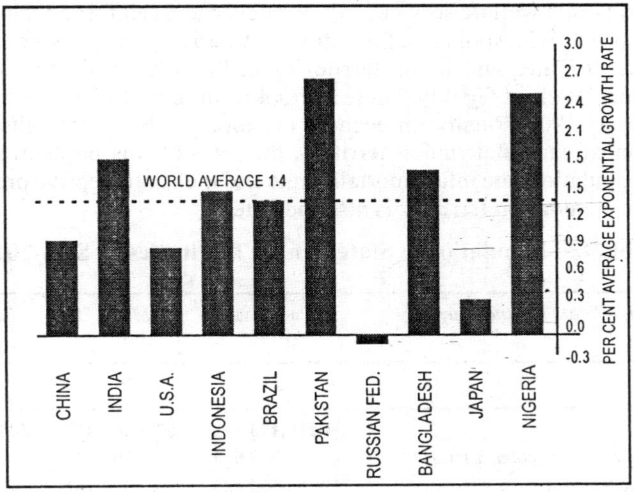

Fig. 4.2: Growth rate of population in India and selected countries (1990-2000)

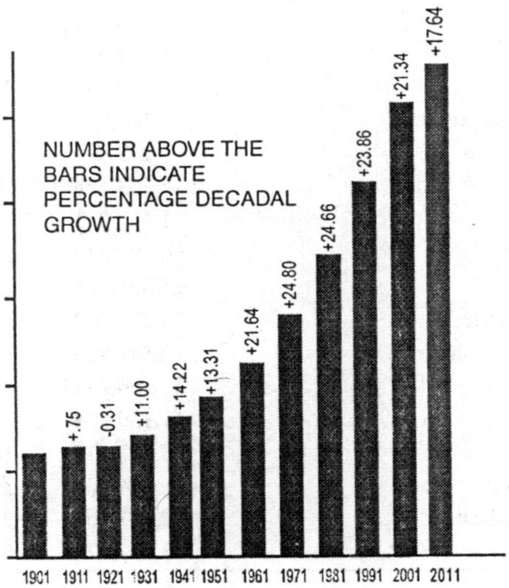

Fig. 4.3: Decadal growth of population in India (1901-2001)

4.4 LARGE SCALE INTERSTATE VARIATIONS IN POPULATION AND STATES' RANKING

India is a country of striking demographic diversity. Substantial differences are visible between states in the achievement of basic demographic indices. This has led to significant disparity in current population size and the potential to influence population increases during 1996-2016. There are wide inter-state, male-female and rural-urban disparities in outcomes and impacts. These differences stem largely from poverty, illiteracy, and inadequate access to health and family welfare services, which coexist and reinforce each other. In many parts, the widespread health infrastructure is not responsive.

At least 9 states and union territories in India have already achieved replacement levels of fertility. These are ranked in accordance with their total fertility rates. Additionally, in each of the three tables below, the current population of each state/union territory, the ratio of this population to the country population, the infant mortality rate and the contraceptive prevalence rate of the state/union territory is also indicated:

Table 4.5: Population of States/Union Territories by Sex--2011

Sr. No.	*India/State or union territory*	*Persons*	*Males*	*Females*
1	2	3	4	5
	India	**1,210,193,422**	**62,27.47,487**	**585,740,244**
1	Andaman and Nicobar Islands	379,944	202,330	177,614
2	Andhra Pradesh	84,665,533	42,509,881	42,155,652
3	Arunachal Pradesh	1,382,611	720,232	662,379
4	Assam	31,169,272	15,954,927	15,214,345
5	Bihar	103,804,637	54,185,347	49,619,290
6	Chandigarh	1,054,686	580,282	474,404
7	Chhattisgarh	25,540,196	12,827,915	12,712,281
8	Dadra and Nagar Haveli	342,853	193,178	149,675
9	Daman and Diu	242,911	150,100	92,811
10	Delhi	16,753,235	8,976,410	7,776,825
11	Goa	1,457,723	740,711	717,012
12	Gujarat	60,383,628	31,482,282	28,901,346
13	Haryana	25,353,081	13,505,130	11,847,951
14	Himachal Pradesh	6,856,509	3,473,892	3,473,892
15	Jammu and Kashmir	12,548,926	6,665,561	5,883,365
16	Jharkhand	32,966,238	15,954,927	15,214,345
17	Karnataka	61,130,704	31,057,742	30,072,962
18	Kerala	33,387,677	16,021,290	17,366,387
19	Lakshadweep	64,429	33,106	31,323
20	Madhya Pradesh	72,597,565	37,612,920	34,984,645
21	Maharashtra	112,372,972	58,361,397	54,011,575

(*Contd.*)

1	2	3	4	5
22	Manipur	2,721,756	1,369,764	1,351,992
23	Meghalaya	2,964,007	1,492,668	1,471,339
24	Mizoram	1,091,014	552,339	538,675
25	Nagaland	1,980,602	1,025,707	954,895
26	Orissa	41,947,358	21,201,678	20,745,680
27	Pondicherry	1,244,464	610,485	633,979
28	Punjab	27,704,236	14,634,819	13,069,417
29	Rajasthan	68,621,012	35,620,086	33,000,926
30	Sikkim	607,688	321,661	286,027
31	Tamil Nadu	72,138,958	36,158,871	35,980,087
32	Tripura	3,671,032	1,871,867	1,799,165
33	Uttar Pradesh	199,581,477	104,596,415	94,985,062
34	Uttarakhand	10,116,752	5,154,178	4,962,574
35	West Bengal	91,347,736	46,927,389	44,420,347

Table 4.6: Five States with Maximum and Minimum Population (2011)

Sl. No.	*States with Maximum Population*		*Sl. No.*	*States with Minimum Population*	
	State	*Population*		*State*	*Population*
1.	Uttar Pradesh	19,95,81,477	1.	Sikkim	6,07,688
2.	Maharashtra	11,23,72,972	2.	Mizoram	10,91,014
3.	Bihar	10,38,04,637	3.	Arunachal Pradesh	13,82,611
4.	West Bengal	913,47,736	4.	Goa	14,57,723
5.	Andhra Pradesh	8,46,65,533	5.	Nagaland	19,80,602

The following table illustrates the ranking of states in population

Table 4.7: Ranking of States/Union Territories by Population Size–2011

Rank in 2011	*India/State or union territory*	*Population in 2011*	*% to Total Population*		
			2011	*2001*	*Rank in 2001*
1	2	3	4	5	6
1	Uttar Pradesh	199,581,477	16.49	16.17	1
2	Maharashtra	112,372,972	9.29	9.42	2
3	Bihar	103,804,637	8.58	8.07	3
4	West Bengal	91,347,736	7.55	7.81	4
5	Andhra Pradesh	84,665,533	7.00	7.27	5
6	Madhya Pradesh	72,597,565	6.00	6.25	7
7	Tamil Nadu	72,138,958	5.96	5.88	6
8	Rajasthan	68,621,012	5.67	5.5	8
9	Karnataka	61,130,704	5.05	5.14	9
10	Gujarat	60,383,628	4.99	4.93	10
11	Odisha	41,947,358	3.47	3.97	11

1	2	3	4	5	6
12	Kerala	33,387,677	2.76	3.1	12
13	Jharkhand	32,966,238	2.72	2.62	13
14	Assam	31,169,272	2.58	2.59	14
15	Punjab	27,704,236	2.29	2.37	15
16	Chhattisgarh	25,540,196	2.11	2.03	17
17	Haryana	25,353,081	2.09	2.05	16
18	Delhi	16,753,235	1.38	1.34	18
19	Jammu and Kashmir	12,548,926	1.04	0.98	19
20	Uttarakhand	10,116,752	0.84	0.83	20
21	Himachal Pradesh	6,856,509	0.57	0.59	21
22	Tripura	3,671,032	0.30	0.31	22
23	Meghalaya	2,964,007	0.24	0.22	24
24	Manipur	2,721,756	0.22	0.23	23
25	Nagaland	1,980,602	0.16	0.19	25
26	Goa	1,457,723	0.12	0.13	26
27	Arunachal Pradesh	1,382,611	0.11	0.11	27
28	Pondicherry	1,244,464	0.10	0.09	28
29	Mizoram	1,091,014	0.09	0.09	30
30	Chandigarh	1,054,686	0.09	0.09	29
31	Sikkim	607,688	0.05	0.05	31
32	Andaman and Nicobar Islands	379,944	0.03	0.03	32
33	Dadra and Nagar Haveli	342,853	0.03	0.02	33
34	Daman and Diu	242,911	0.02	0.02	34
35	Lakshadweep	64,429	0.01	0.01	35

4.5 CENSUSES IN INDIA AND KEY STATISTICS

Conduct of Census: Under Article 246 and listed at serial number 69 of the Seventh Schedule of the Constitution of India, population census is a Union subject. The Census Act, 1948 forms the legal basis for conduct of censuses in independent India. The Census of India, 2001 was the sixth census in independent India and the 14th since 1872 – the first population census in the country.

The Census Organisation under the Union Home Ministry has been functioning on a permanent footing ever since 1961. This Organisation is headed by the Registrar General and Census Commissioner, India. There are permanent Directorate of Censuses in States headed by the Directors of Censuses. A Census hierarchy is set up at all levels by the States.

Significance of Census. The Census throws up benchmark data on the state of human resources in habiting the country, their demography, culture and economic structure. This information is very useful in planning and development of the country.

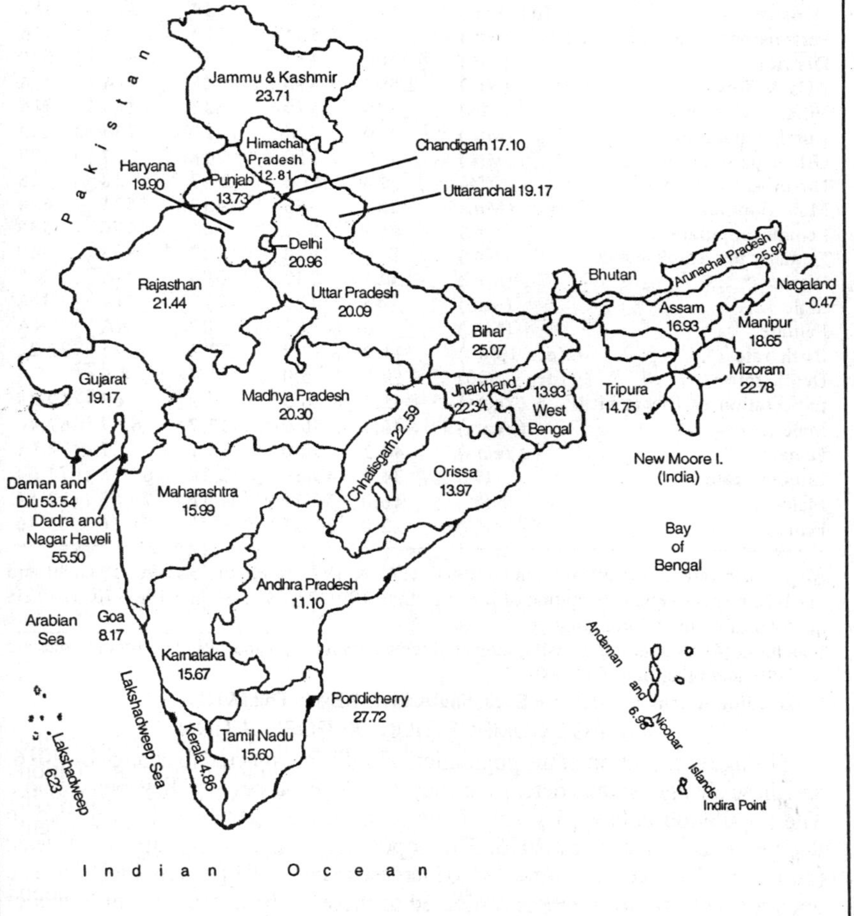

Fig. 4.4: India – Percentage decadal growth of population 1991-2011 (States/UTs)

Table 4.8 : Key Census Statistics (1991 to 2011)

		1971	*1981*	*1991*	*2001*	*2011*
Population	(Mn.)	548	683	846	1027	1210
Density	(per km^2)	177	230*	273*	324	382
Persons per household	(No.)	5.46	5.55*	5.52*	NA	NA
Districts	(No.)	360	412	466	593	640
AUs & Towns	(No.)	2,590	3,378	3,768	NA	NA
Villages (inhabited)	('000s)	576	579	627	NA	NA
Rural population	(Mn.)	439	524	629	734	833
Urban population	(Mn.)	109	159	218	287	377
Urban as % of total ...	(%)	20	23.3	25.7	28	28
Male population	(Mn.)	284	353	439	531	624
Female population	(Mn.)	264	330	407	496	588
Females per 1,000 males	(No.)	930	934	927	933	940
Workers*	(Mn.)	181	242	306	NA	NA
Male	(Mn.)	145	179	219	NA	NA
Female	(Mn.)	36	63	87	NA	NA
Birth rate	(per 1,000)	41.2	37.2	32.5	25	22.22
Death rate	(per 1,000)	19.0	15.0	11.4	8.9	6.4
Expectation of life at birth ..	(Years)	45.6	50.5	58.2	63	69.89
Male	(Years)	46.4	50.9	57.7	62.7	67.46
Female ...	(Years)	44.7	50.0	58.7	63.7	72.61
Literacy rate ..	(%)	34.5	43.6+	52.2#	65.38	74.04
Male ...	(%)	46.0	56.4+	64.1#	75.85	82.14
Female ...	(%)	22.0	29.8+	39.3#	54.16	65.46

Note: Birth rate and death rate under 1991, 1981 & 1971 relate to 1981-90, 1971-80 and 1961-70 respectively; expectation of life at birth to 1991-92, 1971-80 and 1961-70. Workers are total of main and marginal.

In column (4), population, density, male and female population and ratio and literacy rate are for 2001 and other data for 2000.

* Excluding Assam and J&K; + Excluding Assam; # Excluding J&K.

4.6 AGE COMPOSITION OF POPULATION

The age distribution of the population of India is projected to change by 2016, and these changes should determine allocation of resources in policy intervention. The population below 15 years of age (currently 35 per cent) is projected to decline to 28 per cent by 2016. The population in the age group 15-59 years (currently 58 per cent) is projected to increase to nearly 64 per cent by 2016. The age group of 60 plus years is projected to increase from the current levels of 7 per cent to nearly 9 per cent by 2016.

Table 4.9 : Age Composition as Percentage of the Total Population

Year	*Below 5 years*	*Between 0 - 15*	*Between >15-59*	*+60 years*
1991	12.80	37.76	55.58	6.57
2001	10.70	34.33	58.70	6.97
2011	10.10	28.48	63.38	8.14
2016	9.7	27.73	63.33	8.94

4.7 SEX RATIO

India shares a distinctive feature of South Asia and Chinese populations as regards the sex ratio, with a century's old deficit of females. The (female to male) sex ratio has been steadily declining. From 1901 to 1991, the sex ratio declined from 972 to 927. According to 2011 Census, it rose to 940. This is largely attributed to the son preference, discrimination against the girl child leading to lower female literacy, female feticide, higher fertility and higher mortality levels for females, in all age group up to 45.

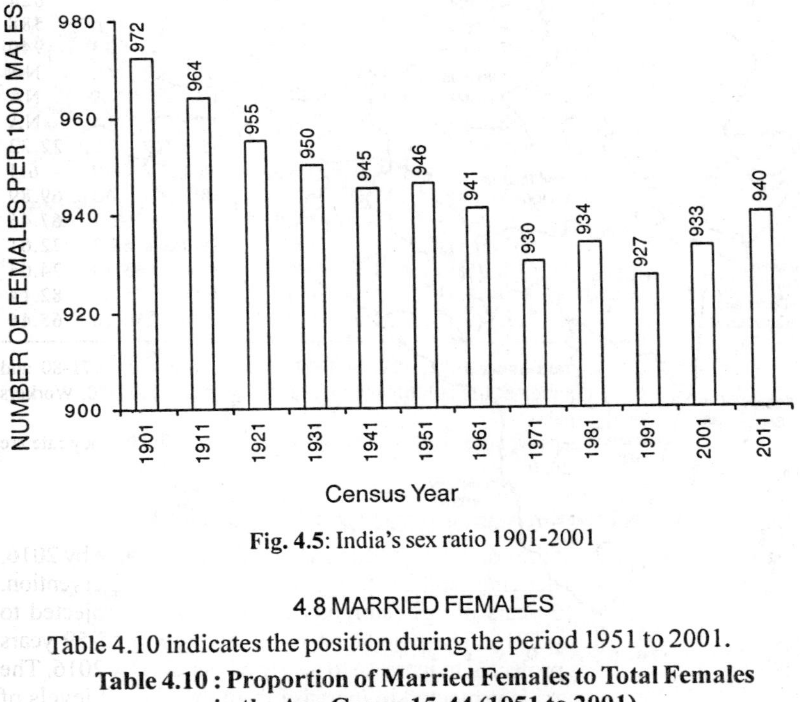

Fig. 4.5: India's sex ratio 1901-2001

4.8 MARRIED FEMALES

Table 4.10 indicates the position during the period 1951 to 2001.

Table 4.10 : Proportion of Married Females to Total Females in the Age Group 15-44 (1951 to 2001)

Year	*Percentage of Population Married*	*Change in Per Centage*
1951	82.94	—
1961	85.75	2.81
1971	83.9	–1.85
1981	80.48	–3.42
1991	77.06	–3.42
2001*	73.64	–3.42

* Estimated

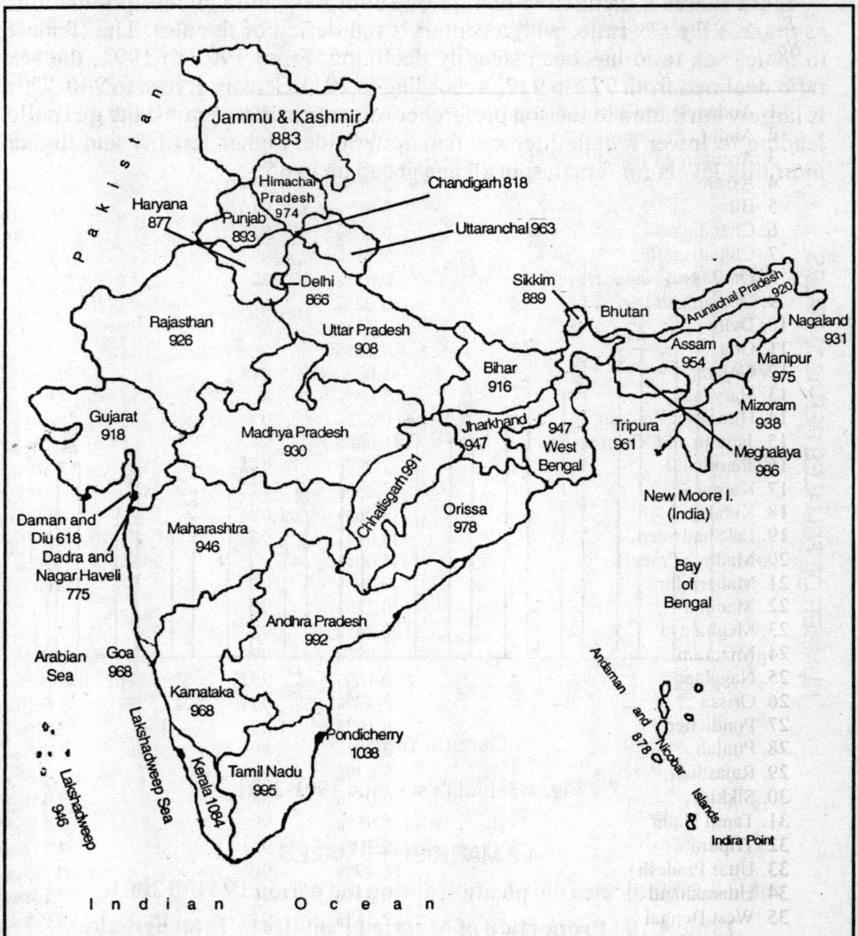

Fig. 4.6: India – Sex Ratio 2011 (States/UTs)

Table 4.11: Distribution of States' Population by Percentage Share in Total Population, Sex Ratio, Density and Decadal Growth – 2011

S. No.	*States and Union Territories*	*Percentage Share in Total Population*	*Sex Ratio*	*Density (per Sq Km)*	*Decadal Growth Rate*
1.	Andaman and Nicobar Islands	0.03%	878	46	6.70%
2.	Andhra Pradesh	7.00%	992	308	11.10%
3.	Arunachal Pradesh	0.11%	920	17	25.90%
4.	Assam	2.58%	954	397	16.90%
5.	Bihar	8.58%	916	1102	25.10%
6.	Chandigarh	0.09%	818	9,252	17.10%
7.	Chhattisgarh	2.11%	991	189	22.60%
8.	Dadra and Nagar Haveli	0.03%	775	698	55.50%
9.	Daman and Diu	0.02%	618	2,169	53.50%
10.	Delhi	1.38%	866	9,340	21.00%
11.	Goa	0.12%	968	394	8.20%
12.	Gujarat	5.00%	918	308	19.20%
13.	Haryana	2.09%	877	573	19.90%
14.	Himachal Pradesh	0.57%	974	123	12.80%
15.	Jammu and Kashmir	1.04%	883	56	23.70%
16.	Jharkhand	2.72%	947	414	22.30%
17.	Karnataka	5.05%	968	319	15.70%
18.	Kerala	2.76%	1,084	859	4.90%
19.	Lakshadweep	0.01%	946	2,013	6.20%
20.	Madhya Pradesh	6.00%	930	236	20.30%
21.	Maharashtra	9.28%	946	365	16.00%
22.	Manipur	0.22%	987	122	18.70%
23.	Meghalaya	0.24%	986	132	27.80%
24.	Mizoram	0.09%	975	52	22.80%
25.	Nagaland	0.16%	931	119	-0.50%
26.	Orissa	3.47%	978	269	14.00%
27.	Pondicherry	0.10%	1,038	2,598	27.70%
28.	Punjab	2.30%	893	550	13.70%
29.	Rajasthan	5.67%	926	201	21.40%
30.	Sikkim	0.05%	889	86	12.40%
31.	Tamil Nadu	5.96%	995	555	15.60%
32.	Tripura	0.30%	961	350	14.70%
33.	Uttar Pradesh	16.49%	908	828	20.10%
34.	Uttarakhand	0.84%	963	189	19.20%
35.	West Bengal	7.55%	947	1029	13.90%

4.9 RURAL-URBAN POPULATION

Table 4.12 shows the population residing in rural and urban areas.

Table 4.12 : Rural-Urban Population (2011)

Area	*% of population*
Rural	68.84 %
Urban	31.16 %

4.10 DENSITY OF POPULATION AND RANKING OF STATES

The density of population is considered as one of the important indices of population concentration. It is defined as the number of persons per square kilometer. The population density of India in 2011 was 368 persons per square kilometer, which implies that now 44 more people live in a square kilometer area in the country than the number that lived a decade ago.

The population density of India from 1901 to 2011 is shown in Table 4.13. At the beginning of the twentieth century i.e. in 1901 the density of India was as low as 77 and this steadily increased from one decade to another to reach 368 in 2011. The persons living in per sq km has increased by 13.6 per cent in 2011 as compared to 2001.

Table 4.13: Density of Population, India (1901-2011)

Census year	*Density (per sq km)*
1901	77
1911	82
1921	81
1931	90
1941	103
1951	117
1961	142
1971	177[1]
1981	216[2]
1991	267[2]
2001	324[2]
2011	368

Notes:

1. While working out the density of India, Jammu & Kashmir has been excluded as comparable figures of area and population are not available for that State.
2. The density has been worked out on comparable data.

Table 4.14: Ranking of States' Population by Density -2011

Sr. No.	*Rank in 2011*	*States and Union Territories*	*Density (per Sq Km)* 2011	2011	*Rank in 2001*
1.	34	Andaman and Nicobar Islands	46	43	34
2.	21	Andhra Pradesh	308	275	21
3.	35	Arunachal Pradesh	17	13	35
4.	15	Assam	397	340	15
5.	6	Bihar	1102	880	6
6.	2	Chandigarh	9,252	7903	2
7.	26	Chhattisgarh	189	154	26
8.	10	Dadra and Nagar Haveli	698	449	10
9.	4	Daman and Diu	2,169	1411	4
10.	1	Delhi	9,340	9294	1
11.	16	Goa	394	363	16
12.	20	Gujarat	308	258	20
13.	11	Haryana	573	477	11
14.	28	Himachal Pradesh	123	109	28

1	2	3	4	5	6
15.	32	Jammu and Kashmir	56	99	32
16.	14	Jharkhand	414	338	14
17.	19	Karnataka	319	275	19
18.	8	Kerala	859	819	8
19.	5	Lakshadweep	2,013	1894	5
20.	23	Madhya Pradesh	236	196	23
21.	17	Maharashtra	365	314	17
22.	29	Manipur	122	107	29
23.	27	Meghalaya	132	103	27
24.	33	Mizoram	52	42	33
25.	30	Nagaland	119	120	30
26.	22	Odisha	269	236	22
27.	3	Pondicherry	2,598	2029	3
28.	13	Punjab	550	482	13
29.	24	Rajasthan	201	165	24
30.	31	Sikkim	86	76	31
31.	12	Tamil Nadu	555	478	12
32.	18	Tripura	350	304	18
33.	9	Uttar Pradesh	828	689	9
34.	25	Uttarakhand	189	159	25
35.	7	West Bengal	1029	904	7

Notes: While working out the density figures for Jammu and Kashmir for 2001 census, the entire area and population of those portions of Jammu and Kashmir which are under illegal occupation of Pakistan and China have not been taken into account.

Table 4.15: Five States with Highest and Lowest Density (2011)

States with Highest Density			*States with Lowest Density*		
S. No.	*State*	*Density*	*S. No.*	*State*	*Density*
1.	Delhi	9340	1.	Arunachal Pradesh	17
2.	Bihar	1102	2.	Mizoram	52
3.	West Bengal	1029	3	Jammu & Kashmir	56
4.	Kerala	859	4.	Sikkim	86
5.	Uttar Pradesh	828	5	Nagaland	119

High increase in density of population puts immense pressure on the natural resources and as such it has become a matter of great concern. It also has an adverse affect on the quality of life of the people.

Among the States, Bihar is the most thickly populated state after Delhi. Here density has gone up from 880 in 2001 to 1102 to 2011.

In 2001, West Bengal was the highest densely populated state but in 2011, it was pushed back to the third position and Bihar became the second highest densely populated state. Bihar's density which was 880 in 2001 rose to 1102 in 2011.

The Eastern region of India has the highest density and the North Eastern region the lowest. The Eastern region includes the States of Bihar, Jharkhand, Odisha, West Bengal and Sikkim.

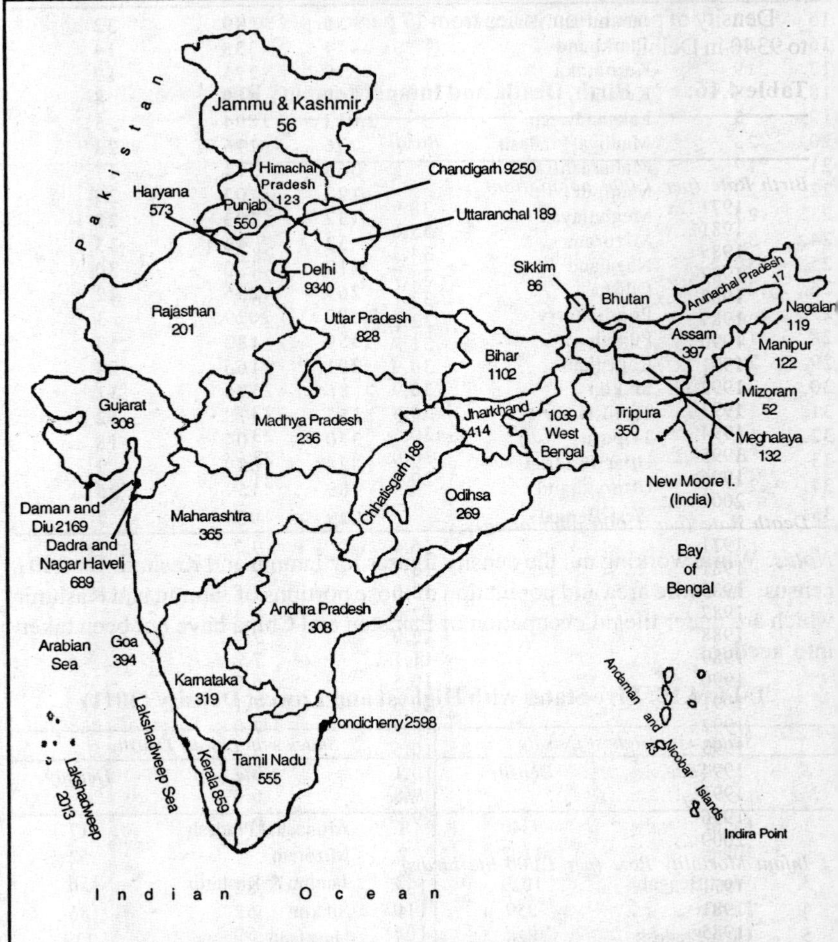

Fig. 4.7: India – Density of population 2011 (States/UTs)

The North Eastern region comprises Arunachal Pradesh, Assam, Meghalaya, Manipur, Mizoram, Nagaland, and Tripura.

Density of population varies from 17 persons per sq km in Arunachal Pradesh to 9340 in Delhi.

Table 4.16: Birth, Death, and Infant Mortality Rate—Rural-Urban

	Rural	*Urban*	*Combined*
Birth Rate (per 1,000 population)			
1971	38.9	30.1	36.9
1981	35.6	27.0	33.9
1985	34.3	28.1	32.9
1987	33.7	27.4	32.2
1988	33.1	26.3	31.5
1989	32.2	25.2	30.6
1990	31.7	24.7	30.2
1991	30.9	24.3	29.5
1992	30.9	23.1	29.2
1993	30.4	23.7	28.7
1994	30.5	23.1	28.7
1995	30.0	22.7	28.3
1996	29.3	21.4	27.4
2009	–	–	22.2
Death Rate (per 1,000 population)			
1971	16.4	9.7	14.9
1981	13.7	7.8	12.5
1985	13.0	7.8	11.8
1987	12.0	7.4	10.9
1988	12.0	7.7	11.0
1989	11.1	7.2	10.3
1990	10.5	6.8	9.7
1991	10.6	7.1	9.8
1992	10.9	7.0	10.1
1993	10.6	5.8	9.3
1994	10.1	6.7	9.3
1995	9.8	6.6	9.0
1996	9.7	6.5	8.9
2009	–	–	6.4
Infant Mortality Rate (per 1,000 life births)			
1971	138	82	129
1981	119	62	110
1985	107	59	97
1987	104	61	95
1988	102	62	94
1989	98	58	91
1990	86	50	80
1991	87	53	80
1992	85	53	79
1993	82	45	74
1994	80	52	74
1995	80	48	74
1996	78	46	72
2009	–	–	30.15

Note : These annual estimates are prepared by the Registrar General of India based on sample registration data. Figures for 1993 to 96 are provisional and exclude J&K, while those for 1995 (prov.) exclude J&K and Mizoram.

4.11 INFANT MORTALITY RATE UNDER ONE YEAR OF AGE AND 5 YEARS OF AGE

Table 4.17 : Infant Mortality Rate (1960 and 1999)

Year	*Mortality Rate under one year of age*	*Infant Mortality Rate under 5 year*
1960	146	242
1999	70	98

4.12 MATERNITY DEATH RATE : 470 PER 1,00,000 BIRTHS

4.13 LIFE EXPECTANCY : IT WAS 69.89 IN 2011

4.14 FERTILITY RATE

Table 4.18: Profile of 12 States and UTs with TFR gr ≥ 3

State	*Total Fertility Rate 1997*	*Infant Mortality Rate 1998*	*Contraceptive Prevalence Rate 1999*
Orissa	3.0	98	39.0
Gujarat	3.0	64	54.5
Assam	3.2	78	16.7
Haryana	3.4	69	49.7
Dadra & Nagar Haveli	3.5@	61	29.1
Tripura	3.9@	49	25.2
Meghalaya	4.8@	52	4.6
Madhya Pradesh	4.0	98	46.5
Rajasthan	4.2	83	36.4
Bihar	4.4	67	19.7
Uttar Pradesh	4.8	85	38.2
Jammu & Kashmir	NA	45	15.0

@ Three year moving average TFR 1995-97.

Table 4.19: Profiles of 11 States and UTs with TFR > 2.1 but < 3

State	*Total Fertility Rate 1997*	*Infant Mortality Rate 1998*	*Contraceptive Prevalence Rate 1999*
Manipur	2.4@	25	20.1
Daman & Diu	2.5@	51	30.2
Karnataka	2.5	58	55.4
Andhra Pradesh	2.5	66	50.3
Himachal Pradesh	2.5	64	48.2
Sikkim	2.5	52	21.9
West Bengal	2.6	53	32.9
Maharashtra	2.7	49	50.1
Punjab	2.7	54	66.0
Arunachal Pradesh	2.8@	47	14.0
Lakshadweep	2.8@	37	9.1

@ Three year moving average TFR 1995-97.

4.15 LITERACY

Literacy and education are the two very important indicators of the development of a country. Higher literacy level of the population act as a catalyst for cultural, economic, political and social development.

Table 4.20 provides comparative data on literacy since independence.

Table 4.20 : Literacy Rate in India (1951-2011)

Census Year	*Persons*	*Males*	*Females*	*Male-Female Gap in Literacy Rate*
1951	18.33	27.16	8.86	18.30
1961	28.30	40.40	15.35	25.05
1971	34.45	45.96	21.98	23.98
1981	43.57	56.38	29.76	26.62
1991	52.21	64.31	39.29	24.84
2001	65.38	75.85	54.16	21.69
2011	74.04	82.14	65.46	16.68

Notes:

1. Literacy rates for 1951, 1961 and 1971 Censuses relate to population aged five years and above. The rates for the 1981, 1991 and 2001 Census relate to the population aged seven years and above.
2. The 1981 Literacy rates exclude Assam where the 1981 Census could not be conducted. The 1991 Census Literacy rates exclude Jammu & Kashmir where the 1991 Census could not be conducted due to disturbed conditions.
3. The 2001 Census, literacy rates exclude entire Kachchh district, Morvi, Maliya-Miyana and Wankaner talukas of Rajkot district, Jodiya taluka of Jamnagar district of Gujarat State and entire Kinnaur district of Himachal Pradesh.

The literacy rates for the country as a whole in 2011 work out to 74.04 per cent for the population aged seven years and over. The corresponding figures for the males and females are 82.14 and 65.46 per cent respectively. Thus three-fourth of the males and more than half of the females aged seven years and above are literate in the country to-day. However, this figure is far below the several countries which have nearly 98 per cent literacy.

The literacy rates in Table 4.20 for the 1951, 1961 and 1971 Census relate to the population aged five years and above, those for the 1981, 1991, 2001 and 2011 relate to the population seven years and above.

As compared with the literacy rates of 1991 there has been a jump of 13.7 per cent points from 52.21 to 65.38 in 2001 and further 8.66% in 2011.

While male literacy rates increased by 6.29 per cent (from 75.85 to 82.14), female literacy rates increased by 11.30 (from 54.16 to 65.46 per cent) during the period 2001 to 2011. Nevertheless there is still a gap of 16.68 per cent between the literacy rates of male and females.

Table 4.21 presents the number of literates and illiterates among population aged 7 years and above and their difference between 1991 and 2001. The total number of illiterates has come down from 328,167,228 in 1991 to 296,208,952.

Table 4.21: Number of Literates and Illiterates Among Population Aged 7 Years and above – India : 1991, 2001 and 2011

Literates/Illiterates	*Persons*	*Males*	*Females*
Literates			
1991	358,402,626	228,983,134	129,419,492
2001	562,010,743	336,969,695	225,041,048
2011 Percentage	74.4%	82.14%	65.49%
Illiterates			
1991	328,167,288	128,099,211	200,068,077
2001	296,208,952	106,654,066	189,554,886
2011	25.96%	17.86%	34.54%

Notes :

1. To make the data comparable shown against literates for the years 1991 and 2001, the corresponding figures for Jammu and Kashmir have not been included in both the years as the data for 1991 Census for Jammu and Kashmir is not available because the 1991 census could not be conducted in this state due to disturbed conditions.
2. To make the data comparable the figures of literates and illiterates shown against 1991 and 2001 do not include the figures for entire district of Kachchh, Morvi, Maliya-Miyana and Wankaner talukas of Rajkot district, Jodiya taluka of Jamnagar district of Gujarat State and entire Kinnaur district of Himachal Pradesh where population enumeration of Census of India, 2001, could not be conducted due to natural calamities.

Table 4.22: State and UT-wiseLiteracy Rate and percentage Increase 2001-2011

Sr. No.	*States/UT*	*Literacy Rates*		*Per cent Increase*
		2011	*2001*	
1.	Andaman & Nicobar	86.27	81.18	6.27
2.	Andhra Pradesh	67.66	61.11	10.72
3.	Arunachal Pradesh	66.95	54.74	22.31
4.	Assam	73.18	64.28	13.85
5.	Bihar	63.82	47.53	34.27
6.	Chandigarh	86.43	81.76	5.71
7.	Chattisgarh	71.04	65.18	8.99
8.	Dadra & Nagar Haveli	77.65	60.03	29.35
9.	Daman & Diu	87.07	81.09	7.37
10.	Delhi	86.34	81.82	5.52
11.	Goa	87.4	82.32	6.17
12.	Gujarat	79.31	69.97	13.35
13.	Haryana	76.64	68.59	11.74
14.	Himachal Pradesh	83.78	77.13	8.62
15.	J & K	68.74	54.46	26.22
16.	Jharkhand	67.63	54.13	24.94
17.	Karnataka	75.6	67.04	12.77
18.	Kerala	93.91	90.92	3.29
19.	Lakshadweep	92.28	87.52	5.44
20.	Madhya Pradesh	70.63	64.11	10.17

Sr. No.	*States/UT*	*Literacy Rates*		*Per cent Increase*
		2011	*2001*	
21.	Maharashtra	82.91	77.27	7.30
22.	Manipur	79.85	68.37	16.79
23.	Meghalya	75.48	63.31	19.22
24.	Mizoram	91.58	88.49	3.49
25.	Nagaland	80.11	67.11	19.37
26.	Odisha	73.45	63.61	15.47
27.	Pondichery	86.55	81.49	6.21
28.	Punjab	76.68	69.68	10.05
29.	Rajasthan	67.06	61.03	9.88
30.	Sikkim	82.2	69.68	17.97
31.	Tamil Nadu	80.33	73.47	9.34
32.	Tripura	87.75	73.66	19.13
33.	Uttar Pradesh	69.72	57.36	21.55
34.	Uttrakhand	79.63	72.28	10.17
35.	West Bengal	77.08	69.22	11.36
	India	**74.04**	**65.38**	13.25

It would be observed from the above Table that Bihar has made phenomenal progress in literacy. Literacy rates rose by 34.27 per cent during the period 2001-2011. However, still its rank is 29. Rajasthan literacy rates rose first by 9.88 per cent, Arunachal Pradesh and J & K have made substantial progress i.e. 22.31 and 26.22 per cent respectively. India's place on the literacy map of the world figures quite low.

Table 4.23: Literacy Rates in States and Union Territory by Sex 2011

Sl. No.	*India/State/UT*	*Literate Persons (%)*	*Males (%)*	*Females (%)*
1.	Andaman & Nicobar Islands	86.27	90.11	81.84
2.	Andhra Pradesh	67.66	75.56	59.74
3.	Arunachal Pradesh	66.95	73.69	59.57
4.	Assam	73.18	78.81	67.27
5.	Bihar	63.82	73.39	53.33
6.	Chandigarh	86.43	90.54	81.38
7.	Chattisgarh	71.04	81.45	60.59
8.	Dadra & Nagar Haveli	77.65	86.46	65.93
9.	Daman & Diu	87.07	91.48	79.59
10.	Goa	87.4	92.81	81.84
11.	Gujarat	79.31	87.23	70.73
12.	Haryana	76.64	85.38	66.77
13.	Himachal Pradesh	83.78	90.83	76.6
14.	Jammu & Kashmir	68.74	78.26	58.01
15.	Jharkhand	67.63	78.45	56.21
16.	Karnataka	75.6	82.85	68.13
17.	Kerala	93.91	96.02	91.98
18.	Lakshadweep	92.28	96.11	88.25
19.	Madhya Pradesh	70.63	80.53	60.02
20.	Maharashtra	82.91	89.82	75.48

Sl. No.	India/State/UT	Literate Persons (%)	Males (%)	Females (%)
21.	Manipur	79.85	86.49	73.17
22.	Meghalaya	75.48	77.17	73.78
23.	Mizoram	91.58	93.72	89.4
24.	Nagaland	80.11	83.29	76.69
25.	NCT of Delhi	86.34	91.03	80.93
26.	Odisha	73.45	82.4	64.36
27.	Pondicherry	86.55	92.12	81.22
28.	Punjab	76.68	81.48	71.34
29.	Rajasthan	67.06	80.51	52.66
30.	Sikkim	82.2	87.29	76.43
31.	Tamil Nadu	80.33	86.81	73.86
32.	Tripura	87.75	92.18	83.15
33.	Uttar Pradesh	69.72	79.24	59.26
34.	Uttarakhand	79.63	88.33	70.7
35.	West Bengal	77.08	82.67	71.16
36.	INDIA	74.04	82.14	65.46

Note:

1. The Literacy rates for India have been worked out by excluding entire Kachchh district, Morvi, Maliya-Miyana and Wankaner talukas of Rajkot district, Jodiya taluka of Jamnagar district of Gujarat State and entire Kinnaur district of Himachal Pradesh where population enumeration of Census of India, 2001, could not be conducted due to natural calamities.

4.16 FERTILITY RATES OF STATES

Table 4.24: Profiles of 9 States and Union Territories of India with TFR ≤ to 2.1

State	Total Fertility Rate 1997	Infant Mortality Rate 1998	Contraceptive Prevalence Rate 1999
Goa	1.0@	23	27.1
Nagaland	1.5@	NA	7.8
Delhi	1.6@	36	28.8
Kerala	1.8@	16	40.5
Pondicherry	1.8@	21	56.9
A & N Islands	1.9@	30	39.9
Tamil Nadu	2.0@	53	50.4
Chandigarh	2.1@	32	35.0
Mizoram	NA	23	34.6

@ Three year moving average TFR 1995-97.

There are 11 States and union territories that have a total fertility rate of more than 2.1 but less than 3.0, ranked accordingly.

The five States of Bihar, Madhya Pradesh, Orissa, Rajasthan and Uttar Pradesh that currently constitute 44 per cent of the total population of India, are projected to comprise 48 per cent of the total population by 2016. In other words, these States alone will contribute an anticipated 55 per cent increase during the period 1996-2016.

4.17 PROJECTED VALUE OF EXPECTATIONS OF LIFE AT BIRTH, TOTAL FERTILITY RATE

Table 4.25 : Projected Values of Expectations of Life at Birth, Total Fertility Rate, and Corresponding Population Projections for Different Periods

Sl. No.	*Indices*	*Period* 1996-2001	2001-2006	2006-2011	2011-2016
1.	Projected values of Expectation of life at birth				
	Males	62.30	63.87	65.65	67.04
	Females	65.27	66.91	67.67	69.18
2.	TFR	3.13	2.88	2.68	2.52
3.	Projected Population*	10124 (2001)	1094.1 (2006)	1178.9 (2011)	1263.5 (2016)

Notes:
1. Population Projection for particular year is shown in millions.
2. Figures in parentheses indicate the end year for which the corresponding projections have been made.
3. *Source* : Population Projections for India and States : 1996 – 2016, Registrar General, India, New Delhi, 1996.

4.18 POPULATION AND DEMOGRAPHIC PROJECTIONS

Right from 1958 the Planning Commission has been constituting an Expert Group on Population Projections prior to the preparation of each of the Five Year Plans so that the information on the population status at the time of initiation of the Plan and population projections for future are available during preparation of the plan. The data from the population projections have been utilised not only for planning to ensure provision of essential necessities such as food, shelter and clothing but also for the prerequisites for human development such as education, employment and health care. Over the years there has been considerable refinement in the methodology used for population projections and substantial improvement in the accuracy of predictions.

In 1996, prior to formulation of the Ninth Plan, the Planning Commission had constituted a Technical Group on Population Projections, under the chairmanship of Registrar General India, to work out the population projections for the country for the period 1996 to 2016 on the basis of census 1991 and other available demographic data. The Group worked out the projections for the population of the country and the major States for the period 1991-2016. The age and sex–wise distribution of the projected population were also worked out. Population pyramids for the period 1971 to 2016 (drawn on the basis of census figures for 1971, 1981 and 1991 and on the basis of population projections for the period from 1996-2016) are shown in Fig. 4.1.

Box 4.2 : Population Projections (1996-2016)

The population will increase from 934 million in 1996 to 1264 million in 2016.

Between the periods 1996-2001 and 2011-2016 there will be a decline of:

CBR	from	24.10	to	21.41
CDR	from	8.99	to	7.48
NGR	from	1.51 %	to	1.39 %
IMR				
Male	from	63	to	38
Female	from	64	to	39

Table 4.26 : Projected Population of India (1996- 2016)

India (in '000)

Year	*Male*	*Female*
1996	484859	449360
1997	492571	457307
1998	500359	465249
1999	508174	473150
2000	515984	480961
2001	523780	488606
2002	531395	496212
2003	539344	504190
2004	547556	512468
2005	555964	520971
2006	564498	529628
2007	573068	538378
2008	581573	546999
2009	590018	555495
2010	598407	563876
2011	606744	572145
2012	614749	580286
2013	622966	588608
2014	631395	597111
2015	640034	605793
2016	648886	614657

Source : Report of the Technical Committee on Population Projections constituted by Planning Commission 1996, Registrar General of India.

Table 4.27 : Percentage Distribution of Projected Population by Age and Sex, 1996-2016, India

	1996			*2001*			*2011*			*2016*		
	M	*F*	*P*	*M*	*F*	*P*	*M*	*F*	*P*	*M*	*F*	*P*
0-4	12.6	13.0	10.6	10.6	10.8	10.7	10.1	10.2	10.1	9.7	9.7	9.7
5-9	13.2	13.3	11.3	11.3	11.6	11.5	9.4	9.4	9.4	9.3	9.3	9.3
10-14	11.9	11.5	12.1	12.1	12.1	12.1	8.9	9.0	8.9	8.7	8.7	8.7
15-19	9.9	9.5	11.0	11.0	10.5	10.8	9.7	9.9	9.8	8.3	8.3	8.3
20-24	8.6	9.0	9.1	9.1	8.7	8.9	10.4	10.3	10.3	9.0	9.1	9.1
25-29	7.8	8.5	7.9	7.9	8.2	8.0	9.4	8.9	9.2	9.7	9.5	9.6
30-34	7.0	7.2	7.2	7.2	7.7	7.4	7.8	7.3	7.6	8.7	8.2	8.5
35-39	6.2	6.0	6.4	6.4	6.6	6.5	6.7	6.9	6.8	7.2	6.8	7.0
40-44	5.3	5.0	5.6	5.6	5.5	5.5	6.0	6.5	6.2	6.2	6.4	6.3
45-49	4.4	4.2	4.7	4.7	4.5	4.6	5.3	5.4	5.4	5.5	5.9	5.7
50-54	3.6	3.4	3.9	3.9	3.7	3.8	4.6	4.6	4.5	4.8	5.0	4.9
55-59	2.9	2.8	3.1	3.1	3.0	3.1	3.7	3.6	3.6	4.0	4.0	4.0
60-64	2.4	2.4	2.4	2.4	2.4	2.4	2.9	2.8	2.9	3.2	3.1	3.1
65-69	1.7	1.8	1.9	1.9	1.9	1.9	2.1	2.1	2.1	2.3	2.4	2.4
70-74	1.3	1.2	1.3	1.3	1.3	1.3	1.4	1.5	1.4	1.6	1.6	1.6
75-79	0.5	0.5	0.8	0.8	0.8	0.8	0.9	1.0	1.0	0.9	1.0	1.0
80+	0.8	0.8	0.6	0.6	0.6	0.6	0.8	0.8	0.8	0.8	0.9	0.9
All	**100.0**	**100.0**	**100.0**	**100.0**	**100.0**	**100.0**	**100.0**	**100.0**	**100.0**	**100.0**	**100.0**	**100.0**

Source: Report of the Technical Committee on Population Projections constituted by Planning Commission, 1996. RGI, India.

Table 4.28: Projected Urban Population of India as on 1st March 1996-2016

(*in '000*)

Year	*Male*	*Female*
1996	133661	120745
1997	137163	124387
1998	140738	128092
1999	144373	131849
2000	148060	135646
2001	151796	139460
2002	155532	143327
2003	159420	147367
2004	163442	151563
2005	167579	155896
2006	171814	160347
2007	176119	164901
2008	180463	169488
2009	184849	1741101
2010	189277	178770
2011	193749	183466
2012	198173	188194
2013	202724	193053
2014	207404	198046
2015	212215	203174
2016	217160	208441

Source: Report of the Technical Committee on Population Projections constituted by Planning Commission 1996, Registrar General of India.

Changes in Population 1971-2016

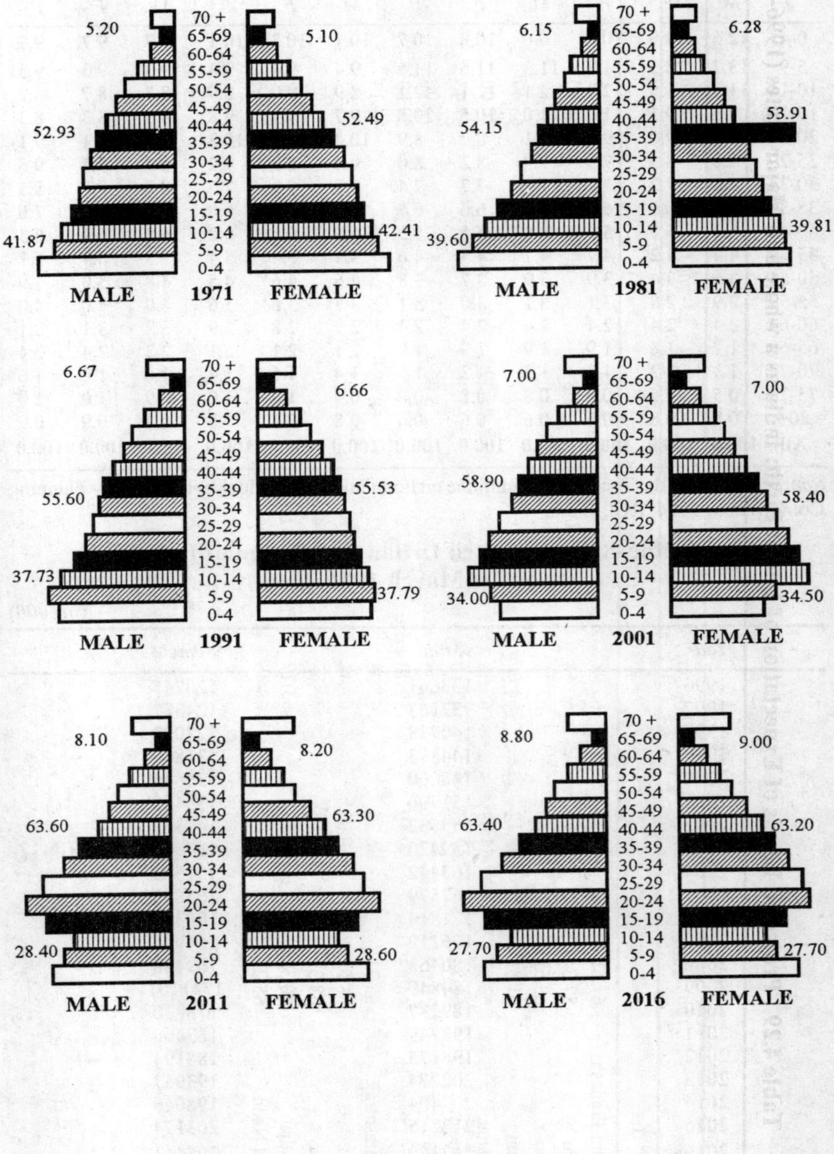

Table 4.29 : Projected Levels of Expectation of Life at Birth: India as a whole and Major States (1996-2016)

	Male				*Female*			
	1996-2001	*2001-2006*	*2006-2011*	*2011-2016*	*1996-2001*	*2001-2006*	*2006-2011*	*2011-2016*
1	2	3	4	5	6	7	8	9
Andhra Pradesh	61.55	62.79	63.92	64.94	63.74	65.00	66.16	67.23
Assam	57.34	58.96	60.44	61.77	58.84	60.87	62.70	64.36
Bihar	63.55	65.66	67.46	69.98	62.07	64.79	67.09	69.05
Gujarat	61.53	63.12	64.60	65.76	62.77	64.10	65.49	66.45
Haryana	63.87	64.64	65.50	66.03	67.39	60.30	70.00	70.00
Karnataka	61.73	62.43	63.10	63.73	65.36	66.44	67.43	68.35
Kerala	70.69	71.67	72.00	72.00	75.00	75.00	75.00	75.00
Madhya Pradesh	56.83	59.19	59.20	60.70	57.21	58.01	59.80	61.40
Maharashtra	65.31	66.75	67.98	69.02	68.19	69.76	71.13	72.00
Orissa	58.52	60.05	61.44	62.70	58.07	59.71	61.23	62.63
Punjab	68.39	69.78	70.88	71.74	71.40	72.00	72.00	72.00
Rajasthan	60.32	62.17	63.79	65.21	61.36	62.80	65.22	66.84
Tamil Nadu	65.21	67.00	68.45	69.64	67.58	69.75	71.54	72.00
Uttar Pradesh	61.20	63.54	65.48	67.10	61.10	64.09	66.60	68.72
West Bengal	64.50	66.08	67.42	68.57	67.20	69.34	71.11	72.00
India (Pooled)	62.30	63.87	65.65	67.04	65.27	66.91	67.67	69.18
India	62.36	64.11	65.36	66.93	63.39	65.43	67.22	68.80

Source : Report of the Technical Committee on Population Projections Constituted by Planning Commission 1996, Registrar General of India.

Table 4.30: Projected Levels of TFRs for Major States and India (1996-2016)

Major States	*SRS*	*Period*			
Year	*1991*	*1996-2001*	*2001-2006*	*2006-2011*	*2011-2016*
Andhra Pradesh	3.00	2.27	2.03	1.88	1.78
Assam	3.50	2.82	2.55	2.33	2.17
Bihar	4.40	2.92	2.53	3.19	2.93
Gujarat	3.10	2.73	2.48	2.26	2.11
Haryana	4.00	3.25	2.93	2.68	2.47
Karnataka	3.10	2.54	2.31	2.14	2.01
Kerala	1.80	1.62	1.61	1.60	1.60
Madhya Pradesh	4.60	3.99	3.72	3.49	3.27
Maharashtra	3.00	2.51	2.28	2.10	1.97
Orissa	3.30	2.64	2.36	2.16	2.01
Punjab	3.10	2.65	2.43	2.25	2.11
Rajasthan	4.60	3.91	3.58	3.30	3.06
Tamil Nadu	2.20	1.87	1.75	1.69	1.65
Uttar Pradesh	5.10	4.75	4.50	4.27	4.05
West Bengal	3.20	2.56	2.31	2.13	1.99
India (Pooled)	3.64	3.13	2.88	2.68	2.52
India	3.60	3.05	2.75	2.52	2.33

Source : Report of the Technical Committee on Population Projections Constituted by Planning Commission 1996, Registrar General of India.

Table 4.31: Year by which TFR of 2.1 will be Achieved

		Year by which Projected TFR will be 2.1
INDIA		**2026***
Andhra Pradesh		2002
Assam		2015
Bihar		2039
Gujarat		2014
Haryana		2025
Karnataka		2009
Kerala	Achieved in 1998	
Madhya Pradesh	Beyond 2060	
Maharashtra		2008
Orissa		2010
Punjab		2019
Rajasthan		2048
Tamil Nadu	Achieved in 1993	
Uttar Pradesh	Beyond 2100	
West Bengal		2009

* Based on Pooled Estimates of TFR.

Source : Report of the Technical Committee on Population Projections Constituted by Planning Commission 1996, Registrar General of India.

Table 4.32 : Projected Levels of Expectation of Life at Birth in Populous States (1996-2016)

	Male			*Female*		
	1996-2001	*2001-2006*	*2011-2016*	*1996-2001*	*2001-2006*	*2011-2016*
Andhra Pradesh	61.6	62.8	64.9	63.7	65.0	67.2
Assam	57.3	59.0	61.8	58.8	60.9	64.4
Bihar	63.6	65.7	70.0	62.1	64.8	69.1
Gujarat	61.5	63.1	65.8	62.8	64.1	66.5
Haryana	63.9	64.6	66.0	67.4	69.3	70.0
Karnataka	61.7	62.4	63.7	65.4	66.4	68.4
Kerala	70.7	71.7	72.0	75.0	75.0	75.0
Madhya Pradesh	56.8	59.2	60.7	57.2	58.0	61.4
Maharashtra	65.3	66.8	69.0	68.2	69.8	72.0
Orissa	58.5	60.1	62.7	58.1	59.7	62.6
Punjab	68.4	69.8	71.7	71.4	72.0	72.0
Rajasthan	60.3	62.2	65.2	61.4	62.8	66.8
Tamil Nadu	65.2	67.0	69.6	67.6	69.8	72.0
Uttar Pradesh	61.2	63.5	67.1	61.1	64.1	68.7
West Bengal	64.5	66.1	68.6	67.2	69.3	72.0
All India	**62.4**	**64.1**	**66.9**	**63.4**	**65.4**	**68.8**

Table 4.33: Projected Levels of Infant Mortality Rate in Populous States (1996-2016)

	Male			*Female*		
	1996-2001	*2001-2006*	*2011-2016*	*1996-2001*	*2001-2006*	*2011-2016*
Andhra Pradesh	65	59	48	56	50	39
Assam	64	53	36	61	51	36
Bihar	54	43	28	55	44	28
Gujarat	46	34	21	44	33	19
Haryana	54	46	34	57	46	31
Karnataka	76	76	75	67	66	64
Kerala	13	10	9	9	8	8
Madhya Pradesh	99	91	76	101	94	83
Maharashtra	46	39	29	46	40	30
Orissa	106	97	81	105	98	87
Punjab	44	39	30	51	45	36
Rajasthan	64	53	37	65	52	35
Tamil Nadu	46	38	26	43	34	23
Uttar Pradesh	64	49	29	74	57	36
West Bengal	54	46	35	56	51	43
All India	**63**	**53**	**38**	**64**	**54**	**39**

Table 4.34 : Projected Population of Major States in India (1996-2016)

	1996	*2001*	*2006*	*2011*	*2016*
			Mn.		
Andhra Pradesh	72.2	76.4	80.6	84.8	88.6
Assam	24.7	26.5	28.4	30.5	32.5
Bihar	93.0	101.8	111.1	121.3	132.3
Delhi	11.7	14.4	17.2	19.5	21.0
Goa	1.4	1.6	1.9	2.0	2.1
Gujarat	45.5	49.0	52.5	56.1	59.3
Haryana	18.5	20.1	21.7	23.4	25.2
Himachal Pradesh	6.0	6.8	7.5	7.9	7.9
Jammu & Kashmir	8.9	10.1	11.1	11.6	11.4
Karnataka	49.3	52.7	56.2	59.6	62.8
Kerala	31.0	32.5	34.2	35.6	36.9
Madhya Pradesh	74.2	81.2	88.6	96.6	105.2
Maharashtra	86.6	92.1	97.3	102.6	107.8
Manipur	2.2	2.6	2.9	3.2	3.3
Meghalaya	2.1	2.5	2.8	3.1	3.2
Nagaland	1.5	1.7	1.9	2.2	2.3
Orissa	34.4	36.2	37.8	39.5	41.0
Punjab	22.4	23.8	25.3	26.7	28.0
Rajasthan	49.7	54.5	59.6	65.3	71.4
Tamil Nadu	59.4	62.2	65.0	67.6	69.9
Tripura	3.3	3.9	4.4	4.8	5.0
Uttar Pradesh	156.7	174.3	194.1	217.1	242.9
West Bengal	74.6	79.9	85.4	90.8	96.2
All India (incl. Others)	934.2	1,012.4	1,094.1	1,178.9	1,263.5

4.19 HIGHLIGHTS OF 2001 CENSUS REGARDING STATES' STATUS

1. Almost half of the country's population lives in five States, namely, Uttar Pradesh, Maharashtra, Bihar, West Bengal and Andhra Pradesh. Uttar Pradesh, Bihar and West Bengal constitute 33 per cent of the total population of India, which was 1.02 billion on March 1, 2001. Uttar Pradesh is followed by Maharashtra and Bihar.
2. While Uttar Pradesh and Maharashtra have held on to the first two positions in terms of their ranking in 2001 as compared to 1991, Bihar has moved on to take the third position from its fifth position pushing West Bengal and Andhra Pradesh to the fourth and fifth places respectively.
3. Kerala has preserved its pre-eminent position in literacy and demographic composition. The state with an average 91 per cent literacy is on top, while the national average is 54.16. The same is with the sex ratio. The sex ratio (proportion of female to male population) has risen to 1058 from 1036 per 1000 in 1991 as against the national average of 933 per 1000 male. More importantly, the decadal population growth was just 9.42 per cent as compared to 21.34 of an all-India average.
4. In just a decade, a population bigger than Canada's has been added to UP's population. If it continues at the same rate, the State's population **would double** in the next 30 years.

UP is way ahead of other states with its population of 16,60,52,859 in March 2001, a 25.80 per cent increase from 1991. The rate of increase in previous decade (1981-91) was 25.55 per cent.

5. West Bengal remains on the top when it comes to the density of population (904). In literacy, it has slipped from the sixth to the eleventh position.
6. Andhra Pradesh has achieved a substantial reduction in growth rate.
7. Bihar has recorded the maximum increase in population growth, whereas Kerala, Tamil Nadu and Andhra Pradesh have recorded the least growth. UP continues to be the most populous State with 16.17 per cent of country's population; followed by Maharashtra with 9.42 per cent and Bihar at 8.07 per cent. West Bengal happens to be the most densely populated state with 904 persons per square km, followed by Bihar with 880 persons.
8. Bihar, with 8.07 per cent of the country's population, has the lowest literacy rate, though it has increased by 10 per cent since 1991.

4.20 POPULATION INCREASE PHENOMENON : DEATH RATE, BIRTH RATE, CONSEQUENCES OF POPULATION EXPLOSION AND REMEDIES FOR CHECKING POPULATION EXPLOSION IN INDIA

Box 4.3: Increase in Population: Phenomenon of Death Rate and Birth Rate

Causes of Decline in Birth Rate	*Causes of High Birth Rate*
1. Decline in the incidence of diseases	1. Universality of marriage
2. Control of epidemics	2. Marriage at an early age
3. Control of famines	3. Religious facts
4. Fall in infant mortality	4. Social factor
5. Expansion of social infrastructure	5. Illiteracy and lack of education
6. Increase in food production	6. Superstition
7. Economic growth and urbanisation	7. Hot and tropical climate
8. Expansion of educational facilities and more awareness towards health	8. Ineffective family planning
	9. Joint family system
	10. Lack of recreational facilities

Box 4.4 : Consequences of Population Explosion

1. Low per capita income.
2. Low rate of capital formation.
3. Unemployment and under-employment.
4. More pressure on land.
5. Increased density of population.
6. Poverty.
7. Low standard of living.
8. Unfavourable balance of payment.
9. Growth of slums.

Box 4.5: Remedies or Methods of Checking of Explosion of Population

Economic Measures	*Social Measures*	*Family Planning*
• Industrial development and expansion • Generation of more employment opportunities • Removal of poverty • Equitable distribution of wealth	• Eradication of illiteracy • Improvement in the condition of women • Raising of minimum age of marriage • Self-control • Change in Social outlook	• Use of media in creating awareness • Early availability of contraceptives • Expansion of health and sanitation services • Increasing male-participation in family planning • Use of incentives and disincentives

5

Population Situation in Developed and Developing Countries

With Special Reference to India

5.1 NOMENCLATURE OF DEVELOPED AND DEVELOPING COUNTRIES

The main characteristics of a developed and a developing country may be summarised as under.

	Developed Countries	*Developing Countries*
1.	Population growth is very low. In some cases it is negative.	Population growth is very high.
2.	Gross National Income is high as compared with population growth.	Gross National income is low.
3.	Per capita income is very high.	Per capita income is very low.
4.	Most of the population is rich.	Most of the population is poor.
5.	Population enjoys a high standard of living.	Majority of the population has a very low standard of living.
6.	People are skilled, literate and gainfully employed.	A large section of the population is illiterate, unskilled and underemployed/ unemployed.
7.	Production in the farms and factories is done by the latest modern techniques.	The techniques of agricultural and industrial production are generally speaking obsolete.
8.	Population is largely dependent on industry.	There is large scale dependence on agriculture.
9.	The distribution of income is relatively even. Even an ordinary person can afford reasonable standard of living.	Most people are very poor. Some people are very rich.

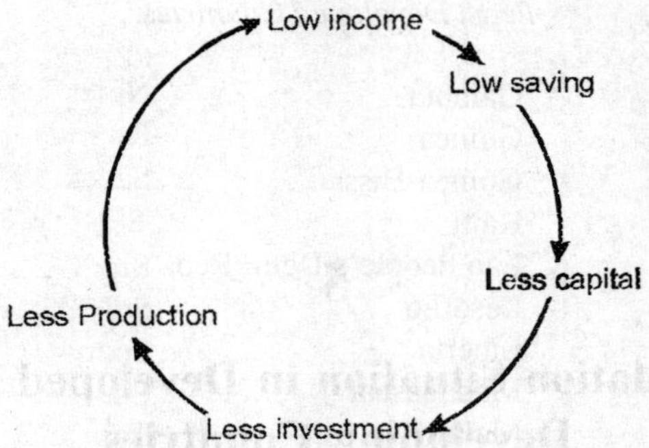

Fig. 5.1: *Economic situation in developing countries*

5.2 INDIA, A DEVELOPING COUNTRY

We all know that an average Indian cannot afford a standard of living as high as an average American or Britisher or a Japanese. This is so because our economy is not developed to that extent. In relation to U.S.A. or Japan, ours is a developing country. According to 1999 estimates, the per capita income in India was the equivalent of only 480 American Dollars while the corresponding figure for an American was 30,600 Dollars. The Swiss had an even higher per capita income of 38,000 Dollars.

This disparity arises out of a number of factors. Our per capita income is relatively low because we have a smaller National Income but a large population. So we suffer from a double disadvantage. A very high percentage of our population is engaged in agriculture which is not able to provide full time employment to all people in the villages. Industrial development is relatively slow and so there are fewer employment opportunities even in the industrial sector of the economy. Fewer goods are produced and even when goods are in plenty, people do not have the money to buy them. In U.S.A. and U.K. only about 2 % of the total population depends on agriculture while in our case this percentage is 73. Pakistan and China also have a very large percentage of population engaged in agriculture. Our agriculture production per hectare is also low in comparison to developed countries. In India, the per capita availability of calories from food is 1998 per day while it is 3652 in U.S.A. and 3537 in West Germany. China, even though a developing country like ours, has a per capita availability of 2472 calories per day.

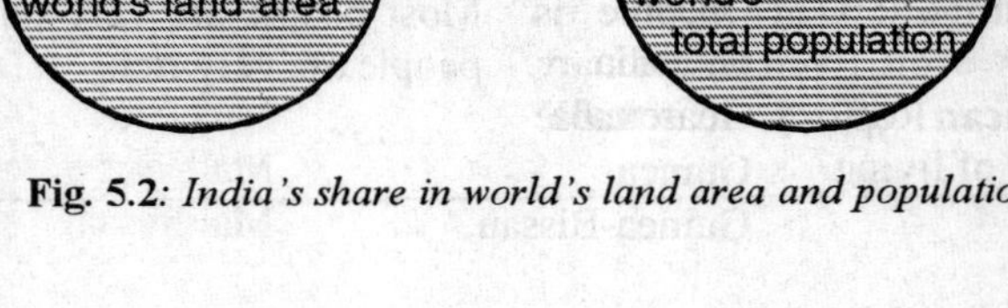

Fig. 5.2: *India's share in world's land area and population*

Least Developed Countries

Afghanistan
Angola
Bangladesh
Benin
Bhutan
Burkina Faso
Burundi
Cambodia
Cape Verde
Central African Rep.
Chad
Comoros
Djibouti
Equatorial Guinea
Ethiopia
Gambia
Guinea
Guinea-Bissau
Haiti
Lao People's Dem. Rep.
Lesotho
Liberia
Madagascar
Malawi
Maldives
Mali
Mauritania
Mozambique
Myanmar
Nepal
Niger
Rwanda
Samoa (Western)
SãoTome'andPrincipe
Sierra Leone
Solomon Islands
Somalia
Sudan
Tanzania, U. Rep. of
Togo
Uganda
Vanuatu
Yemen
Zaire
Zambia

Developing Countries

Afghanistan
Algeria
Angola
Antigua and Barbuda
Argentina
Bahamas
Bahrein
Bangladesh
Barbados
Belize
Benin
Bhutan
Bolivia
Botswana
Brazil
Brunei Darussalam
Burkina Faso
Burundi
Cambodia
Cameroon
Cape Verde
Central African Rep.
Chad
Chile
China
Colombia
Comoros
Congo
Costa Rica
Cote d'Ivoire
Cuba
Cyprus
Djibouti
Dominica
Dominican Rep.
Ecuador
Egypt
El Salvador
Equatorial Guinea
Ethiopia
Fiji
Gabon
Gambia
Ghana
Grenada
Guatemala
Guinea
Guinea-Bissau
Guyana
Haiti
Honduras
Kong Kong
India
Indonesia
Iran, Islamic Rep. Of
Iraq
Jamaica
Jordan
Kenya
Korea, Dem. People's Rep. of
Korea, Rep. of
Kuwait
Lao, People's Dem. Rep.
Lebanon
Lesotho
Liberia
Libyan Arab Jamahiriya
Madagascar
Malawi
Malaysia
Maldives

Mali
Mauritania
Mauritius
Mexico
Mongolia
Morocco
Mozambique
Myanmar
Namibia
Nepal
Nicaragua
Niger
Nigeria
Oman
Pakistan
Panama
Papua New Guinea
Paraguay
Peru
Philippines
Qatar
Rwanda
Saint Kitts and Nevis
Saint Lucia
Saint Vincent
Samoa (Western)
Sāo Tome' and Principe
Saudi Arabia
Senegal
Seychelles
Sierra Leone
Singapore
Solomon Islands
Somalia
South Africa
Sri Lanka
Sudan
Suriname
Swaziland
Syrian Arab Rep.
Tanzania, U. Rep. of
Thailand
Togo
Trinidad and Tobago
Tunisia
Turkey
Uganda
United Arab Emirates
Uruguay
Vanuatu
Venezuela
Vietnam
Yemen
Zaire
Zambia
Zimbabwe

Developed or Industrial Countries

Albania
Armenia
Australia
Austria
Azerbaijan
Belarus
Belgium
Bulgaria
Canada
Czech Rep.
Denmark
Estonia
Finland
France
Georgia
Germany
Greece
Hungary
Iceland
Ireland
Israel
Italy
Japan
Kazakhstan
Kyrgyzstan
Latvia
Lithuania
Luxembourg
Malta
Moldova, Rep. of
Netherlands
New Zealand
Norway
Poland
Portugal
Romania
Russian Federation
Slovakia
Spain
Sweden
Switzerland
Tajikistan
Turkmenistan
Ukraine
United Kingdom
USA
Uzbekistan

Notes

1. All developing countries include least developed countries also.
2. Based on Human Development Report (2000).

5.3 Comparative Data on Important Indicators Regarding Select Countries

Data are presented in Table 5.1.

Table 5.1: Comparative Data on Population and Demography: Developed and Developing Countries

Sl. No.	Country	Population Total (thousand) 2001	Density of Population	Annual Growth Rate Total %	Urban %	Rural %	Under 5 Mortality Rank	Total Fertility Rate	Life Expectancy (1999)
1	2	3	4	5	6	7	8	9	10
	Developed countries								
1.	Australia	19338 (1.9 crore)	03	1.0	0.9	0.7	175	1.8	78
2.	Austria	8075 (81 Lakhs)	96	–0.1	0.5	–0.2	175	1.4	77
3.	Canada	31015 (3.1 crore)	3	0.8	01.11	0.8	165	1.6	79
4.	Denmark	5333 (53 lakhs)	124	0.2	0.2	–0.4	175	1.7	76
5.	France	59453 (6 crore)	108	0.4	0.6	–0.7	175	1.7	78
6.	Germany	82007 (8.2 crore)	230	0.0	0.2	–1.5	175	1.3	77
7.	Italy	57503 (5.8 crore)	191	–0.1	0.1	–0.7	165	1.2	78
8.	Japan	127335 (12.7 crore)	337	0.1	0.3	–0.7	187	1.4	80
9.	Norway	4488 (45 lakhs)	14	0.4	0.9	–0.3	187	1.9	78
10.	Russian federation	144664 (14.4 crore)	8	–0.6	0.2	–1.7	—	—	—
11.	Sweden	8833 (88 lakhs)	20	–0.1	0.3	–0.3	187	1.6	79
12.	Switzerland	7170 (72 lakhs)	174	–0.1	0.6	0.1	187	1.5	79
13.	UK	59542 (6.0 crore)	244	0.2	0.2	–0.6	165	1.7	78
14.	USA	285926 (28.6 crore)	31	0.9	1.0	–0.4	158	2.0	77

S. No.	Country	Population Total (thousand 2001)	Density of Population	Annual Growth Rate			Under 5 Mortality Rank	Total Fertility Rate	Life Expectancy (1999)
				Total %	Urban %	Rural %			
1	2	3	4	5	6	7	8	9	10
	Developing countries								
1.	India	1025096 (102 crore)	312	1.5	2.8	0.8	49	3.0	63
2.	Afghanistan	22474 (2.2 crore)	34	3.7	6.9	4.2	4	6.7	46
3.	Angola	13527 (.3 crore)	11	3.0	4.9	2.1	2	6.6	48
4.	Bangladesh	140369 (14 crore)	975	2.1	4.0	0.9	53	3.0	59
5.	Bhutan	2141 (21 lakhs)	46	2.6	6.0	2.4	45	5.3	62
6.	Brazil	172559 (17.2 crore)	20	1.2	1.8	-1.4	89	2.2	67
7.	China	1284972 (128 crore)	134	0.7	2.3	-0.1	87	1.8	70
8.	Cuba	11237 (1.1 crore)	101	0.3	0.5	-0.3	158	1.6	76
9.	Indonesia	214840 (21.4 crore)	113	1.2	3.6	-0.6	73	2.5	66
10.	Maldives	300 (3 lakhs)	1006	3.0	3.5	2.4	55	5.2	65
11.	Myanmar	48364 (4.8 crore)	71	1.2	2.9	0.4	39	2.3	61
12.	Nepal	23593 (2.3 crore)	168	2.3	5.1	1.8	47	4.3	58
13.	Nigeria	116929 (11.7 crore)	127	2.6	4.1	0.7	15	5.0	50
14.	Pakistan	144971 (14.4 crore)	182	2.5	4.1	1.5	39	4.8	65
15.	Sierralone	4587 (45 lakhs)	64	4.5	4.0	1.1	1	5.9	39
16.	Sri Lanka	19104 (1.9 crore)	291	0.9	2.8	0.4	135	2.1	71

5.4 ANALYSIS OF POPULATION SITUATION IN DEVELOPING AND DEVELOPED COUNTRIES WITH SPECIAL REFERENCE TO INDIA

1. Pressure on Land

While India had a density of only 103 persons in 1941, the figure rose to 267 in 1991 and 324 in 2001. This implies a progressive by increasing pressure on land and resources with consequent overcrowding, squalor, proliferation of slums and jhuggi clusters, which have become breeding grounds for diseases.

Africa in early 2000 had a population of 820 million as compared with India's 1007 millions population, in an area of 30 million sq kms. about 10 times our area of 3.3 million sq kms. Europe too has a population of 730 million with an area of 10 million sq kms or three times the size of India. Similarly, North America and South America with an area of 41 sq kms had a combined population of 824 million. Even China, with a population of 1276 million as against India's 1007 million population has landmass thrice of India's size.

India has nearly 330 million hectares land area. Out of this, it is estimated that ultimately about 190 million hectares are cultivable (113 million hectares of irrigable area and the rest rainfed). In order to feed the increased level of population when it reaches stability of 1.7 billion in 2150 A.D., it will be necessary to produce about 350 million tons of foodgrains. This establishes the need to increase the yield. The average yield in India is 1.7 tons per hectare (for cereals) as compared to 3.5 tons per hectare in some countries like U.S.A. and Egypt. It would be too simplistic to assume the possibility of manifold increase in the yield on a sustainable basis. Several scientific and technological inputs are needed. Management of water resources presents even greater challenge than land resources management in future. It is estimated that out of about 400 million hectare meters of water contributed by rain, snow and inflows from the rivers flowing in from other countries, only about 110 million hectare meters of water is usuable. Under the existing pattern of food production, it will be possible to produce 260 million tons. On the other hand we would need 350 million tons to feed 1.7 billion people. This is based on the present consumption level of 204 kilograms per capita. It may be mentioned that in China, per capita gram consumption is 280 kg. To reach this level, we need to produce 480 million tons.

More than three-fourths of the world's population live in developing countries but they enjoy only 16 per cent of the world's income. One-fourth of the world's population i.e. population of the developed countries enjoy 84% of the world's income. Out of the ten most populous countries in the world, three are developed countries and seven are developing countries. In general, developed countries are less populous countries.

Almost all developed countries are industrially advanced countries and developing countries are industrially backward.

Population of developed countries is more prosperous, and enjoys a better standard of living than the developing countries.

Population of developed countries have more longetivity than the developing countries.

Per capita income is higher in the developed countries as compared with the developing countries.

There is negligible annual growth rate of population of the developed countries. Countries like Austria, Italy, Russian Federation, Sweden and Switzerland have even negative growth rate.

Almost all countries of Europe are developed countries. In the rest of the world, barring a few countries, all others are developing countries.

Some of the developed countries of Europe remained colonial powers for a pretty long period. A large number of Asian and African countries that are now developing countries remained under the domination of the European colonial powers.

Women in the developed countries enjoy better status than the women of the developing countries.

Infant mortality rate is negligible in the developed countries whereas in developing countries it is very high.

2. Maternal Mortality

With 16% of the world's population, India accounts for over 20% of the world's maternal deaths. The maternal mortality ratio, defined as the number of maternal deaths per 100,000 live births, is incredibly high at 408 per 100,000 live births for the country (1997), which is unacceptable when compared to current indices elsewhere in Asia.

Table 5.1: Maternal Mortality Ratios in Asia

Country	*Maternal Mortality Ratio*
Sri Lanka	30
China	115
Thailand	200
Pakistan	340
Indonesia	390
India	437
Bangladesh	850
Nepal	1500

Within India, the inter-state differentials are a matter of concern.

Table 5.2: Inter-State Differences within India in Maternal Mortality Ratios

Country	*Maternal Mortality Ratio*
Kerala	87
Bihar	451
Madhya Pradesh	498
Rajasthan	607
Uttar Pradesh	707
Orissa	739

3. Infant Mortality

It is estimated that about 7 per cent of new-born infants perish within a year. Poor maternal health results in low birth weight and premature babies. Infant and childhood diarrhoeal diseases, acute respiratory infections and malnutrition contribute to high infant mortality rates. Additionally, in India, across the board (rural or urban areas), there are more female deaths in the age group of 0-14 than elsewhere. Although the Infant Mortality Rate (IMR) has decreased from 146 per 1000 births in 1951 to 72 per 1000 (1997), and sex differentials are narrowing. Again there are wide inter-state differences recorded in 1998, as is clear from Table 5.3. In comparison, we may note the infant mortality rates in South Asia and elsewhere:

Table 5.3: Infant Mortality Rates under 5 years in Asia (1999)

Country	*Infant Mortality Rate*
Sri Lanka	19
Thailand	30
China	41
Indonesia	52
India	98
Pakistan	112
Bangladesh	89
Nepal	104

4. Preference for Male Child

In India, the birth of a girl child is generally regarded as a misfortune. Sons are in demand, leading to an uncontrolled growth in their number thus imbalancing gender ratio. Sex ratio in India is 933 i.e. the lowest in the most populous countries. World sex ratio is 986 (sex ratio is the number of females per 1000 males).

Following table reflects the sex ratio in India vis-à-vis some other countries.

Table 5.4: Sex Ratio of Selected Countries

Sl. No.	*Country*	*Sex ratio (Females per 1,000 Males)*
1	2	3
	World	**986**
1	Bangladesh	953
2	Brazil	1,025
3	China	944
4	India	933
5	Indonesia	1,004
6	Japan	1,041
7	Nigeria	1,016
8	Pakistasn	938
9	Russian Fed.	1,140
10	U.S.A.	1,029

5. Baby-Boom and Female Illiteracy

Female illiteracy rates negatively affect their fertility levels and the health of their families. Nearly 54 per cent of females are still illiterate in India. Women in India do not have adequate freedom to accept contraception without their menfolk's approval. A survey conducted by a Mumbai based Institute for Research in Reproduction, (IRR) under the Indian Council of Medical Research in 1996 revealed that India's population control programme is not making much dent because of the 'negative attitude' of men who consider family planning their wives' business. Only 41 per cent women in India use contraceptives as compared with women in countries like Canada (73%), China (92%), U.K. (82%) and U.S.A. (74%).

Following table illustrates the relationship between illiteracy and use of contraceptive by women.

Table 5.5: Illiteracy Rates and use of Contraceptives

From above, it is quite clear that literacy has a positive effect on the use of contraceptives, other things remaining the same.

	Country	*Women Illiteracy Rate as % of Males*	*Use of Contraceptives*
1.	Afghanistan	35%	19%
2.	China	85%	91%
3.	India	62%	41%
4.	Korea, Dem. Republic of	99%	79%
5.	Pakistan	58%	29%
6.	Turkey	79%	64%

6. Fertility Rate

Fertility rate also greatly affects demography.

Table 5.6: Fertility Rate in Select Countries

Sl. No.	*Country*	*Fertility Rate*	*Sl. No.*	*Country*	*Fertility Rate*
1.	Afghanistan (199)	6.7	12.	Nepal	4.7
2.	Bangladesh	3.0	13.	Nigeria	5.0
3.	Canada	1.6	14.	Russian Federation	1.4
4.	Cuba	1.6	15.	Saudi Arabia	5.6
5.	China	1.8	16.	Sri Lanka	2.1
6.	Egypt	3.2	17.	Sweden	1.6
7.	Ethiopia	6.2	18.	Switzerland	1.5
8.	Germany	1.3	19.	UAE	3.3
9.	India	3.0	20.	United Kingdom	1.7
10.	Korea, Republic of	1.7	21.	United States	2.0
11.	Pakistan	3.7			

From the above table, two important points emerge.

1. All advanced and industrialised countries have very low fertility rates.
2. In countries, where majority of the population is Muslim, fertility rate in general is high.
3. India's fertility rate is quite high and needs to be checked.

7. Density of Population

Other things being equal, developing countries with high density of population have low per capita income. Countries like Australia, Canada and New Zealand offer immigration opportunities and a large number of people from India have settled there. Other countries like U.K. and U.K. also encourage immigration, of course according to a fixed quota which is of a limited nature.

Table 5.7: Density of Population in Select Countries (1999)

	Country	*Area in sq km*	*Population*	*Density of Population*
1.	Australia	7,682,300	18,705,000	2.43
2.	Brazil	8,511,965	1,67,988,000	19.73
3.	Canada	9,976,139	3,085,700	3.09
4.	China	9,561,100	12,66,838,000	132.50
5.	Japan	3,77,765	1,26,505,000	33.48
6.	Myanmar	676,553	45,059,000	66.60
7.	Nepal	147,181	23,385,000	158.88
8.	New Zealand	269,057	3,828,000	14.23
9.	Pakistan	796,095	1,52,331,000	191.34
10.	Russian Federation	17,075,000	1,47,196,000	8.62
11.	Sri Lanka	65,610	18,639,000	284.08
12.	U.K.	244,108	58,744,000	240.64
13.	U.S.A.	9,372,614	2,76,218,000	29.47
14.	India	3,287,263	9,98,056,000	303.61

Table 5.8: The 20 Countries With Lowest Singulate Mean Age At Marriage (SMAM) And Largest Gender Difference In SMAM

Region	*Singulate Mean age at Marriage (years)*		*Sex Difference in SMAM (Male Minus Female)*
	Male	*Female*	
Africa	Malawi (23.5) Mozambique (22.6) Niger (23.9) Sao Tome and Principe (23.0) Uganda (22.5)	Angola (19.4) Burkina Faso (18.9) Central African Rep. (19.4) Chad (18.0) Congo (18.4) Democratic Rep. of Congo (16.6) Eritrea (19.6) Gambia (19.2)	Burkina Faso (8.6) Cameroon (6.5) Chad (6.1) Congo (8.6) Côte d'Ivoire (7.2) Democratic Rep. of Congo (8.6) Eritrea (5.7) Gambia (9.2)

Region	*Singulate mean age at marriage (years)*		*Sex difference in SMAM (male minus female)*
	Male	*Female*	
		Malawi (18.4) Mali (18.4) Mozambique (18.0) Niger (17.6) Sao Tome and Principe (17.8) Uganda (18.2)	Liberia (6.5) Mali (7.5) Mauritania (7.7) Niger (6.3) Nigeria (6.9) Senegal (8.1) Sudan (6.4)
Asia	China (23.8) India (23.9) Kyrgyzstan (23.9) Maldives (23.2) Nepal (22.0) Tajikistan (23.1) Turkmenistan (23.8) Ukraine (24.0) Uzbekistan (23.3)	Afghanistan (17.8) Bangladesh (18.1) India (19.3) Maldives (19.1) Nepal (18.8)	Afghanistan (7.5) Bangladesh (6.8)
Europe and North America	Rep. of Moldova (23.7) San Marino (22.2)		
Latin America and Caribbean	Cuba (23.5) Guatemala (23.8) Honduras (23.8)		Montserrat (8.3)
Oceania	Marshall Islands (23.7)		Nauru (7.3)

6

Key Statements About Population

Their Impact on Country's Development and Need for Population Education

6.1 INTRODUCTION

This chapter may be considered as an introductory one dealing with the population problems and concerns and their impact on India's developmental needs. This is intended to provide an overview of programmes and activities involved in understanding and solving population related issues. This brings out the dire need of imparting population education to the students in our country. In fact the entire book revolves round this chapter. The statements are pointers to various concerns and issues relating to population control and education.

6.2 FOUR-FOLD DIVISION OF KEY ISSUES AND STATEMENTS ON POPULATION PROBLEMS

1. Our fast growing population.
2. Growing numbers and our struggle for Better Living or Quality of Life.
3. Population on March, Environment on Retreat.
4. Battle to be fought and won in every family.

6.3 OUR GROWING POPULATION

1. Every sixth person on earth is an Indian.
2. India with 102 crore population is the second largest populous country in the world.
3. India accounts for a meagre 2.4 per cent of the world surface area yet it supports and sustains a whopping 16.7 per cent of the world population.
4. It is estimated that in 2050, India will overtake China and become the most populous country in the world with 17.2 per cent population living here.
5. As against world's 1.4 per cent annual growth rate of population, India's annual growth rate was 1.9 per cent in 1991-2001.

6. The average density of population in India is seven times the world average. India's density is 330 as compared with world's density 55.
7. The rapid growth in our country is due to the widening gap between the birth rate and death rate.
8. The death rate in our country has been brought down substantially on account of improved and extended facilities for public health and medical care.
9. Quite a substantial section of our population is not yet fully convinced about the necessity of bringing down birth rate corresponding to falling death rate.
10. Still the bulk of our population is not aware of the use of scientific methods and techniques of postponing or curtailing births in their families. Child mortality has been greatly reduced in our country on account of better care and health.
11. The average expected span of life of an Indian at one time (beginning of the century) was calculated to be 23 years only. Today it has been increased nearly three times i.e. it is now 63 years.
12. On an average there are three children in an Indian family whereas in many developing countries there is only one child.

The dependent population in India is very large. Thus the per capita income is bound to be low.

6.4 GROWING NUMBERS AND OUR STRUGGLE FOR BETTER LIVING OR QUALITY OF LIFE

* Broadly speaking the total income of the country is the sum total of the income of all the families belonging to that country.
* The total income of the country will increase to the extent every family is able to increase its income.
* The family would be able to increase its income if every grown up member of the family works hard and that in every family the number of dependent young members is kept to a reasonable minimum.
* If the total income of the country is evenly distributed over its entire population, the figure thus arrived is called per capita income. In other words it is an average income per individual or per head.
* Normally per capita income should rise in proportion to the national income.
* In our country per capita income has not risen in proportion to the national income as there was tremendous rise in the population of our country.
* Rapid population growth has been largely responsible for very slow or meagre improvement in the living conditions of an average individual.
* The living conditions of the people are broadly indicated by the food they eat, the clothes they wear, the shelter they live in and the medical and educational facilities that they are able to enjoy.
* India with very hard labour has been able to increase its food production by four times in the last 50 years. Yet bulk of its population

is denied a balanced and nutritious diet, which is a must for healthy, productive and satisfying living.

* Inspite of tremendous increase in the number of schools, teachers and the literate people in our country, the number of illiterate people is on constant increase.
* Now there are many more doctors in our country, yet their number is almost insignificant in terms of the people they are supposed to serve.
* By and large, national savings are the sum total of the savings of all the families put together.
* Generally the national savings would increase only to the extent every family in the country is able to save.
* Since an average Indian family is large in size and has a very large proportion of the dependent population its savings are very meagre.
* When the families and also the countries do not generate sufficient savings they find it difficult to make necessary investments for creating job opportunities.
* During the last fifty years India has created a large number of jobs for its people. Nonetheless, the number of people who are unemployed has been constantly increasing.
* Able bodied unemployed adults are a burden and a source of anxiety to themselves and to the families to which they belong.
* Unemployed people are a threat to the society and its well being.
* Every healthy society is keen to develop dignity of labour amongst its people and to develop proper attitude towards hard and productive work.
* Increased production calls for hard work, careful planning and intelligent use of all the resources at the disposal of the society.

6.5 POPULATION ON MARCH AND ENVIRONMENT ON RETREAT

1. No other species except man on earth has ever tried or succeeded in changing, manipulating and modifying environment.
2. Man has been interfering with his environment in various ways such as clearing forests, breaking grasslands, bringing more and more land under cultivation, digging mining and drilling for minerals.
3. Several changes brought about by man in his environment have had an overall adverse effect.
4. Adverse and harmful changes are like large scale deforestation, over-grazing of grasslands, shifting cultivation, unscientific tilling of land leading resulting in soil erosion, impoverishment of soil, decreasing wild life and disturbing ecological balance in nature.
5. Of late man has been exploiting some of the valuable resources recklessly, for instance mineral oil, natural gas, coal, copper and tin.
6. Man's interference with natural environment has led to extinction of certain animal species.
7. Some of the large scale changes brought about by man in the environment have changed local climates with serious repercussions.
8. Like any other animal, man is a mere consumer of food. He is not a manufacturer of food.

9. Manufacture of food is an exclusive prerogative of the vegatal world or plant kingdom. Plants manufacture food with the help of Sun's energy through the process of photosynthesis.
10. Man has to distinguish clearly between renewable and exhaustible resources and their relevance for continuance of human civilisation.
11. Man has to learn to overcome the temptation to use and thereby exhaust known reserves of exhaustible resources such as coal, mineral oil and natural gas.
12. Man has to learn how best to use natural resources that are renewable, for instance solar energy, water, wind and tidal energy, various forest products and agricultural produce.
13. Man has to learn and use new economics based on recycling like scrap, rags, used paper etc.
14. Every increasing population, desirous of having high standard of living has been responsible for rapid depletion of natural resources, pollution of air, water, soil and deterioration of environment.
15. The widespread use of insecticides, pesticides and chemical fertilizers also adds to pollution of water and results in high concentration of these harmful chemicals in fish, birds and in their eggs, not excluding human beings who eat them.
16. Ignorance and apathy regarding environmental concerns also lead to unhygienic habits such as using sources of potable water for bathing and washing of hands.
17. Man has to learn the laws of nature, secrets and mysteries of nature for making their optimum use to his own advantage.
18. Man cannot live and prosper by being constantly at war with or away from nature. On the other hand, he must learn to live in peace and harmony with nature.

6.6 BATTLE TO BE FOUGHT AND WON IN EVERY FAMILY

1. Food, clothing, shelter, medicine, education, recreation and savings are pillars on which happiness of the entire family rests.
2. Every member of the family needs adequate nutritious and balanced diet.
3. This need is greater and more important in the case of an expectant and nursing mother and growing children.
4. These demands are more difficult to meet where there are many children born in succession.
5. A happy mother is the secret of a happy family.
6. A mother undergoing many and Insufficiently spaced deliveries cannot be expected to maintain good health for herself and her nursing and growing children.
7. For the good health of both the mother and children, there should not only be few deliveries but adequately spaced deliveries.
8. Only a small family is in a better position to provide medical and educational facilities to its members.
9. It is only the healthy and educated members of family who can earn more and be successful in life.

10. Large families not only create problems for themselves but also tend to be more demanding on the community and the state, at least up to such time as their members grow up and are able to learn on their own.
11. People who are convinced of the advantages of a small family norm and have the courage of conviction also can take to planning a family as a way of life.
12. It is the duty of the society and particularly educated people to demand small family norm and advise those who are ignorant about it.
13. The final solution to the population problem lies to accepting and practising a small family norm by each and every family
14. Science and technology which help in fighting and postponing death, also come to our rescue by postponing births as per wishes of the parents.
15. To take help of science and technology in one case and leave the other to the so-called 'Will of the God' is only hypocritic to say the least.

7

National Policy on Education (NPE) and Population Education

7.1 NATIONAL POLICY ON EDUCATION 1986 ON POPULATION EDUCATION

The NPE 1986 took due not of the growing population of India and made recommendations on population in the following paragraphs:

1. Paragraph 1.13
2. Paragraph 3.4

Paragraph 1.13. It states, "The growth of our population needs to be brought down significantly over the coming decades. The largest single factor that could help achieve this is the spread of literacy and education among women".

Paragraph 3.4 on Population Education. The paragraph states as under: "The National system of Education will be based on a national curriculum framework which contains a common core alongwith other components that are flexible. The common core will include history of India's freedom movement, the constitutional obligations and other content essential to nurture national identity. These elements will cut across subject areas and will be designed to promote values such as India's common culture, heritage, egalitarianism, democracy and secularism, equality of sexes, protection of environment, removal of social barriers, observance of the small family norm and inculcation of scientific temper. All educational programmes will be carried on in strict conformity with secular values".

Paragraph 4.11 relating to adult education programmes states that these programmes will be "linked with ...observance of small family norm".

7.2 COMMITTEE FOR REVIEW OF NATIONAL POLICY ON EDUCATION, 1986 ON POPULATION EDUCATION

The government of India appointed in 1990 a Review Committee to review the implementation of the National Policy on Education, 1986. The Review Committee Report is also known as the Ramamurti Committee Report after the name of its chairperson.

Para 4.1.40 regarding 'Empowerment of Women', in its recommendations states: "Along with the means for economic independence for women the issues of women's health, including reproductive health and sexuality, should be included in the parameters for empowerment of women."

7.3 REVISED NATIONAL POLICY ON EDUCATION (1992) AND POPULATION EDUCATION

The entire implementation of the NPE 1986 was evaluated in 1992 and certain modifications were incorporated in it.

1. A new *Para 8.16* was introduced. It stated as under:
   "Population education must be viewed as an important part of the nation's strategy to contain the growth of population starting at the primary and secondary school levels with inculcation of consciousness about the looming crisis due to expansion of population. Educational programmes should actively motivate and inform youth and adults about family planning and responsible parenthood".
2. *Para 4.12 under Adult Education.* It reads as:
   "Since involvement of the participants in the literacy campaigns is of crucial importance, the National Literacy Mission will be geared to the national goals such as alleviation of poverty, national integration, environmental conservation, observance of the small family norm, promotion of women's equality, universalisation of primary education, basic health care etc."

7.4 PROGRAMME OF ACTION–POA (1992) ON NPE (1986,1992) AND POPULATION EDUCATION

The POA included the following paragraphs on population education.

1. *Chapter 1.* In Chapter 1 entitled *Education for Women's Equality*, the Programme of Action (1992) suggested inter alia the following parameter for the empowerment of women:
   "enable women to make informed choices in areas like education, employment and health (especially reproductive health)"

2(2) *Chapter 5 : Adult and Continuing Education. Para 5.1(e)* states, "Propagation of the message of small family norm which has been yet another issue of national concern as also one of the sub-themes of all literacy campaigns would continue to be accelerated. This, along with other measures like importance of delayed marriage, proper spacing, changing existing social biases in favour of the male child in our society, etc. will be integrated into the content of the primer (for adults), content of materials for neo-literates, curriculum and course content of training and orientation of instructional lessons, evaluation, etc."

3. *Chapter 6. Early Childhood Care and Education*
   (i) *Para 6.1.3(v)* stipulates the provision of "Maternal and child health services through primary health centres and sub-centres and other agencies."
   (iv) *Para 6.3.1* stipulates, "Even a modest development process during this period (Early childhood Care and Education – ECCE)

includes care of mother during pregnancy (ante-natal health check-up, nutritional support, control of anaemia, immunisation for prevention of tetanus following delivery etc.) hygienic and skilled birth attendance, nutritional care of mother during lactation, correct infant feeding practices, immunisation of infant from communicable diseases, mother's education in child care, early childhood stimulation, and health and nutritional support throughout."

4. *Chapter 8. Secondary Education*

   Para 8.9.14 Population Education: The NE specified observance of the small family norm as one of the core curricular elements at all stages of education. This has been sought to be achieved through population education programme. Contents relating to population education have been integrated into the syllabi and textbooks of geography, economics, civics, science, and languages at the secondary stage. These contents have been drawn from areas like population and economic development, social development, environment, health and nutrition, family life and population dynamics. These contents are related to six major themes, viz. (i) Family size and family welfare, (ii) Delayed marriage, (iii) Responsible parenthood, (iv) Population change and resource development, (v) Population-related values and beliefs and (vi) Status of women.

7.5 NATIONAL CURRICULUM FRAMEWORK FOR SCHOOL EDUCATION NCERT (2000) ON POPULATION EDUCATION

The National Curriculum Framework for school education points out the need for population education in Chapter 1 and Chapter 5.

1. *Chapter 1.4.10*. Under the caption 'Integrated Diverse Curriculum Concerns,' it states, "At a time when concerns such as 'literacy', 'family system', 'neighbourhood education', 'environmental education', 'consumer education', 'tourism education', 'AIDS education', 'human rights education', 'legal literacy', 'peace education', 'population education', 'migration education', 'global education' and 'safety education' are making a case for separate place in the school curriculum, the best approach would be to integrate these ideas and concepts, after a careful analysis in the existing areas of learning. Appropriate strategies for this integration may be suitably worked out in the detailed subject curricula."
2. *Chapter 2.5*. Under the caption 'general objectives of education', it includes (a) Appreciation of the various consequences of large families and over population and need for checking population growth. (b) Cultivating the power of understanding of and attitude towards healthy sex related issues and respectful attitude toward members of the opposite sex.

7.6 SUMMARY : MAIN ELEMENTS OF POPULATION EDUCATION RECOMMENDED IN THE NPE, PROGRAMME OF ACTION AND NATIONAL CURRICULUM FRAMEWORK

1. Need for bringing down population.
2. Literacy and education to play an important role in bringing down population.
3. Equality of sexes to form an integral part of core curriculum.
4. Small family norm also to form an integral part of core curriculum.
5. Adult education programmes to be linked with small family norm.
6. Reproductive health and sexuality to be included in the parameters of empowerment of women.
7. Population education to start at the primary and secondary levels.
8. Educational programmes for adults and youth to include population education.
9. Social bias in favour of male child to be eliminated.
10. Delayed marriages to be practised.
11. Spacing of children to be attended to.
12. Mother care during pregnancy to be well looked after.
13. Development of health population values to be cultivated in the students.

8

Growing Population

Need and Importance of Population Education in India

8.1 CRITICAL POSITION

India is in a critical position as regards the problems created by its growing numbers. In an earlier chapter we have noted that the population of India during the 20th century increased from 23.8 crore in 1901 to 102.7 crore (March 2011). This increase has posed serious problems of great magnitude. Before we discuss measures to control the growing population, it would be in the fitness of things to dilate upon the causes of its growth.

8.2 CAUSES OR FACTORS OF GROWING POPULATION IN INDIA

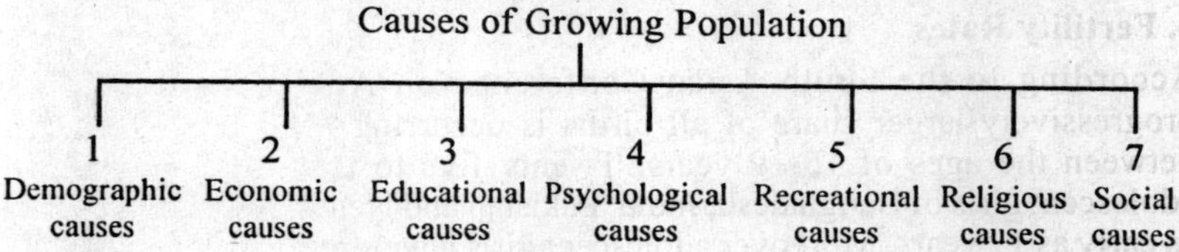

8.3 DEMOGRAPHIC CAUSES

1. Gap Between Birth Rate and Death Rate

It is a healthy sign that death rate in India over the years has been declining. However, in India, which is on the path of economic development, the other variable of population growth i.e. birth rate has not declined proportionately. In the seven decades i.e. 1901-1910 to 1961-70, death rate decreased from 48.6 deaths per 1,000 to 19. However, the birth rate decreased from 48.1 per 1,000 to 41.2 per 1,000 only. During the period 1971 to 2000, the death rate decreased from 17 to 9 and the birth rate from 39 to 25 i.e. by 47 per cent and 36 per cent respectively.

2. Early Marriage Age

Marriage age marks the turning point in reproductive behaviour and signals the onset of sexual activity. Therefore, age of marriage has a great bearing on fertility rates, child bearing and other issues like infant mortality and maternal mortality.

Table 8.1: Birth Rate and Death Rate (1911-2000)

Annual Rate	*Birth Rate per 1,000*	*Death Rate per 1,000*
1911-20	48.1	48.6
1921-30	46.4	36.3
1931-40	45.2	31.2
1941-50	39.9	27.4
1951-60	41.7	22.8
1961-70	41.2	19.0
1971-80	37.2	17.0
1981-90	32.5	11.4
1991-2000	25.0	9.0
2008-09	22.22	6.4

(*See also Table Chapter 4.3*)

The legal age at marriage in India is 18 for females and 21 for males. However, early marriage continues to be the norm. It is estimated that by the age of 15, nearly 26 per cent of females are married. By the age of 18, this figures rises to 54 per cent.

The present incidence of adolescent marriages below 18 years is as high as 71.0 in Bihar followed by Rajasthan, 68.3%. In Manipur and Goa, this percent is as low as 9.9 and 10.1 respectively. (see Fig. 3). Over 50 per cent girls marry before the age of 18. This results in a typical reproductive pattern of "too early, too frequent, too many".

3. Fertility Rates

According to the South Asian Conference on Adolescents (1999), a progressively larger share of all births is occurring from adolescent girls between the ages of 15-19 years. Twenty five to thirty five per cent of adolescent girls of Bangladesh, India, Pakistan and Nepal begin child bearing as early as 17 years. Moreover adolescent girls have shorter spacing intervals between successive births than older women. Thus they add to already high fertility rate among adolescent girls.

4. High Reproductive Age Group

The size of population in the reproductive age-group is large (estimated contribution 58 per cent). An addition of 417.2 million between 1991 and 2016 is anticipated despite substantial reductions in family size in several states, including reduction in family size in several states, also including those which have already achieved replacement levels of total fertility rate (TFR). This momentum of increase in population will continue for some more years because high TFRs in the past have resulted in a large proportion of the population being currently in their reproductive years. It is imperative that the reproductive age group adopts without further delay or exception the "small family norm", for the reason that about 45 per cent of population increase is contributed by births above two children per family.

5. Unmet Demand for Contraceptives

Higher fertility is due to unmet need for contraception (estimated contribution 20 per cent). India has 168 million eligible couples, of which just 44 per cent are currently effectively protected. Urgent steps are currently required to make contraception more widely available, accessible, and affordable. Around 74 per cent of the population lives in rural areas, in about 5.5 lakh villages, many with poor communications and transport. Reproductive health and basic health infrastructure and services often do not reach the villages, and, accordingly, vast numbers of people cannot avail of these services.

6. Child Birth Insurance against High Infant Mortality

High wanted fertility is due to the high infant mortality rate (IMR) (estimated contribution about 20 per cent). Repeated child births are seen as an insurance against multiple infant (and child) deaths and accordingly, high infant mortality stymies all efforts at reducing TFR.

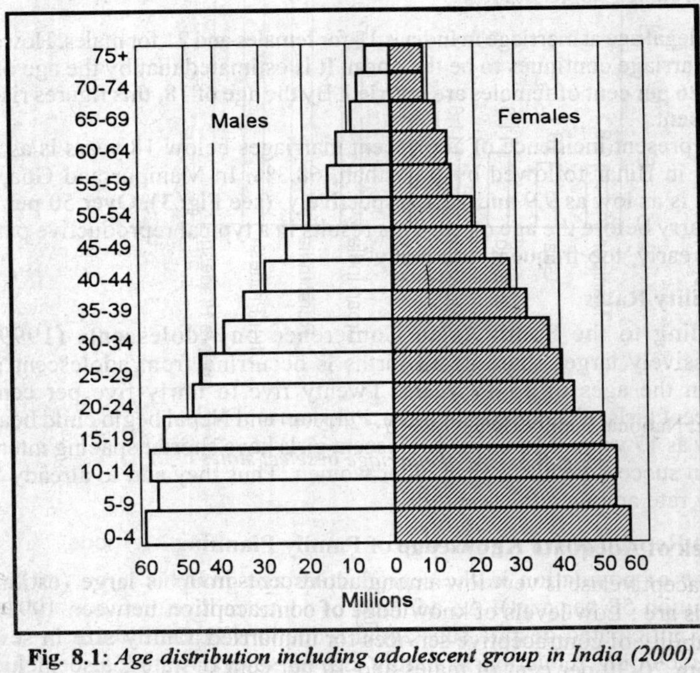

Fig. 8.1: *Age distribution including adolescent group in India (2000)*

Table 8.2: Percentage Distribution of Adolsescents by Sex and Age Group

Age-Group	*1981*		*1991*		*1996*		*2001*		*2006*		*2011*		*2016*	
	M	*F*	*M*	*F*	*M*	*F*	*M*	*F*	*M*	*F*	*M*	*F*	*M*	*F*
0-14	13.2	12.6	11.9	11.6	12.0	11.5	12.1	12.1	10.5	10.6	8.9	9.0	8.7	8.7
5-19	9.9	9.4	9.7	9.1	9.9	9.5	11.0	10.5	11.2	11.2	9.7	9.9	8.3	8.3

Source : Central Statistical Organisation, Youth in India : Profile and Programmes 1998, New Delhi : CSO 1998, page: 23-23.

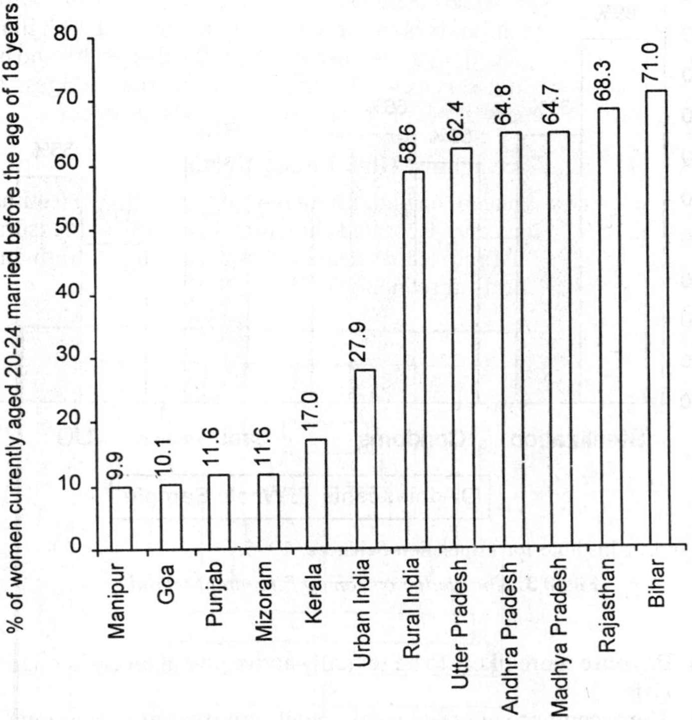

Source: National Family Health Survey - 2, 1998-99

Fig. 8.3: *Age of marriage in select states of India*

7. Lack of Adequate Knowledge of Family Planning Methods

Contraceptive use is very low among adolescents in India. Important reasons for this are : Low levels of knowledge of contraceptive methods and lack of availability of contraceptive services for unmarried adolescents.

With 20-30 per cent of males and 10 per cent of all adolescent females estimated to be sexually active before marriage, there is clearly a need for such services.

8. Sexual Activity and Behaviour

According to studies, following are the main characteristics of sexual activity and behaviour of the adolescents in India:

(i) The magnitude of adolescent sexual activity is significant. It is higher in boys than in girls.

(ii) There is under-reporting of sexual relationships by adolescent girls on account of fears of social disapproval.

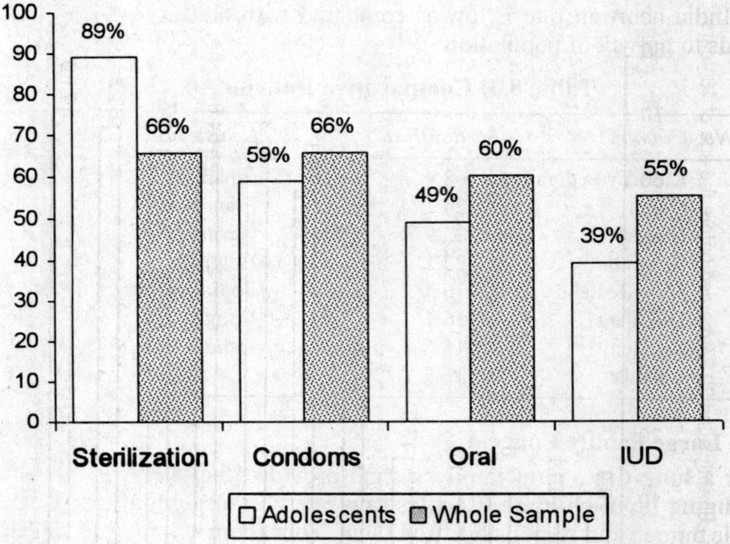

Source: Indian Institute for Population Sciences, 1995.

Fig. 8.3: *Knowledge of Family Planning Methods*

(iii) Boys are more likely to be sexually active and at an earlier age than girls.
(iv) The acceptance of pre-marital sexual activity is greater among boys than girls.
(v) Attitudes on pre-marital sexual activity remain conservative.
(vi) Parents and teachers are usually reluctant to impart information on sexual matters.
(vii) Contraceptive use is low and is seldom used in first-time sexual encounters.
(viii) Contraceptive awareness is usually about sterilisation which is not suitable for most adolescents.
(ix) Knowledge of HIV/AIDS, safe sex and preventive behaviour like use of condoms is low.
(x) Knowledge of sexual and reproductive issues is extremely poor.
(xi) The system of education does not adequately meet the needs for imparting sex education.
(xii) Adolescent girls have very little choice on issues like 'whom to marry' and 'when to marry.'
(xiii) There is lack of adolescent health facilities, information on sex education and counselling services.

9. Less Abortion Rate (Around 1996)

In India abortion rate is low as compared with other countries. This also leads to growth of population.

Table 8.3: Comparative Data on Abortion

Sl. No.	*Country*	*Abortion Rate*	*Sl. No.*	*Country*	*Abortion Rate*
1.	Russian Federation	68.4	9.	Japan	13.4
2.	China	26.1	10.	France	12.4
3.	U.S.A.	22.9	11.	Germany	7.6
4.	Australia	22.2	12.	Belgium	6.8
5.	New Zealand	16.4	13.	Spain	5.7
6.	Denmark	16.1	14.	Bangladesh	3.8
7.	Sweden	15.6	15.	India	2.7
8.	Canada	15.5			

10. Large Family Concept

For a long time, joint family system provided facilities for the care and bringing up of children. Couples saw safety in large numbers. There was little burden and responsibility on them. Thus there was preference for large families. Now this tendency seems to have been weakened on account of various factors.

11. Indifferent Male Attitude Towards Family Planning

Research studies conducted in India show that family planning business is considered by males as 'women' job. Thus almost the entire burden of family planning falls upon women. This indifferent attitude of men contributes to more births.

8.4 ECONOMIC FACTORS

These are as below:

1. *Backward Agricultural Economy.* In India, which practised agriculture of the traditional type for a number of decades, a large number of children was considered as an advantage. Even if a few of them did not survive beyond ten or fifteen years, certain functions of economic nature like tending cattle or carrying out simple tasks in the fields could be fulfilled by the younger ones. By all means emphasis was having more numbers.
2. *Low Standard of Living.* Traditionally rural society in India was not very particular in having a higher standard of living. People were prepared to share their resources. No particular consideration was given to the quantum of each share. This led to small agricultural holdings.

8.5 EDUCATIONAL FACTORS

Two of the most important factors are as under:

1. *General Illiteracy*. Lack of mass education has been undoubtedly an important factor in having large families. Without adequate literacy and education, people remain unacquainted with the benefits of increased knowledge. They believe in superstitions and sometimes think that large families are the gifts of God. They become fatalists.
2. *Neglect of Girls and Women's Education*. Although there has been a steady growth in this context, yet the situation cannot be said to be quite satisfactory. Still nearly 46 per cent of females are illiterate (2001 census figures). The situation in rural areas, hilly areas, slums and tribal areas is particularly disappointing.

Lack of education makes it difficult to communicate ideas about family planning.

8.6 PSYCHOLOGICAL FACTORS

1. *Satisfaction Through Sharing Resources:* Sharing the resources with new entrants in the family gave the members a social pleasure which in part compensated them for the lack of material resources. This tendency also developed among them a fatalistic attitude.
2. *Attitude of Dependence*: People in the past had little hope for a brighter future on account of their stagnating situation. They lost their initiative. Psychologically they resigned themselves to something beyond their control.

8.7 RECREATIONAL FACTORS

1. *Lack of Means of Entertainment*: A substantial section of people for years have remained without adequate recreational facilities. This factor became responsible for them indulging in sexual activity and desiring pleasure from it.
2. *More Leisure Time*: Subsistence agriculture is the occupation of nearly 70 per cent of Indian population. Agriculture is unable to provide employment throughout the year. Thus there is lot of leisure time at their disposal. The easiest pas time for them has ban to occupy themselves in sexual activities, resulting in increased population.

8.8 RELIGIOUS FACTORS

Following are the main factors:

1. *Preference for Sons* : It is believed by the Hindus in particular that their last rites should be performed by the sons, otherwise there will be no *'mukti'* (salvation) for them and they will not merit *'swarg'* (heaven).
2. *God Given Children:* There is a religious belief among some sections of the society, that it is the will of god that has bestowed children to them.

8.9 SOCIAL FACTORS

Important factors are:

1. *Universality of Marriage*. S. Chandrasekhar in *Asia's Population*

Problems (1967) has observed, "Everyone in India sooner or later, usually sooner, gets married. Nearly every adult male and female in the country participates in reproduction."

2. *Joint Family System.* Joint family system has merits and demerits but from the point of view of growth of population, it has acted as a pro-natality factor. It is observed that this system reduced the responsibility of parents for bringing up their children for there are parent's parents to look after the children of the former.
3. *Social Stigma.* Women in particular and men in general face social stigma if they are without children. Those women who do not bear children are considered as a cur upon the family. They are given several epithets.

8.10 SUMMARY

Causes of growing population may be summed up as under:

1. Gap between birth rate and death rate.
2. Early marriage age.
3. High fertility rates.
4. High reproductive age group.
5. Unmet demand for contraceptives.
6. Child birth insurance against high.
7. Lack of adequate knowledge of family planning methods.
8. Sexual activity and behaviour.
9. Less abortion rate.
10. Large family concept.
11. Indifferent male attitude towards family planning.
12. Backward agricultural economy.
13. Low standard of living.
14. General illiteracy.
15. Neglect of girl's and women's education.
16. Satisfaction through sharing.
17. Attitude of dependence.
18. Lack of means of entertainment.
19. More leisure time.
20. Preference for son.
21. God given children.
22. Universality of marriage.
23. Joint family system.
24. Social stigma.

8.11 CONSEQUENCES/IMPACT OF OVER-POPULATION ON INDIA

Increasing population of India has created the following problems for it:

1. Shortage of food for several decades.
2. Qualitative aspects of the food problem – undernourished population.
3. Benefits of planned development in India unevenly distributed.
4. Poverty and subsistence level.

5. Wide gap between the 'haves' and 'have nots'.
6. Uneven age structure i.e. dependent population in a high ratio.
7. Unemployment.
8. Under-employment.
9. Increased pressure on land.
10. Pollution.
11. Unhygienic living condition of the people.
12. Slums and Jhuggi Jhonpris.
13. Unhealthy economy of the country.
14. Heavy imports of some commodities.
15. Illiteracy.
16. Fatalist attitude.

(For details *see chapter* on Resource Generation and Impact of Population Growth).

9

Implementation of Population Education Programme

Role of Various Agencies

9.1 CONSTITUTIONAL PROVISIONS REGARDING POPULATION EDUCATION PROGRAMME

Following are the important constitutional provisions regarding population education programme:

Central List

Entry 69 of the Central List of subject in the seventh schedule of the Constitution relating to Article 246 lists 'Census'.

Concurrent List

Entry 20A of the 'Concurrent List' lists 'population control and family planning'.

Entry 25 of the Concurrent List includes 'Education'.

In others words both the central government as well as the state governments are charged with the responsibility of population control, family planning and population education.

Elements in the Planning Decision Process of Population Education

The government adopts a specific decision making process in the planning and implementation of population education. This process can be shown diagrammatically as per Fig. 9.1.

9.2 ROLE OF THE GOVERNMENT IN POPULATION EDUCATION PROGRAMME

Important functions of the government in Central Government in population education are listed below.

1. To diagnose and appraise the existing educational system in relation to population education.
2. To diagnose and appraise the need and importance of population education in relation to the economic and social situation.
3. To assess the financial resources available for population education.

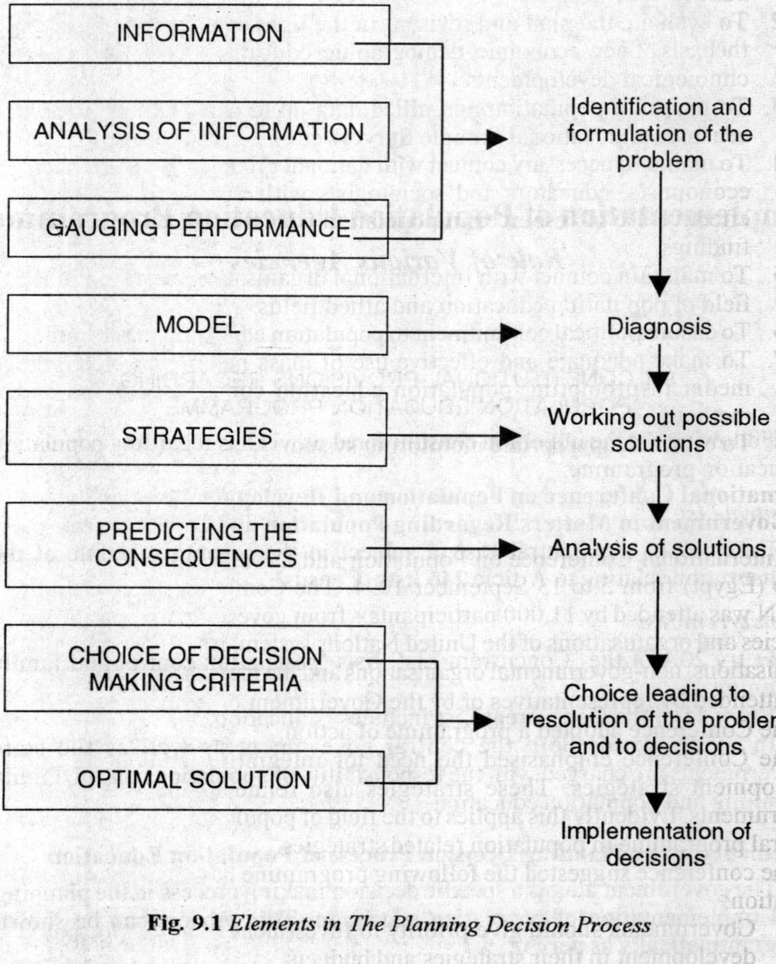

Fig. 9.1 *Elements in The Planning Decision Process*

4. To establish relevant quantitative projections in the light of economic, demographic and social factors.
5. To set basic long term and short term targets of population education.
6. To set basic and special objectives of population education.
7. To formulate the contents, methods and structure of population education programme.
8. To co-ordinate with other national plans.
9. To ensure inter-ministerial co-operation in the implementation of the programme at the central and state level.
10. To ensure participation of non-governmental organisations (NGOs).

11. To implement plans and initiate appropriate action for the same i.e. budget, contracts, etc.
12. To evaluate the plan and revise it in the light of implementation on thebasis of new economic, demographic, educational, political and te chnological developments.
13. To maintain population and allied data up to date through regular censuses and National Sample Surveys etc.
14. To maintain necessary contact with national groups of demographers, economists, educators and sociologists with a view to ensure the effective use of resources in population education through research findings.
15. To maintain contact with international organisations working in the field of population education and allied fields.
16. To ensure political commitment to population education programmes.
17. To make adequate and effective use of mass media and electronic media in promoting population education concept, contents and methods.
18. To establish appropriate monitoring system.

International Conference on Population and Development on the Role of the Government in Matters Regarding Population and Development

The International Conference on Population and Development was held at Cairo (Egypt) from 5 to 13 September 1994. The Conference convened by the UN was attended by 11,000 participants – from governments, specialised agencies and organisations of the United Nations system, inter-governmental organisations, non-governmental organisations and the media. The Conference was attended by representatives of by the Government of India also.

The Conference adopted a programme of action.

The Conference emphasised the need for integrating population and development strategies. These strategies also relate to the role of the Governments. Evidently this applies to the field of population education – an integral programme in population related strategies.

The conference suggested the following programme having a bearing on education:

1. Governments should give priority to investment in human resource development in their strategies and budgets.
2. Programmes should seek to increase people's access to information, education, skill development and employment opportunities.
3. The governments should increase people's access to information regarding reproductive health services, including family planning.
4. The governments should improve the knowledge base through research.
5. The governments should reduce and eliminate unsustainable patterns of consumption and production.
6. The governments should promote appropriate demographic policies.
7. The governments should work for economic growth, and eradicate poverty.

8. Governments should eliminate all forms of discrimination against women as they are the key factors in development and ensuring quality family planning and reproductive health.
9. The government should ensure that population, environment and poverty–eradication factors are integrated into sustainable development policies and strategies.
10. The governments should involve voluntary non-governmental organisations (NGOs) in planning population programmes.
11. The governments should make us of mass media and electronic media in population related programmes.

Population Education Programme

Realising the potential of education in tackling the problems of growing rate of population a Population Education Programme was launched with effect from April 1980. The underlying object of the programme is to create in the younger generation, an adequate awareness of the population problems and realisation of its responsibilities towards the nation in this regard.

The Population Education Programme is a plan scheme in the Central Sector of Ministry of Human Resource Development, Government of India. It has been developed in collaboration with the United Nations Fund for Population Active (UNFPA) and with the active involvement of the Ministry of Health and Family Welfare. (*Discussed separately*)

9.4 NATIONAL COUNCIL OF EDUCATIONAL RESEARCH AND TRAINING (NCERT) IN THE FIELD OF POPULATION EDUCATION

The NCERT is the apex resource organisation to assist and advise the central and state governments on academic matters related to school education including population education at the school level. It is charged with the responsibility of implementation of the National Population Education Project.

It has set up a Population Education Cell to undertake population education programmes. These programmes in the states are implemented through State Councils of Educational Research and Training/State Institutes of Education.

Population Education aims at making young students aware of the inter-relationship between population, development and the quality of life. It further seeks to develop in them a rational attitude and responsible behaviour towards population issues and to foster in them positive value orientation so that they may take informed decisions which, in turn, would promote the small family norm. The project is currently being implemented in 29 States and Union Territories.

The main activities are in the following areas:

— Preparation of training, instructional and supplementary materials.
— Orientation of teacher-educators and intensive training of newly appointed project personal in State Population Education Cells.
— Holding of meetings with the State Education authorities like school boards, textbook bureaux and voluntary organisations etc.

Publications of the Population Unit of the NCERT

1. Readings in Population Education, 1969.

2. National Seminar on Population Education – Second Revised Edition, 1970.
3. Population Education in School Curricula (Social Sciences): A Working Document, 1970
4. Plug-points for Population Education in School Curricula, 1971.
5. Population Education: A Draft Syllabus (Classes I to XI), 1971.
6. A Bibliography on Population Education, 1971.
7. Indian Population Situation, 1971.
8. Population Education: Current Problems in Education Series, 1971.
9. Population Education: Selected Readings, 1972.
10. National Conference on Population Education – Problems of Implementation, 1972.
11. (भविष्य के सपने – A Supplementary Reader in Hindi), 1972.
12. Nutrition and Population Education – A Resource Book for Teachers, 1973.
13. Teaching Units on Population Education, 1973.
14. (दीनू डाकिया – A Supplementary Reader in Hindi), 1973.
15. Population Education for Teachers, 1974.
16. National Bibliography on Population Education, 1975.
17. Indian Population and Development, 1977.
18. Population Education in Classrooms, 1978.
19. Co-ordination between Education and Population Policies – A Case Study of India, 1978.
20. Population Education: A Conceptual Framework (Teachers Manual to My Workbook on Population Studies), 1979.
21. Decade of Population Education Research in India, 1981.

9.5 UNIVERSITIES AND POPULATION EDUCATION

UGC-UNFPA Project on Population and Development Education in the Higher Education System

Aims: The University Grants Commission (UGC) has been providing assistance to Universities and Colleges for the promotion of Population Education Programme since 1983.

The main objective of the programme is to enable the youth in Universities and Colleges and through them the community to comprehend clearly the following issues:

(i) Family size.
(ii) Quality of life.
(iii) Gender equality.
(iv) Reproductive health.
(v) AIDS.
(vi) Impact of population growth on society and the nation.

Population Education Cells: The UGC has set up 17 Population Education Resource Centres (PERCs) in selected universities as a joint project undertaken with the United Nations Fund for Population Activities (UNFPA). These centres provide technical support and support for various activities relating to curriculum development, teaching and learning material.

The second phase ended on June 30, 1998 and the third phase began in January 1999. As per the Third Phase Project Agreement, the UNFPA agreed to provide funds for conducting various activities under the project; and Govt. of India was to contribute towards salaries of the staff employed in the PEU, UGC and 17 PERCs, infrastructural facilities, provision of equipment and other miscellaneous expenditure and also to meet the expenses towards the orientation of college principals. The emphasis is to be on national capacity building, adolescent education and improved management systems to realise the set of objectives in tune with the International Conference on Population and Development goals.

Important concerns and Activities of the Third Phase: In this phase, there is a shift of locus from population control and other demographic concerns to reproductive health, gender equality, adolescence education and quality of life.

1. In the third phase, counselling services have been operating in 16 Population Education Resource Centres. Through this service, qualified doctors, counsellors provide information to university and college students on AIDS, drug abuse and other related matters.
2. In order to create a supportive environment for the institutionalisation of population education, advocacy programmes are being organised for decision-makers, vice–chancellors, college principals etc.
3. Capacity building of the PERCs and their strengthening is being undertaken to consolidate their programme and training capacity. This is being done through development of linkages, workshops, exchange programmes, research materials and publications.
4. Training programme to be organised in order to enhance capacities in research by training in Qualitative Research Methods.
5. Training personnel from different Population Education Research Centres for providing adequate telephone counselling services for developing responsible behaviour among college students.

In order to strengthen the research base for improving Population and Development Education in Higher Education System, an Inter–Sectoral Research Consultative Meet was jointly organised by the UGC with the UNFPA in November 1999. Review of research conducted in the second phase was carried out to identify the gaps in the research in the meeting.

Inter-country study visits were conducted in September 1999 for PERC personnel to two countries namely Indonesia and Sri Lanka to sensitise PERC personnel to population issues and understand different approaches.

An officer from the UGC received training on "Communicating Population and Health Research to Policy Makers", in February-March, 2000 at Bangkok Thailand.

As part of Inter Sectoral–Co-ordination, links and networking have been established with governmental organisations, NGOs, Panchayati Raj Institutions, Opinion leaders etc. Attempts are being made to network with other UN Agencies such as UNESCO, UNICEF and WHO. Further State Level Co-ordination Committees have been formed with the other sectors namely, School and Adult Education.

Material Development is a specialised activity of the Third Phase. Developing Bibliographies for courses is currently being prepared by selected PERCs on the thrust areas namely Adolescence Education, Reproductive Health, HIV/AIDS, Substance Abuse, Environment and Gender Issues.

For the purpose of monitoring and evaluation, two Project Progress Review Meetings were held jointly with the Advisory Committee in the month of March 1999 and January 2000 to provide a good understanding of the achievements of the project and an appreciation of its strengths and weaknesses. During the year 1999-2000, an amount of Rs. 60.98 lakhs was expended towards the activities of the project. (Based on UGC Annual Report 1999-2000)

9.6 ROLE OF NON-GOVERNMENTAL ORGANISATIONS (NGOS) IN IMPLEMENTING POPULATION EDUCATION PROGRAMMES

Role of NGOs in the implementation of population education programme has been accepted all over the world including India. Population education is an area ideally suited to NGOs work. The programme of population education to be implemented is of such dimensions that their mobilisation will play a crucial role in the success of our plans.

Regarding the role of the voluntary organisations, the UNO International Conference on Population and Development (1994) observed, "the non-governmental" organisations are important voices of the people and their association and networks provide an effective and efficient means of better focusing local and national initiatives and addressing pressing population environmental migration and economic and social development concerns."

The conference further observed, "non-governmental organisations, especially those working in the field of sexual and reproduction health and family planning etc. have increased knowledge and services which will contribute towards successful implementation of population and development policies."

The conference also recommended that the project-oriented sector should consider how it might assist non-project NGOs in playing a wider role in society by enhancing or creating mechanisms to provide financial and other support to NGOs.

Main Functions of the Non-government Organisations in Population Education

1. To take responsibility in well-defined areas of population education for promoting it.
2. To organise programmes of population education in selected territorial areas.
3. To organise population education programmes catering to slum and other backward areas.
4. To undertake resource development activities including population education curriculum development, production of teaching and learning material, training of family planning education workers, preparing audio-visual aids including establishment of State Resource Centres, District Resource Units, etc.

5. To take up programmes of experimentation, innovation, action research including application and technology and pedagogic inputs for improvement of population education programmes.
6. To take up programme evaluation including support to institutions of population education research.
7. To help in the creation of environment, through support to the mass media, folk, and traditional media, organisation of 'jathas' etc.
8. To organise symposia, seminars and conferences etc. for the promotion of population education.
9. To train youth and other animators to facilitate implementation of family planning programmes.
10. To undertake such other activities as may be appropriate for achieving the objectives of the National Population Education Policy.
11. To make the optimum use of government grants and submit timely reports and statements of accounts etc.

Five-Year Plans and Non-Governmental and Voluntary Organisations

It is accepted that NGOs have been playing a very important role for the welfare of deprived sections in all areas of national life. Accordingly, NGOs have been helped by the government in a number of ways in the Five Years Plans.

The Ministry of Health and Welfare has installed the following programmes involving the NGOs:

1. Revamping of Mini Family Welfare Centre in areas where couple protection rates are below 35 years.
2. Involvement of Indian System of Medicine (ISM) and Homeopathy System.
3. Area specific IEC activities through NGOs.
4. Establishment of Standing Committees for Voluntary Actions (SCOVAs) to fund NGO projects promptly.
5. Identification of government/NGOs for training of NGOs in project formulation, programme management and monitoring.
6. The Department of Education, Ministry of Human Resource Development, Government of India provides grants, assistance and guidance to NGOs working in the field of adult education to include popularisation of population education as one of their activities.

A Word of Caution

Some times ago an official evaluation of the NGOs revealed that the work of a substantial number of NGOs was not satisfactory. In fact some of them existed on paper only and several of them did not come forward to show their field work, account books or other records related to their work. Suffice it to say that a great care and caution should be exercised while giving grants and other facilities to the NGOs working in the field of population education.

Important NGOs in the Field of Population Education

1. Family Planning Association of India (FPAI), R.K. Puram, New Delhi.
2. Indian Adult Education Association. This organisation has established a National Documentation Centre on Literacy and Population Education, Indraprastha Estate, New Delhi. It was set up by UNFPA.
3. Association for Social Health in India, New Delhi.
4. Population Services International (PSI), New Delhi.

9.7 UN AND OTHER INTERNATIONAL ORGANISATIONS AND ASSOCIATION LIKE UNFPA WORKING IN THE FIELD OF POPULATION EDUCATION

United Nations Population Fund (UNFPA), New York and Geneva

Objectives

The objectives of UNFPA are:

1. To assist countries in providing reproductive health care including family planning and sexual health, on the basis of individual choice.
2. To assist countries in formulating population strategies in support of sustaining development.
3. To assist countries in advocacy of issues related to population, reproduction health.
4. To assist countries in advocacy of autonomy and equality of women.
5. To advance the strategy endorsed by the International Conference on Population Development (ICPD) held in Cairo (Egypt) in 1984.

Programmes

Its programme includes:

1. *Subject Areas.* These are: (i) Reproductive health including family planning and sexual health.

(ii) Population and development studies.

(iii) Advocacy.

2. *Services/Materials Available.* These include (i) Resource Materials.

(ii) T.V. and video production.

(iii) Project support.

The fund began its work in 1969 and it is a subsidiary of the General Assembly.

United Nations Non-Governmental Liaison Service (NGLS), Geneva and New York

NGLS is an interlagency programme of the United Nations that promotes co-operation between the UN system and non-governmental organisations on economic and development issues.

The NGLS publishes several reports and documents. Its publication, a newsletter '*Go Between*' is published six times a year. The newsletter includes a variety of in formation on development activities.

9.8 POPULATION SERVICES INTERNATIONAL (PSI), NEW DELHI

Population Services International (PSI) is an Indian non-profit and non-governmental organisation established in 1988, with a mandate to assist the Government of India in the fields of Reproductive Health, HIV/AIDS prevention and Maternal and Child Health.

Social marketing is one of the strongest tools for empowering low income people to lead healthier lives and PSI/India is one of the world's most cost-effective social marketing operations. Affordable health products, including contraceptives, are badly needed for growing segment of Indian society that does not need to rely on free products from the government and yet cannot afford private sector prices. PSI creates well-informed demand as well as a widely accessible, affordable supply.

PSI has social marketing activities in 14 States and Union Territories throughout India. With a field force of 125, which reaches 130,000 retail outlets for secondary sales and 906 stockists for primary sales, PSI is by far the largest and most successful social marketing organisation in India. Through August 2001, PSI has sold contraceptive products responsible for over 9.7 million Couple Years Protection (CYP), and over 8.7 million sachets of ORS.

PSI is associated with PSI/Europe and with the Washington DC based international non-profit organisation Population Services International, which operates social marketing and communication programs for HIV/AIDS prevention, child and reproductive health in over 50 countries across Africa, Asia, Eastern Europe and South and North America. PSI/India accesses valuable experience and technical resources from PSI's headquarters and country operations worldwide.

Statement of Mission and Vision – PSI India's Mission is to empower low income people to lead healthy lives through the informed use of health products and services, made accessible and affordable to them by the subsidised application of communications and marketing resources and techniques.

PSI India's Vision is to enhance its position as the country's leading social marketing organisation. In co-operation with the Government of India, PSI programmes address priority health issues in the fields of reproductive health and child survival for low income people throughout India, while continuing to set new standards for innovation, efficiency and all-round excellence. PSI's intent is to successfully combine entrepreneurial spirit with its social mission. PSI has a long term commitment to the people of India and to maximising its impact through advocacy, networking and collaboration with other organisations.

What Makes PSI Different: The lower-income and harder to reach populations are carefully targeted in the development and implementation of PSI's projects. One of the primary tenets of social marketing is that communication strategy and distribution efforts are based on the needs expressed by the target groups.

All of PSI's projects are designed and monitored using both quantitative and qualitative types of population and market based research. PSI's activities are consistent with and complementary to those of the government, particularly the Ministry of Health and Family Welfare, with whom PSI has close contact and a formal operating agreement.

Since its inception, PSI India had played an important role in the Government of India's Contraceptive Social Marketing Programme and is still the largest non-profit social marketing organisation in the national programme. But this has not limited its operations to being a contraceptive provider. *Saadhan*, PSI's comprehensive family health network, arose from the need to create a network of users, influencers and providers of appropriate products, services and information to influence individual behaviour and safeguard the health of the family.

Expanded and Informed Choice through *Saadhan* will provide low-income populations with comprehensive information about the benefits and accessibility of a full range of reproductive and child health products and services, enabling them to choose those they need most. Birth spacing, prevention and management of diarrhoeal disease, improved nutrition, safe motherhood and STDs/HIV/AIDS are some of the components of the RCH programme.

PSI recognises that the social and political environment impacts greatly on the success of any development activity, and has thus taken on the important role of advocacy. This includes providing comprehensive information to a wide range of people health professionals, lawyers, journalists and others who influence public opinion and enable people to make informed choices and adopt healthy behaviour. The organisation also actively establishes links between donors, partner NGOs, the private sector, and government.

HIV/AIDS: PSI's social marketing activities include HIV/AIDS prevention in high-risk groups in many States. Started in 1991, the Mumbai PSI project addresses reproductive health concerns related to high risk behaviour groups such as commercial sex workers and their clients, truckers and youth, including STD/AIDS prevention, condom use, caring for and counselling of HIV infected persons and helping them find alternative sources of income. PSI's HIV/AIDS prevention projects are co-ordinated with the National AIDS Control Organisation and the Mumbai District AIDS Cell. The PSI helpline offers objective information and referrals on STDs including HIV/AIDS and other reproductive health concerns by trained phone counsellors.

Today interventions are being carried out at many local industries, the police department, colleges, and Mumbai's four jails. In 1998, a major project was begun in Cotton Green, Asia's largest truck terminus. Over 1,000 truckers, their assistants and other local labourers visit this centre and others every month to learn about how HIV/AIDS is prevented, to visit the STD doctor, for pre- and post -HIV test counselling, and to participate in lucky draws and other entertaining activities. Peer educators walk among the over 5,000 truck telling idle truckers of the centre, talking about HIV/AIDS prevention and selling Masti condoms. Intervention activities are now being carried out at truckers' stops along all the major highways leading to Mombay, from Gujarat, Rajasthan, and Delhi.

Expanding RCH in India: The alarmingly high levels of maternal and infant mortality in India have multiple epidemiological causes. The connection between the use of spacing methods and improved maternal and child health has not yet been established by the general public, government authorities and health providers. PSI recognises that effective interventions, which ensure complete accessibility to essential products and services and behaviour change communication strategies can bring about a difference. In 1998, the organisation began a comprehensive strategic planning process intended to better integrate Child Survival, Maternal and Reproductive Health in its programs throughout India. This resulted in the creation of *Saadhan*; established the need to increase organisational capacity; and cater to the health needs of the urban slum and rural population.

PSI's social marketing activities in India include the delivery and promotion of *Deluxe Nirodh, Masti and Kama Sutra* brands of condoms, *Pearl* and *Mala-D* brands of low dose oral contraceptive pills for women, and a WHO formula packaged oral dehydration solution (ORS) branded *Neotral* and *Neotral Orange.*

Source: PSI: C-445, Chittaranjan Park, New Delhi-110 019.

10

Strategies for Transacting Population Education Curriculum

10.1 MEANING OF POPULATION EDUCATION CURRICULUM

Population education curriculum is the sum total of all the programmes and experiences which an educational institution sponsors or provides for the learners with a view to achieving the objectives of population education. The programmes and experiences are mostly conducted in the school during school hours. However, sometimes they may be undertaken after school hours and outside the school complex. The entire work is done under the guidance and supervision of the teachers.

10.2 POPULATION EDUCATION CURRICULUM: WHY, WHAT, WHOM, WHO, WHEN, WHERE, AND HOW

Box 10.1: Why, What, Who, Where, When, How of Population Education Curriculum}

1.	Why of population education curriculum	For fulfilling the objectives of population education
2.	What of population education curriculum	Contents of the population education curriculum
3.	Whom of population education curriculum	For students
4.	Who of population education curriculum	Role of teachers in curriculum transaction
5.	Where of population education curriculum	Educational institution Non-formal adult education centres
6.	When of population education curriculum	Stage/level or class from which population education curriculum to begin and when to end
7.	How of population education curriculum	Approaches/methods of transacting teaching-learning programmes and activities of population education

10.3 OBJECTIVES OF POPULATION EDUCATION CURRICULUM AS AN INTEGRAL PART OF GENERAL EDUCATION

'Population Education' as an integral part of General Education seeks:

1. to develop an understanding of some demographic concepts and processes.
2. to develop among the younger generation an understanding of the most important phenomenon of the modern world, viz. rapid growth of population and its causes
3. to develop an understanding of the influence of population trends on the various aspects of human life, political, social, cultural and economic.
4. to develop an understanding of the close interaction of population growth and developmental processes, with particular reference to developmental programmes for raising standard of living of people.
5. to develop an understanding of the evil effects of over population on the environment and the concomitant dangers from pollution.
6. to develop an understanding of scientific and medicinal advancement enabling to get an increasing control over famines, diseases and untimely deaths, and the unbalance thus created between death rate and birth rate.
7. to develop an understanding of biological factors and phenomenon of reproduction which are responsible for the continuation of the species.
8. to develop an appreciation of:
   (a) the small family norms as proper and desirable.
   (b) the relation between population size and the quality of life.
   (c) the fact that family size is a matter of deliberate choice and human regulation rather than of accident or forces beyond human control.
9. to develop an attitude of responsibility and natural help and co-operation in all aspects of personal and family living.
10. to develop an appreciation of the relationship between the preservation of the health of mother, the welfare of the children and small size of the family.
11. to develop an appreciation of the fact that the actions of each individual member of the society affect the others, and personal and national decisions concerning family size and population have long range consequences for the whole world.
12. to develop an awareness of the population policies and programmes of the country.
13. to provide the students with a basic demographic vocabulary so that they are able to read and interpret demographic material with some understanding. (*see also chapter 3.5*)

10.4 COMPONENTS OF POPULATION EDUCATION CURRICULUM

For fulfilling the above mentioned objectives of population education, the contents of the curriculum for population education have to be delimited. We have already mentioned that population education is not 'sex education' and 'family planning'. However it is a fact that certain elements of 'sex education' and 'family planning' are included in population education curriculum. According to Prof. Jayasuriya (1972) population education curriculum should include the totality of issues connected with population, ranging from the nature, measurement, causes, determinants and consequences of population growth as well as urbanisation both at the micro level of the family and at the macro level of the community, the nation, or the world at large to the dynamics of the reproductive process and finally the possibility of family size and population growth.

The Asian Regional Workshop (1970) suggested the following three areas of population education curriculum.

1. Determinants of population growth.
2. Demography.
3. Consequences of population growth.

10.5 ISSUES TO BE CONSIDERED IN DESIGNING POPULATION EDUCATION CURRICULUM

An NCERT Publication *Tasks and Challenges* listed the following problems to be considered while designing population education curriculum:

What are the general and specific goals of population education as an area of study at different school stages? What values, perspectives and knowledge should be expected for a large number of students at the end of each possible terminal point of formal education such as primary, middle and secondary?

What are the existing subjects that lend themselves admirably to integrate population education ideas and values?

What are the different ways or patterns that we can follow in development of curriculum, for organising knowledge and development of values?

How can we ensure active participation of students in discussing population problem and its implications for individuals, families and communities?

How best can we identify children's experiences and relate new contents to the same?

How do we spot potential talent and nurture it in the State for the development of curriculum?

What are the systematic procedures of curriculum development?

What range of specific expertise shall we need in developing balanced curriculum?

Would it be ensured by participation of different subject specialists, subject teachers, masters of methods, curriculum specialists, textbook writers and the like?

What needs to be done or emphasised for inculcation of proper attitudes and values related to population education suited to different school stages?

Are there any patterns and models of curriculum and curriculum development in population education? If so, where are they?

Would population education curriculum vary from State to State in view of their varying situations, socio-economic conditions and cultural backgrounds? If so, to what extent and in what manner?

10.6 DESIGNING POPULATION EDUCATION CURRICULUM

(1) Infusing Population Education Curriculum or Permeating Population Education Curriculum or Multidisciplinary Approach

(2) Integrating Population Education Curriculum

(3) Population Education as a Separate Subject in the Curriculum

10.7 INFUSING POPULATION EDUCATION CURRICULUM

Meaning of Infusing Curriculum—According to this design of curriculum planning, population problems are included in subject areas like Social Studies, Health Education, Sciences, Mathematics, Languages etc. Population education is not taught as a separate subject. As a matter of fact, in almost all the books of the subjects mentioned above, some elements of population education always exist. The difference would be in the treatment of the contents and laying stress on the implications of the population issues. Besides, these contents are flexible and can very easily be adapted to the demands and requirements of population education.

Infusing curriculum designed is recommended as it would not entail any extra burden on students as in the case of introducing population as a separate subject. The infusing approach will involve a number of teachers teaching different subjects.

At the high school stage, one unit on population may be provided, students may also undertake population surveys of the school or the locality. At the senior secondary stage, it can be made as one of the elective subjects. At the same time, lessons on demography may be included in the Social Sciences. In Biology, there is a lot of scope for taking up several population related topics.

10.8 MULTIDISCIPLINARY OR INFUSION MODEL OR APPROACH OF POPULATION EDUCATION CURRICULUM

Here concept of population education and problem solving skills are incorporated in various disciplines wherever appropriate. and no separate unit, course or module is created (see Figs. 19.1 and 19.2).

10.9 INTERDISCIPLINARY OR INTEGRATED OR IN FUSED APPROACH OR MODEL OF POPULATION EDUCATION CURRICULUM

Here a distinctive population education unit, course or module is created by selecting, presenting and dwelling upon the relevant components of various

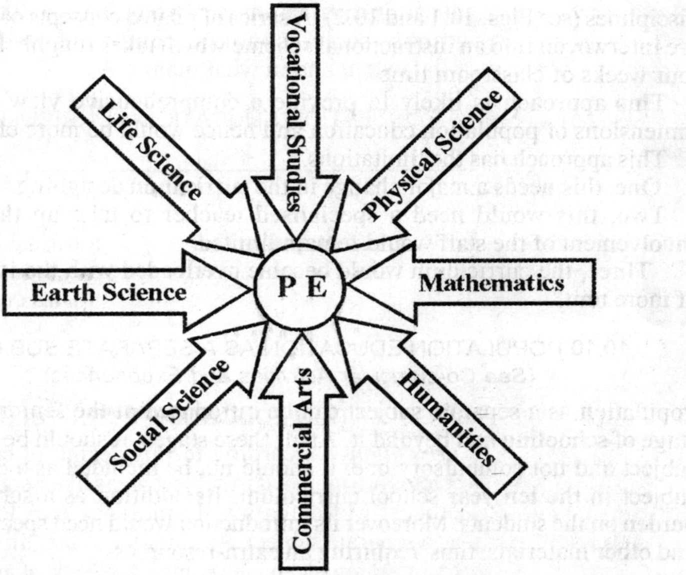

Fig. 10.1 : Interdisciplinary or Infused Model of Population Education

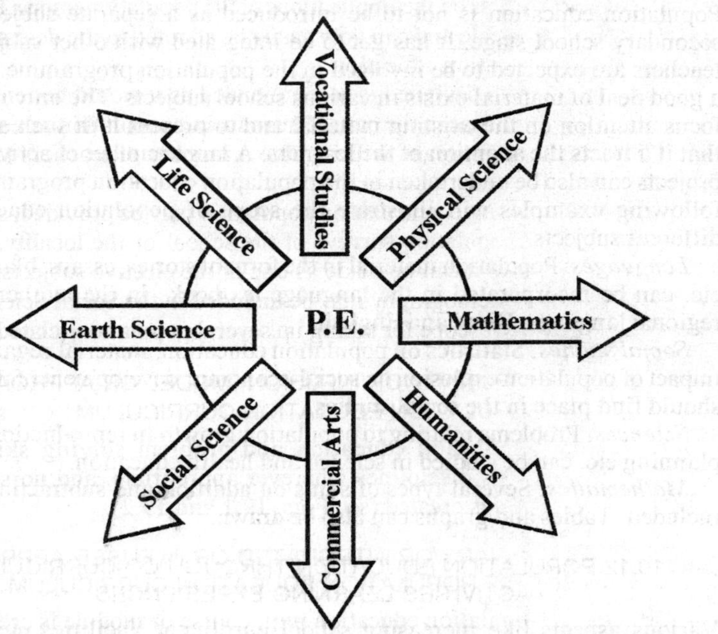

Fig. 10.2 : Multidisciplinary or Infusion Model of Population Education

disciplines (see Figs. 10.1 and 10.2). A series of related concepts of population are interwoven into an instructional scheme which takes roughly from one to four weeks of classroom time.

This approach is likely to provide a comprehensive view of various dimensions of population education and hence would be more effective.

This approach has the limitations.

One, this needs a major change in the curriculum designing.

Two, this would need a specialised teacher to take up this subject. Involvement of the staff would remain limited.

Three, the curriculum would become overloaded with the introduction of more unit.

10.10 POPULATION EDUCATION AS A SEPARATE SUBJECT

(*See Co-curricular Activities and Experiences*)

Population as a separate subject can be introduced at the senior secondary stage of schooling and beyond it. At all these stages, it should be an elective subject and not compulsory one. It should not be included as a compulsory subject in the ten year school curriculum. Its addition as a subject would burden on the students. Moreover its introduction would need special teachers and other materials, thus requiring an extra-resources.

10.11 POPULATION EDUCATION NOT A SEPARATE SUBJECT

Population education is not to be introduced as a separate subject at the secondary school stage. It has got to be integrated with other subjects. All teachers are expected to be involved in the population programme. Already a good deal of material exists in various school subjects. The only need is to focus attention on the existing material and to present it in such a manner that it attracts the attention of the learners. A large number of activities and projects can also be undertaken in the population education programme. The following examples will illustrate the scope of population education in different subjects.

Languages: Population material in the form of stories, essays, blank verses etc. can be incorporated in the language textbooks in the mother tongue, regional language, Hindi and English.

Social studies: Statistics on population education, material regarding the impact of population explosion on social-economic development of the nation should find place in the social studies.

Sciences: Problems relating to population growth in reproduction, family planning etc. can be studied in science and health education.

Mathematics: Several types of sums on addition and subtraction can be included. Tables and graphs can also be drawn.

10.12 POPULATION EDUCATION THROUGH CO-CURRICULAR ACTIVITIES LEARNING EXPERIENCES

Various aspects like increasing school enrolment, facilities etc. can be correlated with population growth. Village and community surveys can be undertaken to find out the impact of growing population.

Summing up. We cannot depend upon one pattern only. At the primary level, simple learning activities regarding population may be provided. At the middle level, one or two chapters in the Social Studies and Sciences may be introduces besides providing activities of a higher order.

10.13 POPULATION EDUCATION THROUGH SOCIAL SCIENCES : AN INTEGRATED APPROACH

Introduction

Social Sciences including History, Civics, Economics and Geography are compulsory and widely read subjects upto the secondary level of schooling. Therefore population education can be easily and effectively imparted through these subjects in an integrated manner. There is a good deal of scope for high-lighting population's cultural economic, historical, moral and political effects in a very comprehensive way. Prof. B.S. Parekh has tried to illustrate this in a paper that appeared in NCERT's publication *Population Education for Teachers* (1974).

The chief features are presented here in a summarised form.

Population Education Unit in Social Studies

Concepts The unit lays stress on the following key concepts relating to population and development:

1. There is close interaction of population growth and development process—with regard to developmental programmes for raising standard of living of people.
2. Population size and quality of life are related.
3. Family size can be chosen. It can be controlled. It is not beyond human control.

This Unit in NCERT books (CBSE syllabus) has three major components.

1. Demography or Population Dynamics.
2. Population Growth and Economic Development.
3. Population Growth and Social Development.

The first component is intended to bring home to the students that population has been growing rapidly as a result of a widening gap between death rate and birth rate.

The second component states it clearly that standard of living depends upon the skill of the people and how they assume responsibility to meet the challenge.

The third component draws our attention to the various social ills, such as superstition and gender bias that affect us.

Population Education through Civics

Some of the important elements of population education that can be introduced in Civics are:

1. More population means more demands and havoc more tension.
2. Rapid population growth leads to several political and social problems besides economic and financial ones.

3. Great influx of unskilled as well as skilled labour into cities takes place in search of jobs when rate of population growth is higher than rate of economic growth in the rural areas.
4. Rapid increase in population results in shortfall of amenities like schooling and health services.
5. Several social customs, traditions, superstitions and tables stand in the way of population control and family size etc.
6. Sometimes ethics of population education like 'no abortion' create population problems.

Population Problems and Education through History

In history, we learn how man has moved from nomadic life to civilised life, how town planning was done in the Indus Valley Civilisation to meet various demands of the urban population etc.

Invention of agriculture led to population growth. For meeting the growing demands, people migrated to other countries and even subjugated other lands.

We learn about the family system and marriage institution.

Population Education through Economics

Following are the various elements that can be incorporated in an Economics lesson:

1. A high rate of economic growth, higher standard of living and greater economic productivity have generally a positive correlation.
2. Optimum utilisation of human resources calls for skilled manpower and it results in higher GNP and GNP per capita.
3. The more the population the less of growth of the economy other things being equal.
4. The most important characteristics of a developed economy is controlled population and low birth rate.
5. Controlled population leads to better quality of life.
6. Population education must develop the habit of balanced saving as it results in getting better amenities. Proper utilisation of savings i.e. its investment also results in economic development.

Population Education through Geography

In Geography, we learn how climatic and other factors influence population. What are the reasons for low density of population and high density of population.

How does migration take place from unproductive regions to productive regions.

How growing population is putting a great burden on the natural resources of a country.

How productivity of land can be increased. What is the impact of growing population on land holdings?

How resources are being depleted to meet the continuous and unprecedented growth of population in a country.

11

Population Education Curriculum at Various Levels (Including Elementary)

11.1 INTRODUCTION

The UNESCO Asian Regional Workshop (1970) arrived at the consensus that elements of population education should eventually be incorporated into all levels of the school system but it also recognised that limitations of human and financial resources demanded that initial programmes be somewhat narrower.

11.2 POPULATION EDUCATION AT THE ELEMENTARY LEVEL

Arguments in Favour of Introducing Population Education at the Elementary Level

Following arguments are given to support population education at this stage:

1. It is universally accepted that at this stage important attitudes towards life and social values are formed among the children. In the developing countries, a large number of children do not go beyond the elementary level of schooling. Therefore, elementary knowledge of population education should be imparted at this stage.
2. In several developing countries like India, a single-teacher system prevails in many elementary schools and particularly at the primary level (Classes I to V). There is also a uniform common curriculum for all students at this stage and there are no optional subjects. Such a situation makes it easy to introduce a population education programme.
3. The majority of population in India lives in the rural areas and there is a great need for the spread of small family norms. With a view to form a broad base of the study of population education, it is essential to introduce population education in elementary classes.

Arguments Against the Introduction of Population Education at the Elementary Stage

Following arguments are advanced against the introduction of population education at the elementary level of schooling.

1. It is very difficult to introduce several concepts of population education at this stage.
2. Concept of population at this stage may suffer from over-simplification on account of the low intellectual level of the students.

3. There is no evidence that an early exposure to population education would affect decision-making and reproductive behaviour a decade later. A large number of students leave before finishing their elementary schooling and the gap in terms of years between their exposure to population education when they are in school and their reaching the reproductive age is so wide that there is no guarantee that they will vote for a small family.
4. The students at the elementary stage are not capable of understanding the significance of small family norms.
5. The attempt to tell the children that two or three children are enough would be not only crude but may also create in the children a feeling of disaffection for their parents and hatred for their brothers and sisters in case they constitute a large family.

11.3 POPULATION RELATED GENERAL EXPERIENCES OF STUDENTS AT THE ELEMENTARY LEVEL THAT FAVOUR THE INTRODUCTION OF POPULATION EDUCATION AT THE ELEMENTARY LEVEL OF SCHOOLING

1. Children are aware of births and deaths taking place in their families and consequent changes in family size.
2. Children are aware of changes in population of their family on account of migrations by way of marriages, deaths, transfers and search for new jobs, etc.
3. Children are aware of certain families or persons coming from outside to live in their village or town and a few others leaving for other places.
4. Some children may be aware of population enumerator visiting their family to collect census information from the head of their families. (In village cattle census is conducted generally every five years).
5. Children are aware that considerable care needs to be taken during pregnancy, delivery and thereafter causing good deal of expenditure.
6. Children are also aware of maternity homes, midwives, nurses and the help they render in ensuring safer deliveries.
7. Children are also aware of constant rush in maternity homes and the need for prior registration, etc., to ensure timely help during deliveries.
8. Children have experience of how lives are saved with proper and timely medical care.
9. Children are also aware of usefulness of various preventive measures such as small pox and cholera vaccines.
10. Children are also aware of the need and actual steps taken to ensure disease-free potable water supply to their families, villages and towns.
11. They have also experienced break of certain epidemics and a sudden spurt in the incidence of death due to them.
12. Children are also aware of child deaths due to malnourishment and lack of medical care and also due to ignorance and superstitions on the part of illiterate and poor people.

13. Children are also aware of primary health centres, family planning and welfare centres, health visitors, doctors, nurses, maternity homes, dispensaries and hospitals, medical stores all of which help in waging war on death and disease.
14. Children are also aware of the family planning campaign and the insistence on accepting a small family norm.
15. Children have seen small and big families and some of the consequences thereof.
16. Children have some idea about difficulties faced by their families in managing their family budgets.
17. They also have some idea of ways of saving for the future and its significance.
18. Some of the difficulties faced in mobilising financial resources for eventualities like marriage serious illness, etc. is within their experience.
19. Children have experience of varying standards of living in different families including their relations.
20. They realise the importance of food, clothing, shelter and medical aid in order to lead a satisfying life.
21. They have generally experienced effects of good crops and bad crops, floods and famines, acute shortages.
22. Children are aware that man is able to tame powerful animals like the elephants, camel and horse, domesticate milih animals like the won and buffalo.
23. Children are also aware of the fact that man can hunt dangerous animals like tiger on land and huge mammals like whale and walrus in the sea.
24. They are also aware of the man's ability to think, imagine, anticipate things in advance, plan for the future, communicate with others and cooperate with fellow beings as well as animals to his own advantage.
25. They are aware of man's ability to change environment at least partially according to his desire or plan.
26. Children are aware of the fact that resources like water are supplied by nature and soil fertility can be restored by planned efforts.
27. They are also aware of the fact that wood is burnt as fuel but its supply can be maintained by planting new trees particularly through those that grow quickly.
28. Children are aware of instances where soil is eroded and certain measures taken to conserve it.
29. They have also seen dams built across the rivers and occasional floods causing great havoc and human misery.
30. Children are aware of the increasing use being made of coal, petroleum and metals like iron or aluminium.
31. Children also know the growing use being made of plastics in place of metals which are becoming costlier every year.
32. Children are aware of growing use of paper which leads to depletion of forests at a much faster rate.

33. Children are aware of pollution caused by big factories and widespread use of DDT.
34. They are also aware of unhygienic conditions prevailing in villages (village ponds, etc.) and in slums in cities.
35. Some children have visited zoos and national parks where animals are protected from hunting.
36. Some children must have seen reserved forests where the trees are felled in a controlled manner and new trees are planted according to a long term plan.
37. Children are also aware of falling water table in their neighbourhood, silting of small dams or tanks and canals.
38. Children are aware of the use of scrap and rags etc. for making certain products out of them.
39. Children are aware of the electricity produced from coal, diesel oil and water.
40. Children are also aware of a gobar gas plant (cow-dung gas plant) which helps not only to produce gas for cooking, lighting and pumping purposes but also for manuring fields.
41. Children experience the need for good food, clothing, shelter, medical care, education and savings for better living.
42. They have seen children and people suffering from malnutrition or under-nourishment.
43. Children also have seen mothers suffering from ill-health due to too many and too frequent births children in succession.
44. Children realise that small families are generally in a better position to meet the needs of all its members.
45. Children realise the importance of savings for meeting emergencies such as illness or death etc. in the family.
46. Children know that some families follow or practise small family norm.
47. Children also know and experience that superstitions do not help in life.
48. Children also know certain people believing in superstition lag behind in life and in the process suffer more than others.
49. Children know that small family norm should not be forced on people. They should be encouraged to adopt it of their free will when they are convinced of its advantages.

Summing up. Simple population related exercises may be taken up in the primary classes (Classes I to V) and simple population concepts may be taken up in Classes VI to VIII (upper primary or middle level). Population education should be imparted through an integrated manner and learning exercises. Elementary stage, therefore, should become the foundation on which further programme of population education may take shape.

11.4 POPULATION EDUCATION AT THE SECONDARY AND HIGHER SECONDARY LEVEL—ARGUMENT FOR ITS INTRODUCTION

Following are the important reasons for introducing population education at the secondary stage of schooling:

1. Students studying at the secondary stage are older than the students of the elementary stage and hence nearer to their reproductive age and also nearer to decisions regarding reproduction. The impact of the population education programme on their minds would retain more freshness than on minds of the students at the elementary stage.
2. The students of the secondary stage constitute the future leaders of the society. After completing their studies, they are likely to occupy the middle-level leadership and as such they may exercise a considerable influence over the masses. They are likely to transmit the knowledge of population education to the lower level of society with a lot of conviction and understanding.
3. It is easier to prepare population education material for the secondary level than the elementary level. This is on account of the fact that the students at the secondary stage are more advanced in age as well as maturity. Moreover, they have a broader knowledge and experience
4. Students at the secondary stage are more developed biologically and physiologically and therefore, it is easier to talk about population problems. It is also easier to explain to them the implications of the population education at the micro-level as well as the macro-level.
5. The teacher teaching at the secondary stage are academically and professionally more equipped than the teachers teaching at the elementary level. At this stage, even controversial topics can be taken up.
6. It is easier to evaluate the population education programme at the secondary level.

11.5 POPULATION EDUCATION AT COLLEGE STAGE

The National Seminar on Population Education (1969) recommended the following steps:

1. At college level, the universities should design a course in demography at the undergraduate level so that those students who are interested in population problems could specialise at the post-graduate level in demography.
2. Guidance Bureaus at the college level should be strengthened by qualified staff to help the students to solve personal problems in connection with family life, and marriage counselling.
3. Universities should organise extension lectures every year in each college on issues related to population education to ensure a wide-spread awareness of the problems among the youth and teachers.

Broad Areas of Population Education Curriculum

Determinants of Poulation Growth	*Determinants of Poulation Growth*	*Determinants of Poulation Growth*	*Determinants of Poulation Growth*	*Determinants of Poulation Growth*	*Determinants of Poulation Growth*	*Determinants of Poulation Growth*
(a) Family Concept of the Society i.e. large or small (b) Fertility (c) Morality (d) Migration (e) Culture or traditions of a socity (f) Religion beliefs (g) Enonomic conditions	(a) Economic (b) Educational (c) Social (d) Individual (e) National (f) International	(a) Censuns reports (b) Birth reports (c) Dealth reports (d) Age pyramids (e) Trends of growth at the local, state, national, and international levels	(a) Human physiology (b) Contraception (c) Social interaction associated with Sexuality	Efforts made in India and Asia to regulate polpulation	End Quality of Life	(a) Life solutions (b) Envirorment poplution

Note: Subject matter could be graded according to schooling level or stage

11.6 POPULATION EDUCATION OUTSIDE FORMAL SCHOOLING

Non-formal education programme should also include population education programmes.

11.7 PROBLEMS IN INTRODUCING AND CONDUCTING POPULATION EDUCATION CURRICULUM

Important problems which arise in introducing and conducting population education are given below:

1. Concept of population being a new concept.
2. Confusion regarding the use of terms like population education, family planning and sex education.
3. Place of imparting population education i.e. why in schools and not in homes.
4. Parents' reaction or conservative and traditional nature of the society.

Usually parents reactions about population are expressed as under.

(i) It is the other name of family planning promotion policy of the Government.

(ii) It is concerned with imparting sex education and hence it will have a degenerating moral influence on the younger generation.

(iii) It is not suited to developmental level of the younger generation as it concerns demographic facts and population dynamics which are difficult subjects for school children.

(iv) It is an imported concept in India at the instance of some foreign agencies and interest.

11.8 POPULARISING POPULATION EDUCATION PROGRAMME IN SCHOOLS

For a successful implementation of the population education programme, concerted and sustained efforts are needed. Among the important measures in this regard, following suggestions are put forward.

1. Creation of a strong favourable climate.
2. Reorientation of teachers.
3. Motivating students.
4. Involvement of the parents.
5. Co-ordinating programmes of population education.
6. Using appropriate teaching-leaning methods of population education.
7. Using of audio-visual aids.

11.9 SELECTED VIEWS ON POPULATION EDUCATION CURRICULUM

NCERT Workshop (1970) suggested the following five areas of curriculum for population education:

NCERT Workshop and Curriculum

1. The population growth.
2. Economic development and population.
3. Social development and population.

4. Health, nutrition and population.
5. Biological factors, family life and population.

Prof. Faneff C.T. on Population Education Curriculum

Feneff. C.T. (Ph.D. thesis 1971) suggested the following curriculum:

1. Birth rate, mortality rate and population.
2. Health and population.
3. Food production and population.
4. Family size and population.
5. Standard of living and population.

D. Gopal Rao on Population Education Curriculum

D. Gopal Rao suggests the following topics forming contents of population education:

1. The history of population growth –world in general, India in particular — causes, trends and implications.
2. An introduction to demography with particular reference to India— components of population growth, population distribution and its composition.
3. Effects of rapid population growth on economic, social, cultural and political aspects of national development.
4. Effects of rapid population growth on individual and family life— standards of living.
5. Effects of rapid population growth on the physical environment, food, natural resources and quality of life.
6. An elementary knowledge of the physiology of reproduction wherever feasible.
7. The population policies and programmes of the world in general.

11.10 CURRICULUM OF POPULATION EDUCATION AS GIVEN IN THE DRAFT SYLLABUS OF NCERT

On the basis of the overall objectives laid down, the following six major areas have been identified which are not exclusive to any particular discipline but draw matter from several social sciences and biological sciences. They also have a wide scope for encompassing most of the concepts related to population education at the school stage. These areas are:

(i) The population growth (determinants and demographic situation).
(ii) Economic development and population growth (consequences).
(iii) Social development and population growth (consequences).
(iv) Health, Nutrition and Population.
(v) Biological factor–family life and population.
(vi) Population programmes– national and international.

Source: Population Education–A Draft Syllabus – Mehta, Saxena, Chandra, NCERT.

Proposed Programme of Population Education

Population Education–Not a Separate Subject

The Population Education Cell, set up by the National Council of Educational Research and Training, has developed a draft syllabus on Population Education for different school stages, which is as under. It may however be stated that population education is not to be treated as a separate subject in the school curriculum. It should be integrated with other subjects.

Elementary Level

1. Growth of population in cities.
2. Over-crowded situation.
3. Economic development and population.
4. Social development and population growth.
5. Importance of good health.
6. Factors responsible for personal hygiene.
7. Life in slums.
8. Control of diseases.
9. Basic food groups.
10. Biological factors and population.

Lower Secondary Level

11. Population growth.
12. Economic development and population growth.
13. Comparisons of national graphs development.
14. Social development and population growth.
15. Health, nutrition and population growth.
16. Biological factors and population.
17. Stages of growth

Higher Secondary Stage

18. Population growth.
19. Economic development and population growth.
20. Health, nutrition and population growth.
21. Social development and population growth.
22. Biological factors and population.

12

Teaching Methodology of Population Education

12.1 SIGNIFICANCE OF TEACHING METHODOLOGY

Modern teaching learning process assigns an important place to student activity and involvement. It is also called child-centred or learner-centred approach. Recent changes in the teaching learning process have led to a new awakening.

12.2 CLASSIFICATION OF TEACHING DEVICES AND TECHNIQUES

Classification of Teaching Devices and Techniques

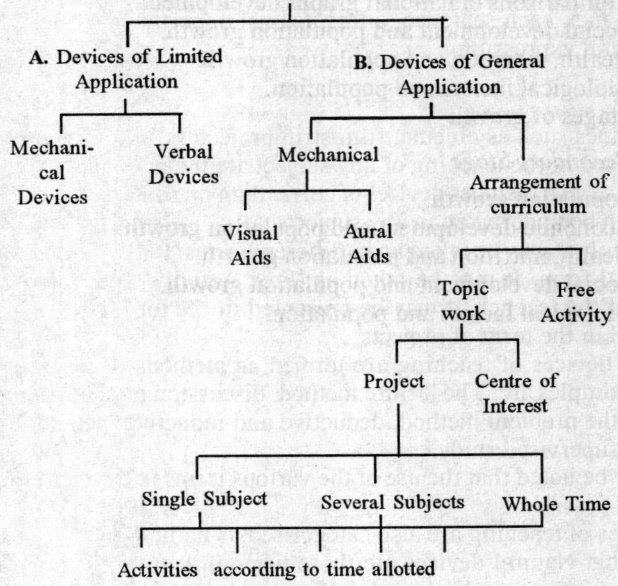

Classification of Devices of Teaching

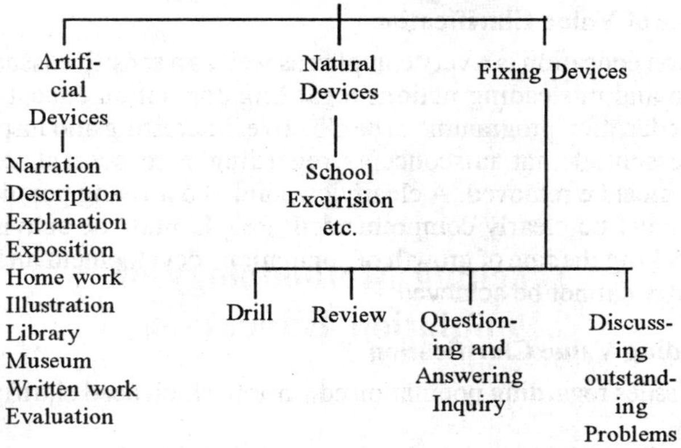

Group A

This category includes both tricks of verbal presentation, suited only to particular facts, and mechanical devices which illustrate single facts or process. "No book can hope to include all the advice needed by teachers in the selection and use of devices in category A."

The mechanical devices of Category A include much specialised apparatus. Counters or counting sticks may be used for teaching of elementary number combinations. Words and letter cards are used in teaching reading. Their application is only to younger children.

Every fact, each sentence, offers its own opportunity for bright imagery and forceful expression.

Group B

Machines such as cinema, film strip projectors, epidiascope, etc. which may be used in the teaching of any subject are included under this heading. This device also includes devices of curriculum presentation, such as projects, which can be undertaken in any subject.

Curriculum may be taken up in different forms. It may be dealt with in the traditional form. It may be taken as 'Free Activity' and without the rigid control of the teacher. It may be presented in the form of 'Topic Work' or presented in the form of projects.

Some devices of teaching are termed as methods of teaching and vice versa. Examples are: The lecture method, discussion method, demonstration method, the problem method, deductive and inductive method, assignment method, supervised study.

It may be noted that the use of the various terms in devices of teaching is arbitrary.

Devices of teaching are also categorised as natural and artificial devices of teaching. Natural devices are those wherein learning is a by-product of direct experience, e.g., in object teaching, outdoor work and school excursions etc. On the other hand artificial devices include oral communication through narration, explanation, exposition and illustration also.

12.3 VALUE CLARIFICATION

Significance of Value Clarification

Population education is a very complex as well as a sensitive issues. People have wrong and misleading notions regarding population education. For a population education programme to be effective, interesting and inspirational, it is very essential that misconcepts regarding it in several sections of population must be removed. A clear viewpoint about rising population and its impact must be clearly comprehended. People must be convinced that without checking the rate of growth of population, development and progress of the country cannot be achieved.

Issues Needing Value Clarification

Important issues regarding population education which need clarification are given below:

1. Rapidly growing population is a curse and not a boon.
2. Growing population can be checked.
3. Population is related to country's progress and development.
4. A small family is the need of the hour.
5. Family planning methods are not injurious to health.
6. Sex element must be imparted at the higher classes of elementary stage.
7. Ethics of population education. (Discussed below)

12.4 VALUE CLARIFICATION AND ETHICS OF POPULATION EDUCATION

Ethics is the art/science of good or evil, right or wrong. Ethics of population education involves the following types of questions:

1. Is it right to impart population education to the students?
2. Is it right to check population?
3. It is against the will of God to check population education?
4. Is it proper to adopt contraceptives?
5. Is abortion not a type of murder?
6. Is it proper to limit the number of members of a family?
7. Are incentives to family planning not a type of bribery?
8. Is marriage for sex satisfaction or reproductive purposes?
9. Is population control not a hindrance to individual freedom?

Most of these problems or ethical considerations have been discussed separately. A concerted effort would be needed to convince the people of the dire need of controlling population to achieve a reasonable standard and quality of life.

Mass and electronic media must be extensively used to popularise population education programmes so that people find these programmes acceptable.

Our approach in value clarification must be rational as well as sustained.

12.5 INQUIRY METHOD

Meaning of Inquiry Method

The inquiry method is a method of development. In this method, the child is led to discover truth for himself. It is a learner-centred approach.

Teacher's Role in the Inquiry Method

The following guidelines are suggested for the teacher to make inquiry method interesting, inspirational and effective.

1. Get them (the students) to define the problem of inquiry clearly.
2. Aid them to keep the problem in mind.
3. Get them to make many suggestions by encouraging them: (a) to analyse the situation in parts, (b) to recall previously known similar cases and general rules that apply, (c) to guess courageously and formulate guesses clearly.
4. Get them time to evaluate each suggestion carefully by encouraging them (a) to maintain a state of doubt or suspended conclusion, (b) to criticise the suggestion by appeal to know facts, minister experiments, and scientific treatises.
5. Get them to organise the material by proceeding (a) to build an outline on the board, (b) to use diagrams and graphs, (c) to formulate concise statement of the net outcome of the discussion.

It has been stated that for the success of the inquiry method of teaching we need "a teacher who has the ability to see problems clearly, the power to analyse with a keen discernment and the faculty to synthesise and draw conclusions with an uncanny accuracy."

Merits of Inquiry Method

Following are the merits of problem solving:

1. It helps in stimulating thinking.
2. It develops reasoning power.
3. It helps to improve knowledge.
4. It helps in developing good study habits.
5. It affords opportunities for participation in social activities. Problems are solved with the joint efforts of many students. The students learn to appreciate the different points of view and thus become tolerant.
6. The students learn to be self-dependent.
7. Discussions help to develop the power of expression of the students.
8. The method provides opportunities to the teachers to know in detail their pupils. They learn which students are shy in nature and which are very active and accordingly they assist the students.
9. Students learn facts which are meaningful and which have been discovered by their own efforts.
10. It helps in the maintenance of discipline. The students remain busy in finding out the answers to their own problem.
11. Knowledge is easily assimilated as it is the result of a purposeful activity.

12. Learning becomes more interesting in place of a dread.
13. It gives the power of critical judgement.
14. It helps to verify an opinion.
15. It satisfies curiosity.
16. It helps to learn how to act in a new situation.

Demerits of Inquiry Methods

The demerits are given below:

1. Generally speaking problem-solving involves mental activity only. There is less of bodily activity.
2. Small children do not possess sufficient background information and therefore they fail to participate in discussions relating to inquiry.
3. There is a lack of suitable reference and source books for children.
4. It involves a lot of time and the teachers find it difficult to cover the prescribed syllabus.
5. Problem method needs very capable teachers to provide effective guidance to students.
6. There is the danger that the inquiry method may lead to the selection of trivial topics and in some instances to those that generate more feeling and emotion than thought.

Approaches to Inquiry Method

Deductive as well as inductive approach is applied to the inquiry method. However, inductive approach is more effective. Here the student remains active. He can display his imagination, initiative and self-confidence.

Inquiry method is quite similar to the problem method of teaching-learning.

12.6 DISCUSSION

Meaning and Significance of Discussion Method

This method has been used in the teaching-learning process since times immemorial. It was widely used at the famous Nalanda University. The Greek scholars in their walk used to discuss various problems and issues with their disciples. Discussion has been described as a thoughtful consideration of the relationships involved in a topic or problem under study. It is concerned with the analysis, comparison, evaluation and conclusions of these relationships. It aims at uniting and integrating the work of the class. It is carried out by organising, outlining and relating the facts studied. It encourages the students to direct their thinking process towards the solution of a problem and to use their experiences for a further clarification and consolidation of learning material.

Discussion is to be distinguished from debate in which the participants seek to prove a point rather than to discover a truth. Debate may also be marked by uncontrolled exchange of verbalism.

Discussion is very important in stimulating mental activity, developing fluency and ease in expression, clarity of ideas in thinking and training in the presentation of one's ideas and facts. An exchange of ideas and opinions offers valuable training to students in reflective thinking.

Discussion may be used for the following purposes:

(i) For planning new work.
(ii) For making decisions concerning future work.
(iii) For sharing information.
(iv) For obtaining and gaining respect for various points of view.
(v) For classifying ideas.
(vi) For inspiring interest.
(vii) For evaluating progress.

Discussion may be formal or informal. Formal discussion is one which proceeds in a predetermined manner and according to set procedures. An informal discussion involves the free verbal interchange of the participants without being governed by predetermined set of rules.

Essential Parts of Constituents of Discussion

These are as under:

1. The leader – the teacher
2. The group – the students
3. The problem or the topic
4. The content – body of knowledge
5. Evaluation – change in ideas, attitudes etc.

Organisation of Discussion

Following are the main techniques of organising discussion:

1. Introducing a topic or a problem by the teacher by giving points or explanations to serve as the basis of discussion.
2. Calling upon a pupil by the teacher to give facts, describe a scene or situation, explain an incident, event or happening for getting the discussion started.
3. Preparing an outline of points co-operatively by the teacher and a few students which may become the starting point for discussion.
4. Asking the students to describe their own experiences connected with the subject, topic or problem and making them points for discussion.
5. Presenting detailed papers by the teacher and discussions thereon.
6. Presenting detailed papers by the students and discussing them in the class.
7. Showing special works and projects to the class and discussing them.
8. Showing some pictures, charts, diagrams or any audio-visual material and discussion about them.

Merits of Discussion

Following are the merits of discussion:

1. It helps in clarifying issues.
2. It helps children in crystallising their thinking.
3. It helps students in discovering what they do not know and what they have overlooked.
4. It engenders more reflection. It is farther from rote learning.
5. It represents a type of pooled knowledge, ideas and feelings of several persons.

6. It develops team spirit.
7. It engenders toleration of views which are at variance.
8. It affords opportunities to the students to learn together, make suggestions, share responsibility, comprehend the topic, evaluate the findings and to summarise results.
9. It provides opportunities to the students to speak distinctly, stand and sit correctly, respect the ideas of others, share interests, ask pertinent questions and comprehend the problem before the group.
10. It helps the teacher in discovering talented students who have potential for becoming good leaders.

Limitations of Discussion

Limitations of discussion are:

1. It is not suitable for all topics.
2. It is likely to be dominated by a few students.
3. It is likely to go off the track.
4. It may lead to unpleasant feelings.
5. It may create emotional tensions.
6. It may involve unnecessary arguments.

Directing Group Discussion

The teacher has to show immense patience and skill to ensure that discussion takes place on right lines and in the appropriate environment. Following points may be considered in this respect:

1. Students should be well acquainted with the significance of the topic, its nature and scope and causes why the class should discuss it.
2. Discussion should be confined to important aspects.
3. Students should be encouraged to take an active part in discussion.
4. Problems for discussion may be invited from the students without embarrassment or pressure.
5. Explanations may be provided where needed.
6. Co-operation rather than competition may be encouraged.
7. Efforts should be made to develop team spirit.
8. Doubts, mistakes and wrong interpretations about ideas and concepts should be made clear by the teacher.
9. Students should be guided to appreciate difference of opinions.
10. Discussion Abound not be dominated by only a few students
11. Students should be given training in discussion by forming small groups so that their hesitation is also removed.
12. Facts and opinions should be evaluated.
13. Personality cult should not be encouraged.
14. Facts and important points should be summarised.
15. Goal of discussion should always be kept in view.

12.7 DEMONSTRATION

Meaning of Demonstration

Demonstration implies the representation of a pre-arranged, series of events or equipments to a group of students for their observation. This is accompanied by explanatory remarks. This device or method is commonly used in science, fine arts and language teaching. Nevertheless it can also be used very profitably in the teaching of population education and other subjects by drawing charts, diagrams, graphs, etc. to illustrate important ideas regarding population education. Some elements involved in family planning and sex education can also be explained through demonstration.

Important Guidelines for a Successful Demonstration

These are given below:

1. Plan all the activities relating to demonstration in great detail.
2. Ensure that all the equipment, illustrations and other relevant materials are procured in time and kept ready before the demonstration begins.
3. Break down the demonstration into suitable steps so that it can be easily understood by the students.
4. Proceed with the demonstration slowly so that all the students may grasp the details.
5. Wherever possible, involve students in demonstration.
6. Ascertain after every step whether the students have grasped the meaning, contents and explanation. Repeat if they have not followed it.
7. Give suitable verbal explanations for heightening the interest of the students.
8. Encourage students to analyse, record and tabulate the results of their observation.
9. Make an assignment based on the Demonstration.

Co-curricular Activities and Learning Exercises for Population Education at the Elementary Level

Co-curricular activities are an integral part of education. At the elementary stages, co-curricular activities play a significant role in providing learning experiences to children regarding population education.

A great care is to be exercised in organising co-curricular activities in population education. Important activities are given below:

Population education curriculum may be seen in terms of the following learning experiences:

1. Children may compare two middle class families one with one earning member and five dependants and the other with two earning members and only two dependant young children and find the difference in their living style.
2. Children may work out per head income of families with equal income but varying sizes.

3. Children with the help of parents, grand-parents and old persons or relations in the family may prepare "family-tree" depicting information of the past three generations about the members in the family-births, deaths, causes of deaths, etc. They may help them to draw some inferences about population trends.
4. Children may also find out from their parents what medicines or treatments were available for certain diseases during their times, the childhood of their parents and those of grand parents. They may discuss their information in the class and arrive at their inferences.
5. Children may collect census figures for their village or town for the past few decades and draw a graph showing increase or decrease in population.
6. Children may also collect figures of school enrolment for the past few years to draw their inferences.
7. Children may collect figures about area population of countries like Australia, Brazil, Canada, China, Japan, Russia, United States of America, etc. and India and compare them in terms of population, area and average density of population.
8. Similar exercise can be done for a few States in India such as Kerala, West Bengal, Bihar, Uttar Pradesh, Tamil Nadu and Rajasthan.
9. Children may draw pictures of average Japanese and Indian family, etc. and compare them in terms of their size and living conditions or standards of living.
10. Budgeting one's pocket expenditure.
11. Presenting two or three imaginary monthly budgets of people drawn from lower middle class families with somewhat equal incomes but what varying family size (children can also be asked to collect data).
12. Finding out broadly the food requirements of our country after 30 years when its population is likely to be doubled. Holding debate and discussion on how and at what cost can this be achieved.
13. Finding out how many additional primary teachers would be required if every year additional 10 million students join the primary schools.
14. Finding out if population remains steady and no new class is required to be opened in their school how can the amount which was otherwise spent on new classes be spent under the new situation.
15. Finding out total number of doctors we would need in a district if there would be one doctor for every 500 people.
16. Children may compare the health and medical facilities available in big towns and small villages. They may draw inferences after discussing the facts among themselves.
17. Finding out what happens when one new job is created in the school or a village. Also finding out what happens when a person loses job against his wish.
18. Comparing life in various respects in two families; one with a working woman and the other only a housewife.
19. Finding out advantages of a family when the mother is educated and the size of the family is small.

20. Comparing standards of living in developed countries like Japan, Germany, UK and USA etc. and developing countries like India and Pakistan. Finding out probable causes that account for vast differences between the two situations.
21. Collecting information on four or five families they know in regard to their basic needs of food, clothing, shelter, medical care and educational facilities. Comparing and drawing inferences in regard to the size of the family and status of meeting their requirements.
22. Undertaking case studies of budgets of two families, one small and one big from the same income group and finding out which of the two is in a better position to save. Children may also find out how their savings are generally used.
23. Comparing two families somewhat closely—one which follows small family norms and the other which does not follow such norms. Children may try to find out the reason for such a behaviour.
24. Undertaking case studies of four or five mothers in respect of their health, number of deliveries and period between them. Consecutive deliveries and drawing inferences.
25. Children may work out and see for themselves what would happen in two generations if in there are two children and in the other four children.
26. Comparing and contrasting powerful wild animals like tiger and elephant on the one hand and man on the other to know their strengths and weaknesses and qualities which put man in a far superior position.
27. Listing various food articles and finding out that ultimately they come from plants growing in the soil.
28. Finding out how even secondary food products like milk, eggs, fish, meat etc. derived from animal world ultimately come from plant food on which the animals live.
29. Drawing pictures or preparing (clay) models of two similar pieces of land one badly managed in terms of deforestation, over grazing, unscientific tilling, soil erosion due to rains and floods, and the other in terms of a nursery, planned afforestation, controlled grazing, proper fencing, dam for flood control and canals for irrigation, generation of hydro-electricity, fishing, navigation and holiday resort to promote tourism, contour ploughing and bunding or terracing, etc.
30. Comparing and contrasting merits and demerits of using coal, petroleum and hydro-electricity from the point of view of pollution and depletion of resources.
31. Listing sources of energy which are replenishable or are almost infinite.
32. Drawing pictures of pollution in affluent and poor countries, and writing notes on how to avoid them.

13

Population Education and Teachers

13.1 SIGNIFICANT ROLE OF TEACHERS IN POPULATION EDUCATION

The active involvement of the teachers would go a long way in promoting population education programmes. Therefore, it is very important that they must be thoroughly acquainted with the various concepts and dimensions of population education programmes. There is considerable scope for incorporating some concepts of population education in teacher education both at the elementary and secondary levels. There is also the need for organising in-service population education programmes for teachers.

Four important points regarding the involvement of teachers must be kept in view:

1. Removing the ignorance of teachers regarding population related issues.
2. Removing the apathy of teachers towards this programme.
3. Removing the resistance of teachers which usually occurs whenever a new programme in the educational system is introduced.
4. Providing incentives to teachers to attend in-service education programmes relating to population education issues.

13.2 ROLE OF TEACHERS IN PLANNING AND GUIDING LEARNING EXERCISES FOR POPULATION EDUCATION

1. Children may compare two families; one with an earning member and five dependants and the other with two earning members and only two dependant young children.
2. They may draw pictures of an average Japanese and Indian family and compare them in terms of their size and living conditions or standards of living.
3. Children may collect census figures for their village or town for the past few decades and draw a graph showing the increase or decrease in population.
4. Children may also collect figures of school enrolment for the past few years to draw their inference.

5. Children may collect figures about area and population of countries like Canada, China, United States of America, Brazil, Australia and India and compare them in terms of population, area and average density of population.
6. Similar exercises can be done for a few states in India, such as, Kerala, West Bengal, Bihar, Uttar Pradesh, Tamil Nadu and Rajasthan. They may arrange them as per average density of population.
7. Presenting two or three imaginary monthly budgets of people drawn from lower middle class families with somewhat equal incomes but with varying family size (children can also be asked to collect data).
8. Working out per head income of families with equal income but varying sizes.
9. Finding out broadly the food requirements of our country after 30 years. Holding debates and discussions on how and at what cost can this be achieved.
10. Finding out how additional primary teachers would be required if every year an additional 10 million students join the primary school.
11. Finding out if the population remains steady and no new class is required to be opened in their schools, how can the amount which was otherwise spent on new classes be spent under the new situation.
12. Finding out the total number of doctors we would need in a district if there would be one doctor for every 500 people.
13. Finding out what happens when one new job is created in the school or a village. Also finding out what happens when a person loses his job against his wish.
14. Comparing life in various respects in two families, one with a working mother and the other only a housewife.
15. Finding out the advantages for a family when the mother is educated and the size of the family is small.
16. Comparing the standards of living in advanced and developing countries. Finding out probable causes that account for vast differences between the two.
17. Children may collect information on four or five families they know in regard to their basic needs of food, clothing, shelter.

Note: Exercises could be graded according to the standard/class. Illustrative aids may be used.

Brief History of In-Service Population Education Programme for Teachers

- 1969 Workshop by M.S. University of Baroda.
- 1969 Workshop organised by Pathfinder Funds (New Delhi).
- 1969 Workshop organised by the Regional College of Education, Bhopal.
- 1976 Workshop organised by Regional College of Education, Ajmer.
- 1977 National Conference on Population Education.

UNESCO Regional Conferences organised from time to time.

At present several Universities in India have introduced population education courses in Teacher Education/Training.

Strategies Needed for Teacher Education Programmes Relating to Population Education

These are as under:

1. Information Centres
2. Lectures
3. Pilot Projects
4. Seminars
5. Workshops
6. Research and Study Groups
7. Curriculum Development Experiments

Population Education Curriculum for Teacher Education/Teacher Training

AIFEA – IATE Workshop on Population Education Curriculum

During May 1970, the All India Federation of Educational Associations (AIFEA) in collaboration with the Indian Association of Teacher Educators (IATE) organised a workshop on Population Education to formulate a special study course on Population Education for the teachers colleges of India. The workshop adopted 'Special Studies Approach' and outlined the following major areas and sub-areas for such a course.

Areas

I. *Population: The Problems and Challenges*
   1. Population in India.
   2. Dynamics of population growth.
   3. Indian population situation in world perspective.

II. *Population Growth and Food Supply*
   1. Food is our basic economic problem.
   2. Foodgrain production in India.
   3. Malnutrition due to over-population.

III. *Health*
   1. Health of people related to population growth.
   2. Over-population leads to over-crowding.

IV. *Standard of Living*
   1. Meaning of standard of living and how it is affected by the size of population.
   2. Economic growth and population growth.

V. *Small Family for Better Living*
   1. Modification of family size is family responsibility.
   2. Family size: factors affecting size.
   3. Population control: need and methods.

VI. *Population Growth and Education*
   1. Over-population and its implications for education.
   2. Education for desirable changes in social values.

Curriculum for Population Education Suggested by the Population Education Centre, Baroda

The Population Education Centre, established in the Faculty of Education and Psychology at the University of Baroda in June 1970 has attempted to devise the following course of special field for trainees:

Unit I. Introduction to Population Education: Its Aims and Objectives

- The problem of population in the world and in India.
- Programmes at national state and district levels (both the government and the non-government programmes).
- Need for special educational programme through purposeful involvement of secondary schools.
- Introducing population education concept in school curriculum.
- Population education as a means of social change geared to national development and progress.
- Population education versus sex-education; population education vis-à-vis family planning education; population education versus education about birth control.
- Major areas of population education: demographic, social and economic.
- Aims and objectives of population education:
  - To create 'population awareness'.
  - To correlate school curriculum with life situations.
  - To impart relevant information.
  - To prepare responsible citizens.
  - To prepare proper attitudes and new values for small family.
- Need and significance of the course in the schools of modern India.

Unit II. Relationship of Population Growth and Education

- Population explosion and its adverse effects on quality of education
- Its impact on education measured in terms of:
  - Adverse student indices
  - Adverse teacher indices
  - Adverse material indices
  - Adverse organisational indices
- Population education as a phase of progressive education meant for developing:
  - Imagination
  - Innovation
  - Creative thinking
  - Problem solving
  - Social change and planned living
- Population control as a key means of quality control in education.

Unit III. Methods and Approaches of Population Education

- Direct versus indirect approach
- Integrated versus specialised approach
- Methods of correlation of the concept of population education through:
  - Curricular activities
  - Co-curricular activities
  - Extra-curricular activities
- Planning lessons in different subjects with a bearing on population education.
- Debates, essay-writing, symposia, group discussions, visits to Centres working on population programmes.
- Projects on population indices, such as, food, housing, education, medical care and health provision, entertainment including recreation, employment, opportunities to learn skills in various trades and leisure time activities.

Unit IV. Curriculum for Population Education in Schools

- Identification of the areas of curriculum for integration of the concept of population education.
- Preparation of teaching units with a bearing on population education.
- Reinterpretation of the present curriculum with reference to the population problems.
- Some important areas of learning in population education like: (a) Population dynamics; birth and death rates, rates of fertility, mortality and migration, (b) health, food and nutrition, (c) standards of living, economic development including employment opportunities, and (d) civic amenities.
- Incorporating ideas on population studies and problems as a bias in textbooks of social studies and languages.
- Elaboration of topics related to human reproduction in science subjects in a simple manner.
- Development of instructional materials with stories, essays, poems and other language components with a focus on population explosion.

Unit V. Evaluation in Population Education

- Testing of pupil's knowledge and information about population dynamics and problems included in the course.
- Various types of tests useful in population education.
- Observation and assessment of the relevant attitudes and values of pupils.
- Interviews with pupils to evaluate the outcomes of the course on population education.
- Identifying area of improvement in approach, methods and curriculum of population education.

Unit VI. Teacher's Role in Population Education

- Teacher as an agent for social change.

- Teacher's faith in national development through proper planning.
- Teacher's conviction and basic belief in the need for checking further growth in population.
- Teacher's faith in education as a strong tool of social change and development.
- Teacher's firm belief in population education programme as a sound measure to achieve national goals.
- Teacher's knowledge of population education areas.
- Teacher's basic understanding about population education concept.
- Teacher's knowledge of socio-economic problems of the country.
- Teacher's knowledge of sex and human reproduction system and its relation to social function of life.
- Teacher's skill in disseminating information according to age and intellectual capacity of students.
- Teacher's characteristics, e.g., being intelligent, liberal, creative, imaginative, innovative and interested in social needs and problems.

Unit VII. Controversies and Issues

- Conceptual differences in meanings (sex education, family planning propaganda, or education about birth control).
- Types of population education for different levels.
- Age-level to be exposed to population education.
- Competence of teachers to deal with the subject.
- Adverse reaction of pupils with different family backgrounds.
- Objection from parents and sections of the society.
- Cultural, religious and political biases against population education.

Suggested Practical Assignments for Trainees

- Drawing lessons for practice teaching with a bias on the theme "Country and its Population."
- Giving population education oriented lessons in the school.
- Gathering data and other demographic information about population of the local community.
- Collecting data on school-going population with regard to the number of schools and enrolment figures.
- Reporting on the visits to:
  - Hospitals and family planning centres
  - Foster homes
  - Beggar homes
  - Employment exchange bureau, etc.

13.5 SAMPLE POPULATION EDUCATION COURSE FOR DIETs

Rationale of Population Education Course

The fast rate of population growth has adverse impact and a great strain on our human material resources. The need of the hour is that the teachers who are charged with the task of educating future citizens, should understand various issues related to population and its impact on society and environment. By doing so they are expected to develop rational attitude and be committed to the desirable size and structure of population among themselves and the students. It is, therefore, important that the teachers themselves first understand and appreciate the concept of population education so that they are themselves able to make rational decisions with regard to their own family size and convey adequately the impact of population dynamics on the individual, family environment and the community as a whole.

Objectives of Population Education Course

On completion of the course, the trainees will be able to:

- Explain the meaning, scope, importance and objectives of population education.
- Explain the impact of population growth on various aspects of human life.
- Appreciate the importance of controlling population growth.
- Appreciate the importance of small family in raising the standard of living and improving the quality of life.
- Appreciate the need for the eradication of population related superstitions and wrong beliefs.
- Develop skills in integrating elements of population education in various curricular and co-curricular activities.
- Develop skill in identifying population education related plug points in different subjects areas.

COURSE OUTLINE

External 40 marks
Internal 10 marks
Time 45 hours

Unit 1: Nature and Scope of Population Education

10 hrs.
10 marks

- Concept, need, and importance of population education at elementary level.
- Population situation in developing countries with special reference to India.
- Recommendations regarding population education in NPE, 1986/1992 and POA.

Unit 2: Implementation of Population Education Programmes and Role of Various Agencies

10 hrs.
10 marks

- Role of Government
- Role of NGO's

Unit 3: Strategies for Transacting Population Education at Elementary level

15 hrs.
10 marks

- Curriculum Designing
  Infusion
- Integration
  Separate Subject
- Teaching Methodology
  Value Clarification
  Inquiry Method
  Discussion
  Demonstration
- Co-Curricular Activities School Based and Community Based activities.

Unit 4: Population and Quality of Life

10 hrs.
10 marks

- Small family norm – significance at individual and societal level.
- Interrelationship between population growth and quality of life.
- Resource generation and Impact of Population Growth.

Practical Work (For Internal Assessment)

7 hrs.
10 marks

Any two of the following:

- Prepare a scrap book on population related superstitions and wrong beliefs.
- A comparative case study of a small and a large family.
- Comparison of population growth of developing and developed countries for a period of five years.
- Preparation of posters/charts graphs/cartoons.
- Organisation of exhibitions/competitions/debates/essays/poetry/slogans/poster making/quiz/cartoon making.

14

Small Family Norm Significance and Societal Level

14.1 IMPORTANCE OF SMALL FAMILY

It is universally concepted that the progress of a nation and that of the family depends upon small families. Most of the developing and least developed countries have large families with the result that they are facing the problems of inadequate food, nutrition, clothing and shelter etc.

Promoting Small Family for Better Living: Population control programmes must be universally accepted in the interest of the family and the nation. The aim of this population control is not merely to cut down population, but to create conditions in which there can be happier families, in which parents are able to give their families the care which is their due. The aim of the family planning is to make family life and the life of children happier, richer, more contented, more prosperous and more progressive. It is to usher a new social order. We want our children to inherit a better world than our own. We should, therefore, realise that family size is controllable and that it can facilitate the development of a higher quality of life in the nation and that a small family size can contribute to the quality of living for the individual family (see also Chapters 22, 3 and 4)

An ancient proverb says:

Where there is harmony at home,
there is contentment in the community;
Where there is contentment in the community,
there is prosperity in the nation;
Where there is prosperity in the nation
there is peace in the world.

14.2 SMALL FAMILY NORMS

The question, "How many children a couple should have"? is most vital for the existence and continuation of every family and the society as a whole. Every society therefore should develop definite behavioural patterns to ensure a certain norm of family size. These behavioural patterns, in the form of emphasis on marriage, age at marriage, preferences for sex, values and roles of children, etc. automatically result in ensuring the normatively desired family size. The two extremes of the family size norm could extend from 'no child family', to 'as many children as God may will'. Within these two extremes, the norm varies from society to society, depending upon its socio-economic and health, particularly mortality status. Logically one could expect change in family size norm corresponding to changes in socio-economic status of any given society. However, this change is not simultaneous because the normative values and behaviour patterns change at a slower pace as compared to economic progress. This cultural lag usually results in increased unhappiness in the individual families as well as society. It is one of the important purposes and goals of the national family planning programmes of every country to bridge this gap and enable individual families to adjust to changing situations so that they can maximise the gains accruing to them as a result of overall socio-economic progress. In simple terms this means that the question of family size and how to regulate it plays a crucial role in deciding upon the progress, development and happiness at both the family and societal level. The present slogan regarding norm is 'हम दो, हमारे दो.' (We are two and we should have two children).

14.3 FAMILY SIZE AND ITS INFLUENCES

Dr. D.C. Dubey and Dr. A. Bardhan (1982) discuss the following influences of family size:

1. *Family Size and Morbidity*. Studies in this field have indicated a clear association between family size and illness. As the family size increases the number of sickness episodes per family and per member of the family also increases. Malnutrition causes several kinds of morbidity among children. Studies in this area have shown that family size is one of the important factors related to malnutrition. Children from large families are more likely to be malnourished. It is obvious that larger the family more the pressure on it because of increased number of illnesses, need for more parental care and higher expenses for treatment.

2. *Family Size and Mortality*. Several mortality studies have analysed relationship between family size and mortality. Invariably all of them indicate a definite association between family size and mortality rate. A study in Punjab found that infant mortality tended to increase with family size. Another study in England found that this increase in mortality with the number of children in a family was true in case of all the social classes. In some studies mortality rates of different birth orders were studied and it was found that higher the birth order higher the mortality. In other words, later births within a large family are likely to experience higher mortality.

3. *Family Size and Physical Growth*. Long term studies in England have established a significant difference in the physical growth of children associated with family size. These differences were further found to be not limited to the lower classes alone. A study suggests that birth of each additional child in a family acts as a check on the growth of all preceding children. In very broad terms it can be said that the larger the family the less the height and weight at all ages of both the earlier and later born children.

4. *Family size and intelligence.* Intelligence is treated as a fairly good indicator of general well being. Because of the importance of intelligence, its association with family size has been examined in several studies. These studies have revealed a remarkable negative correlation between intelligence and family size. Further it is found that this negative relationship holds true in case of all social classes and all age groups. In general terms, it can be stated that intelligence test scores decrease as family size increases.

5. *Consequences of Family Size on Parents.* Not very many studies have been done in this field—but there is some evidence to suggest that family size in certain ways influences the life style and mental and physical health of parents. Here and Shaw found that physical and mental health problems in parents increased with family size. The increase was marked in case of health of the mother. Chen and Gobb found positive relationship between frequency of particulars among parents and number of children. Another study of women shows a positive relationship between arthritis and large family size. Similarly, it was found that the incidence of hypertension increased with the number of children.

Mothers in large family experience repeated pregnancies at short intervals. These pregnancies create heavy lactation demands. Prolonged lactation creates protein deficiency. Failure to meet this protein demand leads to premature ageing and early maternal death. This is particularly true of developing countries.

In India the problem of family size has not been studied extensively and in-depth. To illustrate such studies, mention of two studies—one carried out in North and the other in South, can be made. Gordon and Wyon made the study in Punjab villages (1962) and University of Kerala carried out a detailed study on family growth in Kerala (1968). There is a definite need to undertake more such in-depth studies. In the absence of such studies most of the knowledge in this area come from several KAP (Knowledge, Attitude and Practice) studies carried out in the country. An attempt is made here to summarise some of the important findings of these KAP studies relating to reasons or factors motivating the people to have larger or smaller families.

14.4 FACTORS LEADING TO LARGE FAMILIES

1. Children are considered to be an economic asset by villagers who largely depend upon agriculture.
2. High prevailing mortality among children induces families to have more children as an insurance against it.
3. Children are considered as the only source of old age security.
4. Children improve the strength of the family in village and ensure continuation of family name.
5. Children are gift of God and ensure religious salvation of the parents.
6. Lack of knowledge and information about modern contraceptives to limit family size.

The above findings are mostly from earlier KAP studies carried out immediately after the initiation of family planning programme in the country. The family planning programme has roughly existed in our country for about thirty years now. As a result of intensive education and communication programme carried out in the country, there has been a substantial change in a large number of people in so far as the above factors are concerned. More recent KAP studies show a shift towards preference for a smaller family of 2 or 3 or 4 children. A vast majority of the people now consider smaller family to be ideal family. Similarly, there is a marked improvement in the knowledge and information about modern contraceptives among the urban and rural areas of the country. There is a similar change in the practice of family planning methods. However, this is far less than what is expected. Women in particular have shown a marked change in favour of smaller families.

14.5 PROMOTIONAL AND MOTIVATIONAL MEASURES FOR THE ADOPTION OF THE SMALL FAMILY NORM

The following promotional and motivational measures need to be undertaken:

(i) Panchayats and Zila Parishads to be rewarded and honoured for exemplary performance in universalising the small family norm, achieving reductions in infant mortality and birth rates, and promoting literacy with completion of primary schooling.

(ii) The Balika Samridhi Yojana run by the Department of Women and Child Development, to promote survival and care of the girl child, will continue. A cash incentive of Rs. 500 is awarded at the birth of the girl child of birth order 1 or 2.

(iii) Maternity Benefit Scheme by the Department of Rural Development. A cash incentive of Rs. 500 is awarded to mothers who have their first child after 19 years of age, for birth of the first or second child only. Disbursement of the cash award will in future be linked to compliance with ante-natal check up, institutional delivery by trained birth attendant, registration of birth and BCG immunisation.

(iv) A Family Welfare-linked Health insurance plan to be established. Couples below the poverty line, who undergo sterilisation with not more than two living children, would become eligible (long with children) for health insurance (for hospitalisation) not exceeding Rs. 5,000 and a personal accident insurance cover for the spouse undergoing sterilisation.

(v) Couples below the poverty line, who marry after the legal age of marriage, register the marriage, have their first child after the mother reaches the age of 21, accept the small family norm, and adopt a terminal method after the birth of the second child, will be rewarded.

(vi) A revolving fund to be set up for income-generating activities by village-level self help groups, who provide community-level health care services.

(vii) Crèches and child care centres to be opened in rural areas and urban slums. This will facilitate and promote participation of women in paid employment.

(viii) A wider, affordable choice of contraceptives to be made accessible at diverse delivery points, with counselling services to enable acceptors to exercise voluntary and informed consent.

(ix) Facilities for safe abortion to be strengthened and expanded.

(x) Products and services will be made affordable through innovative social marketing schemes.

(xi) Local entrepreneurs at village levels to be provided soft loans and encouraged to run ambulance services to supplement the existing arrangements for referral transportation.

(xii) Increased vocational training schemes for girls leading to self-employment to be encouraged.

(xiii) Strict enforcement of Child Marriage Restraint Act, 1976.

(xiv) Strict Enforcement of the Pre-Natàl Diagnostic Techniques Act, 1994.

(xv) Soft loans to ensure mobility of the ANMs to be increased.

(xvi) The 42nd Constitutional Amendment has frozen the number of representatives in the Lok Sabha (on the basis of population) at 1971 Census levels. The freeze is currently valid until 2001, and has served as an incentive for State Governments to fearlessly pursue the agenda for population stabilisation. This freeze needs to be extended until 2026.

14.6 CONCLUDING OBSERVATIONS

The above discussion establishes the role and importance of family size in influencing overall family welfare and happiness. Its influence on the well being of children is particularly marked. Large families are likely to experience frequent illness, malnutrition of children, increased mortality of children and mother and lesser intellectual and physical growth. Large families also increase economic and emotional pressure and stress on the parents leading to their increased ill health. As opposed to these, smaller families are likely to minimise the above ill effects and increase chances of higher social, economic and emotional welfare of all the members of the family. To plan for small family with two or three children is to plan for happy family. There seems to be a definite change in favour of smaller families as revealed by recent KAP studies carried out in the country. There is increase in knowledge and practice of family planning although it can be further improved. The continuing improvement in mortality rates is likely to make smaller families still more relevant in modern India.

15

Interrelation between Population Growth and Quality of life

15.1 UN INTERNATIONAL CONFERENCE ON POPULATION AND DEVELOPMENT (1994) ON THE INTERRELATION BETWEEN POPULATION GROWTH AND QUALITY OF LIFE

The All-world UNO conference which went into several aspects of population and development highlighted the interrelation between population and development in these words, "There is general agreement that persistent widespread poverty and serious social and gender inequities have significant influence on, and in turn influenced by demographic factors such as population growth, structure and distribution." It is, therefore, very essential that population policy and concerns must be fully integrated into development strategies of planning at all levels and in all dimensions. The economic growth that results would help meet the needs and requirements of quality of life of the present and future generations. It is also like by to promote social justice and help in the enrichment of life. (*see also Chapter 18*)

15.2 FACTORS AFFECTING THE QUALITY OF LIFE

According to the Conference, among the factors that affect the quality of life are reproductive health services, sexual health care, age groups, literacy etc.

15.3 MEANING OF QUALITY OF LIFE

The concept quality of life has different connotations. In fact it depends upon the way we look at life. For a Jain *Muni*, quality of life may mean almost reduction in wants. Several Jain Munis bear minimum clothes.

Saints like Sant Kabir emphasised purity of life and doing one's duty in an honest manner. They wanted people to live a pure life.

Mirabai is quality of life meant pure and self-devotion to Lord Krishna.

However, for a vast majority of people, quality of life depends upon the following:

1. Reasonable income to sustain oneself
2. Balanced food and nutrition
3. Adequate shelter

4. Proper clothing
5. Availability of cheap health and sanitary services
6. Availability of cheap communication and transport facilities
7. Employment
8. Small family

15.4 INDICATION OF QUALITY OF LIFE

Table 15.1 provides comparative data on quality of life in respect of 14 developed and 16 developing countries including India.

Table 15.1 Selected Indicators of Population growth and Quality of Life: Developing countries (1999)

	Country	*Population (1999) ('000)*	*Under 5 Infant Mortality rate/rank*	*% of Infant with 100 gm weight*	*% of population using improved water facilities*	*% of population having adequate sanitary condition*	*No of radio & and T.V. sets per 1000 population radio*	*TV*
	1	2	3	4	5	6	7	
	Developed Countries							
1.	Australia	18705	175/5	6	100	100	1391	554
2.	Austria	8177	175/5	6	100	100	751	525
3.	Canada	30857	165/6	6	100	100	1067	710
4.	Denmark	5282	175/5	6	100	100	1145	594
5.	France	58886	175/5	5	100	10.	946	595
6.	Germany	82178	175/5	-	100	100	948	567
7.	Italy	57343	165/6	5	100	100	880	528
8.	Japan	126505	187/4	7	100	100	956	686
9.	Norway	4442	187/4	4	100	100	917	462
10.	Russian Federation	147196	123/22	7	99	99	417	410
11.	Sweden	8892	187/4	5	100	100	932	519
12.	Switzerland	7344	187/4	5	100	100	979	457
13.	UK	58744	165/6	7	100	100	1443	521
14.	USA	276218	158/8	7	100	100	2116	806
	Developing Countries							
1.	India	998056	49/98	33	88	31	120	65
2.	Afghanistan	21923	4/257	20	13	12	132	13
3.	Angola	12479	2/295	19	38	44	54	13
4.	Bangladesh	126947	53/149	30	97	53	50	6
5.	Bhutan	2064	45/175	-	62	69	19	6
6.	Brazil	167988	89/40	8	83	72	434	223
7.	China	1266838	87/41	6	75	38	335	321
8.	Cuba	11160	158/8	7	95	95	352	239
9.	Indonesia	209255	73/52	8	76	66	155	68
10.	Maldives	278	55/83	13	100	56	129	28
11.	Myanmar	45059	39/112	24	68	46	96	6
12.	Nepal	23385	47/104	-	81	27	38	6
13.	Nigeria	108945	15/187	16	57	63	226	66

1		2	3	4	5	6	7
14.	Pakistan	152331	39/112	25	88	61	- -
15.	Sierra Leone	4717	1/316	11	28	28	— -
16.	Sri Lanka	18639	135/19	25	83	83	- -

(For Income and Expectation of Life – other indicators of Development *see chapter 5*)

15.5 DEMOGRAPHIC AND POPULATION CHANGES AND THEIR ECONOMIC IMPLICATIONS FOR QUALITY OF LIFE

Population growth and its relation to economic growth has been a matter of debate for over a century. The early Malthusian view was that population growth is likely to impede economic growth because it will put pressure on the available resources, result in deterioration in quality of life. Contrary to the Malthusian predictions, several of the South East Asian countries have been able to achieve economic prosperity and improvement in quality of life in spite of population growth. This has been attributed to the increase in productivity due to development and utilisation of innovative technologies by the young educated population who formed the majority of the growing population. These countries have been able to exploit dynamics of demographic transition to achieve economic growth by using the human resources as the engine driving the economic development; improved employment with adequate emoluments has promoted saving and investment which in turn stimulated economic growth.

Box 15.1 Economic Implications of Demographic Transition

The next two decades will witness:
- Increase in the 15-59 age group from 519-800 million
- Low Dependency ratio

Challenge is to ensure:
- Adequate investment in HRD
- Appropriate employment with adequate emoluments

Opportunity is to:
- Utilise available abundant human resources to accelerate economic development

However, it is noteworthy that not all countries which have undergone demographic transition have been able to transform their economies. Sri Lanka, which underwent demographic transition at the same time as other South East Asian countries, still continues to have poor economic indices. It is likely that population growth or demographic transition can have favourable impact on economic growth only when there are optimal interventions aimed at human resource development and appropriate utilisation of available human resources.

For India the current phase of demographic transition with low dependency ratio and high working age group population represents both a challenge and an opportunity. The challenge is to utilise these human resources fully, give them appropriate jobs with adequate emoluments; if this challenge is met through well planned schemes for employment generation which are implemented effectively, there will be improved national productivity and personal savings rates; appropriate investment of these savings will help the country to achieve the economic transition from low economic growth – low per capita income to high economic growth–high per capita income. It is imperative to make the best of this opportunity so as to enable the country and its citizens to vault to the high income–high economic growth status.

15.6 TYRANNY OF GROWING NUMBERS AND QUALITY IN LIFE IN INDIA

The tyranny of numbers is terrible and poses serious challenges to development planners and implementers.

Sixteen per cent of the world's population lives on two per cent of land in India.

The 1.8 crore addition to the population every year requires the opening of 70,000 new primary schools annually (current figure 6,000), raising foodgrain production from 40 lakh tonnes to 55 lakh tonnes (per capita foodgrain production is a measly 200 kg per year, just about beating the UN standard for famine–like conditions—below 200 kg per person per year) creating 35 lakh new non-agriculture jobs every year and accommodating more than 50 lakh additional labourers in the crowded agro-sector.

15.7 INDEX OF POPULATION GPD AND FOODGRAINS IN INDIA

The following indices illustrates the indices for population, for GDP and for Foodgrains production.

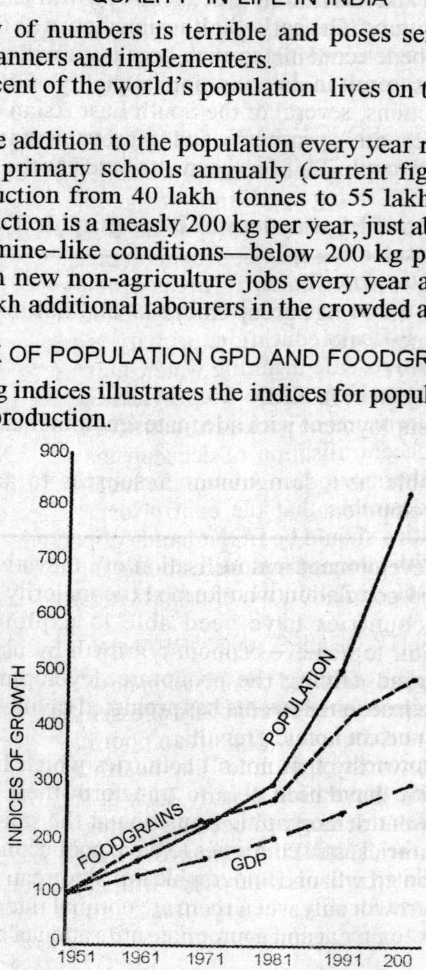

Fig. 15.1: Indices of Growth of Population, GDP and Foodgrains Production (1951 to 2001)

15.8 QUALITY OF LIFE AND FOOD REQUIREMENTS

In the past, food and nutritional security has been largely interpreted to mean adequate availability of basic food products in the country as a whole. The concept of food security now needs to be broadened to include peoples' access to basic nutritional requirements, both physically and economically. This problem is particularly acute in the vulnerable sections for society and in the deficit and inaccessible regions of the country. It is necessary to develop strategies by which such inadequacies can be overcome by integrating the food production and distribution systems with the employment and poverty alleviation programmes. In particular, the Public Distribution System (PDS) will need to be restructured in order to provide foodgrains at substantially lower prices to the poor in a focussed manner and to ensure availability of such commodities in the remote and deficit areas of the country. A widespread, well-established PDS is essential for ensuring food security.

15.9 OTHER SERVICES AND QUALITY OF LIFE

Economic growth and employment opportunities in themselves may not be sufficient to improve the living conditions of the poor. They need to be accompanied by measures which enhance the social and physical conditions of existence. Despite considerable efforts, provision of social infrastructure and services remains inadequate. These are areas which are in the nature of quasi-public goods and in which private initiatives and the market are unlikely to play a significant role. Primary education, primary health care, including the preventive and promotive, safe drinking water, nutrition and sanitation require heavy investment which has to be provided out of public funds. However, since the requirements of social infrastructure vary significantly across regions, greater decentralisation of decision making than exists at present is desirable. Furthermore, recognising the localised nature of these essential services, it is desirable that the control over the operation and maintenance of the facilities should be in the hands of peoples' institutions and local associations, with adequate resources being made available either from the exchequer or through devolution of powers to raise such resources.

15.10 QUALITY OF LIFE AND URBANISATION

In recent years the problems of rapid urbanisation has become acute. There has been a progressive decline in the availability of essential services as well as in the quality of life in urban areas. The urban poor have been the worst affected segment in this process of decline. The health and environmental consequences of increasing population density, lack of safe drinking water inadequate urban sanitation are likely to become further aggravated unless steps are initiated during the Tenth Plan to improve the situation through a well considered and articulated urbanisation policy with identified programme components including those for disease surveillance, epidemic control and urban solid and liquid waste management.

15.11 QUALITY OF LIFE AND ENVIRONMENT, HEALTH AND DEVELOPMENT NEEDS

No development process which leads to an adequate quality of life can be sustained in a situation of deteriorating environmental and ecological conditions. Environmental degradation is usually the outcome of individual actions which do not take into account the externalities imposed on others both in space and time. The market mechanism left to itself does not provide any method of forcing the internalisation of these costs. Indeed, it may actually reinforce such behaviour. As a consequence, it is the responsibility of the government to ensure that the interests of both the current victims of environmental degradation and future generations are adequately protected, without disrupting the process of growth and development. Eventually, the responsibility for preservation of the environment rests on the people themselves. In order for these responsibilities to be properly discharged, however, the rights to a healthy environment have to be unambiguously assigned through legislative action; and people's participation in preservation of the environment fostered through social mobilisation and appropriate organisational structures.

15.12 QUALITY OF LIFE AND BASIC MINIMUM SERVICES

The Minimum Needs Programme (MNP) was launched in the Fifth Five Year Plan. Its objective was to ensure a basic minimum standard of life for all sections of people living in the rural areas of the country. The strategy was to establish a network of facilities to attain an acceptable level of social consumption in respect of selected items within a stipulated time-frame. The rationale was twofold.

First, it was felt that the competing demands for greater investment in other development sectors left relatively small allocations for social services. In the face of resource constraint, the tendency was to impose economy measures or cuts in the allocations for social sectors.

Second there were wide inter-State differences in the provision of social services and infrastructure which called for governmental intervention. Initially, there were eight components of MNP, viz., elementary education, rural health, rural water supply, rural electrification, rural roads, rural housing, environmental improvement of urban slums and nutrition. While adult education was added to the list of MNP components in the Sixth Plan, rural domestic energy, rural sanitation and public distribution system were added during the Seventh Plan.

While in some areas of MNP, great strides have been made since the launching of the programme, for certain other components of the programme, the extent of achievement is below acceptable levels. Further, the inter- State differences in the levels of achievement still remained very high.

Recognising the shortfall in the achievement of the basic minimum standard of life for all sections of the people, a bold initiative was taken by the Chief Ministers Conference held in July, 1996 to ensure access of all to certain Basic Minimum Services (BMS) in a time-bound manner.

The Conference endorsed the seven basic minimum services as of paramount importance in securing a better quality of life for the people, especially those residing in rural areas. Further, it observed that it would be in the best interests of the country, if time-bound action plans are formulated to secure full coverage of the country with these seven basic services by 2000 AD. This was essential for the rapid growth of the economy and for social justice and hence, these basic services were to constitute the core of the social sector development plan.

The seven basic services identified for priority attention are:

1. 100 per cent coverage of provision of safe drinking water in rural and urban areas;
2. 100 per cent coverage of primary health service facilities in rural and urban areas;
3. Universalisation of primary education;
4. Provision of Public Housing Assistance to all shelterless poor families;
5. Extension of Mid-day Meal Programme in primary schools, to all rural blocks and urban slums and disadvantaged sections;
6. Provision of connectivity to all unconnected villages and habitations; and
7. Streamlining of the Public Distribution System with focus upon the poor.

15.13 HIGH POPULOUS INDIAN STATES AND POOR QUALITY OF LIFE

In majority of States with high population growth rates, the performance in the social and economic sectors has been poor. The poor performance could be the outcome of a variety of factors including paucity of natural, financial or human resources. Poverty, illiteracy and poor development co-exist and reinforce each other. In order to promote equity and reduce disparity between States, special assistance has been provided to the poorly performing States. The benefits accrued from such assistance has to a large extent depended upon:

(a) the States' ability to utilise the available funds and improve services and facilities, and

(b) community awareness and ability to utilise the available services.

In spite of the additional assistance provided, improvement in infrastructure, agriculture and industry have been sub-optimal and the per capita income continues to be low in most of the poorly performing States. These States also have high birth rates and relatively low literacy rates. It is imperative that special efforts are made during the next two decades to break this vicious self perpetuating cycle of poor performance, poor per capita income, poverty, low literacy and high birth rate so that the further widening of disparities between States in terms of per capita income and quality of life is prevented. In addition to the special assistance available to poorly performing States, additional Central assistance from Basic Minimum Service (BMS) programme will also be available during the Ninth Plan period for achieving these objectives.

The higher population growth rates and low per capita income in poorly performing States are likely to have a major impact on several social sector programmes. The health status of the population in these Status is poor; the health sector programme will require inputs not only for improving infrastructure and manpower, but also increasing efficiency and improving performance. The Family Welfare Programme has to address the massive task of meeting all the unmet needs for MCH and contraception so that there is a rapid decline in mortality and fertility rates. Due to high birth rate, the number of children requiring schooling will be large. The emphasis in the education sector on primary education is essential to ensure that the resource constraints do not result in an increase in either proportion or number of illiterates. Emphasis on pre-vocational and vocational training in schools will enable these children to acquire skills through which they will find gainful employment later.

Box 15.2: The Seven Basic Minimum Services for Quality of Life

- ❑ Primary health care services
- ❑ Provision of safe-drinking water
- ❑ Universalisation of primary education
- ❑ Housing assistance to shelterless
- ❑ Nutrition support
- ❑ Streamlining of PDS with a focus on the poor
- ❑ Connectivity of unconnected villages.

Box 15.3: Health

Major areas of concern are:

- ❑ Continued high morbidity due to communicable diseases
- ❑ Rising disease burden due to non-communicable diseases
- ❑ Escalating cost for health care

Focus will be on:

- ❑ Providing integrated preventive, promotive, curative and rehabilitative services in primary, secondary and tertiary health care institutions with appropriate referral linkages.

15.14 POPULATION POLICES AND QUALITY OF LIFE

Following points need to be taken note of while planning and implementing population policies so that quality of life can undergo substantial improvement.

1. *Population and Poverty:* Widespread poverty remains the major challenge to development tasks. Poverty is often accompanied by illiteracy, malnutrition, unemployment, low status of women, exposure to environmental risks and limited access to social and health services (reproductive health service including family planning). All these factors contribute to high level of fertility morbidity, mortality, as well as to low level of economic

productivity. Poverty is also related to inappropriate distribution of population in equal use of natural resources and also to serious environmental degradation.

Slower population growth in several countries has increased their ability to attack poverty, protect the environment and build the base for future sustainable development. All these have a considerable positive impact on quality of life.

2. *Population and Environment:* Meeting the basic needs of growing population is dependent on healthy environment. At the same time pressure on the environment may result from rapid population growth, distribution and migration, especially in ecologically vulnerable eco-systems.

In attempting to address population growth, environmental concern will have to be taken note of.

3. *Population: Children and Youth.* Owing to declining mortality rates and the persistence of high fertility levels, a large number of developing countries continue to have a very large proportion of children and young people in their populations. Poverty has a devastating impact on children's health and welfare. The on-going and future demands created by large young populations, particularly in terms of health, education and employment pose major challenges and responsibilities to families, local communities and the country.

Equal educational opportunities must be ensured for boys and girls.

Effective steps will have to be taken to protect children from all types of exploitation and abuse.

First and the foremost responsibility is to ensure that every child is a wanted child and that he is the most valuable resource for the future. He, therefore, must be properly looked after.

4. *Population of Elderly People*: The decline in fertility levels and mortality levels is providing fundamental changes in the age structure of the population of most societies. The steady increase of old age groups or 'ageing of population' poses serious economic and social challenges to all the societies. This implies.

i) To develop appropriate system of health care for the older people.
ii) To develop appropriate systems of economic and social security in old age.
iii) To develop a support system with a view to enhancing the ability to families to take care of elderly people within the family.
iv) To develop the self-reliance of elderly people to facilitate their continued participation in society.
v) *Population of Persons with Disabilities*: Persons with disabilities constitute a significant proportion of population. It has to be recognised that they have a great role to play in all aspects of cultural, economic and social life of the society. Proper conditions must be created to ensure equal opportunities for them. Their dignity and self-respect must be ensured.
vi) *Population Policy and Women Empowerment*: The key to the new approach to population planning would be to empower women and provide them with more choices through access to education and health

services, skill development and employment. Their full involvement in policy decision making and policy implementing must be ensured.

15.15 CONCLUSION

In the new millennium, nations are judged by well-being of their peoples; by levels of health, nutrition and education; by the civil and political liberties enjoyed by their citizens; by the protection guaranteed to children and by provisions made for the vulnerable and the disadvantaged.

The vast numbers of the people of India can be its greatest asset if they are provided with the means to lead healthy and economically productive lives. Population stabilisation is a multi-sectoral endeavour requiring constant and effective dialogue among a diversity of stakeholders, and co-ordination at all levels of the government and society. Spread of Literacy and education, increasing availability of affordable reproductive and child health services, convergence of service delivery at village levels, participation of women in the paid work force, together with a steady, equitable improvement in family income, will facilitate early achievement of the socio-demographic goals. success will be achieved if the Action Plan contained in the NPP 2000 is pursued as a national movement.

16

Resource Generation and Impact of Population Growth

16.1 INTRODUCTION ON POPULATION AND RESOURCE GENERATION

Growing population of our country is a boon or bane for us is a matter of controversy among the scholars. Some scholars who are nick-named as 'doom-sayers' visualise the present pressure of population growth as a great burden on our resources and think that this phenomenon has eaten away the fruit of the spectacular progress that India has made in resource generation. The growing of population has also led to depletion of our resources. It is responsible for environmental degradation. Above all, it has posed serious threats to the earth's resources' capacity to sustain human population. The opposite view of another set of scholars, who are optimistic in nature, view the growing population as an opportunity and predict with confidence that human ingenuity, technological advances and efficient system of use of resources and distribution of wealth will usher in a golden and assured future. They argue that it is the quality of the population that counts. They cite the example of Japan—a country with nearly three times the density of population as compared with India, which has become one of the most advanced countries in the world. Again they argue that China, the most populous country in the world is also ahead of India in progress.

Taking the realities of the situation as it exists in India, it is crystal clear that the growing population in India has diluted the efforts in resource generation. The Census Report 2001 explains the impact of growing of population in these words.

"Rapid population growth has economic, social and political implications. It also affects public education, health and welfare, and the quality of the environment in which people live. It is recognised that the most critical implication of continuing population growth is the demand for food which it generates. India may be in a comfortable position at present but it is doubtful whether we could continue to be so in the long term, particularly because availability of new land is less likely. On the other hand, there are possibilities of loss of good land to urban areas, housing for growing population in the rural areas, industries, highways etc. When population growth is rapid, the number of children grow even more rapidly than the total population which adversely affects school enrolment ratios and improvement in the quality of education.

Quantitative and qualitative improvements of health services require large investments which becomes difficult for want of resources. The physical and mental development of children is often retarded in large families. Rapid urbanisation and growth of slums are also important social evils of rapid population growth. The sum total of all these effects is that malnutrition, poverty and unemployment afflict a large number of people in developing countries like India characterised by high rate of population growth. Indeed the distinction between the developed and developing countries is that in developing countries, a sizeable proportion of population does not have any regular income.

16.2 GROWING POPULATION AND GIGANTIC TASKS AHEAD

At present population of our country is 102 crore. According to the projection of the Registrar General of India, India's population which was 93.4 crore in 1995 would reach to the tune of 126.4 crore by the year 2016. In other words, our population would register an increase of 33 crore in just 20 years. It is worth mentioning here that our population was 34.2 crore in 1947 and it would increase to a little less than four times in 2106. This spectacular increase will not save us from fast approaching Malthusian catastrophy.

According to UN estimates (Medium Rate Projections), the position would be as under:

Year	*Projected Population*	*Increase*
1995	929 million	308 million in 20 years
2000	1007 million	78 million in 5 years
2025	1330 million	323 million in 25 years
2050	1533 million	203 million in 25 years

For meeting the growing needs in different areas of national life we need the following:

(i) Raising our food production to the tune of 50 lakh tonnes every year. At present the increase is only 40 lakh tonnes every year. The quality and quantity of food available is not commensurate with our needs. A substantial section of population will remain underfed and under-nourished.

(ii) Establishing about one lakh new primary schools every year as against nearly 6000 primary schools per year.

(iii) Creating at least 30 lakh new jobs per year in the non-agricultural sector.

(iv) To meet the needs of new houses we will require new technology as we are left with less than 9 million square km for living for the present day population.
With the increase in population the demand for houses will continue to increase and thus the land available for agriculture will be progressively reduced and the consequent result will be huge shortage of food.

(v) Reforestation is reined because in the villages the demand for fire wood would rise to such levels that one wonders if any tree will be left in the coming centuries.

(vi) Steps have to be taken to meet the growing demand for water the potable water is not even adequate for the existing population. The question is from where will the nation get potable water for approximately 261 crore people?

(vii) To meet the growing demands of clothing, we need to increase cloth production.

During the last two decades our Govt. has spent crores of rupees for poverty elimination programmes. Not withstanding this, the hunger seen among the poor people in the states of UP, MP Bihar, Orissa and the esters states brings tears to one's eyes. The main cause for all is: Over population. In sum, our gigantic demographic load is bound to spell doom for our coming generations and the Malthusian nightmare will be very much present in our country which implies acute poverty, starvation, unemployment, illiteracy, diseases and violent conflicts – far worse than what we are confronting now.

16.3 PHENOMENAL EXPANSION OF EDUCATIONAL FACILITIES IN INDIA SINCE INDEPENDENCE STILL FAR BEHIND THE REQUIREMENTS

There has been a phenomenal expansion of educational facilities in India since independence and especially since 1950-51. While primary schools increased by 2.82 times, upper primary schools and higher secondary schools by 13 times. Colleges for general education increased by 18 times and the universities, (including deemed Universities and Institutions of National Importance) by 8 times. The total enrolment at primary stage increased by nearly 6 times while for the girls the increase is 9 times.

At the upper primary stage of education, the increase is 13 times while that of girls the increase is more that 32 times.

At the Secondary and Senior Secondary stage the total increase is 18 times and that of girls it is 49 times.

Whereas in 1950-51, enrolment in higher education was about 3.6 lakhs, in 1998-99, it was 74.17 lakhs. Thus the increase was about 22 times. The enrolment of women students was 24.46 lakhs. At the post-graduate level, the enrolment of women students was 34 per cent of the total enrolment.

The number of school teachers increased by more than 6 times. In the case of female teachers, the increase was more than 13 times.

Literacy rate rose from 16.67 per cent in 1950-51 to 62 per cent in 1997 and 65.38 in 2001.

Still we have not been able to fulfil the requirements of the Article 45 of the Constitution.

At the college level, only 6 per cent population of the age group 19-25 is covered.

Nearly one-third of the population is illiterate.

Drop-out rates at various levels is quite appreciable. This shows that the quality education is lacking.

The above mentioned situation clearly reflects that growing population is a curse.

16.4 AVAILABILITY OF CEREALS BELOW REQUIREMENTS

Keeping in view the grow population at a rapid the of rate, it is unlikely that food production will increase proportionately. Also there is little hope that the international level of nourishing diet would be available to the common man.

Table 16.1: Decadal Net Availability of Cereals (1951 to 2000)

Year	Cereals				Per capita net availability per day (grams) Cereals
	Net production (million tonnes)	Net Imports (million tonnes)	Change in Government stocks (million tonnes)	Net Availability (million tonnes)	
1951	40.1	4.1	(+)0.6	44.3	334.2
1961	60.9	3.5	(–)0.2	64.6	399.7
1971	84.5	2.0	(+)2.6	84.0	417.6
1981	104.1	0.5	(–)0.2	104.8	417.3
1991	141.9	(–)0.6	(–)4.4	145.7	468.5
1992	136.8	(–)0.7	(–)1.6	137.7	434.5
1993	145.8	2.6	(+)10.3	138.1	427.9
1994	149.6	0.5	(+)7.5	142.6	434.0
1995	155.3	(–)3.0	(–)1.7	154.0	457.6
1996	147.1	(–)3.6	(–)8.5	152.1	443.6
1997	162.0	(–)0.6	(–)1.8	163.2	468.2
1998	156.9	(–)2.8	(+)6.1	147.9	417.3
1999(P)	164.7	(–)1.5	(+)7.0	156.2	433.7
2000(P)	168.7	(–)1.0	(+)8.7	159.1	434.8

(P) Provisional

Table 16.2: Comparative Data of Indicators of Development and of Progress in Developed and Developing Countries

Country	Population thousands (1999)	GNP Capita US $ (1999)	Life Expectancy at Birth (1999)	Total Adult Literacy (1999)	Primary School Enrolment Ratio (crores) (1995-99)	% of Population Below $ 1 a day (1990-99)
Developed Countries						
Australia	18705	20050	78	99	101	Almost Nil
Austria	8177	25970	77	99	103	”
Canada	30857	19320	79	97	102	”
Denmark	5282	32030	76	99	101	”
France	58886	23480	78	99	105	”
Germany	82178	25350	77	99	104	”
Italy	57343	19170	78	98	101	”
Japan	126505	32230	80	99	102	”
Norway	4442	32880	78	99	100	”
Russian Federation	147196	2270	67	99	107	7
Sweden	8892	25040	79	99	103	Almost Nil
Switzerland	7344	38350	79	99	107	”
U.K.	58744	22640	78	99	114	”
U.S.A.	276218	30600	77	99	102	”

Country	*Population thousands (1999)*	*GNP Capita US $ (1999)*	*Life Expectancy at Birth (1999)*	*Total Adult Literacy (1999)*	*Primary School Enrolment Ratio (crores) (1995-99)*	*% of Population Below $ 1 a day (1990-99)*
Developing Countries						
India	998056	450	63	58	90	44
Afghanistan	21923	250	46	32	29	--
Angola	12479	220	48	42	88	--
Bangladesh	126947	370	59	56	97	29
Bhutan	2064	510	62	42	72	--
Brazil	167988	4420	67	85	128	5
China	1266838	780	70	84	104	11
Cuba	11160	1170	76	96	97	--
Indonesia	209255	580	66	88	114	15
Maldives	278	1160	65	99	123	--
Myanmar	45059	220	61	83	100	--
Nepal	23385	220	58	45	122	38
Nigeria	108945	310	50	57	70	70
Pakistan	152331	470	65	45	84	31
Sierralone	4717	130	39	32	50	57
Sri Lanka	18639	820	74	90	107	7

Definitions

Population 2001 : The mid-year de facto population.

Population Density: The number of people per square kilometre.

Population Growth Rate: Average annual per centage change in total population size.

Urban Growth Rate: Average annual per centage change in urban population.

Rural Growth Rate: Average annual per centage of rural population.

16.5 RESOURCE GENERATION AND OVERALL INDICATORS OF DEVELOPMENT

The situation in India in all indicators of development and progress as reflected in Table 16.2 cannot be said to be satisfactory in spite of our efforts to use our resources. Population would have to be checked. There is no doubt that there is a limit to resource generation. Our population is not skilled enough to produce more. Several countries of Europe with their skilled population have made tremendous development. In Asia, Japan, has become one of the most advanced countries in the world. Thus our rapidly growing population has sapped our resources.

16.6 EDUCATIONAL PROBLEMS DUE TO OVER-POPULATION

1. *Too Many Pupils at all Levels*: At the elementary stage the per centage of children in age group 6-14 is one of the highest in India, while it is restricted to 15 % in Scandinavian countries and a good many countries of Europe. India is having almost 20 % of the population in 6-14 age group. This has resulted in increased liability in respect of education and does not synchronise with our financial resources to provide the requisite facilities. As a result of it, a large number of children remain unattended and those who get the privilege of admission are packed like goods in a truck, making studies difficult, hindering teacher-pupil contact and preventing wholesome development of the personality of the student.
2. *Poor Buildings, Furniture and Equipment*: Very often, the students are taught either in the open under the scorching sun, or cold waves—having sky as the roof or in dilapidated building—a product of the poverty of resources and ever-increasing student population. Besides buildings, adequate furniture, teaching aids, library facilities, playgrounds etc. are other casualties. Many schools are without proper buildings and students without textbooks. Very often for almost the whole year, four out of five schools are without the facility of even clean drinking water. This is the state of our schools in spite of the fact that expenditure of education has increased enormously. With the growth of population we have to introduce shift-system (two or three times in a day) which lowers the efficiency of teaching too.
3. *Wastage and Stagnation*: Wastage and stagnation like headache, fever, etc. are not the diseases but symptoms of a disease. Even the symptoms have rocked the foundation of elementary education. The premature withdrawal of students, from the completion of the courses results in huge wastage of funds. Not only this, a student taking more time than stipulated causes frustration to himself and to his family and waste of educational expenditure. Besides many reasons responsible for this malady in elementary education, overcrowding is one of the most important which has resulted in making educative experiences poorer, less effective and individual guidance rather difficult and dealing of individual problems a remote idea.

   Wastage has four dimensions: (a) Wastage of the talents of teachers. The talents of the teachers cannot be mobilised and utilised effectively because of overcrowding in classes. (b) Wastage of material resources: The available material resources cannot be availed of because many cannot use them and they remain dormant. (c) Wastage of talented students: The identification of talented students is impossible in a large group which makes the emergence of talented individuals impossible which in itself is a great national waste. Thus, we are deprived of exploring the talents of those not attending the schools as well as those attending them. (d) Wastage due to dropouts: The students fail and discontinue their education. Thus this is a useless investment on their education, wastage of time, and energy.

4. *Unemployment.* Unemployment of the educated is a great problem. Gradually there will be need of skilled manpower owing to scientific and technological advancements all over the world which are influencing us at an ever increasing pace. The present left out school children (6-14) will form tomorrow's army of illiterates, causing a potential danger to prosperity of the nation and the institution of democracy as a whole.
5. *Under-employment of the Educated.* The problem of under employment because of abundance of available manpower is very acute. The misplacement of trained manpower adds another dimension to this explosive problem. While it is, on one hand, a problem of distressing gulf between education and manpower and, on the other hand, it causes frustration to individuals and is a national loss for foregoing the maximum benefits of their services.
6. *Poor Quality of Education.* One of the significant achievements of the post-independence period has been expansion of educational facilities at all levels of education which has on parallel in the history of Indian education. The increased educational facilities meant recruiting lakhs of teachers and providing the minimum necessities. In the absence of the right type of teachers, sub-standard teachers had to be recruited keeping in mind "quality if possible without it if necessary."
7. *Student-indiscipline and other Allied Problems at Various Stages of Education*: Despite the fact that infection of indiscipline has not yet filtered down to the elementary stage, crowd mentality is brewing because of large size of the school growing and classes which render congenial experience as a remote possibility.

16.7 STUDYING THE IMPACT OF POPULATION GROWTH ON EDUCATION

The impact of population growth on education can be studied systematically and measured by several indices of education. The four main indices are:

I. Student Indices
II. Teacher Indices
III. Organisation Indices
IV. Material Indices

The indices show the shortage and lacunae caused by over-population in operating the system of our education or in conducting our programmes of education at different levels. Every category of indices is being elaborated briefly.

Student Indices: Some of these indices are as follows:

Large pupil-teacher ratio (about 50 pupils per teacher).

Low public expenditure of education (nearly Rs. 400 per student, per annum).

Less pupil-attainment (less than 50 % results in the examinations conducted by the Secondary School Boards).

More pupil-wastage (about 60 % at the higher primary stage and 40 % at the higher secondary stage).
Less pupil-guidance (little time and attention given to pupils in large classes).
Poor pupil-health (lack of medical care, lunch programmes and other amenities).
Poor pupil-motivation (lack of interest in learning and absence of encouragement and inspiration).
Teacher Indices. Some of these indices are as follows:
Low-paid teachers (comparatively poorer grades of salaries given to teachers).
Less-qualified teachers (lack of adequate qualifications and training in a number of cases).
Less-motivated teachers (persons seeking employment but not the career coming to teaching).
Poorly-selected teachers (improper selection of teachers).
Poorly-selected teachers (lack of legal or professional security available to teachers).
Poorly-equipped teachers (lack of teaching aids and expert assistance available to teachers).
Poor social recognition of teachers (teachers are not duly respected by society as important workers).
Organisation Indices. Some of the organisational indices are as follows:
Inadequate supervisory staff (inspecting staff is less than the requirements).
Low-paid heads of schools (Headmasters and Principals are not paid adequately).
Less space facilities (buildings of schools are small and without adequate facilities).
Less budget for education (not more than 3 to 4 per cent is spent on education).
More rigid programmes and procedures of work (policies of admission, curriculum; instruction and evaluation are less flexible and more bureaucratic due to large size of the classes).
Less administrative initiative and leadership (Department of Education and its staff are overburdened with the maintenance of services only).
Material Indices. Some of the material indices are as follows: Less facilities of library and laboratory (it is impossible for every student to make full use of the limited resources available).
Poor and limited textbooks and references (there are no sufficient instruction materials for students).
Inadequate and outdated teaching devices (the modern teaching aids like audio-visual techniques, programmed materials are not easily available).
Ill-equipped subject rooms (the special rooms for history, geography, languages etc. are not fully equipped).

Inadequate provision for means and materials for physical development and mental growth (the tools, tests and equipment for developing sound body and sound mind are not available).

16.8 TASKS OF EDUCATION IN CONTROLLING POPULATION GROWTH

1. Education has a great motivational task to perform for promoting the small family in India. First of all education should make people aware of the high rate of growth of population and then warn them of the evil effects that follow afterwards as a result of it.
2. The next step for education will be to give the concept of a small family and how in small families resources of family are shared by a small number of members who can live in peace and happiness. Therefore, social value based on the philosophy supporting the large family have to be changed.

Some Educational Measures: Suitable educational measures need to be adopted to promote desirable changes. The following can be tried:

1. Community forums and voluntary organisations should discuss the drawbacks of large families and the advantages of small families and thus develop a favourable attitude and appreciation for a small family.
2. Children in the elementary stage should also be taught through their courses of study the merits of a small family and demerits of a large family and should develop favourable attitude and appreciation for having a small family when they become adults, because many of the children will not continue their education at the secondary stage. For example, arithmetic sums may be introduced in their teaching.
3. Boys and girls at the secondary stage should be given the knowledge in a scientific way about the reproductive biology system and the sex hygiene as being taught in Biology and Homes Science courses.
4. Appropriate literature for supplementary reading should be prepared and supplied by the agencies concerned.
5. Parent-teacher associations can also take the responsibility of educating the families.
6. Schools should assume the responsibility of educating the community and the families and should collaborate with other agencies for the education of the masses for having small families.

16.9 CONCLUDING OBSERVATIONS

Only incurable optimists will derive consolation from the findings of the 2001 census that the population during the period has grown at an average annual exponential growth rate of 1.93 as against 2.14 per cent during 1981 to 1991. The overall increase this decade is more than 180 million more than the entire population of Pakistan and around two-third of the total population of the United States of America, which should keep the alarm bells ringing. The decadal increase is nearly one and a half times population of Japan.

The provisional census figures set the priorities for the coming decade. The most obvious thing to do is to curtail population growth. Overall, the fact that the population growth rate during the last decade has declined only marginally has implications for the poverty alleviation effect that Yojna Bhavan would not like. Any claims about an improvement in poverty level would be quite meaningless in the reported growth rate during the decade ended March 1, 2001. The challenge of '*garibi hatao*' becomes more daunting.

There has been a slight rise in the sex ratio of women i.e. from 927 in 1991 to 933 in 2001. Nevertheless its implication is that despite all the rhetoric about women's emancipation, the results are not quite encouraging.

There is need for some soul searching to clear doubts that the demographic imbalance reflects deeper social malaise. The Census of 2001 provides a crucial data base for socio-economic planning. There is an urgent need to take vigorous action as envisaged in the National Population formulated in 2000.

Stabilising population is an essential requirement for promoting sustainable development with more equitable distribution. However, it is an much a function of making reproductive health care accessible and affordable for all, as of increasing the provision and outreach of primary and secondary education, extending basic amenities including sanitation, safe drinking water and housing, besides empowering women and enhancing their employment opportunities, and providing transport and communications.

17

Sex Education for Population Control and Quality of Life

17.1 NEED FOR SEX EDUCATION

Talking about sex is ordinarily considered something secretive, sinful or not worthy of mention in sophisticated and so-called cultured society. People feel very much inhibited in talking about sex, but without sex education people cannot live a happy and well-adjusted life because it has been noted that many marital, emotional and mental problems among human beings occur as a result of the misdirection and wrong understanding of the sex urge. Alva Myrdal has observed: "In general more wholesome attitudes towards sex questions will not be created until they are discussed openly and as a matter of fact phenomena." Children ask questions about sex as the subject fascinates them and it is our answer and the way we give them that plays an important part in forming their future attitudes towards sex. Frank and honest response can help them to develop a healthy outlook. Prof. Uday Shankar is of the firm opinion, "population education without sex education is ridiculous as the 'how' of population control cannot be answered without sex education. Sex education is no imposition, it concerns a vital matter in which children are interested. Interest in sex is instinctive and starts from early infancy. In pre-adolescent boys and girls, the sex drives further. Enlightenment on sexual matter is to be given intelligently and pleasantly but gradually and methodically. There need not be 'sex teacher' or 'sex classes' like history or geography classes. There cannot be any general rules as to the time and place or manner of imparting sex education. Through the teaching of general science, biology, physiology or hygiene, a good deal of physiological knowledge about sex differences and about animal and human reproduction, involving all the process of mating, fertilisation, pregnancy or birth can be imparted."

Sex education rightly understood plays an important role in understanding the population dynamics and improving quality of life.

17.2 ROLE OF PARENTS AND TEACHERS IN IMPARTING SEX EDUCATION

Without going into the controversy whether sex education should be imparted or not, an attempt is made here to suggest measures which should be adopted to provide sex education as it plays an important role in controlling population and ensuring quality of life. Simple questions of children are sometimes difficult to answer. When a child is very young one can make up any number of stories to convince them, but young boys and girls are keen to seek answers indepth. They may investigate, adventure or explore to find out the answers. Sometimes they find them out the wrong way.

In a growing child there is development of the body about which he is confused; there is also growth of mind and awareness. Their quest for information needs to be addressed and delivered. Nothing is better than direct communication between parents and youngsters.

Parents and teachers should not be thrown off guard by awkward questions. They should have the presence of mind and answer some questions in fun and some in utter seriousness so that the child gets a positive signal that though sex is a private thing there is nothing shameful about it. In this way children are able to confide in their teacher and parents and look upon them as friends, which in turn keeps the teachers and parents informed about children's activities.

Following points in this respect deserve attention:

1. Documentaries can be shown to teenagers in schools. If made properly they can easily hold their attention.
2. Plays, seminars and workshops organised in school can also achieve this goal where the situations leading to problems can be dealt with.
3. Students can directly approach the teachers or counsellors to have their confessions cleared.
4. Students can be asked to write questions on a paper without revealing their identity so that shy students can have answers too. Teachers may be warned that they are likely to receive a few embarrassing, awkward and may be downright obscene questions or drawings which ought to be taken with an equanimity of mind and understanding. This may need discussion as to why some children do so. Oversupressed, overexposed or those children who are denied recognition by their parents of their sexual development may do these kinds of things and therefore are required to be reassured and gently pushed in the right direction.
5. Specially trained teachers, separately for girls and boys in the initial phase, or doctors can be called to give a few lectures to remove misconceptions and doubts.
6. Goods books are best companions at all ages. They can serve the purpose of educating a curious mind where parents feel restricted in communicating with the child. This way parents also know that whatever a child is reading is healthy and beneficial for him.
7. Guidance from an elderly relative can also serve the very important role of a confidante to the teenager in the family.

17.3 SUGGESTIVE SYLLABUS AND ACTIVITIES FOR SEX EDUCATION

The following syllabus and activities regarding sex education cover different stages/years, content and approach.

It is obvious that in the school, elementary stage is the starting point for imparting sex education to students. Contents and approaches are graded.

Details and Source: *Sex Education: How and Why.* Association for Social Health in India, New Delhi, 1976.

Objectives	*Content*	*Approach*
Age group 1-3 years		
1. To create a sense of discipline and orderliness with regard to personal cleanliness and regularity about toilet and feeds.	1. Developing love and affection for parents among children.	1. With love and affection.
2. To develop affection for parents and other family members, and obey to do small errands for them.	2. Training infant for observing regularity in feeding and for toilet.	2. Training children to observe regularity and prevent unsocial attitudes developing.
3. To develop proper behaviour towards other children and learn to be affectionate and helpful to them.	3. Prevent habit of beating and misbehaving with other children.	3. Observe non-discriminatory attitude towards all children.
	4. Ensuring that there is no discrimination in treatment between boys and girls.	4. Making the child happy and contented by careful handling, giving feeds regularly and playing with it sometime. Children must not be neglected.
Age group 3-5 years		
1. To observe all stated objectives for 1-3 year group.	1. Continue as for 1-3 group.	1. Same as for 1-3 year group.
2. to encourage the child to play with other children and to develop team spirit and a sense of equality among boys and girls.	2. Prevent habit of beating or pinching weaker children.	2. Prevent children to develop aggressive attitudes towards others by strong admonition. Parents themselves should serve as a model by creating harmony and peace among all family members.
3. To show the difference between boys and girls from differences in clothing, modes of dress.	3. Prevent habit of fondling genitals by covering the parts with dress, and diverting its mind by other activities.	3. Parents should develop a habit of imparting information naturally and truthfully. They must not say anything beyond child's understanding or

Objectives	*Content*	*Approach*
	4. Inform about sex differences if the child desires to know, naturally and without emotion.	4. Picture of happy family showing father, mother, a girl and a boy.
	5. Emphasising that father and mother are necessary for a complete happy family.	

Age group 6-8 years

1. To practise all mentioned objectives for earlier group.	1. Same as for earlier group.	1. Same as stated related earlier to daily experience.
2. Need of both father and mother for the babies to give them food, love and to look after them till they grow up.	2. Importance of both male and female for care and growth of babies.	2. Draw child's attention to sexes in different domestic animals, and in human being.
3. To love father and mother as essential for their existence and security.	3. No. discrimination in treatment between boys and girls in the family or in the school.	3. Do Not much of anatomical details at this stage and subject may be presented in the form of stories.
4. To foster proper attitudes in boys of regard and helpfulness towards girls.	4. Emphasising equality of intelligence and proficiency in various activities both in school and at home, among boys and girls.	4. Encourage boys to help mothers and sisters in household work, so that they may not consider such work to be unmanly.
	5. Boys being physically stronger must always help girls and weaker children whenever necessary, in day-to-day life both in the school and at home.	5. Emphasise, ties of love and security between parents and children.
		6. Children should not be left alone.

9-11 years of age

1	To develop a health attitude towards sex.	To develop comradeship and respect towards the opposite sex.	Brothers and sisters should help each other in studies, household work and play as equals.
2.	To Observe that all living organisms, whether of animal or vegetable kingdom, multiply for continuance of species.	Trees and plants multiplying in gardens and jungles. Dogs, cats producing litters and increasing in numbers.	Birth of a baby brother or sister in the family.
3.	To inform about different modes of multiplication of a cell.	Sexual and asexual modes of cell multiplication.	Show cell multiplication of both types in pictures or diagrams as in the book.
4.	To correlate male and female parts of a flower for producing a new plant.	Fertilisation of an egg-cell in a flower.	Exhibit male and female parts of a flower and mode of fertilisation as per book diagram.
5.	To tell that fertilisation of the egg-cell of the female by a seed from the male.	Growth of an animal from a single fertilised cell.	Importance of both male and female in producing offspring.
6.	To tell that in human beings male seed comes from the father and egg cell from the mother.	Both daddy and mummy are necessary for the birth and care of the baby.	Explain in a question-and-answer session. No anatomical details are to be shown. Exhibit diagrams of fertilisation as in the book.
7.	To inform about development of a fertilised egg cell either inside or outside the mother's tummy in different animals.	Development of the fertilised egg-cell outside the female's body as in the case of birds, and inside the mother's tummy as in human female, cows, bitches, cats, etc.	Child should be shown egg of birds, as an example of development outside the body, and explained how to recognise a pregnant cow, bitch or a woman as an example of development inside the tummy of the mother.

Pre-Adolescent 11-13-14 Years Age Group

1. To impart knowledge about body development.	Sudden spurt of body growth. In girls: appearance of pubic hair, breasts and enlargement of hips. Onset of menstruation. In boys: appearance of pubic hair and enlargement of testicles and penis, night pollutions.	Correlating with other subjects like Nature study, Biology and physiology. Illustrate body growth in boys and girls with the aid of pictures, diagrams and charts, as in the book. Discussing this subject separately with boys and girls, to encourage questions and answers by each group.
2. To help in emotional and social adjustment of adolescents.	Clarifying that such body changes are natural at this age and do not produce any disease.	Reassuring the youngsters that the body changes should not cause any anxiety. These prepare them for becoming grown up men and women.
3. To develop desirable health habits.	Observing personal cleanliness and to help parents as desired by them. Develop proper regard and understanding for the opposite sex.	Should spend spare time in healthy outdoor games. Girls may like indoor pursuits such as games, sewing, knitting, etc.
4. To enable pre-adolescents to understand and control sexual tendencies.	Dangers of sex relations at this stage must be emphasised as youngsters are too immature and not in a position to undertake any responsibility. Youngsters must be warned about the adverse psychological and physical effects of the habit of masturbation.	Youngsters should be guided to make suitable friends. Show films or slides of boys and girls playing separately or in mixed groups under supervision. Discussion in question-answer session in separate groups of boys and girls about masturbation.
5. To develop correct behaviour towards members of the opposite sex.	Arrange joint programmes of boys and girls under supervision as mentioned in the book.	By arranging games, plays, dramas, debates and other cultural programmes under direct guidance.

Adult—Above 18 years of Age

1. Recapitulate all items of 14-18 year group.		
2. To develop knowledge about population explosion.	Present rate of population growth and its impact on the life of the country and urgent need to check the same.	Charts to show the trend of birth and death rates as compared with more advanced countries.
3. To tell that planned parenthood is a means to check population growth.	Different methods. Use of contraceptive devices.	Advantages and disadvantages of the different methods of contraception

18

Population Growth and Economic and Human Development in India

18.1 CLOSE RELATIONSHIP BETWEEN POPULATION GROWTH AND ECONOMIC AND HUMAN DEVELOPMENT

The rapid growth in population without corresponding economic and human development growth upsets the entire economic life. The economic life of the family depends upon the size of the family, income accrued to it, the level of consumption of various agricultural and industrial products, clothing, housing etc. Therefore, planned family at the micro level secures better standard of living for the members of the family. At the macro level, the politics adopted by the government in the areas of population growth and economic development decide the economic life of the country.

Under the Five Year Plans, concerted efforts have been made to better the quality of life both individually and collectively. The achievements have not been commensurate with the aspirations and expectations of the people, mainly due to the constant race between the population growth and economic development. The demographic monster has been swallowing the fruits of planned economic development thereby adversely affecting the economic life of a country.

In various earlier chapters and especially chapters 5, 14, 15 and 17, several aspects of population growth and their impact on various dimensions of family life and national developed have been analysed briefly.

Controlled but skilled population leads to steady economic development. Economic development provides opportunities to the population to better quality of life. Reasonable standard of living needs small families. Thus population growth and economic development are interdependent and interrelated.

18.2 ECONOMIC DEVELOPMENT AND HUMAN RESOURCES

The economic development depends upon the optimum use of existing resources. These resources are mainly human resources and natural resources. The labour and organisation constitute human resources which make use of land and capital.

A nation's wealth does not entirely lie on its natural resources like land, forest, mine and water etc., not in its flocks and herds but in its healthy and happy men, women and children. It lies in the energy, initiative and moral fitness of its people. The population of a country is both an asset and a liability depending upon its skill to use resources. The population is a means to economic development. This is in the form of either physical or mental labour. Labour is both skilled and unskilled. It helps to provide workers in the farms, fields, mines, hunting, forestry, etc. The skilled labour is necessary for exploitation of the resources available in a country. It supplies educationists, industrialists, entrepreneurs, technicians, scientists, traders etc. The human resources in collaboration with natural resources assist in the process of economic development. The population is the supply side of the labour. Its demand depends on the demand for goods and services which are required for human well-being. Like other goods, value of labour too is governed by its demand and supply. As a natural consequence, if the supply of labour increases more than what could profitably be utilised, its value diminishes, its productivity diminishes and in turn the per capita income of the labourer diminishes. The supply of labour mainly depends on the growth of the population.

18.3 UNCHECKED POPULATION GROWTH AND ITS IMPACT ON ECONOMIC AND HUMAN DEVELOPMENT

In our country the race between the population growth and economic development is going on resulting in serious disequilibrium in human and natural resources. The fruits of economic development are being swallowed by the rapid growth of population. While the levels of living have not improved substantially, the growing unemployment among the educated and uneducated youth is creating serious economic, social and political problems. There is a serious disequilibrium in all walks of life—floods and draughts, strikes and lockouts, growing urban sky-scrapers and slums, luxurious dinners and starvation deaths, scenic beauty and unhealthy environments, affluence and misery, important to material and spiritual values and several others only reflect poverty amidst plenty.

18.4 INDIA'S POPULATION AND PROGRESS IN HUMAN DEVELOPMENT AT A GLANCE

Box 18.1 reflects the progress and development.

Box 18.1 : Population and Demographic Data : India

1.	Population (2011 Census)	Persons	121.0 crore	
		Males	62.35 crore	
		Females	58.64 crore	
2.	Decadal Population growth	(2001-2011)		*Percent age* 17.64
		Males	91,944,020	20.93
		Females	88,683,339	21.79
3.	Density of Population (2011 Census) (per sq. km)		382	
4.	Sex Ratio (Females per 1000) — 2011 Census		940	
5.	Annual Growth Rate (2001-2010)		1.76	
6.	Crude Death Rate (Number of deaths per 1000)		9 in 1999, 7.9 in 2010	
7.	Crude Birth Rate (Number of Birth per 1000)		25 in 1999, 21.3 in 2010	
8.	Life Expectancy (Average life)		69.89 years in 2009 63 years in 1999 49 years in 1970	
9.	Life Expectancy of Females as a % of males (2009)		107.6%	
10.	Total Fertility Rate (2010)		2.5	
11.	% of population urbanised (2011)		31.16	
12.	Average Annual Growth Rate of Urban Population (%)		2.8 in 1990-99	
13.	% of Infants with low birth		30.15	
14.	% of population using Improved Drinking Water Resources (1999)		88 (Rural 86; Urban 92)	
15.	% of population using Adequate Sanitation Facilities (1999)		Rural 14; Urban 73	
16.	% Contraceptive Prevalence (1995-2000)		41	
17.	% Pregnant Women immunised against Tetanus (1997-99)		73	
18.	% of Births attended by Trained Health Personnel (1995-2001)		34	
19.	Maternal Mortality Ratio (1980-99) (Annual number of deaths from pregnancy-related causes per 10,000 live births)		450	

18.5 INDIA'S POPULATION AND PROGRESS IN HUMAN DEVELOPMENT VIS-À-VIS OTHER COUNTRIES

Box 18.2 provides the comparative picture.

Box 18.2: India's Population and Human Development and Progress in World Context

Indicator of Human Development and Progress	*India*	*Country with Best Indicator*	*India's Rank*
Population (1999) (Population is not an indicator of progress)	998056000 (99.8 crore)	1266838000 (1.27 crore) For 2001 see next page	2
1. GNP per capita US $ (1999)	450	Luxembourg: 44640 (1) Switzerland: 38350 (2)	40/173
2. Under 5-years Mortality Rate (1999) (per 1000 births)	98	Japan, Norway, Singapore, Sweden and Switzerland (4 each)	89/187
3. Life Expectancy (1999)	63 years	Japan (11 – 80) Switzerland, Sweden (21 – 79)	114/165
4. Adult Literacy Rate (1990-95)	58%	Nearly 80 Countries with more than 90% adult literacy rate	135/165
5. Literacy % (2001)	Total : 65.38 Male : 75.75 Female : 54.16	Nearly 80 countries with more than 90% literacy rate	140/160
6. % of Primary School Entrants Reaching Grade 5 (1995-99)	52%	Nearly 80 countries with more than 90%	144/161
7. Population Annual Growth rate (1990-99)	1.8%	Russian Federation 1 (-0.1) UK 2 (0.2%); Japan 3 (0.3%); Germany 4 (0.4%); USA 5 (0.9%); China 6 (1.0%) Brazil 7 (1.4%); Indonesia 8 (1.5%); Bangladesh 9 (1.6%); Pakistan 10 (2.7%) (Note: Populous countries)	98/184

18.6 ECONOMIC AND HUMAN DEVELOPMENT AND OBJECTIVES OF POPULATION EDUCATION

(i) To develop an understanding of the concept of economic life of the country.

(ii) To develop an understanding that economic life of a country depends as much upon human resources as upon natural resources.

(iii) To enable the pupils to understand that the two resources are interconnected one affecting the other.

(iv) To help them to understand that population as a means of economic development, supplies, labour—skilled and unskilled—and entrepreneurs.

(v) To enable them to understand that there has been and there is a rapid growth of population in India.

(vi) To develop an understanding that natural resources, such as land, soil, forest, water, etc. available in a country are limited.

(vii) To enable them to appreciate that the disequilibrium between the human resources and natural resources results in serious repercussions on the economic life of a country.

(viii) To enable the pupils to realise that a planned family is essential for a better economic life.

(ix) To develop the ability to use and interpret the data on human and natural resources rationally.

(x) To develop in the pupils the ability to make correct decisions in matters relating to their economic life.

18.7 POPULATION EDUCATION AND TEACHING OF ECONOMICS

The teaching of Economics provides a lot of opportunity to impart population education. Here a few teaching hints are provided in this regard.

Teaching Hints

Hints to Teachers	*Activities for Pupils*
1. The teacher may gather information regarding the concept of planned economic development and strategies adopted by various countries both capitalistic and socialistic.	The pupils may be involved in planning various activities in a school to stress the concept of planning. Activities like field trips to a factory, a Community Development Centre etc. can be taken up.
2. The teacher may use the statistical abstracts (Government publications) and related charts illustrating quantitative aspects of human resources available in the country.	The pupils may be asked to prepare charts and graphs showing the growth of agricultural labour and industrial labour in select areas.
3. The teachers may use the data showing the increase in population during the last 50 years together with trends in birth and death rates.	The pupils may be informed of the broad trends and significant factors.

Hints to Teachers	*Activities for Pupils*
4. The teacher may display charts showing the increase in mineral and industrial production during the last decade.	The pupils may be asked to gather data on the natural resources available in a local area.
5. The teachers may gather up-to-date information about the Economic Development and Population Growth of India from the view-point of comparison from the latest publications of Government of India. He may further explain the disequilibrium between the two. (This information is available in (i) "India"—A Reference Manual, Published annually by the Ministry of Information and Broadcasting, (ii) Annual Economic Survey, Ministry of Finance, Government of India.	Students may be asked to prepare charts, graphs and tables on the data.

19

Population Education Programme in India

History and Development

19.1 BRIEF HISTORY OF POPULATION PROGRAMME IN INDIA

In 1969 the first national seminar on population education was held at Bombay to develop the objectives and contents of population education. Union Ministers of Education and Health and Family Planning were involved in this seminar. Their involvement in this seminar was indicative of policy level interest, concern, and commitment to this approach. This approach and strategy was further reinforced in the National Population Policy statement issued by the Ministry of Health and Family Planning in 1976 and the New Population Policy in 1977.

In accordance with the recommendations of the first National Seminar on Population Education, a Population Education Cell was developed in the NCERT to find out ways and means of developing and implementing the programmes in schools and teacher-training colleges. Since then NCERT through this Cell has made efforts to develop the concept of population education curriculum for use in schools and teacher-training colleges and has helped to disseminate the knowledge to teachers and teacher educators in various parts of the country through a series of seminars and workshop.

Realising the utility of NCERT Population Education Cell, one Population Education Cell was developed in each State and Union Territory in three phases.

1st Phase State/UTs	*2nd Phase State/UTs*	*3rd Phase State/UTs*
1. Bihar	1. Andhra Pradesh	1. Manipur
2. Gujarat	2. Assam	2. Meghalaya
3. Haryana	3. Himachal Pradesh	3. Nagaland
4. Karnataka	4. Kerala	4. Sikkim
5. Madhya Pradesh	5. Orissa	5. Tripura
6. Maharashtra	6. Uttar Pradesh	6. A and N Islands (UT)
7. Punjab	7. West Bengal	7. Arunachal Pradesh (UT)
8. Rajasthan	8. Delhi (UT)	8. Dadra and Haveli (UT)
9. Tamil Nadu		9. Goa, Daman and Die (UT)
10. Chandigarh (UT)		10. Lakshadweep (UT)
		11. Mizoram (UT)
		12. Pondicherry (UT)

The UNESCO came into the picture in 1970 and made special provisions for training of teacher educators at the Asian Institute for Teacher Education at Quezon City in the Philippines.

State and U.T. Population Education Cells were funded by UNFPE (United Nation's Fund for Population Education), and planned their activities under guidance and in consultation with NCERT Population Education Cell in the beginning. Now they are functioning independently under State and UT Governments.

State and U.T. Population Education Cells have the following objectives.

19.2 OBJECTIVES OF POPULATION EDUCATION CELLS

(i) Long-Term Objectives

1. To develop among the students a keen insight into the inter-relationships between population change and the process of socio-economic development vis-à-vis the individual, the family, the society, the nation and the world.
2. To create among the students and the teachers an awareness about the population situation in the country and the strategies adopted to meet the critical situation.
3. To provide population education its rightful place in the curriculum of the formal as well as the non-formal programme of education.
4. To make curriculum renewal a continuous and on-going process to meet the emerging challenges that confront society from time to time.
5. To reorient the system of education to be helpful in the developmental efforts of the country and forge it as an active agent for social transformation.
6. To develop desirable attitudes and behaviours in the students and the teachers as well as the community at large towards the population issues so as to enable them to arrive at rational decisions about the quality of life that suits them best.

(ii) Short-Time Objectives

1. To set up population education cell in the State or UT with competent and qualified officers and other supporting staff responsible for efficient implementation of the programme.
2. To develop population education curricula and textual materials for primary, middle, secondary and senior secondary classes as well as for the Pre-Primary, Primary and Secondary Teacher Training Institutions.
3. To develop a training package for in-service training of teachers and orienting senior supervisory staff for proper implementation of the programme.
4. To develop instructional materials including teaching-kits and other audio-visual aids for use in classroom at various levels.
5. To orient field officers to administer, supervise, guide, co-ordinate and assess the programme implementation process.

6. To train key persons for launching the population education programme in the State or UT
7. To train teachers, educators and teachers to properly handle the textual as well as the instructional materials in the classroom.
8. To orient Heads of Primary, Middle, Secondary and Senior Secondary schools to intelligently guide and supervise the programme in their schools.
9. To develop a suitable monitoring system for periodic evaluation of the programme.
10. To develop sample lessons in population education for the school Radio and TV Programmes.
11. To conduct research studies on the impact of population education, on the attitude formation and the behavioural patterns of the students.
12. To conduct Action Research Projects for improving the teacher-learning situations and instructional devices in the classroom.
13. To bring out a Newsletter on Population Education to open up a two-day communication channel between the Population Education Cell and the Field Workers.
14. To organise inter-state U.T. visits and study tours within the country for mutual exchange of ideas and comparing of notes.
15 To translate selected population education materials from English and Hindi and o4her regional languages.

19.3 ACTIVITIES OF POPULATION EDUCATION CELLS OF STATE/U.T.

1. Curriculum and Material Development

(i) Development of Curriculum
(ii) Development of Training Package for Key Persons
(iii) Development of Audio-Visual Aids
(iv) Development of Kits for the training of:
  (a) Primary School Teachers
  (b) Secondary School Teachers
  (c) Educational Administrators
(v) Development of Teachers' Guides for:
  (a) Primary School Teachers
  (b) Secondary School Teachers
(vi) Development of Textual Material for:
  (a) Primary Students
  (b) Middle Students
  (c) Secondary Students
(vii) Try-out Modification of the Materials
(viii) Newsletter

2. Training

(i) Training of Population Education Project Personnel
(ii) Training of Key Persons
(iii) Orientation of Educational Administrators

(iv) Training of Heads of
- (a) Primary Schools
- (b) Middle Schools
- (c) Secondary Schools

(v) Training of Teachers of:
- (a) Primary Schools
- (b) Secondary Schools

3. Research and Evaluation

(i) Status Studies of Population Education and Allied Problems
(ii) Appraisal Seminars
(iii) Programme Evaluation and Reporting

19.4 UNFPA'S POPULATION AND DEVELOPMENT PROGRAMME IN INDIA

The United Nations Population Fund (UNFPA) is the lead agency assisting the Government of India in reaching its population and development goals. UNFPA's assistance to India dates back to 1974. Over $220 million during 1974-1975 under 4 country programme cycles. Currently, $100 million have been allocated for Country Programme V (1997-2001), the largest UNFPA programme funded in the world.

UNFPA country programmes have made a major contribution to population and development policy and the family welfare programme. They have helped in improving family planning services, integration with mother and child health, and local production of contraceptives. Intensive support to few States was given through area development projects. In the last few years, UNFPA's support has become multi-sectoral and it now includes income generation, female literacy, community participation and empowerment activities.

To facilitate the Government's efforts to broaden its approach to health care, a Programme Review and Strategy Development (PRSD) exercise was undertaken by UNFPA in August 1996. The PRSD mission consisted of experts from the field of reproductive health, population and development, advocacy, gender, and population and environment. Country Programme V was designed to coincide with the Ninth-five year plan of GOI and the fifth programme cycle of UNDP. The CPV has three major sub-programmes: Reproductive Health, Population and Development Strategy, IEC and advocacy.

The main purpose of the proposed programme is to complement GOI's efforts to operationalise the Reproductive Health (RH) approach and replace the target oriented family welfare programme of the past. The programme assists the Government in meeting its national goals of improving the reproductive health of India's women, men and adolescents and of achieving an early stabilisation of the country's population.

The Country Programme operates at two levels—the district and national levels. Over and above these, district/town-level projects have also been formulated in 6 major states of the country viz., Rajasthan, Maharashtra, Kerala, Gujarat, MP and Orissa. These Integrated Population and Development projects (IPDs) go beyond reproductive health and cover education, gender and community development issues. In this manner, UNFPA supports district based projects in six states. Some of these districts and urban slums were chosen because they have particularly unfavourable reproductive health indicators, while others e.g. Kerala were selected to develop programmes for replication elsewhere. These interventions are intended to have an immediate impact on districts where they are implemented. Projects have been developed through a decentralised participatory planning process and on the basis of needs. Over $50 million have been budgeted for both IPDs and District Reproductive Health Projects. In view of the increasing incidence of HIV/AIDs in the country, UNFPA's programme puts special attention on HIV/AIDs issues at the district/state and national levels.

At the national level, the programme assists GoI in promoting integration of population issues within a wider developmental context; implementing the national policy for empowerment of women and special programmes to improve women's status and address gender disparities; and strengthening the logistics for distribution of contraceptives as well as increase contraceptive method choice. The programme aims at strengthening Government's advocacy efforts in favour of reproductive health to incorporate the concepts and approaches of ICPD (International Conference on Population and Development 1994.)

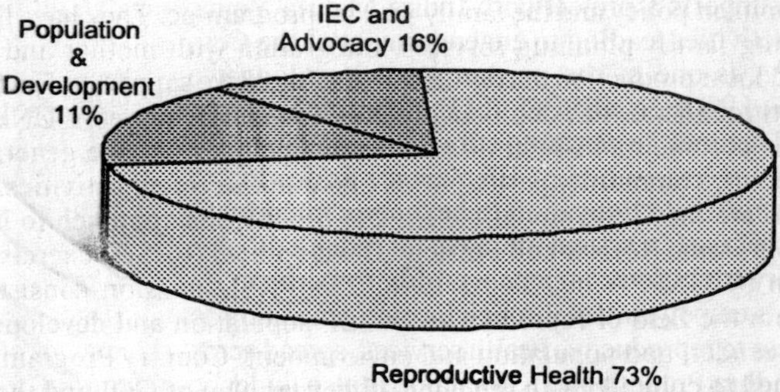

Fig. 19.1: UNFPA, India Country Programme Budget

Reproductive Health: The IPD projects support the goal of Government in reducing material and infant mortality and increasing contraceptive prevalence rates by meeting unmet needs of people. In order to increase the participation of NGOs in implementation, 10 per cent funds are being programmed through NGOs. Under Reproductive Health, the package of reproductive child health (RCH) services includes prevention of unwanted fertility, safe motherhood, including neonatal and infant survival, prevention and management of complications of unsafe abortions, prevention and management of reproductive tract infections (RTIs) and sexually transmitted infections (STIs) including HIV/AIDS. Problems related to access, service environment and supplies are also addressed. To improve the quality of client provider interaction, service providers are trained in interpersonal communication skills. Information, Education and Communication (IEC) activities are targeted towards specific communities and groups. To promote male participation, the No Scalpel Vasectomy (NSV) project envisages training of surgeons in performing this type of sterilisation, which is simple and easy and a stitch-free method for male sterilisation. For strengthening the logistics systems for distribution of contraceptives and other supplies, a logistics project has been launched in 4 states of the country. SOSVA, an NGO, is also being funded to establish a network of NGOs to strengthen delivery of RH services in different parts of the country.

Population and Development Strategy: The ICPD programme of Action is the expression of policy reorientation from demographic goals as an end in themselves to reaffirming the centrality of individual well being, including access to health, education, political and economic empowerment, particularly of women. Under the population and development sub-programme, the Integrated Women's Empowerment and Development project became operational in three districts of Haryana. The project activities aim at bringing about a change in the present scenario by generating awareness, mobilising women in groups, creating leadership and bringing men into the fold in order to enlist their support for women's activities. In IPD projects, NGOs have been identified to initiate schemes for income generating activities through establishment of Self Help Groups in the districts. In the state of Maharashtra, UNFPA supports a project with Indira Mahila Yojna (IMY), UNFPA also support activities leading to engenderment of the Census in 2001.

UNFPA is one of the partner agencies along with four UN agencies (UNICEF, UNDP, UNESCO, ILO), to provide programme support, in a co-ordinated manner, to on-going efforts undertaken by the Government of India towards Universalisation of Elementary Education (UEE), UNFPA would ensure Family Life Education to be incorporated in primary education.

As part of the UN system initiative for India, a programme for strengthening the primary education component is also in operation. An NGO project aiming at women's empowerment through income generation activities and increasing their access to reproductive health services, spread across three states of Tamil Nadu, Andhra Pradesh and Karnataka, is also under consideration.

IEC & Advocacy: Population Education projects with UNFPA assistance have been implemented in India since 1980. Three projects for School education, Higher education and Adult and continuing education have been successful in that Population Education has now been accepted as an integral part of the Indian educational system at all levels.

In the past, UNFPA has supported GOI in three major areas of population education programmes. Projects on NPEP (National Population Education Programme), Population Education in higher education and Population Education in adult literacy programme have attempted to incorporate population education issues in the curricula. Programmes in the present country programme are being reoriented in the light of post ICPD concepts. Objectives of the sub-programme are related to continuously promoting follow-up of ICPD programme goals through creating better understanding within GOI, public representatives, NGOs, professional agencies and media groups. Advocacy initiatives for gender equity and quality also find support. A unique 26 episode radio experiment on reproductive health including family planning, HIV/AIDS issues, based on enter-education approach has been initiated along with the Government of Rajasthan. Various media events, press conferences, public speaking engagements, release of the State of World Population Report and holding functions to mark World population day, International Women's day and World AIDS day are also planned.

The programme is largely carried out through national modalities drawing on the large pool of human and institutional resources available in the country which include central, state and local governments, research institutions and NGOs. Major emphasis is on the decentralised planning and implementation mechanism in the districts.

Population Education Project 1981-84

A population education project has been sponsored by the Government of India, NCERT with UNESCO support from April 1980 to March 1983 to cover 143 millions school children in primary, secondary and senior secondary schools in the country.

Target Audience at a Glance

Students in the age group of 6 to 17	93 million
Students in Universities	2 million
Out of school children in the age group of 6-14	45 million
Number of teachers in the country	3 million (Approximately)
The total number of audience to be covered under this project (excluding adults in the age group of 15-35)	143 million
Population in the age group of 15-35	100 million (to be taken care of by National Adult Educational Programme

Budget Summary (In Dollars)

	1980	1981	1982	1983	Total
1. Project personnel	42,210	53,480	44,480	11,070	151,240
2. Sub-contract	773,650	1586,000	2092,000	476,250	4927,900
3. Training	50,170	52,560	51,560	390	154,680
4. Equipment	31,100	3,00	2,500	700	37,300
5. Misc.	20,000	15,000	12,000	3,500	50,500
Grand Total	**917,130**	**1710,040**	**2,202,540**	**491,910**	**5,321,620**

19.5 CP-V (1997-2000): UNFPA'S COUNTRY PROGRAMME IN INDIA

Over the years, UNFPA has provided commodity assistance for contraceptives and equipment, helped to improve communication programmes and introduced population education on a major scale.

UNFPA's fourth programme (1991-96) focused on material and child health (MCH) and family planning (FP) projects in three states – Rajasthan, Himachal Pradesh and Maharashtra; advocacy and information education communication initiatives; and innovative interventions to enhance women's role in development. Over the years, UNFPA's support to India has increased. In the Fifth Country Programme CP-V UNFPA proposes to spend $ 100 million in India. Out of this amount, $ 50 million will go to Integrated Population Development (IPD) projects that have been launched in six states. The Programme draws its approach from the recommendations of the Programme of Action of the International Conference on Population and Development (ICPD), Cairo, 1994. In Cairo, there emerged a consensus on the linkages between population and development. The Programme of Action called for inputs in reproductive health services, education, women's empowerment and overall development in order to achieve stable populations.

UNFPA's assistance of $100 million will be utilised for the three core "sub-programme" areas. These are Reproductive Health (including family planning and sexual health), population and development strategies and advocacy. The main purpose of CP-V is to complement the government's efforts in operationalising the reproductive health (RH) approach, so as to replace the target-oriented programmes of the past. The programme will assist the government in meeting its national goals of improving the reproductive health of India's women, men and adolescents and of achieving early stabilisation of India's population. The RH approach places individual men and women at the centre – it recognises certain reproductive rights of individuals and couples while attempting to provide a range of services for meeting their varying needs over the life cycle.

In the present situation, most states of India have a heavy burden of reproductive morbidity and mortality. The situation is aggravated by inadequate access to services among marginalised groups like landless labourers, tribals, migrants and slum dwellers. The RH needs of adolescent boys and girls as well as men have not been adequately addressed. There is continuing cause for concern with respect to areas covered by RH services – family planning, maternal and child health, reproductive tract infection and sexually transmitted diseases, gynaecological problems of older persons etc. In 1997, by abolishing the demographic contraceptive targets and removal of provider incentives, and introducing the community needs assessment (CAN) approach, the government institutionalised a major policy change.

Following the RH approach, UNFPA first started district reproductive health projects (DRHPs) in five districts of India. They were to be the pilots for the new RH approach. The districts were Malappuram in Kerala, Patna in Bihar, Sirmour in Himachal Pradesh, Wardha in Maharashtra and Bundi in Rajasthan. After the DRHPs were found to be successful, UNFPA launched full-fledged IPD projects in 33 districts and four urban slums of India. These districts are in six states of India – Kerala, Maharashtra, Gujarat, Orissa, Madhya Pradesh and Rajasthan. Of these, the Kerala and Rajasthan projects were launched towards the end of 1998. IPD projects for the other four states were concurred to by the Government of India in June this year.

Another sub-programme is on population and development strategies. UNFPA has a mandate to assist countries in developing policies and programmes that integrate population and development concerns. This approach emphasises the need to address poverty, to improve the status of women and reduce gender discrimination in the context of economic and development policy.

The third sub-programme, on advocacy, has weaved in the new people-centred approach towards development, such as improving gender equality and equity, education of girls, empowerment of women and addressing reproductive health needs of adolescents and men through various available media and methods like population education, training of journalists, electronic media initiatives and advocacy with policy planners and opinion leaders.

20

Population Education and Environment Education

20.1 NATURE OF HUMAN INTERACTION WITH ENVIRONMENT

Man's influence upon the natural environment started from the moment he appeared in the biosphere. The early man, afraid of lightning, thunder, dense forests and darkness, started worshipping different aspects of nature. His activities or interaction with the environment had very little impact on it. Gradually man started making radical changes in the environment to suit his needs. The phenomena reached their summit, so to say on a worldwide scale in the twentieth century. The modern development of science and technology combing different ways of world economic development led too often to a wasteful intensification of the exploitation of natural resources.

A simplified diagram of this process of man's influence upon the natural environment is given in Fig. 20.1.

20.2 POPULATION ON MARCH AND ENVIRONMENT ON RETREAT

(See the 'Key Statements Population—on March and Environment on Retreat' in Chapter 6)

Table 20.1: Comparative Data on Population and Environment of Select Countries

Sl.No.	*Country*	*Population (thousands) 2001*	*Water Resources Per capita (Avg.) annual cubic metres 2000*	*Forest Cover annual change (%) 1990-2001*	*Crop per capita (hectares) 1996-98*
1	2	3	4	5	6
1.	Afghanistan	22474 (2.2 crores)	2421	0.0	0.39
2.	Bangladesh	140369 (14 crores)	813	1.3	0.07
3.	Bhutan	2141 (21 lakhs)	44728	0.0	0.08
4.	Canada	31015 (3.1 crores)	87971	0.0	1.51

1	2	3	4	5	6
5.	China	1284972 (128.5 crores)	2201	1.2	0.11
6.	Democratic Republic of Congo	52522 (5.2 crores)	18101	-0.4	0.16
7.	Egypt	69080 (6.90 crores)	34	3.4	0.05
8.	Ethiopia	64459 (6.4 crores)	1758	-0.8	0.18
9.	France	59453 (5.9 crores)	3047	0.4	0.33
10.	Germany	82007 (8.2 crores)	1301	0.2	0.15
11.	Japan	127335 (12.7 crores)	3393	0.0	0.04
12.	India	1025096 (102.5 crores)	1244	0.0	0.18
13.	Iran (Islamic Republic of)	71369 (7.1 crores)	1898	0.0	0.29
14.	Iraq	23584 (2.4 crores)	1523	0.0	0.26
15.	Israel	6172 (61.7 lakhs)	121	4.9	0.07
16.	Myanmar	48364 (4.8 crores)	19306	1.4	0.23
17.	Nepal	23593 (2.3 crores)	8282	-1.8	0.13
18.	Nigeria	116929 (11.7 crores)	1982	-2.6	0.30
19.	Pakistan	144971 (14.4 crores)	541	-1.1	0.15
20.	Russian Federation	144664 (14.5 crores)	29358	0.0	0.87
21.	South Africa	43792 (4.3 crores)	1110	0.0	0.41
22.	Sri Lanka	19104 (1.9 crores)	2656	-1.6·	0.10
23.	Turkey	67632 (6.8 crores)	2943	0.2	0.45
24.	United Arab Emirates	2654 (2.7 crores)	61	2.8	0.04
25.	United Kingdom	59542 (5.9 crores)	2465	0.8	0.11
26.	United States of America	285926 (28.6 crores)	8838	0.2	0.66

Unbalanced population growth means depletion of resources—material and non-material. It implies environmental pollution of earth, water, air, space, etc.

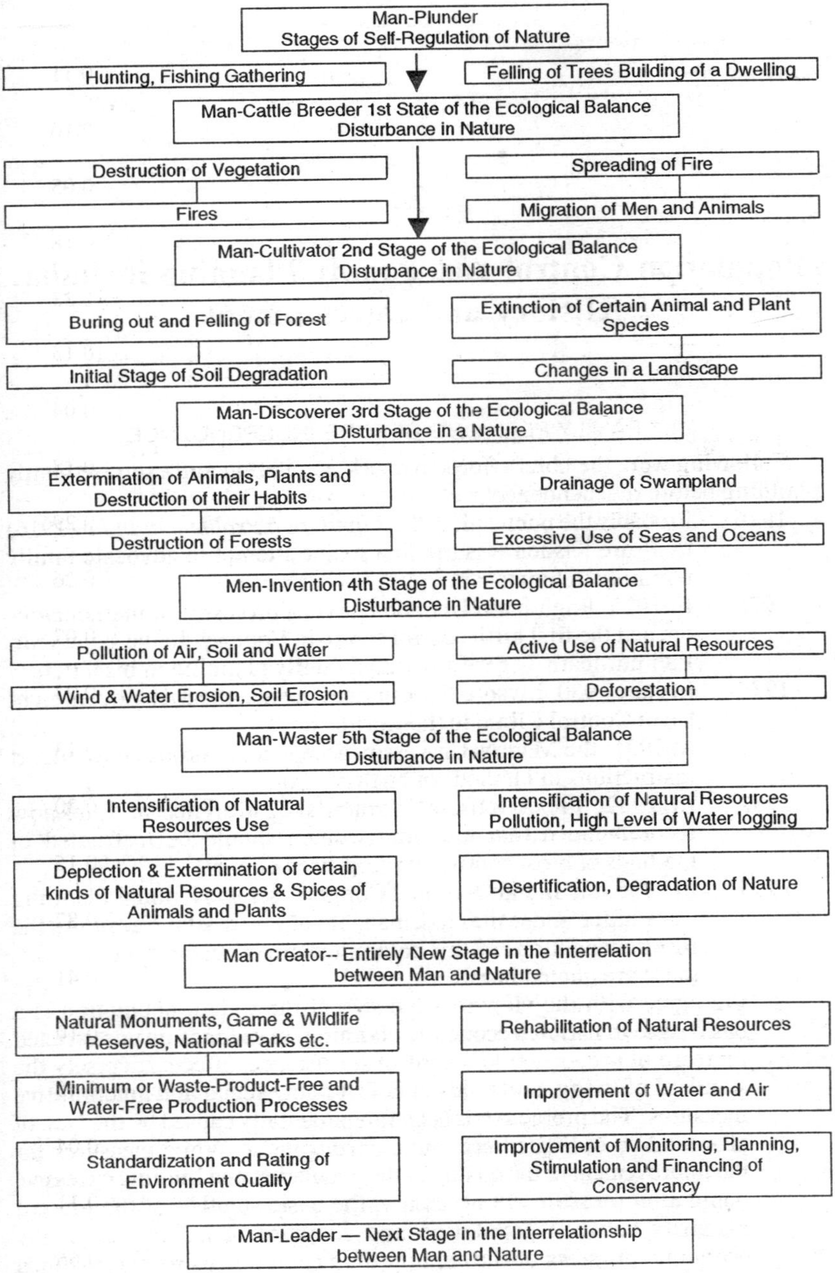

Fig. 20.1: Man-nature Interrelation States

21

Population Control and Family Planning in India: History and Development

21.1 FAMILY PLANNING BEFORE INDEPENDENCE

Following were the chief efforts to check population and exercise family planning before independence.

1916 Probably the publication *The Population Problem in India* (1916) by Pyare Kishen was the first major attempt to advocate family planning in India.

1925 In 1925, Raghunath Dhondo Karve, a professor of mathematics opened the first birth control centre in Bombay. In the same year, Rabindranath Tagore advocated family planning in his letters.

1930 In June 1930, Mysore Government opened the first Government Birth Control Clinic in the world.

1931 In 1931, the Madras University accepted the proposal to impart instructions in methods of birth control.

1932 In 1932, the All India Women's Conference at Lucknow recommended that men and women should be instructed in methods of birth control in recognised clinics.

1935 In 1935, the Indian National Congress set up National Planning Committee under the chairmanship of Jawaharlal Nehru. As the recommendations of this committee are of historic importance, these are quoted here:

"1. We agree with the view that the size of the Indian population is a basic issue in national economic planning, in so for as its unrestricted increase of proportion to means of subsistence, affects adversely the standard of living, and tends to defeat many social and ameliorative measures. The problem has been fundamentally caused by the lack of all-round co-ordinated economic development. While measures for the improvement of the quality of the population and limiting excessive population pressure are necessary, the basic solution of the present disparity between population and standard of living lies in the economic progress of the country on a comprehensive and planned basis.

2. In the interest of social economy, family happiness and national planning, family planning and limitation of children are essential; and the state should adopt a policy to encourage these. It is desirable to lay stress on self-control as well as to spread knowledge of cheap and safe methods of birth control. Birth control clinics should be established and other necessary measures taken in this behalf to prevent the use of or advertisement of harmful methods.
3. We consider that a gradual raising of the marriage age and discouragement of polygamy are desirable in the interests of the limitation of the size of the family.
4. An eugenic programme should include the sterilisation of persons suffering from transmissible diseases of a serious nature, such as insanity or epilepsy.
5. The maintenance of vital statistics and the carrying out of periodic demographic surveys on comprehensive lines are necessary; and appropriate machinery should be devised for the purpose."

(*See* also Chapter 6)

21.2 BEGINNING OF FAMILY PLANNING IN INDEPENDENT INDIA

1952 India was the first country to start Family Planning which became an integral part of five year plans.

1976 Family Planning was done more or less through compulsion by the government.

1977 In 1977, there was a political revolution, when Mrs. Gandhi was voted out of power. In came Morarji Desai Government. This government changed the name of Family Planning to Family Welfare. It was committed to the programme of population control but ruled out any compulsion in it.

A population policy statement was prepared but it was not placed in the Parliament (for details *see chapter 24* on National Population Policy).

21.3 FAMILY PLANNING PROGRAMME IN INDIA : STRUCTURE AND DIMENSIONS

The following are the main points regarding Family Planning in India:

1. Organisational Structure
2. Approaches to Implementation
3. Family Planning Methods
4. Achievements

1. *Organisational Structure*: The family planning programme was started in 1952. It is the responsibility of Union Ministry of Health and Family Welfare. It is a centrally sponsored and financed programme implemented by the States.

In 1966, a full-fledged Department of Family Planning was established within the Central Ministry which was redesignated as the Ministry of Health and Family Planning and a Minister of Cabinet rank was appointed to look after its work. There is a Cabinet Committee of Family Planning. Then there is a Family Planning Council with the Minister of Health and Family Planning as its Chairman. The Council has a Standing Committee. Similar councils have been set up in the States as well. These council are mainly meant to review the progress of the Family Planning programmes and to make policy decisions.

At the District level, there are Family Planning Bureaus.

In 1977, there was change of nomenclature—from Family Planning to Family Welfare.

2. *Approaches to Implementation*: Many approaches have been followed:

(a) *The Clinical Approach or the Planned Parenthood Model*: The clinic approach was the approach of 1960s. It leaned heavily in favour of services for women rather than for couples. It also leaned heavily on medical personnel. It reached only a fraction of population and did not make much impact on birth rates.

(b) *The Extension Approach*: The credit for this goes to Lt. Col. B.L. Raina. Extension approach was initiated in 1963. It is an educational approach which tries to bring about change in the knowledge, attitudes and behaviour of people in regard to family planning. Here the leaders of the people are identified and their help taken to make people accept family planning. The help of panchayats is also to be taken. There are three conditions which have to be satisfied if extension approach is to work:

(i) Group acceptance;
(ii) Knowledge about family planning; and
(iii) Easy availability of supplies and services.

(c) *The Integrated Approach*: It was stated in Second Five Year Plan, "Family Planning Service is likely to succeed if the clinics are associated with maternity and child health work or with centres which provide medical aid and welfare services." In the Fifth Five Year Plan, the Family Planning Programme formed an integral part of Maternal and Child Health (MCH) and Nutrition Services. With this change in strategy, it was expected that programme will find wider acceptance among the people. The principle of integration of family planning services with maternity and child health services has thus been accepted since long. The basis of integration is that infant will be protected. He will not be allowed to die. Full care is to be taken of the mother and child—hence please limit your family. One sub-centre covers a population of 5000 people. "It is envisaged that under this scheme, integration and health and family planning services and nutrition, education will take place from the sub-centre through the PHC (Primary Health Centre) and District levels to the States."

Another facet of integrated approach is the *post-partum* programme, which is restricted to hospitals, where women are admitted/enrolled for delivery and abortion. The all India *Post-Partum* Programme was initiated in January 1970. Sub-district Hospitals were also covered by it by 1980. The rationale behind this programme is that when women go to hospitals for maternity care, they are in a positive frame of mind to receive family planning education.

(d) *The Cafeteria Approach*: Like in a cafeteria, all sorts of snacks are available, one has to pick according to one's choice—similarly applied to family planning it means that all sorts of family planning devices are available, one has to pick the one that suits you. The cafeteria approach was very popular during 1970s.

(e) *The Camp Approach:* It implies mass vasectomy camps. Large number of operations are performed in a single day. Vasectomy is a permanent method of limiting one's family.

21.3 METHODS OF FAMILY PLANNING FOR A SMALL FAMILY

Methods of Family Planning

Physical	Chemical	Mechanical	Oral pills	Sterilisation	Abortion
1	2	3	4	5	6
(i) Coitus	(i) Foam tablets	(i) Condom	interrupts	(i) Vasectomy for males	Oral pills
(ii) Safe period	(ii) Jellies	(ii) Diaphragm		(ii) Tubectomy for females	
	(iii) Pastes	(iii) Intra-Uterine Contraceptive device			
	(iv) Cream				

Temporary methods or Methods of Spacing and Permanent Methods of Family Planning

1. Temporary methods include the following:
   (i) Physical methods
   (ii) Chemical methods
   (iii) Mechanical methods
   (iv) Oral pills methods
2. Permanent methods
3. Abortion
4. Abstinence

(i) *Physical Methods:* (a) *Coitus Interruptsus* — In this method semen is not allowed to be discharged into the vagina.

The main drawback of this method is that the precoital secretions may contain sperm and further, the slightest delay in withdrawal may led to deposition of certain amount of sperm into the vagina. In addition, this may lead to dissatisfaction on the part of either husband or wife.

(b) *Safe Period* — The consideration in the method is that the time of ovulation can be found out either by recording the basal body temperature which shows a rise of 0.5°C immediately after ovulation (usually between the 13-16 the day of the menstrual cycle) or by calculation based on the longest and the shortest cycle of the woman. The fertile period starts from the day as figured by deducting 18 from the shortest cycle and ends on the day as figured by deducting 11 from the longest cycle. The day of the cycle is counted from the day menstrual period starts. The rest of the period is the safe period. As for example if any woman had the longest cycle as 31 days

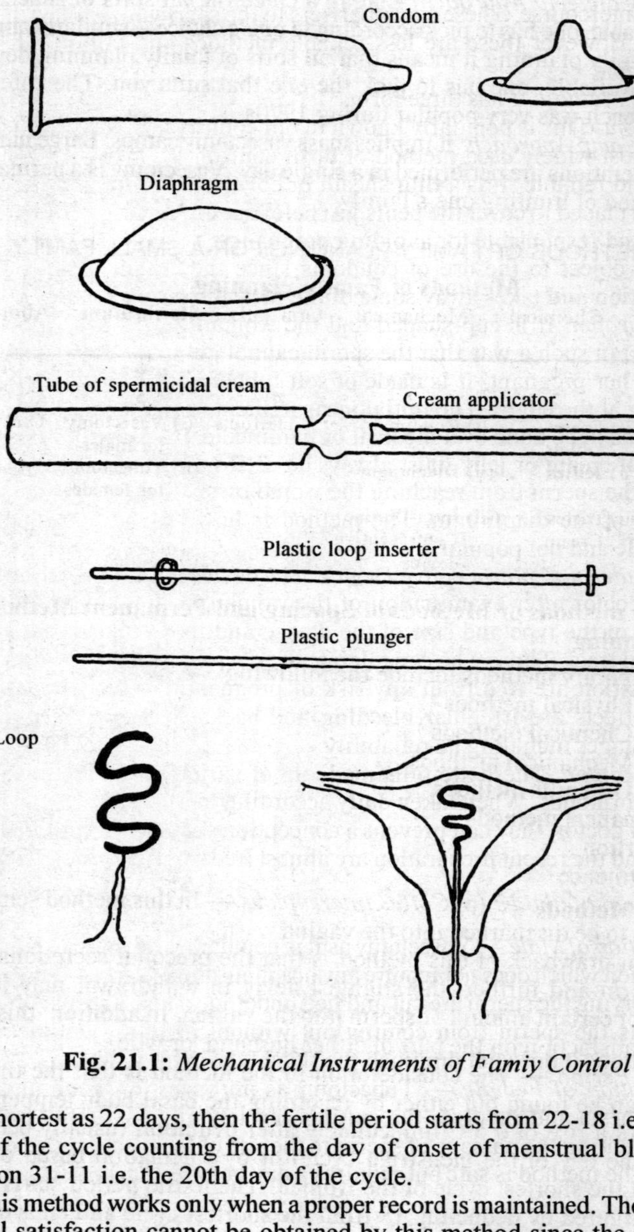

Fig. 21.1: *Mechanical Instruments of Famiy Control*

and shortest as 22 days, then the fertile period starts from 22-18 i.e. the fourth day of the cycle counting from the day of onset of menstrual bleeding and ends on 31-11 i.e. the 20th day of the cycle.

This method works only when a proper record is maintained. The maximum sexual satisfaction cannot be obtained by this method since the intercourse needs to be avoided during the most receptive period.

(ii) *Chemical Method*: Various foam tablets, jellies, pastes and creams having spermicidal properties are available which can be introduced into the vagina before intercourse. These act as barriers to the spermatozoa as well as toxic to them. However these are less reliable methods and failure rate is quite considerable.

Mechanical Method: It has three forms:

(i) *Condom*: This is popularly known in our country as 'Nirodh' and is the most widely used method of birth control. It is very simple to use and reliable. It is a thin sheath or cover of high quality rubber and is placed to cover the penis just before sex relation. It makes the husband responsible for avoiding pregnancy.
Some object to the use of condoms since they think it dulls the sensation and takes away some of the pleasure of sex.

(ii) *Diaphragm*: It is cup-shaped and the woman places it inside the vagina in such a way that the sperm cannot get into the womb and make her pregnant. It is made of soft rubber with a rubber coated spring at the edges. The initial measurement to find out the proper size has to be done by a medical or paramedical personnel. A birth control cream or jelly must always be used with the diaphragm to keep the sperm from reaching the womb by swimming around the edges of the diaphragm. The method is however, not absolutely reliable and not popular.

(iii) *Intra-uterine Contraceptive Device*: The device needs to be inserted by a doctor after examination of the woman for her suitability in terms of the type and size of the device and the conditions of the genital tract. Those who can tolerate the device and have the device in position are free from any risk of pregnancy. While the main side-effects are irregular bleeding and backache there are many advantages including its reliability.

Oral-pills Method. These are pills made up of various combinations of synthetic sex hormones. When taken daily according to a specific regime as prescribed by a doctor, they can prevent a conception very successfully. It is most reliable and the recent preparation are almost free from any side-effects.

2. Permanent Methods

(a) *Sterilisation of Male* — Vasectomy as it is popularly known is a simple, and safe operation which does not require any hospitalisation. The vas deferens or the ducts carrying the sperm are cut and tied under local anaesthesia. Since it only prevents the sperm from coming out without affecting any of the testicular functions it does not diminish the sexual desire or power.

(b) *Sterilisation of Female* — Tubectomy is an operation done under general anaesthesia and involves the cutting and legating of the fallopian tubes thus preventing the passage of sperm to the site of fertilisation and ova to the uterus. The method is safe but requires a day or two of hospitalisation.

3. Abortion

Abortion or the medical termination of pregnancy (MTP) may not be called a method for family planning since this cannot be performed repeatedly and ethically this is not permitted. However, unwanted pregnancies may be

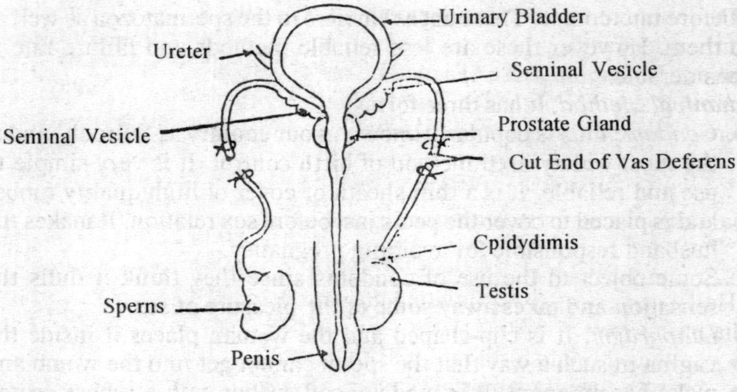

Fig. 21.2: *Vesectomy of Male*

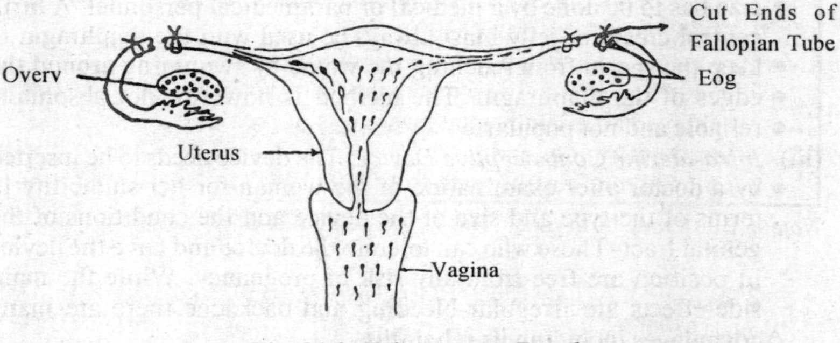

Fig. 21.3: *Tubectomy in Female*

terminated when the health of the mother is threatened or when the mother does not want a child for social and moral reasons or when the child is expected to have some hereditary defects. In exceptional cases, this may be resorted to in cases of failure of other contraceptives. The procedure is simple evacuation of the womb by vacuum suction under local anaesthesia, or the use of chemicals intravaginally, intrauterine or intravenously.

Abstinence

All the above mentioned methods either require some extraneous device, material, or surgical interference. It is, however, possible to discard all these, if a couple can exercise self-control.

Choosing a Method

Any of the methods as enumerated above may be chosen considering whether a permanent method is required or a method for spacing is necessary. The couple should feel free to try different methods as they want and choose one that suits them best. The doctors' advice is freely available all over the country. Cost is not an important factor since most of the methods are available in family welfare clinics almost free of charge.

The failure of family planning methods is mostly due to (i) taking a chance, (ii) misunderstanding between husband and wife, (iii) being caught without supplies, (iv) improper use of a method or (v) defective materials. In addition, certain per centage is added due to contraceptive failure, which varies in different methods which are less reliable to most reliable.

21.5 ACHIEVEMENTS IN FAMILY PLANNING

India's achievements in birth control rate etc. are given in Box 21.1.

Box 21.1: India's Demographic Achievement

Half a century after formulating the national family welfare programme, India has:

- reduced crude birth rate (CBR) from 40.8 (1951) to 25 (1999);
- halved the infant mortality rate (IMR) from 146 per 1000 live births (1951) to 72 per 1000 live births (1998);
- quadrupled the couple protection rate (CPR) from 10.4 per cent (1971) to 44 per cent (1999);
- reduced crude death rate (CDR) from 25 (1951) to 9.0 (1999)
- added 25 years to life expectancy from 37 years to 63 years (1999);
- achieved nearly universal awareness of the need for and methods of family planning; and
- reduced total fertility rate from 6.0 (1951) to 3.0 (1999)

Note: CBR. Crude birth rate; CDR. Crude death rate; IMR. Infant mortality rate

21.6 POPULATION CONTROL: INDIA HAS A LONG WAY TO GO

Arvind Bhandari (Hindustan Times, September 13, 1996) analysed the impact of population control measures as under.

1. The Washington-based Population Research Bureau, a non-government organisation observed that India's three-decade old effort to control its population has miscarried. India has the dubious distinction of being in the vanguard of the Third World Countries whose efforts on the family planning front have failed because of their refusal to go beyond education and propaganda.
2. According to Bhandari, the psychology behind the 'soft approach policy' can be explained in terms of three phenomena:
   (a) The policy continues to be hamstrung by a backlash of the emergency days.
   (b) The government initiative has been invariably marked by slothfulness.
   (c) The third phenomenon is what was prognosticated in the fifties by Gunnar Myrdal, renowned Swedish economist, in his three volume tome "Asian drama: An Analysis into the Poverty of Nations". The strand running through his thesis on India was that this country would be a "soft state". By this he did not mean that India would be lacking in cruelty, violence and brutality. What he meant was India would not be able to throw

> up political leadership having the calibre, vision and altruism to take tough, albeit politically inconvenient, measures necessary for the betterment of the general mass of the population. Considering the way things are being allowed to aside on almost all fronts, he has been proved right to the hilt.

The writer commended the policy China of 'Carrot-and stick' incentive—disincentive policy in family planning.

There is a great need to involve menfolk in a big way to achieve substantial result in family planning.

22

Reproductive Health

22.1 MEANING OF REPRODUCTIVE HEALTH

Reproductive health implies that people are able to have a satisfying and safe sex life and that they have the capability to reproduce and the freedom to decide 'if', 'when' and 'how' often to do so.

22.2 SCOPE OF REPRODUCTIVE HEALTH CARE

Reproductive health care includes the following types of services

(i) Family planning counselling, information, education, communication and services.
(ii) Education and services for prenatal care, safe delivery.
(iii) Education and services for post-natal care, especially breast-feeding and infant and women's health care.
(iv) Prevention and appropriate treatment of infertility.
(v) Abortion including prevention of abortion and management of the consequences of abortion.
(vi) Treatment of reproductive tract infections.
(vii) Information, education and counselling on human sexuality, reproductive health and responsible parenthood.
(viii) Referral for family planning services and further diagnosis and treatment for pregnancy, delivery and abortion etc.
(ix) Active discouragement of harmful practices such as female genital mutilation etc.

22.3 OBJECTIVES OF FAMILY PLANNING

1. To help couples and individuals promote family well-being.
2. To help them promote their health.
3. To help them and respect their dignity and right to choose the number, spacing and timing of the birth of their children.
4. To prevent unwanted pregnancies
5. To reduce the incidence of high risk pregnancies and morbidity and mortality
6. To make quality Family Planning services affordable, acceptable and accessible to all who need them. Confidentiality is to be maintained.

7. to improve the quality of Family Planning advice, information, education, communications, counselling and services.
8. To increase the participation and sharing of responsibility of men in the actual practice of Family Planning.
9. To promote breast-feeding to enhance birth spacing.

22.4 SUGGESTIONS FOR PROMOTING FAMILY PLANNING

1. All possible means should be used to popularise and support the principle of voluntary choice in Family Planning.
2. Universal access to a full range of safe and reliable Family Planning methods should be provided for all.
3. Non-governmental organisations should play an active role in mobilising community and family support.
4. All barriers related to the inadequacy, poor quality and cost of existing Family Planning services should be removed.
5. Unnecessary legal, medical, clinical and regulatory barriers to information and access to family-planning services and methods should be removed.
6. All political and community leaders should play an active role in promoting the use of family planning and reproductive health services.
7. It should be recognised that methods of family-planning for couples and individuals vary according to their age, family-size preference and other factors.
8. It should be ensured that people have access to the widest range of safe and effective family-planning method, in order to enable them to exercise free and informed choice.
9. Family Planning services should be made safer, affordable, convenient and accessible.
10. Privacy and confidentiality should be ensured.
11. Formal and informal training in sexual and reproductive health care and Family Planning for all health care providers, health educators and others engaged in this work should be upgraded and expanded.
12. Appropriate follow-up care, including treatment for side-effects of contraceptive use should be ensured.
14. Availability of related reproductive health services on site or through a strong referral mechanism should be ensured.
15. There should be effective evaluation of Family Planning services.
16. Family Planning and reproductive health services should emphasis breast-feeding education and support services which can simultaneously contribute to birth spacing, better maternal and child health and child survival.
17. Appropriate steps should be taken to help women avoid abortion.
18. Abortion, in no case should be promoted as a method of Family Planning.
19. Human treatment and counselling of women who have had uric to abortion should be provided.

20. Private sector and non-governmental organisations should be involved in providing reproductive health services.
21. An efficient co-ordination system with the help of international agencies should be established in order to meet the substantial increase in demand for contraceptives for the next decade and beyond.
22. Appropriate assistance and guidance in various dimensions of planning, especially quality and safety etc should be secured from the World Health Organisation.

22.5 SEXUALLY TRANSMITTED DISEASES (STDs) AND PREVENTION OF HUMAN IMMUNE DEFICIENCY VIRUS (HIV)

Problem

The Word-Wide incidence of STDs is quite high. The situation has become very serious with the emergence of HIV epidemic.

Women are especially vulnerable to these diseases. They are exposed to high-risk sexual behaviour of their partners. For them, the symptoms of infections from sexually transmitted diseases are often hidden. Health consequences are often greater and they are faced with increased risk of infertility and ectopic pregnancy. The risk of transmission from infected men to women is also greater than from infected woman to men, woman are also powerless to take steps to protect them selves.

Objectives of Programmes

1. To prevent and reduce the incidence of STDs and HIV.
2. To provide treatment.
3. To avoid complications such as infertility with special reference to girls and women.

Action Programmes

1. Reproductive health programmes should increase their efforts to prevent, detect and treat STDs and other reproductive tract infections, especially at the primary health care level.
2. Special outreach efforts should be made to those who do not have access to reproductive health care programmes.
3. Specialised training in the prevention, detection and counselling regarding STDs and HIV should be provided to all health–care providers including all Family Planning providers.
4. Information, education and counselling for responsible sex behaviour and effective prevention of STDs and HIV should be made an integral components of all reproduction and sexual health services.
5. Promotion and the reliable supply and distribution of high quality condoms should also become integral components of all reproductive health services.

22.6 HUMAN SEXUALITY AND GENDER RELATIONS

Introduction

Responsible sexual behaviour, sensitivity and equity in gender relations particularly when formed during adolescence enhance harmonious partnerships between men and women. They are also very helpful in improving the quality of life of individuals.

Objectives of the Programme

1. To promote adequate development of responsible sexuality.
2. To promote relation of equity and mutual respect between the genders.
3. To ensure that women and men have access to the information, education and services needed to achieve good sexual health.
4. To ensure that women and men have the necessary knowledge and access to services to exercise their reproductive rights and responsibilities.

Actions

1. Efforts for providing integral sexual education and services for young should begin within the family, in the community and in the schools at an appropriate age. They must also reach adults through non-formal education.
2. Active and open discussion of the need to protect women, youth and children from any abuse, including sexual abuse, exploitation, trafficking and violence must be encouraged.
3. Government should set the necessary conditions and procedures to encourage victims of sexual abuse to report violations of their rights.
4. Laws addressing these concerns should be suitably enacted, strengthened and enforced.
5. Appropriate rehabilitation services should be provided to the victims.
6. Government should also prohibit the production and trade of child pornography.
7. Urgent steps should be taken to stop the practice of female genital mutilation and protect women and girls from all such similar dangerous practices. People should be informed of the harmful effects on girl's and women's health. Appropriate treatment and rehabilitation services for girls and women who have suffered mutilation should be provided.

22.7 ADOLESCENTS

Introduction

The health needs of adolescents as a group have been largely ignored by the existing reproductive health services. Sexually active adolescents are specially vulnerable but they are poorly informed of the high risks of contracting STDs, including HIV/AIDS.

Objectives of the Programme

1. To address adolescent sexual and reproductive health issues.
2. To provide services and counselling suitable for adolescents.
3. To reduce substantially all adolescent pregnancies.

Actions

1. To educate the parents to accept their responsibilities to provide direction and guidance to the adolescents in sexual and reproductive manners.
2. In collaboration with non-governmental organisations The Government should establish appropriate programmes to respond to the needs of the adolescents in sexual and reproductive matters.

23

Population Control : Education and Empowerment of Women

23.1 INTIMATE CORRELATION BETWEEN FEMALE EDUCATION AND POPULATION GROWTH

The right to education is one of the most important means of empowering women with the knowledge, skill and self-confidence necessary to participate fully in the development process. Education enables women to respond to opportunities, to change their traditional roles, and to change their life circumstances. Promoting the education of women and girls contributes to postponement of their age of marriage, and to reduction in the size of their families. Education builds life skills for acquiring timely and relevant information.

Functional literacy and basic education are pre-requisites for accessing information and services for good health. While there is a correlation between educational status of women and their family size, fertility preferences, child care practices and, it has now been established that even in the non-formal education programmes, raising the functional literacy level of a community leads to a demonstrable decline in fertility and infant mortality rates. Educational interventions through formal and non-formal programmes are investments for population stabilisation and ensuring human rights, including reproductive rights.

The overall infant mortality rate declines sharply with increasing education of mothers. A strong positive relationship has been established between mother's education and children's immunisation. Only 28 per cent of children of illiterate mothers had fully vaccinated their children compared with 73 per cent of children of mothers who had completed high school. Education has been found to be a key factor influencing contraceptive use. Modern spacing methods account for 6 per cent of contraceptive use by illiterate women compared to 35 per cent by women with at least a high school education.

23.2 EMPOWERING WOMEN FOR IMPROVED HEALTH AND NUTRITION

1. Create an enabling environment for women and children to benefit from products and services disseminated under the reproductive and

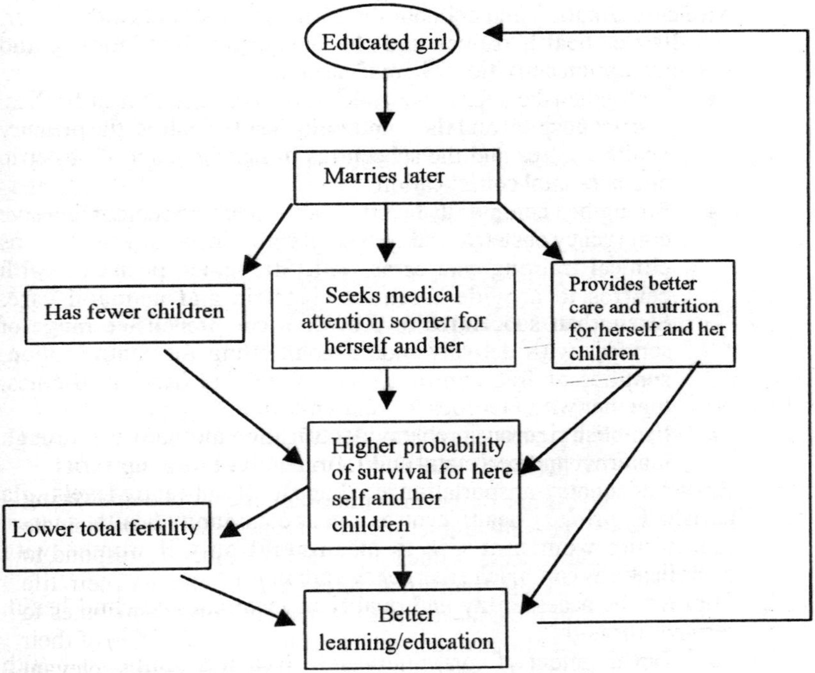

Source: The State of World's Children 1999, UNICEF.

Fig. 23.1 *Female Education and Quality of Life*

child health programme. Cluster services for women and children at the same place and time. This promotes positive interactions in health benefits and reduces service delivery costs.

2. As a measure to empower women, open more child care centres in rural areas and in urban slums, where a woman worker may leave her children in responsible hands. This will encourage female participation in paid employment, reduce school drop-out rates, particularly for the girl child, and promote school enrolment as well. The anganwadis provide a partial solution.
3. To empower women, pursue programmes of social afforestation to facilitate access to fuel wood and fodder. Similarity, pursue drinking water schemes for increasing access to potable water. This will reduce long absences from home, and the need for large numbers of children to perform such tasks.
4. In any reward scheme intended for household levels, priority may be given to energy saving devices such as solar cookers, or provision of sanitation facilities, or extension of telephone lines. This will empower households, in particular women.

5. Improve district, sub-district and panchayat-level health management with co-ordination and collaboration between district health officer, sub-district health officer and the panchayat for planning and implementation activities. There is need to
   - Strengthen the referral network between the district health office, district hospital and the community health centres, the primary health centres and the subcentres in management of obstetric and neo-natal complications.
   - Strengthen community health centres to provide comprehensive emergency obstetric and neo-natal care. These may function as clinical training centres as well. Strengthen primary health centres to provide essential obstetric and neonatal care. Strengthen subcentres to provide a comprehensive range of services with delivery rooms, counselling for contraception, supplies of free contraceptives, ORS and basic medicines, together with facilities for immunisation.
   - Establish rigorous problem identification mechanisms through maternal and peri-natal audit, from village level upwards.
6. Ensure adequate transportation at village level, subcentre levels, zila parishads, primary health centres and at community health centres. Identifying women at risk is meaningful only if women with complications can reach emergency care in time.
7. Improve the accessibility and quality of maternal and child health services through:
   - Development of community midwives and additional health providers at village levels; cluster services for women and children at the same place and time, from village level upwards, e.g. ante-natal and post-partum care, monitoring infant growth, availability of contraceptives and medicine kits; and routinised immunisations at subcentre levels.
   - Strengthen the capacity of primary health centres to provide basic emergency obstetric and neo-natal health care.
   - Involve professional agencies in developing and disseminating training modules for standard procedures in the management of obstetric and neo-natal cases. The aim should be to routinise these procedures at all appropriate levels.
   - Improve supervision by developing guidance and supervision checklists.
8. Monitor performance of maternal and child health services at each level by using the local area maternal and child health monitoring system, which includes monitoring the incidence and coverage of ante-natal visits, deliveries assisted by trained health care personnel and post-natal visits, among other indicators. The ANM at the subcentre should be responsible and accountable for registering every pregnancy and child birth in her jurisdiction, and for providing universal ante-natal and post-natal services.
9. Improve technical skills of maternal and child health care providers by:

- Strengthening skills of health personnel and health providers through classroom and on-the-job training in the management of obstetric and neo-natal emergencies. This should include training of birth attendants and community midwives at district-level hospitals in life-saving skills, such as management of asphyxia and hypothermia.
- Training in integrated management of childhood illnesses for infants (1 week-2 weeks).

10. Support community activities such as dissemination of IEC material, including leaflets and posters, and promotion of folk jatras, songs and dances to promote healthy mother and healthy baby messages, along with good management practices to ensure safe motherhood, including early recognition of danger signs.
11. Programme development, comprising:
    - Partnership in family health and nutrition. The anganwadi worker will identify women and children in the villages who suffer from malnutrition and/or micro-nutritional deficiencies, including iron, vitamin A, and iodine deficiency; provide nutritional supplements and monitor nutritional status.
    - Convergence, strengthening, and universalisation of the nutritional programmes of the Department of Family Welfare and the ICDS run by the Department of Women and Child Development, ensuring training and timely supply of food supplements and medicines.
    - Include STD/RTI and HIV/AIDS prevention, screening and management in maternal and child health services.
    - Provide quality care in Family Planning, including information, increased contraceptive choices for both spacing and terminal methods; increased access to good quality and affordable contraceptive supplies and services at diverse delivery points; counselling about the safety, efficacy and possible side effects of each method, and appropriate follow-up.
12. Develop a health package for adolescents.

24

National Population Policy (2000 A.D)

24.1 MILESTONES IN THE FORMULATION OF NATIONAL POPULATION POLICY

I. India, the First Country in the World to start Policy Family Planning (1952)

In 1952, India launched a national programme of Family Planning for reducing birth rates to stabilise the population at a level consistent with the requirement of national economy. The policy did not yield the desired results.

II. Statement of National Population Policy (1976)

In 1976, a statement of National Population Policy was laid on the Table of the House in Parliament but never discussed or adopted.

III. National Health Policy (1983)

The National Health Policy of 1983 emphasised the need for "securing the small family norm, through voluntary efforts and moving towards the goal of population stabilisation". While adopting the Health Policy, Parliament emphasised the need for a separate National Population Policy.

IV. Committee on Population 1991

The National Development Council appointed a Committee on Population with Shri Karunakaran as Chairman. The Karunakaran Report [Report of the National Development Council (NDC) Committee on Population] endorsed by NDC in 1993 proposed the formulation of a National Population Policy to take a "a long-term holistic view of development, population growth and environmental protection" and to "suggest policies and guidelines for formulation of programmes" and "a monitoring mechanism with short, medium and long-term perspectives and goals" (Planning Commission 1992). Specifically, is was recommended that "a National Policy of Population should be formulated by the Government and adopted by Parliament."

V. Draft National Population Policy (1993)

An Expert Group headed by Dr. M.S. Swaminathan was asked to prepare a draft of a national population policy. The Report on a National Population Policy by the Expert Group headed by Dr. Swaminathan was circulated among Members of Parliament, and comments requested from central and state agencies. It was anticipated that a national population policy approved by the Parliament would help produce a broad political consensus.

VI. Approval of the Policy

During 1997 Cabinet approved the draft National Population Policy with the direction that this be placed before parliament. However, this document could not be placed in either House of Parliament as the respective Houses Stood adjourned followed by dissolution of the Lok Sabha.

VII. Finalisation of the National Population Policy (2000)

Another round of consultations was held during 1998, and another draft National Population Policy was finalised and placed before the Cabinet in March, 1999. Cabinet appointed a Group of Ministers (headed by Deputy Chairman, Planning Commission) to examine the draft Policy. The GOM met several times and deliberated over the nuances of the Population Policy. In order to finalise a view about the inclusion/exclusion of incentives and disincentives, the Group of Ministers invited a cross-section of experts from among academia, public health professionals, demographers, social scientists, and women's representatives. The GOM finalised a draft population policy, and placed the same before the Cabinet. This was discussed in the Cabinet on 19 November, 1999. Several suggestions were made during the deliberations. On that basis, a fresh draft was submitted to the Cabinet. It was approved in 2000 and the policy declared.

24.2 CHIEF FEATURES OF THE NATIONAL POPULATION POLICY NPP (2000)

Chief features of National Population Policy are :

1. Objectives of National Population Policy
2. National Socio-Demographic goals for 2010
3. Expected Results from the implementation of NPP
4. NPP 2000 Action Plan.

24.3 OBJECTIVES OF THE NATIONAL POPULATION POLICY (NPP)

These are divided into:

(i) Immediate objective of NPP
(ii) Medium term objective of NPP
(iii) Long term objective of NPP

(i) *Immediate Objective of NPP*: The immediate objective of the NPP 2000 is to address the unmet needs for contraception, health care infrastructure, and health personnel, and to provide integrated service delivery for basic reproductive and child health care.

(ii) *The Medium-Term Objective of NPP*: To bring the TFR to replacement levels by 2010 through vigorous implementation of inter-sectoral operational strategies.

(iii) *The Long-Term Objective*: This is to achieve a stable population by 2045 at a level consistent with the requirements of sustainable economic growth, social development, and environmental protection.

24.4 NATIONAL SOCIO-DEMOGRAPHIC GOALS FOR 2010. THESE ARE PRESENTED IN THE BOX 24.1

Box 24.1 : National Socio-Demographic Goals for 2010

1. Address the unmet needs for basic reproductive and child health services, supplies and infrastructure.
2. Make school education up to age 14 free and compulsory, and reduce drop-outs at primary and secondary school levels to below 20 per cent for both boys and girls.
3. Reduce infant mortality rate to below 30 per 1000 live births.
4. Reduce maternal mortality ratio to below 100 per 100,000 live births.
5. Achieve universal immunisation of children against all vaccine preventable diseases.
6. Promote delayed marriage for girls, not earlier than age 18 and preferably after 20 years of age.
7. Achieve 80 per cent institutional deliveries and 100 per cent deliveries by trained persons.
8. Achieve universal access to information/counselling, and services for fertility regulation and contraception with a wide basket of choices.
9. Achieve 100 per cent registration of births, deaths, marriage and pregnancy.
10. Contain the spread of Acquired Immuno Deficiency Syndrome (AIDS) and promote greater integration between the management of reproductive tract infections (RTI) and sexually transmitted infections (STI) and the National AIDS Control Organisation.
11. Prevent and control communicable diseases.
12. Integrate Indian Systems of Medicine (ISM) in the provision of reproductive and child health services, and in reaching out to households.
13. Promote vigorously the small family norm to achieve replacement levels of TFR.
14. Bring about convergence in implementation of related social sector programmes so that family welfare becomes a people centred programme.

24.5 NATIONAL POPULATION POLICY (2001 : ACTION PLAN)

This includes the following strategies:

1. Decentralised planning and programme implementation.
2. Convergence (Integrating and Co-ordinating) of Service Delivery at village levels i.e. combining with Integrated Child Development Scheme (ICDS), Centrally Sponsored Schemes of (a) Department of

Women and Child Development, Ministry of HRD (b) Ministry of Rural Development (c) Ministry of Environment and Forests.

3. Empowering women for improved health nutrition.
4. Improving Child health and survival.
5. Meeting the unmet needs for family welfare services.
6. Providing health services and facilities for under served population groups i.e. (a) urban slums (b) tribal communities, hill areas population, displaced and migrant populations (c) meeting adolescents' needs (d) ensuring participation of men in planned parenthood.
7. Ensuring diverse health care providers i.e. trained medical and health personnel at various levels.
8. Collaborating with NGOs and industry.
9. Promoting contraceptive technology and research.
10. Mainstreaming Indian systems of medicine and Homeopathy.
11. Providing health and other services for the older population.
12. Strengthening information education and communication.

24.6 STABILISING POPULATION AND FOLLOW-UP ON NPP (2000)

Following are the major initiative taken to achieve objectives as laid down in NPP 2000.

- For the first time in independent India, a comprehensive National Population Policy was adopted by the Government in 2000 with the objective of improving the quality of life of the citizens, by reaching out to them with an enhanced package of services and supplies that will inter alia serve to stabilise the unregulated growth of population.
- National Commission on Population has been constituted directly under the chairmanship of Prime Minister with Chief Ministers of all States/UTs, demographers, non-government organisations and public health professionals as members to advise in operationalising the National Population Policy.
- An Empowered Action Group, constituted under the chairmanship of the Union Health and Family Welfare Minister, is focusing attention on improving the coverage and outreach of services in the 8 states of Uttar Pradesh, Uttaranchal, Bihar, Jharkhand, Rajasthan, Orissa, Madhya Pradesh and Chhatisgarh, involving voluntary associations, community organisations and Panchayati Raj Institutions in this national effort.
- Series of consultations have been held with all stakeholders—the State Health and Family Welfare Ministers, State Secretaries, professional medical associations and medical experts, NGOs, media persons, Corporate sector and Civil society for implementation of the National Population Policy, 2000 and action being taken.
- In order to arrest the adverse sex ratio, an intensive campaign has been launched against the practice of female foeticide through the mass media—print and electronic as well as through the voluntary organisations for stricter enforcement of the Law. The Pre-Natal Diagnostics Act, 1994 is being amended as well.

- Male participation in the programme has increased manifold with the growing popularity of No Scalpel Vasectomy—a much improved method.

Upgradation of Health Infrastructure

- In the two years 2000-01 and 2001-02 the prime minister's gramodaya yojana has provided Central allocation of Rs. 809 crores for the maintenance and upkeep of primary health infrastructure in rural India.

Integrated Service Delivery: Reproductive Health

- Immunisation is key to the health of children by reducing infant mortality. RCH cutreacn services such as immunisation, ante and post natal check ups, information and counselling, as well as contraceptive services are being provided. This scheme which covered 50 districts in 2000 was extended during year 2001 to 101 additional districts.

24.7 EXPECTED RESULTS FROM THE IMPLEMENTATION OF NPP

If the NPP 2000 is fully implemented, we anticipate a population of 1107 million (110 crores) in 2010, instead of 1162 million (116 crores) projected by the Technical Group on Population Projections:

Table 24.1: Anticipated Growth in Population (million)

Year	*If current trends continue*		*If TFR 2.1 is achieved by 2010*	
	Total Population	*Increase in Population*	*Total Population*	*Increase in Population*
1991	846.3		846.3	—
1996	934.2	— 17.6	934.2	17.6
1997	949.9	15.7	949.0	14.8
2000	996.9	15.7	991.0	14.0
2002	1027.6	15.6	1013.0	11.0
2010	1162.3	16.8	1107.0	11.75

Similarly, the anticipated reductions in the birth, infant mortality and total fertility rates are:

Table 24.2 : Projections of Crude Birth Rate, Infant Mortality Rate, and TFR, if the NPP 2000 is fully implemented

Year	*Crude Birth Rate*	*Infant Mortality Rate*	*Total Fertility Rate*
1997	27.2	71	3.3
1998	26.4	72	3.3
2002	23.0	50	2.6
2010	21.0	30	2.1

25

India's Population, Progress and Human Development: An Overview

25.1 INTRODUCTION

In this chapter, an attempt is made to illustrate the progress India has made during the last several decades in various fields in the wake of growing population. Data covered are:

1. India's Population : Demographic data
2. Economic Indicators of Development
3. Education Indicators
4. Health Indicators
5. Nutrition Indicators
6. Family Planning and Women Education Indicators
7. Communication Indicators

It is hardly necessary to stress that all the above indicators have great bearing on quality of life.

25.2 INDIA'S POPULATION : DEMOGRAPHIC INDICATORS

Sl. No.	*Indicator*	*Development (Number/Per centage etc.)*
1.	Total population (2011)	1,21,01,93,422 (121 crore)
	(a) Males	62,37,24,248
	(b) Females	58,64,69,174
2.	Annual growth rate (%)	
	(a) 1970 – 90	2.1 %
	(b) 1990 – 99	1.8 %
	(c) 2001-2011	1.76%
3.	Population under 6 years (2011)	15,87,89,287 (15.9 crore)
	(i) Males	8,29,52,135
	(ii) Females	7,58,37,152

Sl. No.	*Indicator*	*Development (Number/Percentage etc.)*
4.	Proportion of child population in the age group 0–6 to total population (2011)	13.12 %
	(i) Males	6.85 %
	(ii) Females	6.27 %
5.	Density of population (2011)	382
6.	Under–5 mortality rate (1990)	242
	Under–5 mortality rate (2010)	65
7.	(a) Infant mortality rate under 1 (1960)	146
	(b) Infant mortality rate under 1 (2010)	48
8.	(a) Crude death rate (1970)	17
	(b) Crude death rate (2010)	7.9
9.	Crude birth rate (1970)	39
10.	Crude Birth rate (2010)	21.3
11.	(a) Life expectancy (1970)	49
	(b) Life expectancy (2009)	69.89
12.	Total fertility rate (2010)	2.5
13.	% of population urbanised (2011)	31.16

25.3 ECONOMIC INDICATORS OF DEVELOPMENT

1.	GNP Growth 2011-12	6.9%
2.	Annual rate of inflation 2011	7.21 %
3.	Population below $ 1 a day (1990-91)	44 %
4.	Population below $ 1 a day (2010)	32.7%

25.4 EDUCATION INDICATORS OF DEVELOPMENT

1.	Adult literacy rate	
	(a) 2005-10	63%
	(b) 1947	12%
	(c) Literacy rate 2001:	65.38%
	(d) Literacy rate 2011	74.04 %
2.	Primary school enrolment ratio	
	(a) 1995-99 (Net) :	
	Males	78 %
	Females	64 %
	(b) 2007-10 (Net)	
	Males	97%
	Females	94%
	(c) Women Education	
	1981	28.5%
	2001	50%
3.	Net primary school attendance (2005-10)	
	Males	85 %
	Females	81 %
4.	Secondary school enrolment ratio-gross (2005-10)	
	Males	59 %
	Females	49 %

5. Higher Education – GER

1960-61	1.4%
2011-12	15%

25.5 HEALTH INDICATORS OF DEVELOPMENT

1. Under–5 mortality rate :

1999	98
2010	63

2. Infant mortality rate under 1 :

1999	70
2010	48

3. Population using improved drinking water sources (2008):

Total	88%
Urban	96%
Rural	84%

4. Population using adequate sanitary facilities (2008) :

Total	31%
Urban	54%
Rural	21%

5. 1-year old children fully immunized (2010) again:

TB	87%
DPT	83%
Polio	70%
Measles	74%
Tetanus Pregnant women	87%

25.6 NUTRITION INDICATORS OF DEVELOPMENT

1. Infants with low birth weight (2006-10) :	28%
2. Children who are (2006-10)	
(a) Exclusively breastfed (0-3 months) :	46%
(b) Breastfed with complementary food (6-9 months):	57%
(c) Still breastfeeding (20-23 months) :	77%
3. Under five suffering from (2006-10)	
(a) underweight; moderate and severe :	43%
(b) Underweight : severe :	16%
(c) Wasting : underweight : severe :	20%
(d) Stunting : moderate and severe :	48%
4. Vitamin A supplementation coverage rate 6-59 months (2006-10) :	34%
5. Households consuming iodised salt (2006-10) :	51%

25.7 FAMILY PLANNING AND WOMEN EDUCATION INDICATORS

1.	Contraceptive prevalence (2006-10) :	54 %
2.	Birth attended by trained health personnel (1995-2000) :	34 %
3.	Maternal mortality rate (2006-10) :	250
4.	Life expectancy of females as a % of males (2010) :	105 %
5.	Adult literacy rate of females as a % of males (2005-2010):	68 %
6.	Enrolment ratio of female as % of males Secondary school (2007-10) :	88 %

26

World Population, Environment, Development and Poverty

26.1 INDICATORS OF POPULATION AND DEVELOPMENT

I. Population

1. *Total Population*: The twentieth century witnessed an extraordinary growth of world population from 1.6 billion in 1900 to 6.1 billion in 2001. Almost 80 per cent of that increase has occurred since 1950. It took only 12 years (1987 to 1999) for the world to add the most recent billion people. This was the shortest period in world history for a billion people to be added. The developing countries and regions account for 80 per cent of the world's inhabitants.

2. *Population Density*: World population density increased from 13 persons per square kilometre in 1900 to 19 persons per square kilometre in 1950 and to its current level of 45 persons per square kilometre. Sharp differences distinguish the more developed regions—with 23 persons per square kilometre—from the less developed regions, where density is almost three times higher at 60 persons per square kilometre.

3. *Population Growth Rate*: The world's population is currently growing at 1.2 per cent annually. Ninety-five per cent of current population growth is taking place in the less developed regions. Whereas more developed regions are barely growing at 0.2 per cent annually, less developed regions are growing at an annual rate of 1.5 per cent. In the least developed countries, which are still at an early stage in the demographic transition, population growth is estimated at 2.5 per cent per year, which yields a population doubling time of 29 years.

4. *Urban Population Growth*: The world is becoming increasingly urbanised. Except for Africa, virtually all future population growth is now concentrated in urban areas. Urban population growth for the period 2000-2005 is estimated at 2.0 per cent per year. The proportion of urban-dwellers climbed from 30 per cent of total population in 1950 to 47 per cent in 2000. The population of urban-dwellers is projected to equal the population of rural-dwellers by 2007. The process of urbanisation is very advanced in more

developed regions, where 76 per cent of the population lives in urban areas. Although the level of urbanisation is considerably lower in less developed regions (40 per cent), urban areas in less developed regions are growing much more rapidly (2.7 per cent per year) than in more developed regions (0.5 per cent per year).

5. *Rural Population Growth*: The population residing in rural areas fell from 70 per cent in 1950 to 53 per cent in 2000. On a global basis, rural populations are growing at a rate of only 0.4 per cent a year, while in more developed regions, the rural population is shrinking at a rate of 0.8 per cent annually.

II. Environment

5. *Average Annual Internal Renewable Water Resources Available Per Capita*: Demand for fresh water has steadily risen with increasing population and socio-economic development. Consequently, the per capita availability of fresh water on a global basis has fallen to nearly to nearly one third of its 1950 level. At present, agriculture accounts for some 70 per cent of freshwater consumption worldwide. Globally, fresh water is abundant, but is unevenly distributed among and within countries.

6. *Water Stress*: Chronic water shortages exist in many areas where precipitation is low or unreliable and/or where withdrawals have significantly increased to meet additional demand from expanding irrigation, industry or urban population. Assessments of the world's water resources are commonly measured in terms of the ratio of water withdrawals to water supply (on the comprehensive assessment of the freshwater resources of the world). A ratio of less than 10 per cent indicates few water resource management problems; a ratio of between 10 and 19 per cent points to water availability's becoming a limiting factor. When water withdrawals are in the range of 20 to 40 per cent, management of both supply and demand will be needed to guarantee sustainability. Use in excess of 40 per cent of available water indicates serious scarcity and usually an increasing dependence on desalination and a situation where groundwater is being used faster than it is being replenished. Water use has been growing at more than twice the rate of the population increase during the twentieth century. About one-third of the world's population lives in countries that are experiencing medium-high to high levels of water stress.

7. *Forest Cover*: Up to half of the forests that originally covered the Earth have been cleared. Although some 90 million hectares of forest were lost between 1990 and 2000, the pace of deforestation is estimated to have been lower in the 1990s than during the 1980s. Deforestation has been arrested and even reversed in Europe and North America. Forests are critical because they house indigenous cultures, shelter global bio-diversity, provide ecosystem services, store carbon, contribute to economic growth and meet recreational needs.

8. *Cropland Per Capita*: The amount of cropland available per capita is decreasing in all world regions, as population increases. The global availability of cropland has fallen by some 25 per cent over two decades. Farmers have traditionally satisfied increasing demand by ploughing new land, but in many

regions opportunities for expansion are now limited. Boosting productivity has therefore become crucial for increased food production.

9. *Poverty Rate*: The total number of the poor in 1998 was greater than it had been a decade earlier. Almost one fourth of the population of developing regions and economies in transition—1.2 billion people—live in absolute poverty. Poverty is most pervasive in sub-Saharan Africa and South-central Asia and is related to a wide range of factors, including income, health, education, gender and ethnicity.

10. *Development and Poverty: Per centage undernourished*: Some 792 million people in developing countries and 34 million in developed countries and those with economies in transition are undernourished. Inadequate access to food results from poverty, political instability, economic inefficiency and social inequity. Almost two thirds of the undernourished live in Asia and Oceania, while about one quarter are in sub-Saharan Africa. The problem is most severe in Central, Eastern and Southern Africa, almost one half of the population is undernourished.

11. *Gross Domestic Product per Capita*: Domestic product per capita — the total amount of goods and services produced per person within the domestic territory of a country —increased almost six fold over the twentieth century; but for the poorest quarter of world population, per capita income grew less than threefold.

12. *Commercial Energy Consumption per Capita*: Energy consumption is a function of economic growth and level of development and is therefore very unequally distributed in the world. Although the share of developed market economies has fallen slightly in recent years as the rest of the world progresses along the path to development, these economies, comprising some one fifth of the world's population, consume almost three fifths of the world's primary energy. As a consequence of development and rapid replacement of traditional energy sources by commercial (mainly fossil) sources, some developing countries, particularly in Asia, have consumption patterns similar to those of developed market economies. Nevertheless, per capita consumption in developing countries still lags far behind that of developed market economies.

13. *Number of Motor Vehicles per 1,000 Population*: During the twentieth century, there was a major shift from rail and water transport to road and air transport. Since the 1940s, the number of vehicles on the road has grown from some 40 million to 680 million. The most rapid per centage increase in the number of motor vehicles is now in less developing regions, where automobile ownership is still low. Transport now accounts for one quarter of world energy use and one half of the world's oil consumption and is a major contributor to greenhouse gas emissions, urban air pollution, urban congestion and health hazards.

14. *Carbon Dioxide Emissions per Capita*: The intensive use of fossil fuels has led to substantial growth in global emissions of carbon dioxide (CO_2) and the build-up of greenhouse effects, a contributing factor in global warming. It is estimated that since 1751, over 265 billion tons of carbon have been released to the atmosphere, one half of these emissions having occurred

since the mid-1970s. Annual global emissions of CO_2 from the burning of fossil fuels have been steadily rising and have quadrupled since 1950. The highest per capita emissions are in North America. Europe's per capita emission levels are less than one half as high. Continuation of these upward trends in emissions may pose serious risks of climate change, especially global warming, possibly inducing surges in sea levels, flooding of low-lying coastal areas, migration of ecosystems, the spread of vector-borne diseases and reductions in agricultural yields.

Source: Adapted from wall chart '*World Population 2000*'. Population Division, United Nation, New York, 2000.

Definitions and Meaning of Indicators

Adult Literacy Rate: Percentage of persons aged 15 and over who can read and write.

GNP per Capita: Gross net per capita is the gross national product divided by the mid-year population of a country.

Gross Primary School Enrolment Ratio: The number of children enrolled in primary schools, regardless of age, divided by the population of the age group that officially corresponds to primary schooling.

Infant Mortality Rate: Deaths before one year of age per 1,000 live births.

Under 5 Mortality Rate: Deaths between births and 5 years of age per 1,000 live births.

Low Weight: Less than 2,500 grams.

DPT: Diphtheria, Pertussis (Whooping cough) and tetanus.

EPI: Expanded Programme on Immunisation.

Net Primary School Attendance: Per centage of children in the age group that officially corresponds to primary schooling who attend primary school.

Life Expecting at Birth: Average life span of an individual.

Crude Death Rate: Annual number of deaths per 1,000 population.

Crude Dirth Rate: Annual number of births for 1,000 population.

ORS use: Per centage of all cases of diarrhoea in children under 5 years of age treated with oral dehydration salt or home fluids.

Primary School Entrants Reaching Grade 5: Percentage of the children entering the first grade of primary school who eventually reach grade 5.

Per cent of Population Below $ 1 a Day: Percentage of population living on less than $ 1 a day.

Contraceptive Prevalence: Percentage of married women aged 15-49 years using contraceptives.

Total Fertility Rate: The number of children born per woman.

Births Attended: Percentage of births attended by midwives, nurse physicians or primary health workers trained in midwifery skills.

Maternal Mortality Rates: Annual number of deaths of women from pregnancy related cases per 1,00,000 birth.

26.2 WORLD POPULATION MILESTONES (1804 TO 2150) AND WORLD POPULATION BY REGION AT A GLANCE

Box 26.1 indicates the milestones in increase in world population

Box 26.1 World Population Milestones

World population reached :		
1 billion in	1804	
2 billion in	1927	(123 years later)
3 billion in	1960	(33 years later)
4 billion in	1974	(14 years later)
5 billion in	1987	(13 years later)
6 billion in	2000	(13 years later)
World population may reach:		
7.8 billion in	2025	(25 years later)
8.9 billion in	2050	(25 years later)
9.3 billion in	2075	(25 years later)
9.4 billion in	2100	(25 years later)
9.6 billion in	2125	(25 years later)
9.74 billion in	2150	(25 years later)

Source: Population Division, United Nations.

Fig 26.1 and 26.2 show world population by region in 2001.

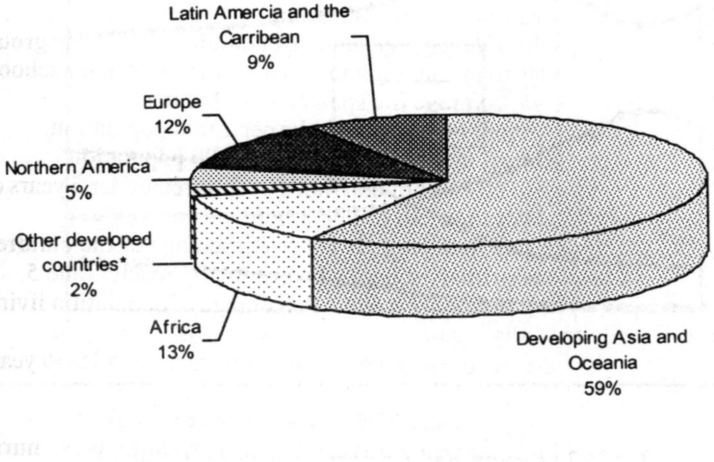

Fig. 26.1 : *World Population by Region, 2001*

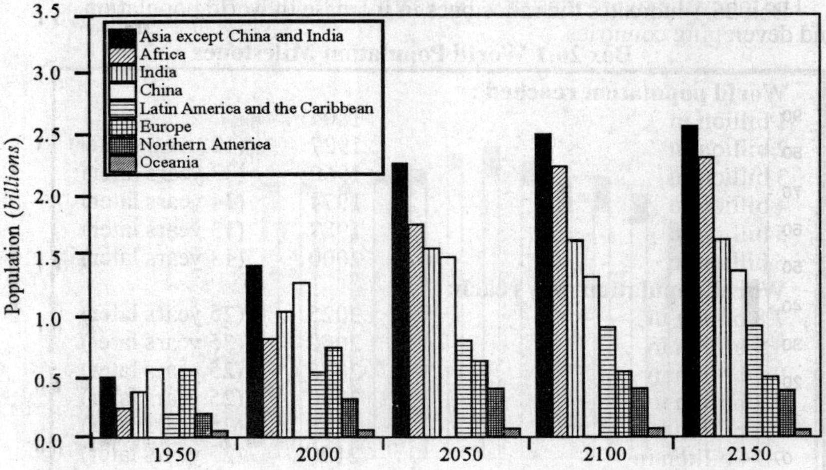

Fig 26.2 : *Population Size of Major World Areas, Medium Scenario,* 1950-2150

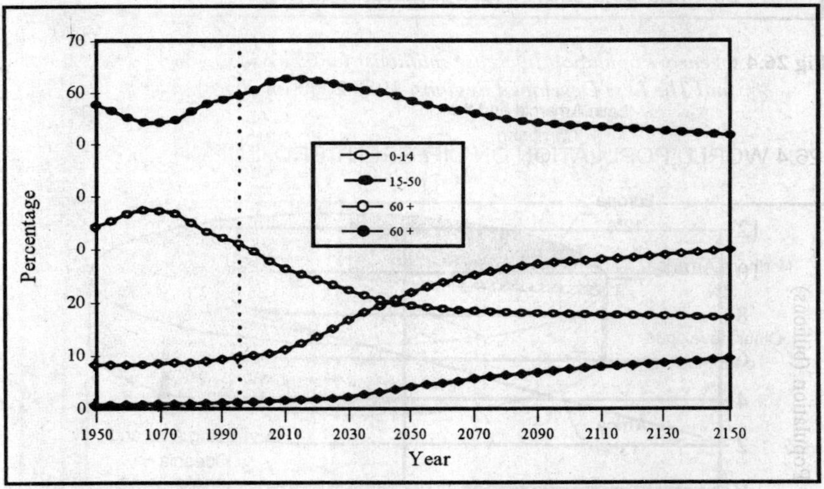

Fig 26.3 : *Percent of World Population by Age Group,*
Medium Scenario (1950-2150)

26.3 YEARLY POPULATION INCREASE IN DEVELOPED AND DEVELOPING REGIONS (1950-2050)

The following figure illustrates the yearly population increase in developed and developing countries.

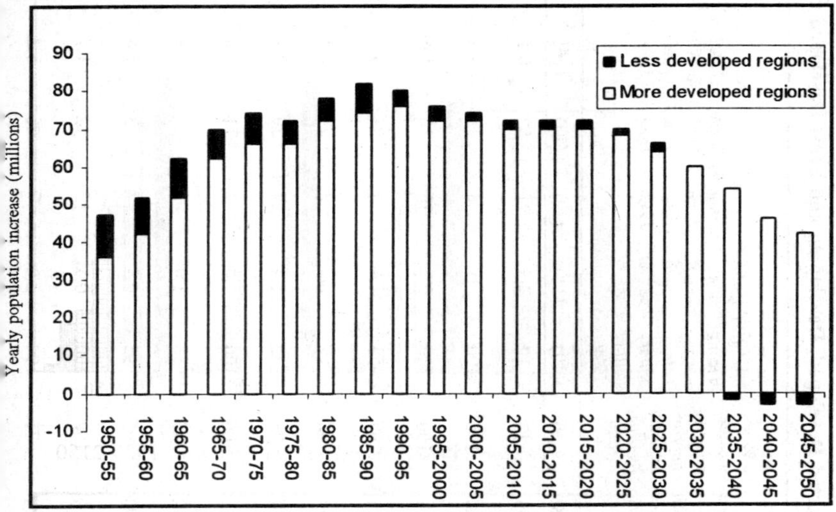

Fig 26.4 : *Yearly Population Iincrease (millions) for The More Developed Regions and The Less Developed Regions,* 1950-2050 *(medium variant)*

26.4 WORLD POPULATION ON DIFFERENT PROJECTION (1950-2050)

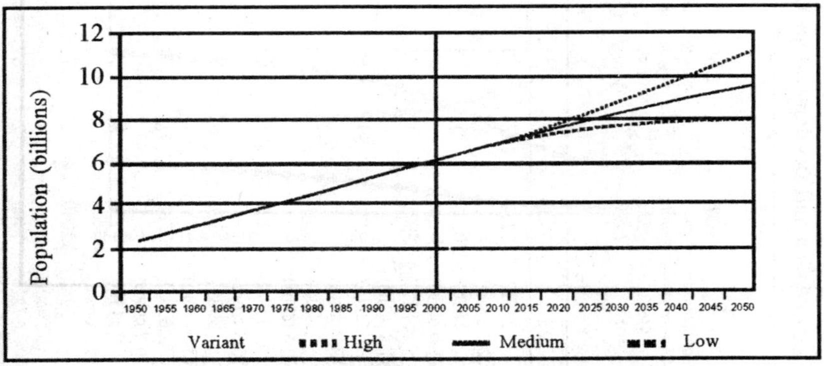

Fig. 26.5 : *World Population (billions) 1950-2050*

Table 26.1 : Population and Development on 12 Indicators : Selected Developed, Developing and Least Developed Countries

Country	*Population (thousand) 1999*	*GNP per capita (US $ 1999)*	*Under 5 mortaliy rate 1999*	*Life expect-ecy at birth (years)*	*Total Adult literacy rate 1995-99*	*% of primary school entrants reachin grade 5 1995-99*	*Access to health serives 1995*	*% of populati on using improv-ed water facilities 1999*	*% of populati on using adequ-ate sanitary facilities 1999*	*Populat-ion annual growth rate (%) 1990-99*	*Crude death rate 1999*	*Crude birth rate 1999*	*Total fertility rate 1999*	*Maternal mortality ratio (1990-2000)*
(1)	(2)	(3)	(4)	(5)	(6)	(7)	(8)	(9)	(10)	(11)	(12)	(13)	(14)	(15)
Afghanistan	21923 (2.2 crore)	250	257	46	32	49	99	13	12	4.4	21	52	6.7	--
Australia	18705 (1.9 crore)	20050	5	78	99	99	NA	100	100	101	8	13	1.8	--
Austria	8177 (81.8 lakhs)	25970	5	77	99	99	NA	100	100	0.7	10	10	1.4	--
Bangladesh	126947 (12.7 crore)	370	89	59	56	70	45	97	53	1.6	9	28	3.0	480
Bhutan	2064 (20.6 lakhs)	510	175	62	42	64	65	62	69	2.2	9	37	5.3	380
Brazil	167988 (16.8 crore)	4420	115	67	85	71	NA	83	72	1.4	7	20	2.2	180
Canada	30857 (3.0 crore)	19320	6	79	99	99	NA	100	100	1.2	7	11	1.6	--
China	1266838 (126.7 crore)	780	41	70	84	91	92	75	38	1.0	7	16	1.8	58
Cuba	11160 (1.1 crore)	1170	8	76	96	96	98	95	95	0.5	7	13	1.6	27
Denmark	5282 (52 lakh)	32030	5	76	99	100	NA	100	100	0.3	12	12	1.7	10
Egypt	67226 (6.7 crore)	1400	52	67	56	92	NA	71	94	2.0	7	26	3.2	120

(1)	(2)	(3)	(4)	(5)	(6)	(7)	(8)	(9)	(10)	(11)	(12)	(13)	(15)	(17)
Fiji	806 (8 lakh)	2210	22	73	91	92	NA	47	43	1.2	5	22	2.8	38
Finland	5165 (51.6 lakh)	23780	5	77	99	99	NA	100	100	0.4	10	11	1.7	6
France	58886 (5.9 crore)	23480	5	78	99	99	NA	100	100	0.4	9	12	1.7	10
Germany	82178 (8.2 crore)	25350	5	77	99	99	NA	100	100	0.4	11	9	1.3	8
India	998056 (99.8 crore)	450	98	63	58	52	85	88	31	1.8	9	25	3.0	410
Indonesia	209295 (20.9 crore)	580	216	66	88	85	80	76	66	1.5	7	22	2.5	450
Japan	126505 (12.7 crore)	32230	4	80	99	99	NA	NA	NA	0.3	8	10	1.4	8
Maldives	278 (2.8 lakh)	1160	83	65	99	98	NA	100	100	28	7	35	5.2	350
Myanmar	45059 (4.5 crore)	220	112	61	83	45	60	68	46	1.2	9	21	2.3	230
Nepal	23385 (2.34 crore)	220	104	58	45	44	NA	81	27	2.4	10	42	4.3	540
Pakistan	152331 (15.2 crore)	470	112	65	45	50	55	88	61	2.7	7	35	4.8	NA
Russia Federation	147196 (14.7 crore)	2270	22	67	99	99	NA	99	NA	–01	14	10	1.4	50
Sri Lakna	186339 (1.9 crore)	820	19	74	90	97	93	83	83	1.0	6	18	2.1	60
South Africa	39900 (4 crore)	3160	69	52	67	65	NA	86	86	1.8	14	35	3.1	NA
Sweden	8892 (89 lakh)	25040	4	79	99	99	NA	100	100	0.4	11	10	1.6	5
Switzerland	7344 (73 lakh)	38350	4	79	99	99	NA	100	100	0.8	9	11	1.5	5
United Kingdom	58744 (5.9 crore)	22640	6	78	99	98	NA	100	100	0.2	11	12	1.7	7
United States	276218 (27.6 crore)	30600	8	77	99	95	NA	100	100	1.0	8	14	2.0	8

26.5 WORLD POPULATION BY MAJOR AREA (INCLUDING INDIA) MEDIUM SCENARIO (1995-2050)

Table 26.2 indicates the population projections of the regions for the period (1995 to 2050)

Table 26.2 World Population By Major Area, Medium Scenario, (1995-2050)

Year	*Total*	*Africa*	*Europe*	*Latin America and the Caribbean*	*Northern America*	*Oceania*	*Asia excl. China & India*	*China*	*India*
				Population (millions)					
1995	5666	697	728	480	297	28	1282	1221	934
2000	6055	784	729	519	310	30	1391	1278	1014
2025	7824	1298	702	697	364	40	1912	1480	1330
2050	8909	1766	628	809	392	46	2262	1478	1529
2075	9319	2077	549	857	390	48	2423	1386	1589
2100	9459	2215	515	877	388	49	2476	1340	1600
2125	9573	2264	508	894	390	50	2512	1338	1617
2150	9746	2308	517	912	398	51	2558	1361	1642
				Percentage					
1995	100	12	13	8	5	1	23	22	16
2000	100	12	13	8	5	1	23	22	16
2025	100	13	12	9	5	1	23	21	17
2050	100	17	9	9	5	1	24	19	17
2075	100	20	7	9	4	1	25	17	17
2100	100	22	6	9	4	1	26	15	17
2125	100	23	5	9	4	1	26	14	17
2150	100	24	5	9	4	1	26	14	17

Source: Population Division of the Department of Economic and Social Affairs of the United Nations Secretariat, "Long-range world population projections: based on the 1998 revision" (ESA/P/WP 153), 1999.

26.6 WORLD POPULATION : DEVELOPED AND DEVELOPING COUNTRIES (MID 2000) AND COUNTRIES WITH MORE THAN 100 MILLION INHABITANTS IN 1950, 2000 AND 2050.

Table 26.3 : World Population

Sl.No.	*Country or Area*	*Population*
1.	World Total 2011	703.5 crore
2.	Developed Region 2000	119.1 crore
3.	Developing or less developed regions 2000	486.6 crore
4.	Least developed are included at 3 above	65.8 crore

Table 26.4 : Countries with More Than 100 Million Inhabitants in 1950, 2000 and 2050 (Population in Millions)

1950			2000			2050		
Rank	*Country*	*Population*	*Rank*	*Country*	*Population*	*Rank*	*Country*	*Population*
1.	China	555	1.	China	1275	1.	India	1572
2.	India	358	2.	India	1009	2.	China	1462
3.	United States of America	158	3.	United States of America	283	3.	United States of America	397
4.	Russian Federation	103	4.	Indonesia	212	4.	Pakistan	344
			5.	Brazil	170	5.	Indonesia	311
			6.	Russian Federation	145	6.	Nigeria	279
			7.	Pakistan	141	7.	Bangladesh	265
			8.	Bangladesh	137	8.	Brazil	247
			9.	Japan	127	9.	Dem. Rep. of Congo	204
			10.	Nigeria	114	10.	Ethiopia	186
						11.	Mexico	147
						12.	Philippines	128
						13.	Viet Nam	124
						14.	Iran (Islamic Republic of)	121
						15.	Egypt	114
						16.	Japan	109
						17.	Russian Federation	104
						18.	Yemen	102
						19.	Uganda	102

27

Evaluation in Population Education

27.1 MEANING OF EVALUATION

The word 'evaluation' is now being increasingly used in current educational literature in place of the word 'examination'. In a simple language, evaluation may be described as a process by means of which changes in the behaviour of students are studied and guided towards the attainment of pre-determined objectives.

Evaluation relates to all aspects of education.

In population education like any other area of education, evaluation is concerned with knowledge, attitudes and skills.

27.2 METHODS OF EVALUATION IN POPULATION EDUCATION

Important methods of valuation education are:

(i) Essay Type Tests
(ii) Short Answer Type Questions
(iii) Objective Type Questions
(iv) Interview or Viva Voce

27.3 QUESTION BANK : SHORT ANSWER TYPE QUESTIONS WITH ANSWERS

Q. 1. Name the factors which affect the distribution of population in the world.

Ans. Following factors affect the distribution of population in the world:

(i) Physical features
(ii) Climate of the region
(iii) Cultural factors
(iv) Political factors
(v) Emigration and immigration
(vi) Fertility of soil
(vii) Availability of water

Q. 2. What is the reason for uneven distribution of population in the world?

Ans. The pattern of distribution of population is the result of growth and spread of population in the past.

Q. 3. Where does the 90 per cent of the world population live?

Ans. North Hemisphere.

Q. 4. State the three major regions on the basis of density of population

Ans. (a) *Sparsely populated areas* : Australia, Canada, North America, South America, New Zealand etc.

(b) *Moderately populated areas*: Central and Southern Europe, coastly low land regions in mid-latitudes of South America and South Africa.

(c) Densely populated regions: Eastern and Southern Asia, North-West Europe and U.S.A.

Q. 5. Why are some regions thinly populated?

Ans.
(i) Newly discovered lands.
(ii) Unfavourable climate.
(iii) Less increase in population

Q. 6. Why are some regions thickly populated?

Ans.
(i) Higher birth rate than growth rate
(ii) More dependence on agriculture.

Q. 7. What is the impact of population distribution on environment?

Ans. The impact on environment is adverse in regions where the population density is higher.

Q. 8. How does level of technological development affect the environment?

Ans. Environmental disturbances are much sharper in technically developed societies than in developing economies.

(Population levels are much higher in industrial towns than in rural areas)

Q. 9. Which hemisphere of the earth has more population?

Ans. About 90 % of earth's population is concentrated in the Northern hemisphere.

Q. 10. Name five countries with population exceeding 100 million

Ans. China, India Bangladesh, United States of America, Indonesia.

Q. 11. List the regions of high population density

Ans.
(i) South-East Asian countries including India, Pakistan and Bangladesh
(ii) East Asian countries including China and Japan.
(iii) North-west Europe including Britain, France, Germany and Netherlands.
(iv) North-eastern parts of United States of America.

Q. 12. Explain how population density, birth rate, and death rate are calculated?

Ans. Population Density : $\dfrac{\text{Total population}}{\text{Area in sq.km}}$

Birth Rate : $\dfrac{\text{Number of live births} \times 1000}{\text{Total Population}}$

Death Rate : $\dfrac{\text{Number of deaths} \times 1000}{\text{Total Population}}$

Growth Rate : $\frac{\text{Birth rate} - \text{Death rate}}{10}$

(While birth and death rates are expressed/1000, growth rate is expressed in %)

Q. 13. Why is northern hemisphere more populated than southern hemisphere?

Ans. (i) Two-thirds land of the world is in northern hemisphere and one-third in southern hemisphere

(ii) There is additional evidence of ancient civilization in the northern hemisphere

Q. 14. Which are the two most populous countries of the world. Give their population in the year 2001.

Ans. 1. China – 1,284 million

2. India – 1027 million

Q. 15. What was the total population of the world in 2001? State its annual growth rate?

Ans. (1) 6.1 million (2) 1.2 per cent.

Q. 16. State the distribution of world population according to major regions?

Ans. (i) Asia 61 per cent (ii) Africa 13 per cent (iii) Latin America and the Caribbean 9 per cent (iv) Northern America 5 per cent (v) Europe 12 per cent.

Q. 17. According to United Nations' Projections medium fertility rate when is India expected to have the largest population in the world? What will be its population at that time?

Ans. (i) Year 2050 (ii) Population 1.53 billion as compared with china's 1.48 billion.

Q. 18. What was the total population of India according to 1991 Census? Also state the population of India in March 2001.

Ans. (i) 846 million (ii) 1027 million.

Q. 19. What is the approximate average annual increase in population in India?

Ans. 180 lakhs.

Q. 20. What is meant by the rate of population growth? What is the rate of population growth in India?

Ans. (i) The difference between the birth rate and the death rate is called the population growth rate.

(ii) According to 1991 Census, birth rate in India was 29.5 per thousand and death rate 9.8 per thousand. So, the growth rate was 29.5-9.8 = 19.7 per thousand or 1.97 per hundred.

In 1998, India's birth rate was 23 per cent and death rate 7 per cent. so the growth rate was 23-7=16 per cent. This means that there has been some check on population growth in India in recent years.

Q. 21. What is the meaning of infant mortality rate? what is its relation with the overall progress of a nation? Give two examples in this regard.

Ans. Infant mortality rate implies the rate of death of children between birth and one year of age expressed per 1,000 births. In India infant mortality rate was 69 in 1998 as compared with 144 I 1960. The comparative figures for Norway were 4 and 19. For Japan these were 4 and 31. In other words, the lower the infant mortality rate, the more developed and advanced a country is.

Q. 22. What percentage of world land area does India occupy? What percentage of world's population does India have?

Ans. (i) 2.4% of the world land area (ii) 16.7%

Q. 23. Distinguish between birth rate and growth rate

Ans. Birth rate is the number of people born in a region or country during the certain period of time, usually considered one year or one decade. It is measured in terms of per thousand people.

Growth rate is the rate at which the population of a region or country increases during the certain period of time. It is the difference between the birth rate and death rate. It is also called the natural growth rate.

Q. 24. Explain two reasons why rural population is migrating to urban areas?

Ans.
1. Increasing unemployment in rural areas and more changes of employment in urban areas.
2. Availability of better basic amenities of daily life in urban areas.

Q. 25. Compare the population growth of developed with that of developing countries.

Ans. Roughly one-fifth of the world population currently lives in the more developed regions and countries including Australia/,New Zealand. Europe, Japan and North America. The remaining 80 per cent life in the developing countries of Africa (13 %), Asia and Oceania (58 %) and Latin America and the Caribbean (9 %).

Q. 26. Explain the term emigration and immigration

Ans. Emigration implies that population which goes out of country and immigration that comes into a country.

Q. 27. What is the technical term for the following?

The average number of inhabitants living within a specified unit of area, such as square kilometre.

Ans. Density of population.

Q. 28. Why are central and southern Europe moderately populated?

Ans. These regions mostly have agricultural and pastoral occupations.

Q. 29. List four types of regions where population density is low.

Ans.
(i) Extremely cold polar regions.
(ii) High mountain plateaus
(iii) Rain forest regions
(iv) Tropical deserts

Q. 30. Why is population density low in areas where grazing animals remains the major occupation?

Ans. Large areas are required for grazing cattle.

Q. 31. River valleys and deltas are associated with high population density.

Ans. High yields of food grains in these regions enable more people to live over smaller areas.

Q. 32. Why has Australia a low population density?

Ans. It has been recently populated by people who migrated from Europe and other countries.

Q. 33. Why was population growth nearly balanced during early periods of human history?

Ans. Scarcity of food and a number of epidemics and diseases led to a high death rate. This balanced the birth rate.

Q. 34. Population growth was slow even after man learned to grow food grains. Why?

Ans. Even with a high birth rate, the population growth was slow as people had new lands to migrate. The death rate was moderated leading to only a slow increase in human population.

Q. 35. How do birth and death rates affect population growth?

Ans. Population grows when the birth rate exceeds the death rate.

Q. 36. Differentiate between migration and immigration

Ans. Migration refers to people going from one country to another. Immigration on the other hand refers to migration of persons into a country from other countries.

Q. 37. What is annual growth rate?

Ans. Expressed in percentage, it indicates the excess of birth over death.
(Ex : Birth rate 35 per 1,000
Death rate 15 per 1,000
Growth rate = 35–15/10 = 2 %)

Q. 38. List four countries of population growth below 1 %

Ans. Japan, Australia, New Zealand, Russia.

27.4 OBJECTIVE TYPE TEST ITEMS

1. The country with a larger population than that of India is
   (a) Indonesia
   (b) China
   (c) Russian Federation
   (d) United States of America
2. For the past several years the population of India has been
   (a) exploding
   (b) almost constant
   (c) fluctuating
   (d) declining
3. In the nineteenth century population of India did not rise appreciably because
   (a) many people settled in other countries
   (b) many people used to die of hunger, disease and epidemics
   (c) there were no industries to provide goods for all
   (d) there were fewer births than what they are today
4. The availability of food per head in our country has not improved during the recent past because
   (a) our agricultural production has not increased substantially
   (b) our population has increased at a faster rate than that of food production.
   (c) we have been exporting several food items to other countries.
   (d) we are laying far more stress on increasing industrial production.

5. The average size of the family in India should not have more than
   (a) three children
   (b) two children
   (c) only one child
   (d) four children
6. India is considered as a densely populated country because
   (a) its population is very large for the area it possesses
   (b) its population is the second largest in the world
   (c) it is a very big country in area
   (d) it has more than half a million villages
7. The huge population of India implies
   (a) a little less work for each one of us
   (b) a matter of pride for us all
   (c) a need for hard work on the part of all
   (d) a very bleak future for us all
8. The popukation of India has been growing very rapidly since 1921 because
   (a) both the birth rate and death rate has been falling
   (b) the birth rate has been rising since then
   (c) both the birth rate and the death rate have been rising
   (d) the birth rate has been almost steady whereas the death rate has been falling appreciably
9. The best way to slow down the growth rate of our population is
   (a) to bring down the birth rate of population in our country
   (b) to encourage people to migrate to other countries
   (c) to redistribute our population more evenly
   (d) to reverse the current trend of bringing down the death rate
10. The national income of India since Independence has been
    (a) stagnant
    (b) rising steadily
    (c) not rising steadily
    (d) fluctuating
11. The food production in India which was about 55 million tonnes at the time of Independence,
    (a) almost the same
    (b) even less than what it has then
    (c) almost four times
    (d) 80 million tonnes
12. At the time of Independence there were 15 per cent literate people in our country; today
    (a) the percentage of literate persons has increased four times
    (b) the percentage of the literates has gone down
    (c) the percentage of the literates has remained almost the same
    (d) there is cent per cent literacy
13. Countries like Japan have been able to raise their standard of living because
    (a) they have a very sparse population
    (b) they have been able to achieve zero growth rate of population

(c) they have abundant natural resources
(d) primarily they have been able to improve the quality of their labour force.

14. The statement given below is followed by four alternatives. Only one is incorrect. Tick off the incorrect alternative. the average span of life in the past was relatively very short because
    (a) there were large number of deaths before the children could complete one year
    (b) there were too many cases of suicides and murders
    (c) many people continued to suffer from under nutrition
    (d) there were deaths on a mass scale due to epidemics and famines
15. Given below are four statements. Only one is correct. Tick mark the correct statement.
    (a) both national income and per capita income are rising at the same rate
    (b) both per capita income and national income are falling at the same rate
    (c) per capita income is rising at a higher rate than the national income
    (d) national income is rising at a higher rate than the per capita income
16. We have a large number of illiterates than what we had at the time of independence because
    (a) rapid increase in population has overtaken the growth in literacy
    (b) there are not sufficient schools for our children
    (c) people are not convinced of the utility of education
    (d) there is a shortage of paper for books, etc.
17. Given below are a few statements about Japan indicating it to be a developed country. One of these statement is incorrect. Tick mark the incorrect statement.
    (a) average life expectancy in Japan is not very high
    (b) Japan has a large population
    (c) Japan has almost cent per cent literacy
    (d) per capita income in Japan is very high
18. Given below are a few statements about the role of a mother in a small family. One of these is incorrect. Tick mark the incorrect one. When size of the family is small, the mother is in a position to
    (a) improve her qualification and abilities
    (b) contribute economically to the well being of the family
    (c) take care of children more effectively
    (d) be indifferent to her family responsibilities
19. Unemployment in India has been increasing because
    (a) growing population makes it rather difficult to save and invest in new ventures which create jobs
    (b) there are no more natural resources which can be developed
    (c) machines stand in the way of creating new jobs.
    (d) there is no demand for Indian products

20. The primary source of our food is
(a) plants
(b) animals
(c) poultry
(d) fish

21. The only renewable source of energy is
(a) coal
(b) uranium
(c) petroleum
(d) water

22. Man is the most dominant species because
(a) he is very strong
(b) he can think
(c) he can hear and see
(d) he can run fast

23. Tick mark the only incorrect statement for the following
(a) Forests help us in conserving water
(b) Forests help us in conserving soil
(c) Forests help us in preserving wild life
(d) Forests rob us of the fertile land suitable for agriculture

24. Man is essentially
(a) a producer of food
(b) a distributor of food
(c) a consumer of food
(d) a decomposer of food

25. The real manufacturers of food are
(a) farmers
(b) owners of food processing industries
(c) animals
(d) plants

26. Given below are four statements one of which only one is insignificant. Tick off one which is insignificant
In highly industrialised countries the major source of pollution is
(a) smoke and waste materials of big factories
(b) widespread use of insecticides and pesticides
(c) food adulteration
(d) noise created by aeroplanes

27. Our relationship with nature should be based on
(a) submission to nature
(b) conquering nature
(c) harmony with nature
(d) fear and awe for nature

28. A good diet is one which is
(a) adequate in quantity
(b) balanced
(c) costly
(d) tasty

29. A good shelter is one which is
(a) very big and multi-storeyed
(b) made of cement concrete, iron, glass etc.
(c) clean, airy and well lit
(d) located in the heart of the town or city

30. Happiness in the family largely depends upon several factors. Tick off from the list the one that is incorrect
(a) good health of the mother
(b) parents' ability to pay attention to all members
(c) wealth amassed by the family
(d) meeting the needs and requirement of all the members

31. The families with equal income but unequal in size differ remarkably in many ways. In what regard they are likely to differ the least?
(a) their ability to save
(b) their ability to educate all their children
(c) their ability to cater to the health and medical requirements of all
(d) their ability to feed all members

32. If there are four children each in two families consecutively for three generations the total number of families at the end of three generations would be
(a) two
(b) four
(c) six
(d) eight

33. In the above case the total population at the end of three generations would be:
(a) twelve
(b) forty eight
(c) twenty four
(d) thirty six

34. Today, a big family is an indication of
(a) social irresponsibility
(b) God's grace or kindness
(c) good health of parents
(d) prosperity and high status enjoyed by parents.

ANSWERS

1. (b)	**2.** (a)	**3.** (b)	**4.** (b)	**5.** (b)	**6.** (b)
7. (b)	**8.** (d)	**9.** (c)	**10.** (c)	**11.** (c)	**12.** (a)
13. (d)	**14.** (b)	**15.** (d)	**16.** (a)	**17.** (a)	**18.** (d)
19. (a)	**20.** (a)	**21.** (d)	**22.** (a)	**23.** (d)	**24.** (c)
25. (d)	**26.** (c)	**27.** (c)	**28.** (b)	**29.** (c)	**30.** (c)
31. (d)	**32.** (d)	**33.** (b).	**34.** (a).		

28

Population Dynamics: Distribution and Density

28.1 MEANING OF POPULATION DYNAMICS

Population dynamics implies pattern of change of population or pattern of growth of population.

28.2 SCOPE OF POPULATION DYNAMICS

Scope of population dynamics is very wide. Generally speaking it includes the following dimensions of population.

1. Population composition—Age, Sex, Rural/Urban.
2. Factors Affecting Population Growth—Fertility, Mortality and Migration (Mobility)

The study of population dynamics may relate to one or more of these aspects or attributes or characteristics.

Population dynamics is usually equated with population structure and its characteristics.

28.3 SIGNIFICANCE OF UNDERSTANDING POPULATION DYNAMICS

As a result of analysis of population dynamics of a country, we may ask some pertinent questions like the following and take appropriate action in the light of analysis.

1. What is the proportion distribution of males and females in a region or in the country?
2. How are children, young adults and aged/elderly people distributed in a population?
3. What percentage of children of different age groups is literate?
4. What is the state of adult literacy?
5. What is the percentage of literacy among different sexes? What is the state of women?
6. What is the percentage of literacy in the rural and urban areas?
7. What is the impact of urbanisation?
8. What are the problems of the rural population?
9. What is the incidence of fertility, mortality and migration?
10. Why do people migrate?

28.4 OBJECTIVES OF POPULATION RELATING TO POPULATION DYNAMICS

These include as under:

1. To enable the students to understand that the population becomes stable when there is little difference between the birth rate and the death rate.
2. To create an awareness among the students that the present population explosion in developing countries, especially India, is on account of the comparatively steady birth rate as against rapidly falling death rate over the past few decades.
3. To impress the students that the use of science and technology has helped us in bringing down the death rate, and that the same can help us in bringing down the birth rate as well.
4. To develop among students a healthy, rational and scientific attitude towards the natural phenomena of births and deaths.
5. To assist the students realise the socio-economic burden involved in bringing up large families usually resulting in deterioration in quality of living.
6. To develop among the students a realisation that the natural growth in population is due to the difference between the number of births and deaths taking place in a given period over a specified area.
7. To help the students develop an idea that populations by their nature are dynamic and never static.

Source: *'Population: A Draft Syllabus'*, NCERT, 1971)

28.5 SOURCES OF DATA ON POPULATION DYNAMICS

Important sources on population are:

1. Census.
2. Registration of records of vital statistics on birth and deaths etc. of local panchayats and local self government offices—Registrar General of India.
3. National Sample Surveys.
4. The National Family Health Survey (NFHS), Ministry of Health and Welfare, New Delhi.
5. UN and its agencies like UNICEF and W.H.O. etc.

28.6 CENSUS AS THE MAIN SOURCE OF OBTAINING DATA ON POPULATION DYNAMICS

Census is the most importance source of obtaining data on population dynamics. India is one of the few countries in the world where regular decennial census has been conducted since 1881, the process having remained uninterrupted even during 1941 when the Second World War was in progress. The 2001 census was the 14th in the series as reckoned from 1872 and 13th as reckoned from 1881.

Census in India is conducted every ten years.

Significances and Utility of the Census

Some of the areas where census data have to be frequently referred to may be identified as follows:

1. *Vital Demographic*: Census data can be very helpful in projecting the future size and demographic character of the population in any given region. Birth and death and rates identify areas for accelerating provision of medical facilities and family planning programmes.
2. *Planning*: Economic and Social Planning is now a universally practised phenomenon, irrespective of political culture of the country or the state. Census data provide a huge wealth of statistical date for the Planning Commission and a number of other agencies functioning at the state and district levels.
3. *Agriculture, Business and Industry*: Census data provide information about availability of labour and their employment status which can be a very rational basis of starting new industries. Similarly reliable estimates of consumer demands can be worked out from census data to the advantage of industry.
4. *Housing Plans*: These have to be related to the needs of the people as reflected through the census. Areas where housing facilities are most neglected get identified and come to focus for the attention of the government and private agencies involved in nation's housing programmes.
5. *Administration*: A number of administration decisions, e.g., delimitation of constituencies, identification of recognised categories of Scheduled Castes and Tribes, have to be based on census data.
6. *Electoral Rolls*: Census data provide valuable base for preparing and updating of electoral rolls.
7. *Research*: Research workers depend on census data for a variety of studies. Often that is the only reliable source since individual scholars cannot afford surveys on such a mass scale.

28.7 DISTRIBUTION OF POPULATION

In Chapter 4, we have given the population of India as a whole and of States during 1991 and 2001. Table 28.1 in this chapter provides the population of States from 1951 to 2001. For the year 2001, three new States formed in 2000 are not included separately. They are included in Bihar, Madhya Pradesh and Uttar Pradesh. Tables in Chapter 4 provide data for all the 35 States and Union Territories for the years 1991 and 2011.

Table 28.1: Population of India: 1951-2011

(*in thousand*)

S. No.	States/Union	1961	1971	1981	1991	2001	2011
1.	Uttar Pradesh	73755	88341.52	110862.5	139112.3	166053	199581
2.	Maharashtra	39554	50412.24	62782.82	78937.19	96752	112372
3.	Bihar	46447	56353.37	69914.73	86374.47	82879	103804
4.	West Bengal	34926	44312.01	54580.65	68077.97	80221	91347
5.	Andhra Pradesh	35983	43502.71	53551.03	66508.01	75728	84665
6.	Tamil Nadu	33687	41199.17	48408.08	55859	62111	72138
7.	Madhya Pradesh	32372	41654.12	52178.84	66181.17	60385	72597
8.	Rajasthan	20156	25765.81	34361.86	44005.99	56473	68621
9.	Karnataka	23587	29299.01	37135.71	44977.2	52734	61130
10.	Gujarat	20633	26697.48	34085.8	41309.58	50597	60383
11.	Orissa	17549	21944.62	26370.27	31659.74	36707	41947
12.	Kerala	16904	21347.38	25453.68	29098.52	31839	33387
13.	Assam (2)	10837	14625.15	18041.25	22414.32	26638	31169
14.	Punjab	11135	13551.06	16788.92	20281.97	24289	27704
15.	Haryana	7591	10036.43	12922.12	16464	21083	25353
16.	Delhi	2659	4065.698	6220.406	9420.644	13783	16753
17.	J & K (3)	3561	4616.632	5987.389	7718.7	10070	12548
18.	Himachal Pradesh	2812	3460.434	4280.818	5170.877	6077	6856
19.	Tripura	1142	1556.342	2053.058	2757.205	3191	3671
20.	Manipur	780	1072.753	1420.953	1837.149	2389	2721
21.	Meghalaya	769	1011.699	1335.819	1774.778	2306	2964
22.	Nagaland	369	516.449	774.93	1209.546	1989	1980
23.	Goa	590	857.771	1086.73	1169.793	1344	1457
24.	Arunachal Pradesh (1)	337	467.511	631.839	864.558	1091	1382
25.	Pondicherry	369	471.707	604.471	807.785	974	1244
26.	Chandigarh	120	257.251	451.61	642.015	901	1054
27.	Mizoram	266	332.39	493.757	689.756	891	1091
28.	Sikkim	162	209.843	316.385	406.457	540	607
29.	A & N Islands	64	115.133	188.741	280.661	356	379
30.	D & N Haveli	58	74.14	103.676	138.477	220	342
31.	Daman & Diu	37	63	79	101	158	242
32.	Lakshadweep	24	31.81	40.249	51.707	61	64
	All India	**439235**	**548160**	**684329**	**846302**	**10270155**	**1210193**

Notes:

1. Censuses for the first time in 1961.
2. The 1981 Census could not be held in Assam. Total population for 1981 has been worked out by interpolation.
3. The 1991 Census could not be held in Jammu & Kashmir. Total population for Jammu & Kashmir as projected by Standing Committee of Experts on Population Projection. (Oct. 1989).

Source: Office of the Registrar General of India, Ministry of Home Affairs.

28.8 ANALYSIS AND OBSERVATIONS ON DISTRIBUTION OF POPULATION: INDEX OF POPULATION CONCENTRATION

The index of population concentration is 16.17 per cent in UP—the highest. For Lakshadeep it is 0.01—the lowest.

After U.P. comes Bihar with 8.07 per cent followed by Maharashtra 9.42 and Bihar 8.07 in 2001.

Amongst the lowest after Lakshadeep are: Nagaland 0.09 per cent, Meghalaya 0.22, Manipur 0.23.

Note: For details on 35 States including the 3 new States formed in 2002, see Table 4.4, 4.5, 4.6, 4.7 (pages 28 to 31) and Table 4.11 (page 35).

28.9 DENSITY OF POPULATION AND RANKING OF STATES

The density of population is considered as one of the important indices of population concentration. It is defined as the number of persons per square kilometer. The population density of India in 2011 was 382 persons per square kilometer, which implies that now 58 more people live in a square kilometer area in the country than the number that lived a decade ago.

The population density of India from 1901 to 2011 is shown in Table 4.13. At the beginning of the twentieth century, i.e., in 1901 the density of India was as low as 77 and this steadily increased from one decade to another to reach 382 in 2011. The percentage of persons living per sq km also increased by 21.3 per cent in 2001 as compared to 1991.

High increased in density of population puts immense pressure on the natural resources and as such it has become a matter of great concern. It also has an adverse affect on the quality of life of the people.

Among the States, West Bengal is the most thickly populated state. Here density has gone up from 767 in 1991 to 904 to 2001.

In 1991, Kerala was the second highest densely populated State but in 2001, it was pushed back to the third position and Bihar became the second highest densely populated State. Bihar's density which was 685 in 1991 rose to 880 in 2001. (Excluding Union Territories).

(See Table 4.11 for details regarding density of States)

28.10 VARIATIONS IN THE DENSITY OF POPULATION

With an average density of 382 persons per sq km, India is considered to be one of the high densely populated countries of the world.

Density of population has been increasing since 1921.

Table 28.2: Density of Population (Density per sq. km.)

Year	*Density (1901-2011)*
1901	77
1911	82
1921	81
1931	90
1941	103
1951	117
1961	142
1971	177
1981	216
1991	267
2001	324
2011	382

State Level Patterns. Significant variations in population density are observed between the States of India.

Area of High Density. The density of population varies in direct proportion to the productivity of land. The areas having fertile alluvial soil including the great plains and the Eastern and Western coastal plains have the highest densities in the country. These plains contain more than 38 percent of the country's population, although the region occupies only about 19 percent of the country's area. The reasons for higher densities are:

(i) Rich fertile alluvial soil.
(ii) A large number of perennial rivers which supply water for the irrigation.
(iii) Availability of large quantity of food grains, pulses, oilseeds, cotton, jute and sugarcane.
(iv) Easy development of means of transport and communication.

According to 2001 census West Bengal is the most densely populated State of the country, i.e., 904 persons per sq. km. The high density is attributed to sound industrial base, jute cultivation and industries and two ports of international importance namely Kolkata and Haldia. Other states having high densities are:

(2) Bihar	880 persons per sq. km
(3) Kerala	819 persons per sq. km
(4) Uttar Pradesh	689 persons per sq. km
(5) Punjab	482 persons per sq. km
(6) Haryana	477 persons per sq. km

Areas of Moderate Density. With few exceptions, the peninsular plateaus bound by the Aravalli and Sahayadri ranges in the West, Eastern Ghats in the east, North of Kerala and Tamil Nadu, all districts of Andhra Pradesh and Maharashtra have a medium population density. Most of the settlements in this region are concentrated in broad river valleys and low flat-topped plateaus where dry farming is practised by the population. Following states have medium density:

(1) Assam	340 persons per sq. km
(2) Maharashtra	314 persons per sq. km
(3) Tripura	304 persons per sq. km
(4) Andhra Pradesh	275 persons per sq. km
(5) Karnataka	275 persons per sq. km
(6) Orissa	236 persons per sq. km

Areas of Low Density. The remote high altitude districts in the Himalayas, the rugged forest-covered hill tracts in the States and Union Territories east of West Bengal, and in the Peninsular plateaus and the arid districts of Rajasthan and Gujarat have a low population density. The reasons for low densities in these regions are:

(i) Climate hazards either too hot or too cold.
(ii) Rugged and sandy terrain resulting in a very low economic development.
(iii) Hard means of livelihood.
(iv) Underdeveloped means of transport and communications.

According to 2001 census Arunachal Pradesh recorded the lowest density with only 13 persons per sq. km. The reasons for low density are hilly and rugged terrain, poor soils, low level of economic development. Thickly forested parts restrict the development of means of transport and communications.

The States having low density are:

(i) Madhya Pradesh 196 persons per sq. km
(ii) Rajasthan 165 persons per sq. km
(iii) Himachal Pradesh 109 persons per sq. km

On the face of it variations in the density of population appear to have been caused by following factors:

1. Physical factors such as relief, climate, water supply, fertility and agricultural productivity.
2. Social, economic, demographic, political and historical factors.

District Level Patterns

A study of the district level density of population reveals that there are striking contrasts from region to region. These variations are found mainly because of the uneven nature of distribution of natural resources and unequal rate of economic development.

The district wise variation in the density of population may be analysed by grouping the districts into the following five categories:

(i) Very Low Density
(ii) Low Density
(iii) Medium Density
(iv) High Density
(v) Very High Density

29

Population Composition: Age, Sex, Rural and Urban

29.1 AGE COMPOSITION

Nature of age data. A UN publication *'Principles and Recommendations for the 1970 Population Census'*, Statistical papers, 1967 defined age as "the estimated or calculated interval of time between the date of birth and the date of census, expressed in complete years." The census also records the date of birth of an individual, i.e., day, month and year. The age is collected by asking the individual about the age completed on the last birthday.

29.2 SIGNIFICANCE OF AGE STRUCTURE

The age structure helps to estimate dependency ratio. The children and the aged people depend upon the bread earners. These groups are consumers. In the economic sense they are the burden. Thus the knowledge of age structure helps to understand the economic, social and political implications. Age structure also indicates the nature of educational planning. Age structure indicates the nature and extent of dependency ratio; statewise picture also emerges.

(*See Table 4.9 and Table 4.27 percentage of Distribution of Projected Population by Age and Sex 1996-2016: India*)

It is observed from the Table 4.9 and 4.27 that the proportion of population of children has been going down since 1996 and of the other groups going up. Proportion of the old increases at a great speed.

(*See Table 4.7 and Table 4.11 Figures at Page 48 contain the sex pyramid*)

29.3 FACTORS DETERMINING THE AGE STRUCTURE OF POPULATION

1. Fertility
2. Mortality
3. Migration

29.4 CHILD POPULATION IN THE AGE GROUP 0-6 YEARS

The collection and compilation of data on child population in the age group 0-6 although primarily intended for calculating the literacy rates, allows us to broadly analyse its possible linkages with growth of population. Table 29.1 gives the child population for 2001 and also its proportion to the total population for 1991 and 2001 by sex. Simple correlation co-efficient between growth rate and proportion of child population in the age group 0-6 in case of major States (with population of more than thirty million) for 1991 and 2001 works out to be +0.78 and +0.92 respectively. There is a strong positive relationship between the growth rate and the child population in the age group 0.6.

It can also be assumed with a fair amount of confidence that the child population in this age group is least likely to be affected by inter-State migrations. In a population that is not greatly affected by huge changes in age structure, adult migration or child mortality between two points of time, a significant fall in proportion of children in the age-group 0-6 is broadly indicative of fall in fertility during the period. In India, the proportion of children in the age group 0-6 decreased from 17.94 per cent in 1991 to 15.42 per cent in 2001. In case of males, the percentage dropped by 2.30 points and for the females by 2.76 points. "The distribution of States and Union territories by their ranges of the proportion of child population in the age group 0-6 for the censuses of 1991 and 2001 is given Table 29.1.

It would be of interest to note that in 1991 only four States/Union territories had the percentage of child population in age group 0-6 less than fourteen with a share of about 10 percent of India's population. This number of States/Union territories swelled to sixteen in 2001 and a share of forty four per cent. The number of States and Union territories having child population less than sixteen per cent increased from six with a share of about ten per cent of India's population in 1991 to twenty four with a share of fifty six percent in 2001. These results perhaps broadly indicate a drop in fertility across the country.

It will be of some topical interest to know about the changing patterns in the absolute number of children in the age group 0-6. For the country as a whole (excluding Jammu and Kashmir), there had been an increase by about 6.4 million children during the decade 1991-2001. However, in as many as thirteen States/Union territories a decline in the absolute number of children during this period had been observed. These are, Himachal Pradesh (59,521) and Punjab (250,753) in the north; Tripura (70,110), Assam (71,263), West Bengal (429,473) in the east and Andhra Pradesh (1,291,114), Karnataka (651,443), Lakshadweep (604), Kerala (183,322), Tamil Nadu (630,390) and Andaman and Nicobar Islands(1,675) in the south. The most impressive decline of about 1.3 million children is observed for Andhra Pradesh. It is also obvious that in the contiguous four major South Indian States fertility decline appears to have become well established, stretching to neighbouring Maharashtra on the west and Orissa and West Bengal in the east, whereas in other regions it is rather scattered.

Table 29.1 : Population and proportion of child population in the age group 0-6 by sex: 1991 and 2001

State/UT Code	India/States/Union territories*	Child population in the age group 0-6			Proportion of child population in the age group 0-6 to total population					
		2001			1991			2001		
		Persons	Males	Females	Persons	Males	Females	Persons	Males	Females
1	2	3	4	5	6	7	8	9	10	11
	INDIA[1]	157,683,145	81,911.041	75,952,104	17.94	17.77	18.12	15.42	15.47	15.36
1	Jammu & Kashmir	1,431,182	738,839	692,343	N.A.	N.A.	N.A.	14.21	13.94	14.52
2.	Himachal Pradesh	769,424	405,618	363,808	16.26	16.47	16.03	12.84	13.34	12.32
3.	Punjab	3,055,492	1,704,142	1,351,350	14.92	14.06	16.00	12.13	11.66	12.75
4.	Chandigarh	109,293	59,238	50,055	14.92	14.06	16.00	12.13	11.16	12.75
5.	Uttaranchal	1,319,393	692,272	627.121	18.33	18.22	18.46	15.56	16.04	15.06
6.	Haryana	3,259,080	1,790,758	1,468,322	18.98	18.84	19.14	15.46	15.81	15.05
7.	Delhi	1,923,995	1.031,584	892.411	17.06	16.28	18.01	13.96	13.63	14.37
8.	Rajasthan	10,451,103	5,474,965	4,976,133	20.13	20,06	20.21	18.51	18.63	18.37
9.	Uttar Pradesh	30,472,042	15,903,900	14,568,142	20.38	19.84	20.99	18.35	18.18	18.54
10.	Bihar	16,234,539	8,375,532	7,859,007	20.70	20.21	21.24	19.59	19.41	19.78
11.	Sikkim	77,170	38,856	38,314	18.37	17.56	19.29	14.28	13.48	15.19
12.	Arunachal Pradesh	200,055	102,010	98,045	21.12	19.82	22.64	18.33	17.77	18.96
13.	Nagaland	280,172	141,852	138,320	17.15	16.23	18.19	14.09	13.62	14.61
14.	Manipur	312,691	159,448	153,243	16.69	16.55	16.83	13.09	13.21	12.97
15.	Mizoram	141,537	71,817	69,720	18.60	18.15	19.09	15.88	15.62	16.17
16.	Tripura	427,012	216,244	210,768	18.03	17.82	18.25	13.38	13.22	13.55
17.	Meghalaya	457,442	231,571	225,871	22.18	21.84	22.54	19.84	19.83	19.84
18.	Assam	4,350,245	2,215,104	2,135,144	19.73	19.20	20.29	16.33	16.07	16.62
19.	West Bengal	11,132,824	5,671,152	5,461,672	16.98	16.56	17.45	13.88	13.67	14.10
20.	Jharkhand	4,796,188	2,440,025	2,356,163	20.17	19.59	20.80	17.82	17.60	18.05
21.	Orissa	5,180,551	2,656,046	2,524,505	16.89	16.93	16.85	14.11	14.27	13.85

1	2	3	4	5	6	7	8	9	10	11
22.	Chhatisgarh	3,469,774	1,756,441	1,713,333	19.34	19.36	19.33	16.68	16.80	16.36
23.	Madhya Pradesh	10,618,323	5,504,422	5,113,901	19.94	19.64	20.27	17.58	17.50	17.58
24.	Gujarat	6,867,958	3,656,956	3,211,002	16.48	16.53	16.43	14.19	14.51	13.85
25.	Daman & Diu	20,012	10,394	9,618	15.53	15.62	15.44	12.66	11.24	14.67
26.	Dadra & Nagar Haveli	39,173	19,856	19,317	20.46	19.84	21.12	17.77	16.31	19.57
27.	Maharashtra	13,187,087	6,878,579	6,308,508	17.11	17.00	17.23	13.63	13.67	13.59
28.	Andhra Pradesh	9,673,274	4,926,200	4,747,074	16.49	16.46	16.51	12.77	12.87	12.68
29.	Karnataka	6,826,168	3,501,499	3,324,669	16.63	16.63	16.63	12.94	13.04	12.85
30.	Goa	142,152	73,547	68,605	11.74	11.75	11.72	10.58	10.73	10.42
31.	Lakshadweep*	8,860	4,488	4,372	18.30	18.32	18.28	14.62	14.42	14.83
32.	Kerala	3,653,578	1,861,669	1,791.909	13.19	13.71	12.68	11.48	12.04	10.95
33.	Tamil Nadu	6,817,669	3,515,562	3,302,107	13.33	13.51	13.15	10.98	11.24	10.71
34.	Pondicherry*	113,010	57,722	55,288	13.67	13.78	13.55	11.60	11.86	11.35
35.	Andaman & Nicobar Islands*	44,674	22,733	21,941	16.51	15.22	18.09	12.54	11.78	13.44

Note:

1. While working out the proportion of child population for 1991 Census in the age group 0-6 for India, the population in the age group 0-6 of areas Himachal Pradesh and Gujarat affected by natural calamities have been excluded. The details of affected areas are given in Notes 2 and 3 below.
2. The proportion of child population for 1991 Census in the age group 0-6 shown against Himachal Pradesh for 1991 excludes population in the age group 0-6 of Kinnaur district to make the data comparable with 2001 Census.
3. The proportion of child population for 1991 Census in the age group 0-6 shown against Gujarat excludes the population data of entire Kachchh district, Morvi, Maliya-Miyana and Wankaner talukas of Rajkot district, Jodiya taluka of Jamnagar district of Gujarat State to make the data comparable with 2001 Census.

Table 29.2 Distribution of States and Union territories by their ranges of the proportion of child population in the age group 0-6 for the years 1991 and 2001 Census

Range of proportion of child population in the age group 0-6	*Number of States/Union territories 1991*	*Percentage of population to total population 1991*	*Number of States/Union territories 2001*	*Percentage of population to total population 2001*
1	2	3	4	5
Less than 12.00	1	0.14	4	9.37
12.00-13.99	3	10.13	12	34.72
14.00-15.99	2	0.09	8	11.72
16.00-17.99	12	43.68	5	13.14
48.00 and above	16	45.05	5	30.07

Note: Jammu and Kashmir is excluded from 1991 and 2001 for the sake of comparability.

29.5 AGEING POPULATION AND ITS IMPLICATIONS

The *'Population Newsletter'* (December 2001) published by the population Division Department of Economic and Social Affairs of the UN presented the following major findings of the world population ageing during 1950-2050.

1. Population ageing is unprecedented without parallel in the history of humanity. Increase in the proportion of older persons (60 years and older) are being accompanied by decline in the proportions of the young (under age 15). By 2050, the number of older persons in the world will exceed the number of young.

2. Population ageing is pervasive, a global phenomenon affecting every man, woman and child. The steady increase of older age groups in national populations, both in absolute numbers and in relation to the working-age population, has a direct bearing on the inter-generational and intra-generational equity and solidarity that are the foundations of society.

3. Population ageing is profound, having major consequences and implications for all facets of human life. In the economic area, population ageing will have an impact on economic growth, savings, investment and consumption, labour markets, pensions, taxation and inter-generational transfers. In the social sphere, population ageing affects health and health care, family composition and living arrangements, housing and migration. In the political arena, population ageing can influence voting patterns and representation.

4. Population ageing is enduring. During the twentieth century the proportion of older persons continued to rise, and this trend is expected to continue into the twentyfirst century. For example, the proportion of older persons was 8 per cent in 1950 and 10 per cent in 2000, and is projected to reach 21 per cent in 2050.

5. The trend towards older populations is largely irreversible, with the young populations of the past unlikely to occur again.

6. The increase in the older population is the result of the demographic transition from high to low levels of fertility and mortality.

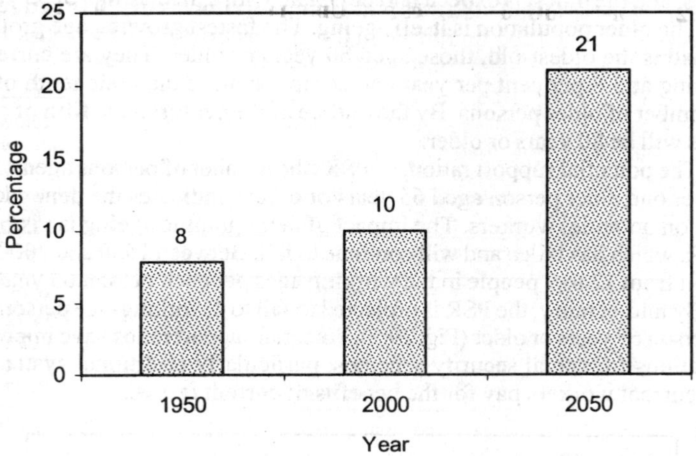

Fig. 29.1: Proportion of population 60 years or older: World, 1950-2050

Source: World Population Ageing: 1950-2050 (United Nations Publication, Sales No. E02 XIII, 3

7. As the twenty-first century began, the world population included approximately 600 million older persons, triple the number recorded fifty years earlier. By mid-century, there will be some 2 billion older persons—once again, a tripling of this age group in a span of 50 years.

8. Globally the population of older persons is growing by 2 per cent each year, considerably faster than the population as a whole. For at least the next twenty-five years, the older population is expected to continue growing more rapidly than other age groups. The growth rate of those 60 or older will reach 2.8 per cent annually in 2025-2030. Such rapid growth will require far-reaching economic and social adjustments in most countries.

9. Marked differences exist between regions in the number and proportion of older persons. In the more developed regions, almost one fifth of the population was aged 60 or older in the year 2000; by 2050, this proportion is expected to reach one third. In the less developed regions, only 8 per cent of the population is currently over the age of 60; however, by 2050 older persons will make up nearly 20 per cent of the population.

10. As the pace of population ageing is much faster in developing countries than in developed countries, developing countries will have less time to adjust to the consequences of population ageing. Moreover, population ageing in the developing countries is taking place at much lower levels of socio-economic development than was the case in the developed countries.

11. Today the median age for the world is 26 years. The country with the youngest population is Yemen, with a median age of 15 years, and the oldest is Japan, with a median age of 41 years. By 2050, the world median age is expected to have increased by ten years, to 36 years. The country with the youngest population at that time is projected to be Niger, with a median age of

20 years, and the oldest is expected to be Spain, with a median age of 55 years.

12. The older population is itself ageing. The fastest growing age group in the world is the oldest-old, those aged 80 years or older. They are currently increasing at 3.8 per cent per year and comprise more than one tenth of the total number of older persons. By the middle of the century, one fifth of older persons will be 80 years or older.

13. The potential support ration, or PSR (the number of persons aged 15-64 years per one older person aged 65 years or older), indicates the dependency burden on potential workers. The impact of demographic ageing is visible in the PSR, which has fallen and will continue to fall. Between 1950 and 2000, the PSR fell from 12 to 9 people in the working ages per each person 65 years or older. By mid-century, the PSR is projected to fall to 4 working-age persons for each person 65 years or older (Fig. 29.2). Potential support ratios have important implications for social security schemes, particularly traditional systems in which current workers pay for the benefits of current retirees.

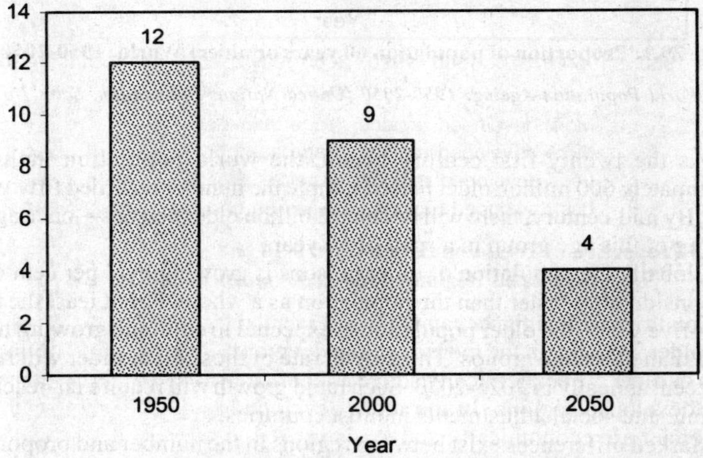

Fig. 29.2: Potential support ratio: World, 1950-2050

Source: World Population Ageing: 1950-2050 (United Nations Publication, Sales No. E02, XIII, 3)

14. The majority of older persons are women, as female life expectancy is higher than that for men. In 2000, there were 63 million more women than men aged 60 or older, and at the oldest ages, there are two to five times as many women as men (Fig. 29.3).

15. The health of older persons typically deteriorates with increasing age, inducing greater demand for long-term care as the numbers of the oldest-old grow. The parent support ratio, the ratio of the population 85 or older to those aged 50-64, provides an indication of the support families may need to provide to their oldest members. Globally, there were fewer than 2 persons aged 85 or older for every 100 persons aged 50-56 in 1950. By 2000, the ratio had increased to 4 per 100, and it is projected to reach 11 by 2050.

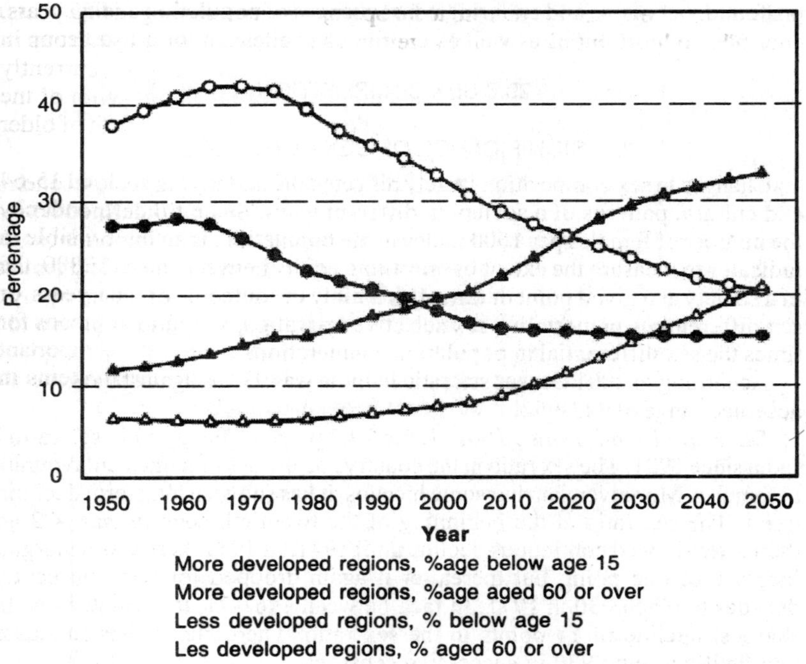

Fig. 29.3 Proportion of Total Population Aged 0-14 and 60 and over, More and Less Developed Regions, 1950-2050 (*medium variant*)

16. Countries with high per capita incomes tend to have lower participation rates of older workers. In the more developed regions, 21 per cent of men aged 60 years or older are economically active as compared to 50 per cent of men in the less developed regions. In the more developed regions, 10 per cent of older women are economically active, compared to 19 per cent in the less developed regions. Older persons participate to a greater extent in labour markets in the less developed regions, largely owing to the limited coverage of retirement schemes and the relatively small incomes when provided.

17. Although literacy has been increasing among the older population, illiteracy is still common. In the less developed regions, as of 2000, about half of all persons 60 or older were literate. Only about one third of older women and about three fifths of older men could read and write at a basic level of competence. In the more developed regions, literacy approached universality in all but a few countries.

In conclusion, it is evident that unprecedented demographic changes, which had their origins in the nineteenth and twentieth centuries and are continuing well into the twentyfirst century, are transforming the world. The declines in fertility reinforced by increasing longevity have produced and will continue to produce unprecedented changes in the structure of all societies, notably the historic reversal in the proportions of young and older persons. The profound, pervasive and enduring consequences of population ageing present enormous opportunities as well as enormous challenges for all societies.

29.6 SEX COMPOSITION

29.7 SIGNIFICANCE OF SEX COMPOSITION

Changes in sex composition largely reflected the underlying socio-economic and cultural patterns of a society in different ways. Sex ratio defined here as the number of females per 1000 males in the population, is an important social indicator to measure the extent of prevailing equity between males and females in a society at a given point of time. It is mainly the outcome of the interplay of sex differentials in mortality, sex selective migration, sex ratio at birth and at times the sex differential in population enumeration.

According to 2001 Census sex ratio in India was 933 as against the generally accepted range of 943-952.

Sex Ratio in India since 1901: Table 29.3 presents the trend in sex ratio in India since 1901. The sex ratio in the country had always remained unfavourable to females. Moreover, barring some hiccups, it has shown a long term declining trend. The sex ratio at the beginning of the twentieth century was 972 and thereafter showed continuous decline until 1941. In 1951 there was a marginal increase of one point, but thereafter it again dropped for two consecutive decades to reach 930 in 1971. In fact, between 1961-71, the country saw the sharpest decline of 11 points in the sex ratio. Thereafter, it has fluctuated marginally around 930 in successive censuses.

Table 29.3 Sex ratio, India: 1901-2011

Census year	*Sex ratio (females per 1,000 males)*
1901	972
1911	964
1921	955
1931	950
1941	945
1951	946
1961	941
1971	930
1981	934
1991	927
2001	933
2011	940

The sex ratio of Indian population has always been of topical interest for the demographers, social scientists, womens groups, research scholars and various planners and policy makers. Why is it that India has such uneven composition of population as compared to most of the developed countries in the world? Several reasons are adduced to explain the consistently low levels of sex ratio and their further decline in the country. Some of the important reasons commonly put forward are listed below:

- Neglect of the girl child resulting in their higher mortality at younger ages

- High maternal mortality
- Sex selective female abortions
- Female infanticide
- Change in sex ratio at birth

The imbalance in the number of males and females begins in the beginning. It is now a well-established law of nature that the males exceed females at the time of birth. It is believed that generally 943-952 female births take place for every 1000 male births, which in effect would mean that there is a deficiency of about 50 females per 1000 males in every birth cohort. Many demographers believe that left on its own, this is an unalterable constant.

Some likelihood of differential under registration of female births over time notwithstanding, the data on sex ratio at birth for the past many years is indicative of a larger than usual shortfall in female births as compared to male births. The three years moving average sex ratio at birth worked out for India as a whole for the period 1982-98 leaves around 900. During the decade 1981-90 sex ratio at birth were above 900 whereas in the succeeding decade it has shown definite sign of a decline below 900. Thus, for recent period there is some primary evidence that sex ratio at birth in the country as a whole is possibly lower than the generally accepted range of 943-952 but it needs to be corroborated by some more data.

The overall sex ratio of India is dependent on the sex ratios obtained in different States and Union territories and their relative weights in terms of size of population. Table 29.4 gives the sex ratio of the total population, sex ratio in the age group 0-6 and sex ratio of population aged 7 and above for 1991 and 2011 for all the States and Union territories. The diversity in sex ratio among the States and Union territories is phenomenal. At the Census of India, 2001 the sex ratio among the major States ranged from 861 in Haryana to 1058 in Kerala. In 1991 also, Haryana with a sex ratio of 865 was at the bottom with Kerala (1036) at the top. The changes in sex ratio over time, therefore, are dependent on the changes in the ratios of the individual States and Union territories and their relative share in population.

Table 29.4 Sex ratio of total population and child population in the age group 0-6 : 1991 and 2011

State/ UT code	*India/States/Union Territories**	*Sex ratio (females per 1,000 males)*							
		Total population		*Child population in the age group 0-6*			*Population aged 7 and above*		
		1991	2001	1991	2001	2011	1991	2001	2011
1	2	3	4	5	6	8	8	9	10
	INDIA	927	933	945	927	914	923	935	944
1.	Jammu & Kashmir	N.A.	900	N.A.	937	859	N.A.	894	887
2.	Himachal Pradesh	976	970	951	897	906	980	981	899
3.	Punjab	882	874	875	793	846	883	886	983
4.	Chandigarh*	790	773	899	845	867	772	763	812
5.	Uttaranchal	936	964	948	906	886	933	976	975

1	2	3	4	5	6	7	8	9	10
6.	Haryana	865	861	879	820	830	862	869	885
7.	Delhi*	827	821	915	865	866	810	813	866
8.	Rajasthan	910	922	916	909	883	908	925	935
9.	Uttar Pradesh	876	898	927	916	889	863	895	910
10.	Bihar	907	921	953	938	933	895	916	912
11.	Sikkim	878	875	965	986	944	860	858	883
12.	Arunachal Pradesh	859	901	982	961	960	829	888	913
13.	Nagaland	886	909	993	975	944	865	899	929
14.	Manipur	958	978	974	961	934	955	981	995
15.	Mizoram	921	938	969	971	971	911	932	976
16.	Tripura	945	950	967	975	953	940	947	–
17.	Meghalaya	955	975	986	975	970	947	974	989
18.	Assam	923	932	975	964	957	910	926	953
19.	West Bengal	917	934	967	963	950	907	929	946
20.	Jharkhand	922	941	979	966	943	908	936	948
21.	Orissa	971	972	967	950	934	972	976	985
22.	Chhatisgarh	985	990	984	975	964	986	992	995
23.	Madhya Pradesh	912	920	941	929	912	905	918	933
24.	Gujarat	934	921	941	929	886	905	918	923
25.	Daman & Diu*	969	709	958	925	909	971	682	589
26.	Dadra & Nagar Haveli*	952	811	1,013	973	924	937	779	752
27.	Maharashtra	934	922	946	917	883	831	923	931
28.	Andhra Pradesh	972	978	975	964	943	972	980	997
29.	Karnataka	960	964	960	949	943	960	966	973
30.	Goa	967	960	964	933	920	967	964	973
31.	Lakshadweep	943	947	941	974	908	943	943	951
32.	Kerala	1,036	1,058	958	963	959	1,049	1,071	1099
33.	Tamil Nadu	974	986	948	939	946	978	992	1000
34.	Pondicherry*	979	1,001	963	958	965	982	1,007	1047
35.	Andaman & Nicobar Islands*	818	846	973	965	966	790	830	868

Notes:

1. While working out sex ratio of child population for 1991 Census in the age group 0-6 and population aged 7 and above for India, the population in the age group 0-6 and population aged 7 and above of areas of Gujarat and Himachal Pradesh affected by natural calamities have been excluded. The details of affected areas are given in Note numbers 2 and 3 below.
2. To make the data comparable with Census of India, 2001, the proportion of child population for 1991 Census in the age group 0-6 and population aged 7 and above shown against Himachal Pradesh for 1991 excludes population in the age group 0-6 and population aged 7 and above of Kinnaur district where population enumeration of Census of India, 2001, could not be conducted due to natural calamity.
3. To make the data comparable with Census of India, 2001, the proportion of child population for 1991 Census in the age group 0-6 and population aged 7 and above shown against Gujarat excludes the population data of entire Kachchh district, Morvi, Maliya-Miyana and Wankaner tatukas of Rajkot district and Jodiya taluka of Jamnagar district of Gujarat state where population enumeration of Census of India, 2001, could not be conducted due to natural calamity.

29.8 SEX RATIO OF INDIA AND OF SELECTED COUNTRIES

Table 29.5 presents sex ratio of 10 most populated countries of the world. A study of the trends in sex ratio of a few selected countries for the period 1950-2000 shows that the sex ratio in U.S.A., Indonesia, Russian Federation and Japan has always remained above unity for the last half century. The most dramatic decline of about 200 points in the sex ratio is seen in the Russian Federation. In U.S.A., it has shown an improvement from 1002 to 1029 in the last fifty years. Bangladesh has shown a continuous improvement in its sex ratio to reach from 880 in 1950 to 953 in 2000. Pakistan and China have also shown an improvement. Thus among the major nations of the world, India is the only exception. Sex ratio in India is a matter of concern. This reflects negative attitude towards the females. This gender bias must be removed. Reasons for this have already been mentioned. These must be attended to urgently to maintain balance.

Table 29.5 Sex ratio of selected countries

Sl. No.	*Country*	*Sex ratio (females per 1,000 males)*	
		2001	2011
	World	986	984
1.	China	944	926
2.	India	933	940
3.	U.S.A.	1,029	1025
4.	Indonesia	1,004	988
5.	Brazil	1,025	1042
6.	Pakistan	938	943
7.	Russian Fed.	1,140	1167
8.	Bangladesh	953	978
9.	Japan	1,041	1055
10.	Nigeria	1,016	987

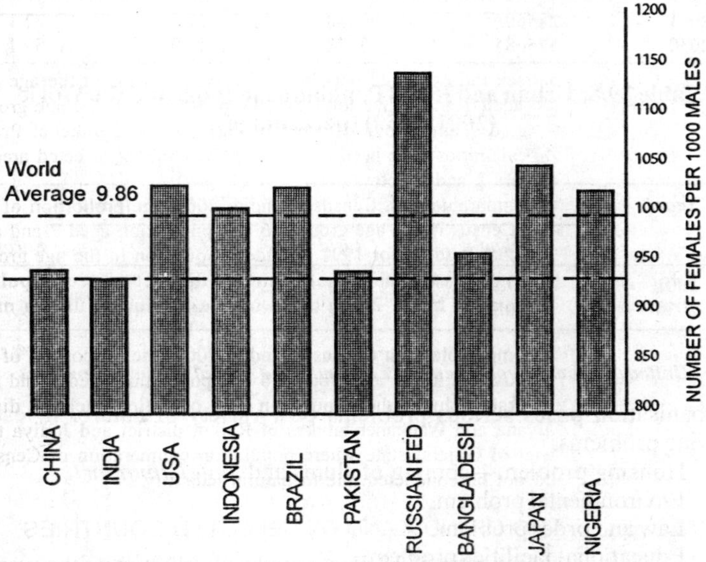

Fig. 29.4 Sex Ratio of Selected Countries

29.9 RURAL AND URBAN POPULATION

Table 29.6: Rural and Urban Population: 1901-2011

Census Year	*Population (Million)*		*Percentage of Total Population*	
	Rural	*Urban*	*Rural*	*Urban*
1901	213	26	89.2	10.8
1911	226	26	89.7	10.3
1921	223	28	88.8	11.2
1931	246	33	88.0	12.0
1941	275	44	86.1	13.9
1951	299	62	82.7	17.3
1961	360	79	82.0	18.0
1971	439	109	80.1	19.9
1981	524	159	76.7	23.3
1991	629	218	74.3	25.7
2001	741.5	285.6	72.2	27.8
2011	833.08	377.10	68.83	31.16

Table 29.6 presents the rural and urban population in India since 1901.

Table 29.7 gives the projected figures for India for 2030 and Table 29.8 compares the same for the world.

Table 29.7: Urban and Rural Population in India (2001-2030)

Year	*Population (Thousand)*		*Percentage*	
	Urban	*Rural*	*Urban*	*Rural*
2001	285608	739488	27.9	72.1
2030	575684	833238	40.9	59.1

Table 29.8: Urban and Rural Population in India and the World (2001-2030) (percentage)

Year	*India*		*World*	
	Urban	*Rural*	*Urban*	*Rural*
2001	27.9	72.1	47.7	52.3
2030	40.9	59.1	60.3	39.7

Source: *United Nations, Department of Economic and Social Affairs, New York.*

Urbanisation poses serious problems of a variety of nature. It leads to following problems.

1. Housing problem—coming of slums and *Juggi Jhunpari*.
2. Environmental problem.
3. Law and order problem.
4. Educational facilities problem.
5. Infrastructure provision problem.

29.10 URBANISATION IN THE WORLD AND ITS IMPLICATIONS

The UN Population Division, in *'World Urbanisation Prospectus: 2001 Revision'* has drawn the following conclusions regarding urbanisation since 1950.

Key Findings

1. The world's urban population reached 2.9 billion in 2000 and is expected to rise to 5 billion by 2030. Whereas 30 per cent of the world population lived in urban areas in 1950, the proportion of urban dwellers rose to 47 per cent by 2000 and is projected to attain 60 per cent by 2030 (Table 29.8). At current rates of change, the number of urban dwellers will equal the number of rural dwellers in the world in 2007.

2. Virtually all the population growth expected at the world level during 2000-2030 will be concentrated in urban areas. During that period the urban population is expected to increase by 2.1 billion persons, just slightly below the 2.2 billion persons that will be added to the world population (Table 29.8).

3. Almost all of the population increase expected during 2000-2030 will be absorbed by the urban areas of the less developed regions whose population will likely rise from approximately 2 billion in 2000 to just under 4 billion in 2030. The urban population of the more developed regions is expected to increase slowly, passing from 0.9 billion in 2000 to 1 billion in 2030.

4. During 2000-2030, the world's urban population is projected to grow at an average annual rate of 1.9 per cent, nearly double the rate expected for the total population of the world (1 per cent per year). At that rate of growth, the world's urban population will double in 38 years (Table 29.8).

5. Population growth will be particularly rapid in the urban areas of less developed regions, averaging 2.4 per cent per year during 2000-2030, consistent with a doubling time of 29 years. In contrast, the rural population of the less developed regions is expected to increase very slowly, at just 0.2 per cent per year during 2000-2030.

6. Rural-urban migration and the transformation of rural settlements into cities are important determinants of the high population growth expected in urban areas of the less developed regions over the next thirty years. In combination with the universal reduction of fertility levels that is expected to occur in the future, these changes will lead to the eventual reduction of the rural population of the less developed regions whose growth rate will become negative in 2025-2030 for the first time. Therefore, it is expected that the rural population of the less developed regions will reach a peak around 2025 and then begin to decline, just as the rural population of the more developed regions has done since 1950.

7. The process of urbanisation is already very advanced in the more developed regions, where 75 per cent of the population lived in urban areas in 2000. Nevertheless, the concentration of population in cities is expected to increase further so that, by 2030, 83 per cent of the inhabitants of the more developed countries will be urban dwellers (Table 29.2).

8. The level of urbanisation is considerably lower in the less developed regions, where 40 per cent of the population lived in urban areas in 2000. This

Table 29.8: Selected indicators for the Urban and Rural Population by Development Group, 1950-2030

	Population billions				*Growth rate (percentage)*		*Doubling time (years)*	
Development group	*1950*	*1975*	*2000*	*2030*	*1950-2000*	*2000-2030*	*1950-2000*	*2000-2030*
				A. Population size and growth				
Total population								
World	2.52	4.07	6.06	8.27	1.75	1.04	40	67
More developed regions	0.81	1.05	1.19	1.22	0.76	0.07	91	998
Less developed regions	1.71	3.02	4.87	7.05	2.10	1.24	33	56
Urban population								
World	0.75	1.54	2.86	4.98	2.68	1.85	26	38
More developed regions	0.45	0.73	0.90	1.00	1.40	0.38	50	185
Less developed regions	0.30	0.81	1.96	3.98	3.73	2.35	19	29
Rural population								
World	1.77	2.52	3.19	3.29	1.18	0.10	59	714
More developed regions	0.37	0.31	0.29	0.21	-0.45	-1.09	--	--
Less developed regions	1.40	2.21	2.90	3.08	1.46	0.20	48	352
				B. Urban indicators				
	Percentage urban				*Urbanization rate (percentage)*		*Doubling time (years)*	
	1950	*1975*	*2000*	*2030*	*1950-2000*	*2000-2030*	*1950-2000*	*2000-2030*
World	29.8	37.9	47.2	60.2	0.92	0.81	75	86
More developed regions	54.9	70.0	75.4	82.6	0.63	0.31	—	—
Less developed regions	17.8	26.8	40.4	56.4	1.63	1.11	42	62

proportion is noticeably higher than it was in 1950 (18 per cent) and is expected to rise substantially, to reach 56 per cent by 2030. Thus, by 2030, the less developed regions will reach a level of urbanisation similar to that exhibited by the more developed regions in 1950.

9. There are marked differences in the level and pace of urbanisation among the major areas constituting the less developed regions of the world. Latin America and the Caribbean as a whole is highly urbanised, with 75 per cent of its population living in urban settlements in 2000, a proportion higher than that of Europe. Moreover, this proportion is twice as high as the one estimated for Africa or Asia. With 37 per cent of their respective populations living in

urban areas in 2000, Africa and Asia are considerably less urbanised and, consequently, are expected to experience rapid rates of urbanisation during 2000-2030. It is expected that by 2030, 53 per cent and 54 per cent, respectively, of their inhabitants will live in urban areas. At that time, 84 per cent of the population of Latin America and the Caribbean will be urban, a level similar to that of Northern America, the most highly urbanised area of the world by 2030 (Table 29.9).

Table 29.9: Selected Indicator for the Urban and Rural Population by Major Area, 1950-2030

Major area	*Population (millions)*				*Growth rate (percentage)*		*Doubling time (years)*	
	1950	*1975*	*2000*	*2030*	*1950-2000*	*2000-2030*	*1950-2000*	*2000-2030*
				A. Population size and growth				
Total population								
Northern America	172	243	314	396	1.21	0.77	57	89
Latin America and the Caribbean	167	322	519	723	2.27	1.11	31	63
Oceania	13	21	31	42	1.77	1.05	39	66
Europe	548	676	727	670	0.57	-0.27	123	—
Asia	1399	2397	3672	4950	1.93	0.99	36	70
Africa	221	406	794	1489	2.56	2.10	27	33
Urban population								
Northern America	110	180	243	335	1.59	1.07	44	65
Latin America and the Caribbean	70	198	391	608	3.44	1.47	20	47
Oceania	8	15	23	32	2.14	1.19	32	58
Europe	287	455	534	540	1.24	0.04	56	1947
Asia	244	592	1376	2679	3.46	2.22	20	31
Africa	32	102	295	787	4.42	3.27	16	21
Rural population								
Northern America	62	64	71	61	0.28	-0.49	251	—
Latin America and the Caribbean	97	124	127	116	0.55	-0.33	127	—
Oceania	5	6	8	10	0.98	0.61	71	114
Europe	261	221	193	131	-0.60	01.31	—	—
Asia	1155	1805	2297	2271	1.37	-0.04	50	—
Africa	188	304	498	702	1.94	1.14	36	61

B. Urban indicators

	Percentage urban				*Urbanisation rate (percentage)*		*Doubling time (years)*	
	1950	*1975*	*2000*	*2030*	*1950-2000*	*2000-2030*	*1950-2000*	*2000-2030*
Northern America	63.9	73.8	77.4	84.5	0.38	0.30	—	—
Latin America and Caribbean	41.9	61.4	75.4	84.0	1.18	0.36	—	—
Oceania	61.6	72.2	74.1	77.3	0.37	0.14	—	—
Europe	52.4	67.3	73.4	80.5	0.68	0.31	—	—
Asia	17.4	24.7	37.5	54.1	1.53	1.23	45	57
Africa	14.7	25.2	37.2	52.9	1.86	1.17	37	59

10. In Europe and Northern America, the percentage of the population living in urban areas is expected to rise from 73 per cent and 77 per cent respectively in 2000 to 81 per cent and 85 per cent in 2030. The increase in Oceania is likely to be smaller, from 74 per cent in 2000 to 77 per cent in 2030.

11. Despite their high levels of urbanisation, the combined number of urban dwellers in Europe, Latin America and the Caribbean, Northern America and Oceania (1.2 billion) is smaller than the number in Asia (1.4 billion), one of the least urbanised major areas of the world in 2000. Furthermore, by 2030, Asia and Africa will each have higher numbers of urban dwellers than any other major area of the world, and Asia will account for 54 per cent of the urban population of the world, up from 48 per cent in 2000 (Table 29.9).

12. Asia also has and is expected to have the largest rural population of the world during 2000-2030, amounting to 2.3 billion persons both in 2000 and in 2030. Africa, with 498 million rural inhabitants in 2000, is expected to see its rural population rise to 702 million by 2030, remaining the major area with the second largest rural population during the period. Except for Africa and Oceania, all major areas are expected to experience a reduction in their rural population between 2000 and 2030 (Table 29.8). As a consequence of regional trends, the world rural population will remain virtually stable during 2000-2030, varying between 3.2 billion and 3.3 billion (Table 29.8).

13. Although urban areas will encompass an increasing share of the world population, the proportion of people living in very large urban agglomerations or mega-cities is still small. In 2000, 3.7 per cent of the world population resided in cities of 10 million inhabitants or more and by 2015 that proportion is expected to rise to 4.7 per cent. In addition, 2.8 per cent of the world population in the year 2000 lived in cities with population ranging from 5 million to 10 million inhabitants, and the projected figure for 2015 is 3.7 per cent. On the whole, by 2015, merely 8.4 per cent of the world population is expected to reside in large urban agglomeration of 5 million inhabitants or more. (Table 29.10)

Table 29.10: Distribution of the World Population and that of more and less developed Regions by area of Residence and size of Urban Settlement, 1975, 2000 and 2015

Development group	*Area of residence and size class of urban settlement (number of inhabitants)*	*Population (millions)*			*Percentage distribution*		
		1975	*2000*	*2015*	*1975*	*2000*	*2015*
World	Total	4066	6057	7207	100.0	100.0	100.0
	Urban area	1543	2862	3869	37.9	47.2	53.7
	10 million or more	68	225	340	1.7	3.7	4.7
	5 million to 10 million	122	169	264	3.0	2.8	3.7
	1 million to 5 million	332	675	960	8.2	11.1	13.3
	500,000 to 1 million	176	290	354	4.3	4.8	4.9
	Fewer than 500,000	844	1503	1950	20.8	24.8	27.1
	Rural area	2 523	3195	3338	62.1	52.8	46.3
More developed regions	Total	1048	1191	1214	100.0	100.0	100.0
	Urban area	734	898	954	70.0	75.4	78.6
	10 million or more	36	67	71	3.4	5.7	5.8
	5 million to 10 million	62	39	45	5.9	3.3	3.7
	1 million to 5 million	145	216	243	13.9	18.1	20.0
	500,000 to 1 million	69	77	74	6.5	6.5	6.1
	Fewer than 500,000	422	498	522	40.3	41.8	43.0
	Rural area	314	294	259	30.0	24.6	21.4
Less developed regions	Total	3017	4865	5994	100.0	100.0	100.0
	Urban area	809	1964	2915	26.8	40.4	48.6
	10 million or more	32	158	270	1.1	3.2	4.5
	5 million to 10 million	60	130	218	2.0	2.7	3.6
	1 million to 5 million	186	458	718	6.2	9.4	12.0
	500,000 to 1 million	108	213	280	3.6	4.4	4.7
	Fewer than 500,000	422	1005	1429	14.0	20.7	23.8
	Rural area	2209	2901	3078	73.2	59.6	51.4

14. In both the more and less developed regions, the proportion of people living in large urban agglomeration (5million inhabitants or more) is low, amounting to 5.9 per cent in the less developed regions and to 9 per cent in the more developed regions in 2000. By 2015, the relative increase in that

proportion will be greater for less developed regions, where it will rise to 8.1 per cent, a level closer to the 9.5 per cent expected for the more developed regions.

15. The proportion of the world population living in small cities is considerably larger, though it is increasing at a slower pace. In 2000, 24.8 per cent of the world population lived in urban settlements with fewer than 500,000 inhabitants and by 2015 that proportion will likely rise to 27.1 per cent (Table 29.10). Furthermore, 52.5 dwellers lived in settlements with fewer than 500,000 inhabitants in 200, a proportion that is expected to decline slightly by 2015 but still remain over 50 per cent. Consequently, the trend towards concentration of the population in larger urban settlements has not yet resulted in a market decline of either the proportion or the number of persons living in smaller urban settlements.

16. In more developed regions, the concentration of population in small urban settlements is even more market than at the world level. Thus, in 2000, 41.8 per cent of the urban settlement with fewer than 500,000 inhabitants and by 2015 that proportion is expected to rise to 43.0 per cent. In less developed regions, where the majority of the population still resides in rural areas, the proportion of people living in small cities was 20.7 per cent in 2000 and will likely rise to 23.8 per cent by 2015 (Table 29.10).

17. Not only do the largest cities account for relatively low proportions of the world population but in addition their share of the annual growth of the urban population is expected to be moderate. During 2000-2015, cities of 5 million inhabitants or more are expected to absorb 20.9 per cent of the annual increment in the urban population, whereas urban settlements with fewer than 500,000 inhabitants will absorb 44.4 per cent (Table 29.11). In both cases, cities in the less developed regions will absorb most of that increase. Thus the large cities of developing countries are projected to account for 19.9 per cent of the increase in the world's urban population and small cities in those countries will account for 42 per cent of that increase. Overall, the largest shares of the increase in the world urban population will be attributed to urban settlements with fewer than 500,000 inhabitants and cities with a population ranging between 1 and 5 million inhabitants.

18. With 26.5 million inhabitants, Tokyo is the most populous urban agglomeration in the world in 2001, followed by São Paulo (1803), Mexico City (18.3), New York (16.8) and Mumbai (16.5). By 2015, Tokyo will remain the largest urban agglomeration with 27.2 million inhabitants, followed by Dhaka, Mumbai (Bombay), São Paulo, Delhi and Mexico City, all of which are expected to have more than 20 million inhabitants (Table 29.12).

Table 29.11 Distribution of the Annual Urban Increment by size class of Urban settlement and Development Group, 1975-2000 and 2000-2015

Development group	*Size class of urban settlement (number of inhabitants)*	*Average annual population increment (millions)*		*Percentage distribution of the overall urban increment)*	
		1975-2000	*2000-2015*	*1975-2000*	*2000-2015*
World	Total	79.6	76.7	—	—
	Urban area	52.8	67.2	100.0	100.0
	Cities of 10 million or more	6.3	7.7	11.9	11.5
	Cities of 5 million to 10 million	1.9	6.3	3.6	9.4
	Cities of 1 million to 5 million	13.7	19.1	26.0	28.4
	Cities of 500,000 to 1 million	4.5	4.3	8.6	6.4
	Cities with fewer than 500,000	26.3	29.8	49.9	44.4
More developed regions	Total	5.7	1.5	—	—
	Urban area	6.6	3.8	12.4	5.6
	Cities of 10 million or more	1.3	0.2	2.4	0.3
	Cities of 5 million to 10 million	-0.9	0.4	-1.7	0.6
	Cities of 1 million to 5 million	2.8	1.8	5.4	2.6
	Cities of 500,000 to 1 million	0.4	-0.2	0.7	-0.3
	Cities with fewer than 500,000	3.0	1.6	5.7	2.4
Less developed regions	Total	73.9	75.2	—	—
	Urban area	46.2	63.4	87.6	94.4
	Cities of 10 million or more	5.0	7.5	9.5	11.1
	Cities of 5 million to 10 million	2.8	5.9	5.3	8.8
	Cities of 1 million to 5 million	10.9	17.3	20.6	25.7
	Cities of 500,000 to 1 million	4.2	4.5	7.9	6.7
	Cities with fewer than 500,000	23.3	28.2	44.2	42.0

Table 29.12: Population of Cities with 10 million Inhabitants or more, 1950, 1975, 2001 and 2015 (millions)

1950		*1975*		*2001*		*2015*	
City	*Population*	*City*	*Population*	*City*	*Population*	*City*	*Population*
New York	12.3	Tokyo	19.8	Tokyo	26.5	Tokyo	27.2
		New York	15.9	São Paulo	18.3	Dhaka	22.8
		Shanghai	11.4	Mexico City	18.3	Mumbai (Bombay)	22.6
		Mexico City	10.7	New York	16.8	São Paulo	21.2
		São Paulo	10.3	Mumbai (Bombay)	16.5	Delhi	20.9
				Los Angeles	13.3	Mexico City	20.4
				Calcutta	13.3	New York	17.9
				Dhaka	13.2	Jakarta	17.3
				Delhi	13.0	Calcutta	16.7
				Shanghai	12.8	Karachi	16.2
				Buenos Aires	12.1	Lagos	16.0
				Jakarta	11.4	Los Angeles	14.5
				Osaka	11.0	Shanghai	13.6
				Beijing	10.8	Buenos Aires	13.2
				Rio de Janeiro	10.8	Metro Manila	12.6
				Karachi	10.4	Beijing	11.7
				Metro Manila	10.1	Rio de Janeiro	11.5
						Cairo	11.5
						Istanbul	11.4
						Osaka	11.0
						Tianjin	10.3

19. The population in large urban agglomerations will rise not only as a result of population growth in today's populous cities but also because the number of such cities is expected to keep on rising. Thus the number of cities with 5 million inhabitants or more is expected to increase from 40 in 2001 to 58 in 2015. Among those cities, the number of mega-cities (those with 10 million inhabitants or more) will likely rise from 17 in 2001 to 21 in 2015 (Table 29.12). Most of the large cities are located in developing countries. Just 9 of the 40 cities with 5 million inhabitants or more in 2001 were located in developed countries and the equivalent figures are 10 out of 58 in 2015.

20. Large urban agglomerations do not necessarily experience fast population growth. In fact, some of the fastest growing cities have small populations and, as population size increases, the growth rate of a city's population tends to decline. However, some of todays mega-cities have experienced high rates of population growth over the past 25 years. Thus, Dhaka in Bangladesh grew at an average annual rate of 7 per cent during 1975-2000 and Delhi in India increased at a rate of 4.1 per cent annually over the same period. But they are exceptional cases. Among the 17 mega-cities of 2001, just 5 grew at rates above 3 per cent per year during 1975-2000 and 8 experienced moderate or low growth (below 2 per cent per year). In the future, just four of today's mega-cities are projected to exhibit growth rates of 3 per cent or more (Dhaka, Delhi, Jakarta and Karachi) and 9 will likely experience very low growth, at below 1 per cent per year.

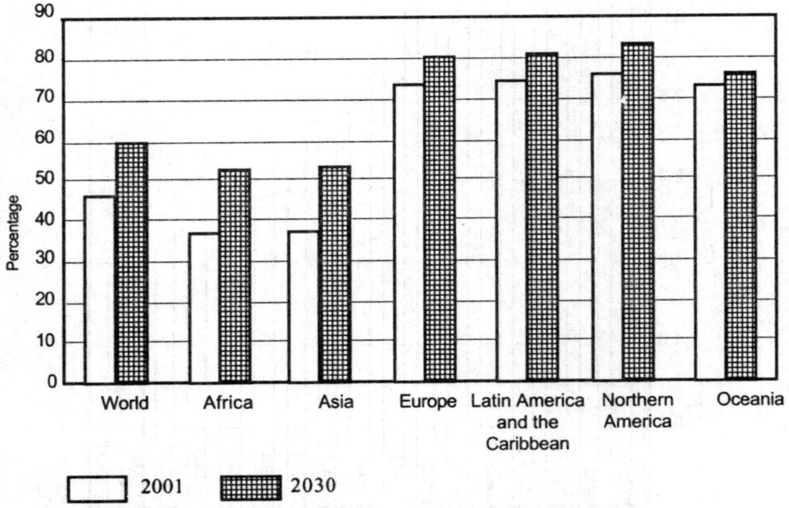

Fig. 29.1: Percentage of Population Living in Urban Areas, 2001 and 2030

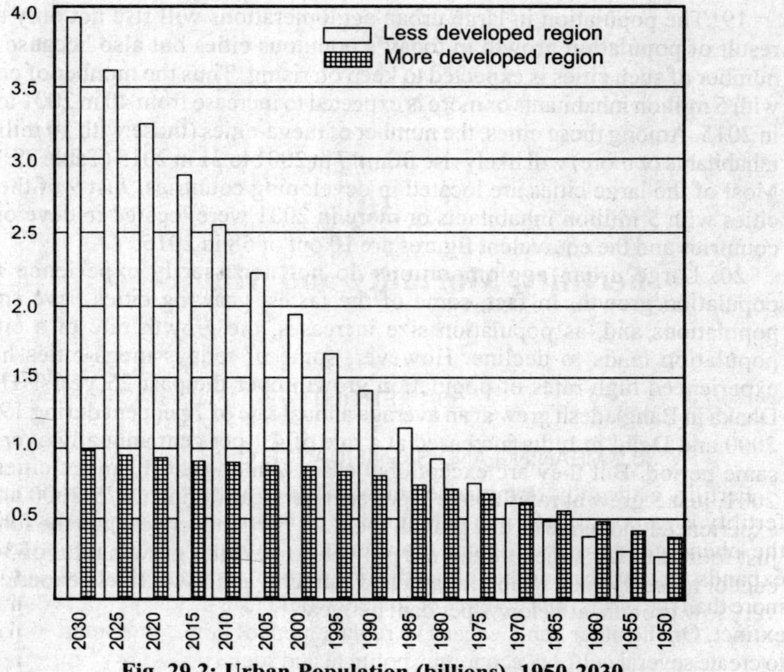

Fig. 29.2: Urban Population (billions), 1950-2030

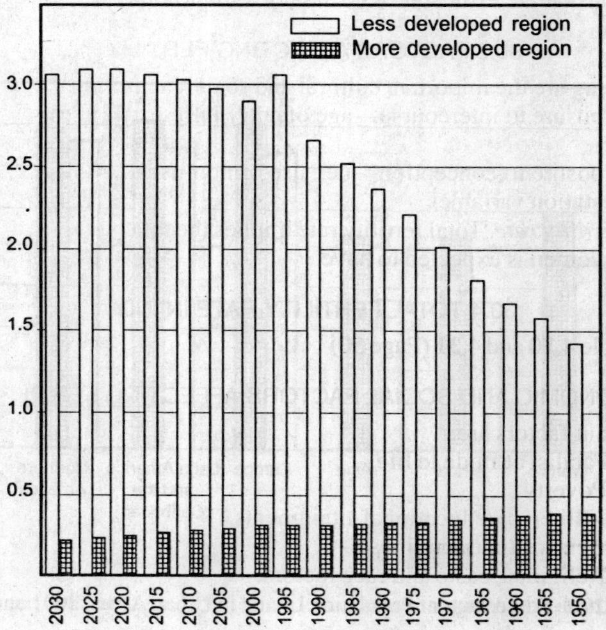

Fig. 29.3: Rural Population (billions), 1950-2030

30

Fertility, Mortality and Migration

30.1 FERTILITY

30.2 MEANING AND SIGNIFICANCE OF FERTILITY

Fertility is the most dominant element in the growth of population. Human fertility is responsible for the maintenance of humanity. It is concerned with the phenomenon of biological replacement. Through fertility population expands. In case the number of deaths in a particular country continues to be more than the births, that country or society would face the danger of becoming extinct. On the other hand, excessive replacement of human numbers is likely to create several cultural, economic, political and social problems for a country.

While a man or a woman or a couple who has given birth to at least one live child, is considered fertile, one who has not a single child is considered sterile.

30.3 FACTORS AFFECTING FERTILITY

Following are the important cultural and social factors affecting fertility:

1. Exposure to intercourse—age of entry into sexual unions, abstinence etc.
2. Exposure to conception—i.e., use or non-use of contraceptives.
3. Gestation variables

Total fertility rate. Total fertility rate implies the total number of children a cohort of women is expected to have.

30.4 TOTAL FERTILITY RATE IN INDIA

See Table 4.30 and 4.31 (Page 50)

30.5 ECONOMIC AND SOCIAL FACTORS AFFECTING FERTILITY RATE

Important factors are;

One—Fatalist attitude to life.

Two—Poverty

Three—Illiteracy/educational attainments.

Four—Leisure-time activities.

Five—Religious, caste and race factors.

Six—Rural-urban factor

Seven—Regional factor.
Eight—Employment of wife.

30.6 FERTILITY RATE IN SELECT COUNTRIES

(See page 64 also)

30.7 FERTILITY RATE OF SELECT COUNTRIES

Table 30.1 reflects the fertility rate of the world and 74 countries.

Table 30.1: Fertility Rate of Select Countries

Major area and country	*Total fertility*		*Fertility decline per decade*
	1950-1955	1995-2000	
World	**5.01**	**2.82**	**0.5**
Africa	*6.71*	*5.27*	*0.4*
1. Réunion	5.65	2.30	0.9
2. Tunisia	6.93	2.31	1.4
3. South Africa	6.50	3.10	0.8
4. Algeria	7.28	3.25	1.2
5. Egypt	6.56	3.40	1.0
6. Morocco	7.18	3.40	0.8
7. Cape Verde	6.60	3.56	1.0
8. Libyan Arab Jamahiriya	6.87	3.80	1.5
9. Botswana	6.50	4.35	0.7
10. Western Sahara	6.53	4.40	0.5
11. Ghana	6.90	4.60	0.5
12. Kenya	7.51	4.60	1.0
13. Lesotho	5.84	4.75	0.3
14. Swaziland	6.50	4.80	0.4
15. Sudan	6.50	4.90	0.4
Asia	*5.88*	*2.70*	*0.7*
1. Lebanon	5.74	2.29	1.4
2. Vietnam	5.75	2.50	1.2
3. Indonesia	5.49	2.60	0.8
4. Bahrain	6.97	2.63	1.3
5. Mongolia	6.00	2.70	1.9
6. Turkey	6.90	2.70	0.9
7. Brunei Darussalam	7.00	2.80	0.9
8. Uzbekistan	5.97	2.85	1.1
9. Kuwait	7.21	2.89	1.5
10. Kyrgyzstan	4.51	2.89	0.7
11. Israel	4.16	2.93	0.3
12. United Arab Emirates	6.97	3.17	0.8
13. Iran (Islamic Republic of)	7.00	3.20	0.8
14. Malaysia	6.83	3.26	0.9
15. Myanmar	6.00	3.30	0.6
16. India	5.97	3.32	0.6
17. Turkmenistan	6.00	3.60	0.9
18. Philippines	7.29	3.64	0.8
19. Qatar	6.97	3.70	0.7
20. Tajikistan	6.00	3.72	1.2
21. Bangladesh	6.70	3.80	0.9

Major area and country		Total fertility		Fertility decline per decade
		1950-1955	1995-2000	
22.	Syrian Arab Republic	7.09	4.00	1.3
23.	East Timor	6.44	4.35	0.9
24.	Jordan	7.38	4.69	0.9
25.	Nepal	5.75	4.83	0.4
Europe		*2.66*	*1.41*	*0.3*
1.	Albania	5.60	2.60	0.8
Latin America and the Caribbean		5.89	2.69	0.9
1.	Suriname	6.56	2.21	1.0
2.	Brazil	6.15	2.27	0.9
3.	Uruguay	2.73	2.40	0.2
4.	Bahamas	4.05	2.40	0.6
5.	Chile	4.95	2.44	0.7
6.	Guyana	6.68	2.45	1.1
7.	Jamaica	4.22	2.50	1.1
8.	Argentina	3.15	2.62	0.4
9.	Panama	5.68	2.63	0.9
10.	Saint Lucia	6.00	2.70	1.1
11.	Mexico	6.87	2.75	1.1
12.	Colombia	6.76	2.80	0.9
13.	Costa Rica	6.72	2.83	1.1
14.	Dominican Republic	7.40	2.88	1.0
15.	Peru	6.85	2.98	0.9
16.	Venezuela	6.46	2.98	1.0
17.	Ecuador	6.70	3.10	0.8
18.	El Salvador	6.46	3.17	1.1
19.	Belize	6.65	3.41	0.7
20.	French Guiana	5.00	4.05	1.1
21.	Paraguay	6.50	4.17	0.7
22.	Honduras	7.50	4.30	0.7
23.	Nicaragua	7.33	4.32	0.7
24.	Bolivia	6.75	4.36	0.5
25.	Haiti	6.30	4.38	0.4
26.	Guatemala	7.09	4.93	0.5
Oceania		*3.87*	*2.41*	*0.4*
1.	French Polynesia	6.00	2.60	1.1
2.	New Caledonia	5.00	2.60	0.8
3.	Fiji	6.63	3.20	0.9
4.	Guam	5.53	3.95	1.5
5.	Samoa	7.30	4.51	0.6
6.	Vanuatu	7.60	4.59	0.7
7.	Papua New Guinea	6.24	4.60	0.5

30.8 MORTALITY

Mortality is an important factor in population dynamics

30.9 IMPORTANCE OF THE STUDY OF MORTALITY

Mortality, fertility and migration are the three components of population change or population dynamics. The study of mortality helps us in analysing current demographic conditions as well as determining the potential changes in mortality in the future. Public health programmes are undertaken on the study of mortality. Mortality statistics become the basis for formulating insurance policies. It affects the life span of an individual.

30.10 MEANING OF MORTALITY

Morality implies the number of deaths in a given time or place.

Mortality rate implies the proportion of deaths to population, the rate of loss of numbers.

30.11 CLASSIFICATION OF FACTORS AFFECTING MORTALITY

(1)	(2)	(3)	(4)	(5)
Biological Factors	Cultural Factors	Economic Factors	Religious Factors	Social Factors

30.12 SIGNIFICANT MEASURES OF MORTALITY

Broadly speaking following are the important measures of mortality.

(1) Crude Death Rate
(2) Average Expectation of Life at Birth.
(3) Infant Mortality Act
(4) Infant Mortality Rate underone year of age
(5) Infant Mortality Rate under five years of age.

Death Rate. Crude death rate is a ratio of the total registered deaths of a specified year to the total mid-year population, multiplied by 1,000. Crude death rate is computed as under.

$$\frac{D}{P} \times K$$

where

D is the total number of deaths registered during a calendar year. P is the total population at the middle of the year.

K is 100.

Under 5 Mortality Rate. Probability of dying between birth and exactly five years expressed per 1,000 life birth.

Infant Mortality Rate under one year. Probability of dying between birth and exactly per 1,000 life births.

Life Expactancy at birth. The number of years new born children would live subject to the mortality risks prevailing for the cross-section of population at the time of their birth.

30.13 SIGNIFICANCE OF INFANT MORTALITY

The UNICEF assigns more importance to measure human as well as economic progress on the basis of infant mortality rates. Following are the important reasons for favouring this indicator of infant mortality.

First, it measures an end result of the development process rather than an input such as school enrolment level, per capita calories availability or the number of doctors per thousand population—all of which are measures to an end.

Second, the U5MR (under 5 years mortality rate) is known to be the result of a variety of inputs, the nutritional health and the health knowledge of mothers, the level of immunisation and ORT use; the availability of maternal and child health services, the availability of clean water and safe sanitation, and the overall safety of the child's environment.

Third, the U5MR is less susceptible than say, per capita GNP to the fallacy of the average. This is because the natural scale does not allow the children of the rich to be one thousand times as likely to survive, even if the man-made scale does permit them to have one thousand times as much income. In other words, it is much move difficult for a wealthy minority to affect a nation's U5MR. It, therefore, presents a more accurate if far from perfect picture of the health states of the majority of children of society as a Whole.

30.14 MORTALITY RATE IN INDIA

See pages 39 and 40 also.

Table 30.2 Infant Mortality Rate in India (1960, 1990 and 2001)

Year	*Morality Rate under one year of age*	*Mortality Rate under 5 years (U5MR)*
1960	146	242
1999	70	98
2001	67	93

Source: *The State of the World's Children 2003*, UNICEF

Table 30.3 : State-wise and Sex-wise Infant Mortality 0-4 years (1961, 1991 and 2001)

Sl. No.	*States/Union Territories*	*1961*			*1981*			*2001*
		Male	*Female*	*Person*	*Male*	*Female*	*Person*	*Person*
(1)	(2)	(3)	(4)	(5)	(6)	(7)	(8)	(9)
1.	Kerala	55	46	50	45	41	42	16
2.	Pondicherry	77	68	73	32	35	34	21
3.	Mizoram	73	65	69	51	56	53	23
4.	Manipur	31	33	32	29	27	28	25
5.	A & N Islands	78	66	72	71	61	69	30
6.	Lakshadweep	124	86	118	100	78	91	30
7.	Chandigarh	53	53	53	50	47	48	32
8.	Goa	60	56	50	56	48	51	36
9.	Arunachal Pradesh	141	111	120	111	103	91	44
10.	J & K	78	78	78	N.A.	N.A.	N.A.	45
11.	Maharashtra	96	89	92	72	76	74	48
12.	Tripura	106	115	111	81	84	82	49
13.	Delhi	66	70	67	55	51	54	51
14.	Meghalaya	81	76	79	79	82	80	52
15.	Sikkim	105	87	91	58	62	60	52
16.	Tamil Nadu	89	82	86	55	51	54	53
17.	West Bengal	103	57	95	75	51	62	53
18.	Punjab	74	79	77	81	53	74	54

(1)	(2)	(3)	(4)	(5)	(6)	(7)	(8)	(9)
19.	Karnataka	87	74	81	74	72	74	58
20.	D & N Haveli	102	93	98	84	73	81	61
21.	Gujarat	81	84	84	74	82	78	64
25.	Haryana	87	119	94	57	54	52	68
27	Assam	N.A.	N.A.	N.A.	96	87	92	78
28.	Rajasthan	114	114	114	94	79	87	83
29.	Uttar Pradesh	121	128	130	98	104	99	85
30.	Madhya Pradesh	158	140	150	131	136	133	97
31	Orissa	119	111	115	129	111	125	98
32.	Nagaland	76	58	68	51	52	51	N.A.
33.	Daman & Diu	60	56	57	61	50	56	N.A.
	All India	122	108	115	74	79	77	71

Note:

(a) The estimates for Goa and Daman & Diu are aggregated.

(b) Female and Male Infant Mortality Rate not available from 1996.

(c) The estimates are not available for smaller States/Union territories.

(d) N.A.: Not available.

Sources: *Office of the Registrar General of India, Ministry of Home Affairs.*

30.15 HEALTH AND MORTALITY

The world experienced remarkable reductions in mortality during the twentieth century. In the second half of the century alone, global life expectancy at birth increased from 46.5 years in 1950-1955 to 65.4 years in 1995-2000 (Table 30.4). In the more developed countries, where substantial increases in longevity had already occurred by 1950, life expectancy at birth increased from 66.6 to 74.9 years since the early 1950s. In contrast, most countries in the less developed regions did not begin to experience mortality declines until after 1950; however, their transition thereafter was more rapid. Life expectancy at birth in the less developed regions is estimated to have jumped an impressive 22.4 years, from 40.9 years in 1950-1955 to 63.3 in 1995-2000. Even among the least developed countries, life expectancy increased over this period by 14.9 years, from 35.6 years to 50.5 years.

The decline in mortality during the twentieth century has been attributed to a number of factors, including increases in income and nutritional intake advances in sanitation and water supply, and disease prevention and public-health reforms that improved living conditions. In the less developed regions where the key feature of the mortality transition is a massive reduction in infant and child mortality in the second half of the twentieth century, public-health programmes have played a major role. Of particular importance has been the application of new technologies in disease prevention and management (*World Health Organization, 1997; 1999*).

Mortality decline has also been strongly linked to the expansion of educational opportunities. Education, in particular that of women, has been shown to have effects on infant and child mortality that are larger than the combined effects of income, improved sanitation and modern sector employment. A recent study of the sources of the global mortality decline

Table 30.4: Trends and Sex Differentials in Life Expectancy at Birth, World and Major Areas, 1950-1955, 1975-2000

Major area	*Life expectancy, both sexes (years)*			*Sex differential (female-male life expectancy)*		
	1950-55	*1975-80*	*1995-2000*	*1950-55*	*1975-80*	*1995-2000*
World	46.5	59.7	65.4	2.7	3.5	4.4
More developed regions	66.6	72.1	74.9	5.0	7.4	7.6
Less developed regions	40.9	56.8	63.3	1.7	2.0	3.2
Least developed countries	35.6	45.3	50.5	1.3	1.8	1.9
Africa	37.8	48.0	51.4	2.7	3.2	2.8
Asia	41.3	58.5	66.3	1.4	1.6	3.1
Europe	66.2	71.2	73.3	5.1	7.7	8.2
Latin America and the Caribbean	51.4	63.1	69.2	3.4	5.2	6.5
Northern America	69.0	73.3	76.9	5.8	7.8	6.6
Oceania	60.9	68.2	73.8	3.8	5.6	4.9

Source: World Population Prospects. The 1998 Revision, vol. 1, Comprehensive Tables (United Nations publication, Sales No. E. 99 XIII.9).

found that one third of the increase in male and female life expectancy between 1960 and 1990 in 110 low- and middle-income countries could be attributed to gains in the educational attainment of females.

Although most of the factors accounting for twentieth century mortality declines have improved the living conditions of both males and females, life expectancy has increased faster for females everywhere, and female life expectancy at birth in 1995-2000 exceeds that of males in nearly all countries (*United Nations,* 1999a). Globally the female advantage in life expectancy at birth in 1995-2000 is estimated to be 4.4 years, but the differential is larger in the more developed regions (7.6 years) than in the less developed regions (3.2 years). The least developed countries exhibit even smaller differentials of about 1.9 years.

Among the developed countries, the sex differential in life expectancy is smallest—less than five years—in Iceland, Malta, Sweden and the former Yugoslav Republic of Macedonia. The largest sex differentials—greater than 11 years—are estimated for Belarus, Estonia, Latvia, Lithuania and the Russian Federation. The higher levels of mortality and the large sex differentials in life expectancy in Eastern Europe reflect the prolonged stagnation and reversals of mortality decline that have occurred in that region since the mid-1960s, particularly among males.

Although life expectancy has been increasing faster for females than for males in the more developed regions as a whole, in a number of countries, including Canada, Finland, New Zealand, Sweden, the United Kingdom and the United States of America, the differential between the sexes has narrowed.

In the more developed regions, Japan and Sweden, the two countries with the highest life expectancy at birth in the world in 1995-2000, exemplify the diversity in the size and trend in the female survival advantage. Although female life expectancy was around 78 years for females in both Japan and Sweden in 1975-1980, by 1995-2000 female life expectancy in Japan exceeded that of Sweden by 2 years, while male life expectancy increased at about the same pace in both countries.

30.16 MIGRATION

30.17 MEANING OF MIGRATION

In technical terms migration denotes the movement of an individual from one place to another with no clear intentions to come back in a relatively short period. The person who moves is known as migrant.

The United Nations Multilingual Demographic Dictionary defines migration as, "Migration is a form of geographical mobility or spatial mobility between one geographical unit and another, generally involving a change in residence from the place of origin or place of departure to the place of destination or place of arrival; such migration is called permanent migration and should be distinguished from other forms of movement which do not involve a permanent change."

Place of origin and destination. The place from the where the person migrates is known as place of origin and the place where he migrates to is known as place of destination.

International migration. In case the places of origin and destination are in two countries, this type of migration is known as international migration.

Broad categories of Migration

- Internal and external migration
- Inter-state and intra-state migration
- Rural and urban migration
- Hill and plain migration
- Non-industrial and industrial migration
- Non-developed area migration to developed area

30.18 FACTORS EFFECTING MIGRATION

1. *Demographic Factors.* The people from areas of high density where quality of life has deteriorated wish to migrate to areas where it is less.
2. *Economic Factors.* It is the most important factor in so far as migration is concerned. The people leave their birth place in search of better economic opportunities, jobs and better living conditions.
3. *Geographical Factors.* Geographical factors considerable help in migration process. The people migrate to places where there is better climate or where minerals are found in abundance. Similarly people do not wish to live at places where the chances of floods and fires or

earthquakes are quite frequent.

4. *Industrialisation.* Regions which get industrialised receive many migrants who leave their native home to permanently settle down in newly rising industrial towns and cities, e.g., the people migrated to Rourkela and Bokaro steel towns.
5. *Political Factors.* People leave their country or place where there is fear of war, internal conflicts or disturbances or where the government has failed to check inflation, price rise and to maintain law and order.
6. *Social Factors.* The people leave the place of their origin where social barriers are very rigid and do not allow proper development.
7. *Miscellaneous Non-Economic Factors.* People also migrate because of marriages, for better education facilities, legal advices or for availing services which the nearby town provide.

Migration Trends in India

Trends in the migration of population in India may be studied by grouping the migrant population into two categories:

Intra-state Migration. Intra-state migration implies the movement of people within the same state. Bulk of the migrants in India belong to this category. Another interesting feature is that the people mostly move from one small area to another. This is so because of marriages. Females migrate from one place to another.

Inter-state Migration. Interstate migration implies the movement of population from one state to another state. It is on a lesser scale than the intra state migrants. The male migration is more in the inter-state migration because males migrate due to get more employment.

30.19 CONCLUSIONS

Following important conclusions are drawn on the basis of above discussion:

1. About 85% of all migrants in the intra-state category are born in rural areas. But in inter-state migration this proportion is nearly 60 per cent.
2. Women form three-fourths of all migration because of marriages.
3. Half of the male migrants at the intra-state level usually move from rural to rural area only. A high proportion of such migrants belong to relatively less developed States of Uttar Pradesh, Bihar, Orissa, Madhya Pradesh and Rajasthan.
4. The States from where out-migration takes place are Rajasthan, U.P., Bihar, Andhra Pradesh, Tamil Nadu and Kerala. On the other hand, the States of West Bengal and Maharashtra as well as Chandigarh and Delhi are mostly in-migrating regions. Punjab also comes under this category as far labour migration is concerned.

	Pull Factors of Migration	Push Factors of Migration
1.	These factors result in immigration	These factors results in out migration.
2.	Migration caused by the attraction of a city or a town offering better economic opportunities life.	People are forced to leave their homes on account to unemployment, hunger and starvation.
3.	These factors attract the population of nearby or distant towns for better education, living conditions, recreation, and health care facilities etc.	When people do not find means of livelihood in their village homes are being rejected as surplus population because rural resources of land are not able to sustain them any longer.
4.	Millions of people have migrated from far off villages to the big cities of Kolkata, Mumbai or Delhi because these cities offered vast economic opportunities. Migration to these towns is still going on.	People have outmigrated from parts of Bihar, interiors of Madhya Pradesh, Rajasthan to big cities for better employment.

Table 30.5 Distribution of Migration by Reason (Percentage)

Reasons	1981		1991		2001 (Rough Estimate)	
	Female	Male	Female	Male	Female	Male
1. Marriage	73.4	3.3	76.1	5.0	80.0	5.0
2. Employment	1.9	31.8	1.8	27.0	2.0	30.0
3. Education	1.0	5.1	0.8	4.5	1.5	5.0
4. Family moving	14.3	30.3	11.0	26.8	12.0	28.0
5. Others	9.4	29.5	10.3	36.7	4.5	32.0

30.20 INTERNATIONAL MIGRATION

International migration is of two types:

Emigration. Emigration implies migrating of Indian residents to other countries. Among the important factors are: (1) Higher emoluments (2) Better working conditions. Skilled as well as unskilled Indian workers migrate to foreign countries. Skilled personnel include engineers, computer engineers, doctors, software engineers, etc. This phenomenon of skilled personnel going abroad is called 'Brain Draw' from India.

Immigration. Immigration means people from other countries coming to India. For example, a large number of residents of Bangladesh, Nepal, etc. have migrated to India.

It is said that illegal immigration from Bangladesh is posing a security threat to India.

30.21 CHARACTERISTICS OF INTERNATIONAL MIGRATION

A fundamental characteristic of people has been their movement from place to place. The right to move was recognised globally over a half-century ago with the adoption of the Universal Declaration of Human Rights. The Declaration states in article 13 that "Everyone has the right to freedom of movement and residence within the borders of each state" and "Everyone has the right to leave any country, including his own and to return to his country."

As noted in the 1994 International Conference on Population and Development, orderly international migration can have positive impacts on both the communities of origin and the communities of destination. Migration also has the potential of facilitating the transfer of skills and contributing to cultural enrichment. Today the number of people residing outside their country of birth is at an all-time high of about 175 million, more than double the number a generation ago. The vast majority of migrants are making meaningful contributions to their host countries. At the same time, however, international migration entails the loss of human resources for many countries of origin and may give rise to political, economic or social tensions in countries of destination.

The United Nations system is addressing the various dimensions of international migration. For example, the United Nations Secretariat has focused on the collection, analysis and dissemination of information on the levels, trends and national policies of international migration. Other parts of the United Nations have been concerned with issues of human rights, internally displaced persons, family reunification, undocumented migrants, trafficking and the social and economic integration of migrants. In addition, specialised agencies have focused on issues related to their expertise and mandates, such as labour flows, refugees and asylum-seekers and remittances.

Since 1994, the United Nations General Assembly has addressed on a variety of occasions the issue of international migration and development. Recently, the General Assembly, in its resolution 56/203 of 21 December 2001, called upon the United Nations system and other relevant organisations to continue to address the issue of international migration and development and to provide appropriate support for processes and activities on international migration and development. In response to this resolution, and also to provide further information on international migration to the General Assembly, the United Nations Secretariat organised in July 2002 the first system-wide Coordination Meeting on International Migration.

International migration, with its intricate web of demographic, social, economic and political consequences, is at the forefront of national and international agendas. However, the many questions arising from growing concerns about international migration have few clear answers and are posing unprecedented challenges. In addressing some of these questions, the United Nations can contribute to and facilitate meaningful dialogue and cooperation among nations, build capacities to manage migration, and hence effectively tackle these unprecedented challenges.

Total population. At the close of the twentieth century, world population stood at 6.1 billion. The less developed regions account for 80 per cent of the world's inhabitants, with China and India together (2.3 billion) representing 38 per cent of the world total. The current annual increase for the world is 77 million, of which 97 per cent is taking place in less developed regions. Six countries account for half of the world's annual population growth, i.e., India (21 per cent), China (12 per cent), Pakistan (5 per cent), Nigeria (4 per cent), Bangladesh (4 per cent) and Indonesia (3 per cent).

Migrant stock. Around 175 million persons currently reside in a country other than where they were born. The number of migrants has more than doubled since 1975. Sixty per cent of the world's migrants currently reside in the more developed regions and 40 per cent in the less developed regions. Most of the world's migrants live in Europe (56 million), Asia (50 million) and Northern America (41 million). Migrants currently make up about 3 per cent of the world population. Almost 1 of every 10 persons living in the more developed regions is a migrant. In contrast, nearly 1 of every 70 persons in developing countries is a migrant.

Number of refugees. The number of refugees in the world at the end of 2000 stood at 15.9 million, of whom 12.0 million are under the mandate of UNHCR and 3.9 million under the mandate of UNRWA. Three million of the refugees are in developed countries and 12.9 million in developing countries. The largest number of refugees was found in Asia, 9.1 million. Africa hosted the second largest refugee population in the world, 3.6 million.

Net migration. During 1995-2000, the more developed regions of the world, on an annual basis, gained an estimated 2.3 million migrants from the less developed regions, or 11.6 million over the whole period. The greatest gains in terms of net numbers of international migrants were made by Northern America, which absorbed 1.4 million migrants annually. It was followed by Europe with an annual net gain of 0.8 million and then by Oceania, with a more modest net intake of 90,000 migrants annually. The net migration rate was highest for Northern America, at an annual average of 4.6 migrants per 1,000 population during 1995-2000. Oceania's net migration rate was only slightly lower at 3 migrants per 1,000, with Europe recording a low of 1 migrant per 1,000. The net emigration rate was highest for Latin America and the Caribbean, where it amounted to a loss of 1 migrant per 1,000 population. For Africa and Asia, the net emigration rates were estimated to be lower, at 0.6 and 0.4 migrants per 1,000 population, respectively.

Workers' remittances. Remittances are the amount of migrants' earnings sent back from the country of employment to the country of origin. For some countries, remittances are a major source of foreign exchange earnings and are an important addition to gross domestic product. For example, in 2000, remittances from abroad augmented GDP by over 10 per cent for such countries as El Salvador, Eritrea, Jamaica, Jordan, Nicaragua and Yemen. Remittances can be used to import capital goods and provide investment funds for entrepreneurs. At the microlevel, remittances can add to household income and savings and be used for the purchase of consumer products.

Government views and policies on immigration. Beginning in the late 1970s, major changes in Governments' views on the level of immigration have been taking place, as a result of growing concerns with the economic, political and social consequences of immigration. By 2001, almost one quarter of all countries viewed immigration levels as too high. Although developed countries are more inclined towards lowering immigration, developing countries are also moving in a similar direction towards more restrictive policies. In 2001, 44 per cent of developed countries had policies aiming to lower immigration levels, as did 39 per cent of developing countries.

Government views and policies on emigration. Developed and developing countries are strikingly similar in their views and policies concerning levels of emigration. About three quarters of both developed and developing countries view their level of emigration as satisfactory. One in five countries have policies in place to lower levels of emigration.

Parties to United Nations instruments. While not creating a right to asylum, the 1951 Convention relating to the Status of Refugees, ratified by 141 countries, was a landmark in setting standards for the treatment of refugees. It established legal protections and a clear definition of the status of refugees. It also prohibited the expulsion or forcible return of persons accorded refugee status. The 1967 Protocol relating to the Status of Refugees, ratified by 139 countries, was formulated to extend the scope of the 1951 Convention, which benefited only persons who became refugees as a result of events occurring prior to 1 January 1951. The 1967 Protocol extended the application of the Convention to persons who became refugees after that date. The 1990 International Convention on the Protection of the Rights of All Migrant Workers and Members of Their Families has been ratified by 19 countries. For the Convention to enter into force, 20 Member States need to ratify it. This Convention established for the first time an international definition of the different categories of migrant worker and represented a major step forward in formalising the responsibility of receiving States in regard to upholding the rights of migrants and assuring their protection. In recent years, trafficking in human beings and its close linkage to transnational organised crime have arisen as new challenges to migration management. The 2000 Protocol to Prevent, Suppress and Punish Trafficking in Persons, Especially Women and Children, supplementing the United Nations Convention against Transnational Organized Crime, ratified by 18 countries, aims to prevent and combat trafficking in persons, paying particular attention to women and children; to protect and assist the victims of such trafficking; and to promote cooperation among States, parties to meet these objectives. The 2000 Protocol against the Smuggling of Migrants by Land, Sea and Air, supplementing the United Nations Convention against Transnational Organized Crime, ratified by 17 countries, provides an effective tool to combat and prevent the smuggling of human cargo, reaffirming that migration in itself is not a crime, and that migrants may be victims in need of protection.

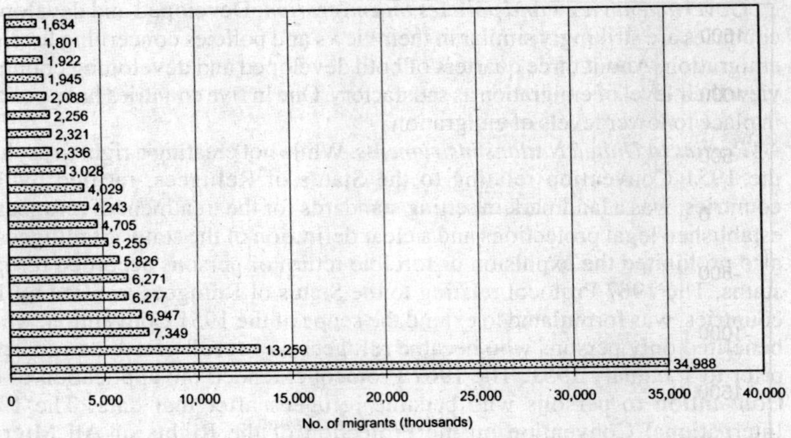

Fig. 30.1: Countries with the largest international migrant stock, 2000

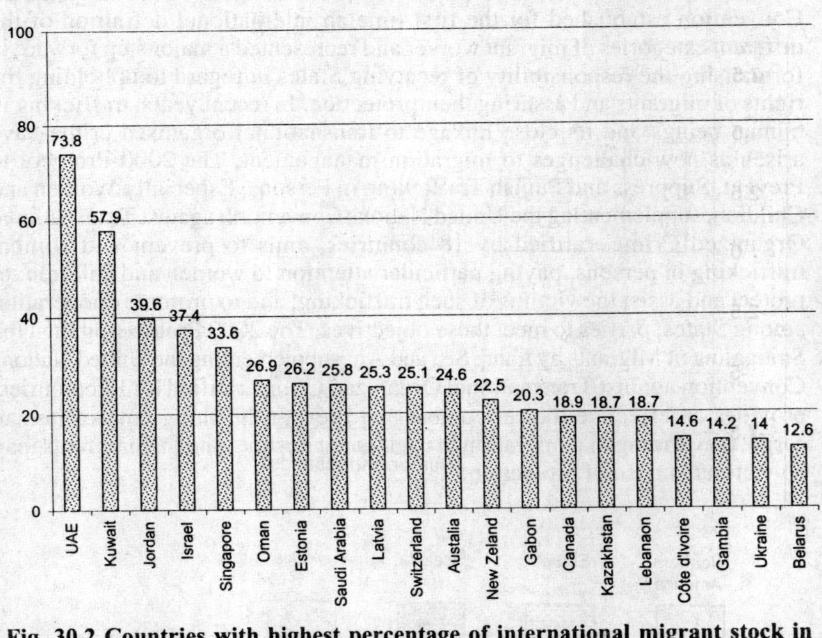

Fig. 30.2 Countries with highest percentage of international migrant stock in total population 2000

(*countries with population of one million or more inhabitants*)

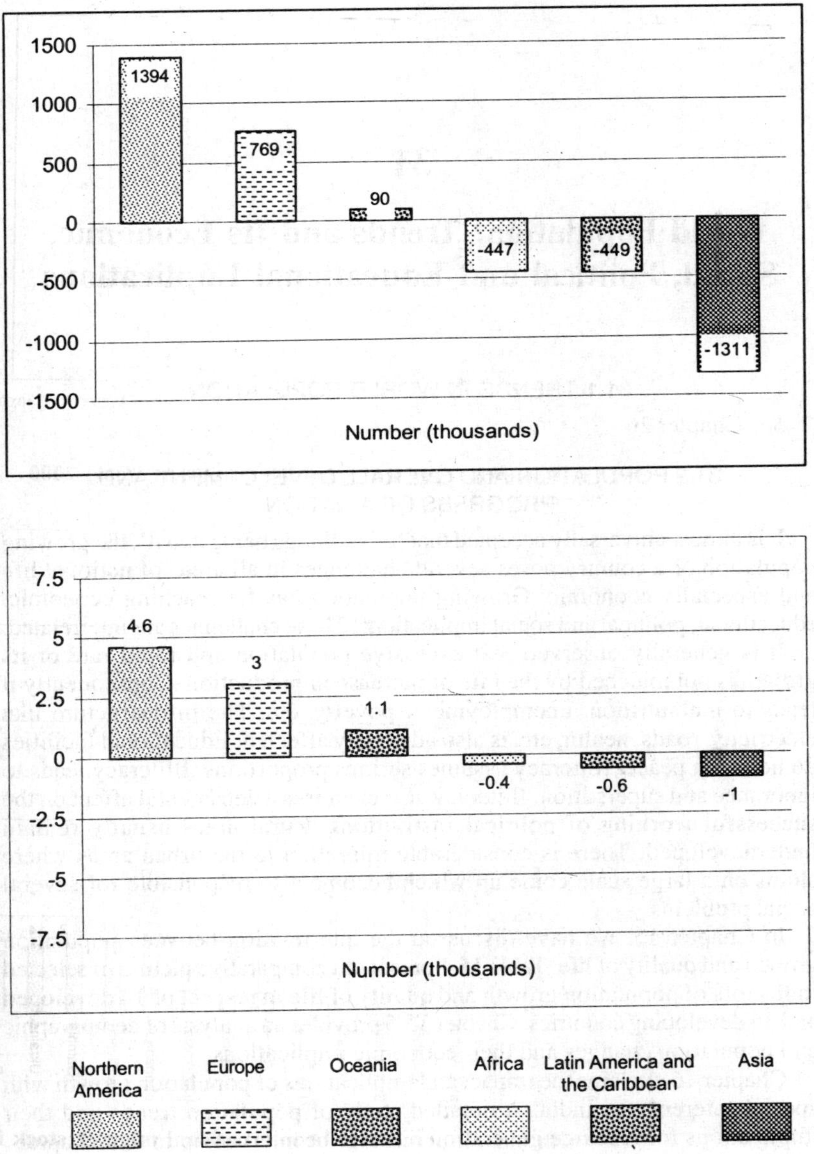

Fig. 30.3: International migration flows and migration rates in the world's major areas, 1995-2000

Source: *International Migration, 2002* (Wall Chart). Population Division of the United Nations, New York.

31

World Population: Trends and Its Economic, Social, Political and Educational Implications

31.1 TRENDS IN WORLD POPULATION

See Chapter 26

31.2 POPULATION AND OVERALL DEVELOPMENT AND PROGRESS OF A NATION

It is almost universally accepted that 'other things being equal', the growing population of a country poses several challenges in all areas of national life and especially economic. Growing population has far-reaching economic, educational, political and social implications. These challenges are interrelated.

It is generally observed that excessive population and rapid rate of its growth is not matched by the rate of increase in production. Consequently it leads to malnutrition, unemployment, poverty, etc. The infrastructure like electricity, roads, health, etc. is also adversely affected. Educational facilities do not keep peace. Illiteracy assumes serious proportions. Illiteracy leads to ignorance and superstition. Illiteracy also exercises a detrimental affect on the successful working of political institutions. Rural areas usually remain underdeveloped. There is considerable migration to the urban areas where slums on a large scale come up which become also responsible for several social problems.

In Chapter 15, we have discussed the interrelation between population growth and quality of life. Table 15.1 presents a comparative picture of selected indicators of population growth and quality of life in respect of 14 developed and 16 developing countries. Chapter 15.5 provides an analysis of demographic and population changes and their economic implications.

Chapter 16 explains the impact and implications of population growth with special reference to India. A detailed study of population trends and their implications for resource generation has also been taken up in that chapter.

31.3 POPULATION AND ECONOMIC IMPACT

Over-population affects the economy in the following manner:

1. Over-population increases investment requirements.
2. Over-population reduces the rate of capital investment.
3. Over-population reduces per capita availability of capital.

4. Over-population leads to food problem and malnutrition.
5. Over-population becomes responsible for unemployment.
6. Over-population adversely affects overall standard of life and living.
7. Over-population puts pressure on agriculture.

31.4 OVER-POPULATION AND SOCIAL IMPLICATIONS

Social implications are:

1. Fatalist outlook on life.
2. Paucity of social security measures.
3. Rise of slums.
4. Degradation in moral standards.
5. Rise of evil practices like child infanticide.

31.5 EDUCATIONAL IMPLICATIONS

1. Lack of educational facilities.
2. Overcrowding in classes.
3. Lack of instructional material.
4. Lack of school buildings.
5. Lack of playgrounds.

(see pages 151-155)

31.6 POLITICAL IMPLICATIONS

1. Increase in the number of voters leading to the creation of a huge election machinery.
2. Illiterate voters and their impact on the working of political institutions.

31.7 OVERALL DEVELOPMENT AND PROGRESS: DEMOGRAPHIC DATA OF SOME SELECT COUNTRIES.

Table 31.1 compares the development and progress of select countries in relation to demographic situation. Its analysis would provide the importance of achieving a balanced relationship among different indicators. It also indicates the economic, educational and social implications for following developmental policies in various fields.

Following are the important indicators included in Table 31.1

1. Under-five Mortality Rate
2. Infant Mortality Rate
3. Total Population
4. GNP Per Capita
5. Life Expectancy
6. Total Adult Literacy Rate
7. Net Primary School Enrolment Attendance
8. Annual Population Growth Rate
9. Crude Death Rate
10. Crude Birth Rate
11. Total Fertility Rate
12. Percentage of Population Urbanised
13. Average Annual Growth Rate of Urban Population

Table 31.1: Progress and Development: Demographic Data of selected country

Countries and territories	Under-five Mortality Rate	Infant Mortality Rate	Total Population	GNP Per Capita	Life Expectancy	Total Adult Literacy Rate	Net Primary School Enrolment Attendance	Annual Population Growth Rate	Crude Death Rate	Crude Birth Rate	Total Fertility Rate	Percentage of Population Urbanised	Average Annual Growth Rate of Urban Population
	2001	2001	2001	2001	2001	2000	1995-2001	1990-2001	2001	2001	2001	2001	1990-2001
	1	2	3	4	5	6	7	8	9	10	11	12	13
Afghanistan	257	165	2247	250	43	36	24	4.5	22	48	6.8	23	6.5
Argentina	19	16	37488	6960	74	97	100	1.3	8	19	2.5	88	1.5
Australia	6	6	19338	19770	79	-	95	1.2	7	13	1.8	91	1.9
Bangladesh	77	51	140369	370	60	41	79	2.2	9	31	3.6	26	4.6
Bhutan	95	74	2141	640	62	47	53	2.1	9	35	52	7	5.4
Brazil	36	31	172559	3060	68	85	97	1.4	7	19	2.2	82	2.2
China	39	31	1284972	890	71	85	93	1.0	7	15	1.8	37	3.6
Denmark	4	4	5333	31090	76	-	99	0.3	11	11	1.7	85	0.4
Egypt	41	35	69080	1530	68	55	86	1.9	6	24	3.0	43	1.7
Ethiopia	172	116	64459	100	44	39	30	2.8	20	44	6.8	16	4.8
Finland	5	4	5178	23940	78	-	100	1.2	5	25	3.0	50	2.9
France	6	4	59453	22690	79	-	100	0.4	9	12	1.8	76	0.8
Germany	5	4	82007	23700	78	-	87	0.3	11	9	1.3	88	0.5
India	93	67	1025096	460	64	56	76	1.8	9	25	3.1	28	2.6
Indonesia	45	33	214840	680	67	87	91	1.5	7	21	2.4	42	4.4

Countries and territories	1	2	3	4	5	6	7	8	9	10	11	12	13
	2001	2001	2001	2001	2001	2000	1995-2001	1990-2001	2001	2001	2001	2001	1990-2001
Iran (Islamic Republic of)	42	35	71369	1750	69	77	97	1.8	5	22	2.9	65	3.1
Iraq	133	107	23584	217x	63	58x	93	2.8	8	35	4.9	88	2.8
Italy	6	4	57503	19470	79	98	100	0.1	11	9	1.2	67	0.2
Japan	5	3	127335	35990	81	-	100	0.3	8	9	1.4	79	0.5
Korea, Republic	5	5	47069	9400	75	98	97	0.8	6	13	1.5	82	1.8
Maldives	77	58	300	2040	67	96	98	3.0	6	36	5.5	28	3.8
Mexico	29	24	100368	5540	73	91	100	1.7	5	23	2.6	75	2.0
Myanmar	109	77	48364	220x	56	85	68	1.8	12	24	3.0	28	2.8
Nepal	91	66	23593	250	59	41	66	2.4	10	35	4.6	12	5.2
Nigeria	183	110	116929	290	52	64	56	2.8	14	40	5.6	45	5.1
Pakistan	109	84	144971	420	60	43	46	2.5	10	37	5.2	34	3.4
Poland	9	8	38577	4240	74	100	97	0.1	10	10	1.3	63	0.4
Russian Federation	21	18	144664	1750	66	99	93x	-0.2	15	9	1.2	73	-0.3
Spain	6	4	39921	14860	79	98	95	0.1	10	9	1.1	78	0.4
Sri Lanka	19	17	19104	830	72	92	97	1.0	6	17	2.1	23	1.8
Sweden	3	3	8833	25400	80	-	100	0.3	11	9	1.4	83	0.3
Switzerland	6	5	7170	36970	79	-	99	0.4	10	9	1.4	67	1.5
Turkey	43	36	67632	2540	70	85	88	1.7	6	21	2.4	66	2.4
United Kingdom	7	6	59542	24230	78	-	99	0.3	11	11	1.6	90	0.4
United States	8	7	285926	34870	77	-	95	1.0	8	13	2.0	77	1.3
Zimbabwe	123	76	12852	480	43	93	80	2.1	18	36	4.7	36	4.3

32

Malthusian Theory of Population

32.1 BRIEF LIFE SKETCH OF THOMAS ROBERT MALTHUS (1766-1834)

Malthus was born on February 14, 1766. He received his early education at home. At the age of eighteen, he entered Jesus College at Cambridge. He became a Fellow of the college at the age of 27 in 1793. He took the holy order in 1797. He married in 1804 at the age of 38. In 1804 itself he was appointed Professor of History and Political Economy at the Hailebury College of the East India Company. He had three children. He died at the age of 68 in 1834.

32.2 A LANDMARK PUBLICATION: *'ESSAY ON POPULATION'* (1798)

Malthus, when he was a curate of a Small Survey Parish, published in 1798 his *'Essay on Population'*. The complete title of the Essay was *'An Essay on the Principles of Population as it Affects the Future Improvement of Society, with remarks on the speculations of Mr. Godwin, M. Clandereet and others.'*

As observed by Asha A. Bhende and Tara Kanitkar in *'Principles of Population Studies (2001)'*, Malthus's essay was mainly directed against the optimistic views of William Godwin, an English writer and philosopher, and against Marie Antonie Condorcet, a French mathematician, economist and philosopher. It is of interest to note that this work was published anonymously.

Malthus's work on population is considered as a landmark in the history of population studies and there is no wonder that all writers on population invariable refer to this. Not only this, his years contained in this essay has attracted the attention of leading philosophers, social reformers, sociologists, Statesmen and thinkers. The Sixth Edition of the book titled '*An Essay on the Principle of Population or a view of Its Past and Present Effects on Human Happiness, With an Enquiry Into Our Prospects Respecting the Future Removal or Mitigation of the Evils which It occasions*' was published in 1826.

32.3 ESSENCE OF MALTHUSIAN THEORY

Population when unchecked reproduces at a geometric ratio (2, 4, 8, 16, 32......) while food increases at an arithmatic ratio 1, 2, 3, 4, 5......). The ultimate result would be the lack of enough food to support such a huge population and hence individuals would face death due to starvation and malnutrition. The natural disaster would then, control the size of population.

32.4 POSTULATES OF MALTHUS REGARDING POPULATION

While propounding his theory, he had in mind the following postulates.

First, food is necessary to the existence of men.

Second, the passion between the sexes is necessary and will remain nearly in its present form.

According to Malthus, these laws are fixed by nature.

32.5 MALTHUS' ARGUMENTS AND HIS THEORY OF POPULATION

Malthus explain his views as under :

1. Assuming that my postulates, as granted, say that the power of population is definitely greater than the power in the earth to produce subsistence for man. Population when unchecked increases in a geometric ratio. Subsistence increases only in an arithmetical ratio. A slight acquaintance with numbers will show the immensity of the first power in comparison with the second.
2. Population is necessarily limited by the means of subsistence.
3. Population invariably increases where the means of subsistence increase unless prevented by some very powerful and obvious checks.
4. These checks, and the checks which repress the superior power of population and its effects on a level with the means of subsistence, are all resolvable into moral restraint, vice and misery.
5. Population tends to double itself every twentyfive years, thus increasing it in a geometrical ratio. On the other hand even under the most favourable conditions, agricultural produce increases each twentyfive years only by an equal quantity, thus increasing only in an arithmatical ratio.
6. Taking the whole earth the human species would increase as the numbers 1, 2, 4, 8, 16, 32, 64, 128, 256 and the subsistence as numbers 1, 2, 3, 4, 5, 6, 7, 8, 9. In two centuries the population would be to the means of subsistence as 256 to 9.
7. There are two types of checks, i.e., preventive checks and positive checks.
8. Preventive checks are (i) Moral Restraint (2) Vice.
9. Moral restraint implies abstinence from marriage, either for a time or permanently.
10. Vice means prevention of the birth of children.
11. Positive checks are those checks which tend to shorten human life. These are (i) unwholesome occupation, (ii) severe labour and exposure to the seasons, (iii) bad and insufficient food, (iv) insufficient clothing, (v) bad child care or nursing of children, (vi) excesses of all kinds, (vii) great town, (viii) great manufactories, (ix) common diseases and expidemics, (x) wars, (xi) infanticide, (xii) plague, (xiii) famine.
12. Two broad categories of positive checks are: (i) Natural causes, (ii) Causes brought by man.
13. There was no need for poor laws providing relief to the poor for the poor themselves should provide remedy by prudently delaying marriage.

32.6 CONTRIBUTION OF MALTHUSIAN THEORY: MERITS

The Malthus Theory of Population has the following merits:

1. *Development of Theory of Population.* Malthus was the first thinker to thoroughly and systematically apply the inductive method to social science.
2. *Relationship of Population and Socio-econo-politico Developments.* Malthus discussed his ideas in a larger framework and examined the interrelation between population growth and socio-economic—politico developments.
3. *Initiator of Discussion on Population Issues and their Impact.* It is true that his essay on population was in response to the views of some contemporary thinkers, but his views became so widespread that volumes of literature on various facets of population began to be published.
4. *Forerunner of Population Policy.* Malthus' view attracted so much attention that the policy workers in due course thought of formulating population policies for its regulation and thereby facilitating the achievement of ideals of quality living.
5. *Self Help.* Malthus very rightly advocated that in the ultimate analysis, the poor themselves should strive to improve their condition.

32.7 CRITICISM OF MALTHUSIAN THEORY

Several thinkers and writers have discussed Mlthusian Theory threadbare and have often criticised him very severely. Important points of criticism are given here in brief.

1. *Malthus concept of Geometrical and Arithmetical Ratios.* It is argued that these two ratios were based on very slender foundation and were never really proved. The case of population growth in India. According to the theory of Malthus, population of India which was nearly 36 crore in 1950-51 should have reached 72 crore in 1975-76 and 144 crore in 2000-2001. However, it was 68 crore in 1981, 84 crore in 1991 and 103 crore in 2001.
2. *Under Emphasis on Limited Land.* His emphasis on the limitation of the supply of land was out of proportion. He could not visualise the occurrence of agricultural revolution leading to increased production. Moreover in various countries there were great possibilities of making additional land available for cultivation by making barren land useful for cultivation. New types of fertilisers came to be used. Rotation of crops came into being. Irrigation facilities increased. All these measures led to tremendous increase in food production. In the case of India, population during the period 1950-51 to 2001 increased from nearly 36 crore to nearly 103 crore, i.e., less than 3 times whereas foodgrains increased from nearly 51 million tonnes to nearly 212 million tonnes, i.e., more than four times.
3. *Underestimating the Importance of Industrial Development.* Malthus did not take into consideration the potential of 'Industrial Revolution' ushering in an era of faster industrial growth.

4. *Malthus's Religious Beliefs*. The religious beliefs of Malthus prevented him from understanding the possibility of the widespread use of contraceptives.
5. *Aspiration Explosion*. There has been a revolutionary change in the perception of the people regarding quality of life since Malthus times. Now people have intense desire for a high standard of living which automatically puts a check on population growth.
6. *Malthus and Birth Control*. While suggesting preventive checks on growth of population, Malthus advocated postponement of marriage and even permanent abstinence from sex. He said, "I should always reprobate any artificial and unnatural modes of checking population on account of immorality." This view is not generally accepted now.

32.8 SUMMIMG UP: BALANCED VIEW OF MALTHUS'S WORK

We may sum up the discussion by quoting Charles Emile Strangleland: "Malthus's work was a great one written in an opportune time, and though it cannot lay any claim to any considerable originality as far as the theories presented are concerned, it was successful in that it showed more fully, perhaps more clearly, and certainly more effectively than had any previous attempt, that population depends on subsistence and its increase is checked by want, vice and disease as well as by moral restraint and prudence." Charles Emile strangleland, *'Pre-Malthusian Doctrines of Population; A study in the History of Economic Theory'*. Columbia University Press, New York, 1904.

32.9 POPULATION GROWTH CURVES

When the number of organisms in a population is plotted against the time, it produces the population growth curve. The growth curve could be J-shaped or S-shaped depending on the environmental resistance.

1. *J-shaped curve*. It is also called as the exponential growth curve. When the factors of environmental resistance do not exert any influence, i.e., there is plenty of food and much less number of deaths due to infection or predation, the population grows exponentially or at the geometric rate. The growth curve takes the shape of letter J (Fig. 32.1). Initially the growth is slow as the animals are few in number but then the population grows at a rapid rate. The rapid rate proceeds till enough food is available and can soar towards infinity.

In nature with limited resources, such a situation never arises and various factors of environmental resistance check the population growth rate.

2. *S-shaped or Sigmoid curve* (Fig. 32.2). Sigmoid or S-shaped curve is a typical growth curve characteristic of many species when introduced into a new habitat. Initially the growth is slow, also called lag phase as it takes time for the individuals to get adapted. It leads into a rapid period of growth, the log phase where the rate of growth is proportional to the food available. It grows like this for quite some time until the individuals become so numerous that their further multiplication is checked by the factors of environmental resistance. Now the population growth begins to decline until the zero population growth is achieved. This is known as the stationary phase when overall growth has ceased completely. It signifies the maximum size of

population that an environment can carry or sustain. It is also referred as the carrying capacity.

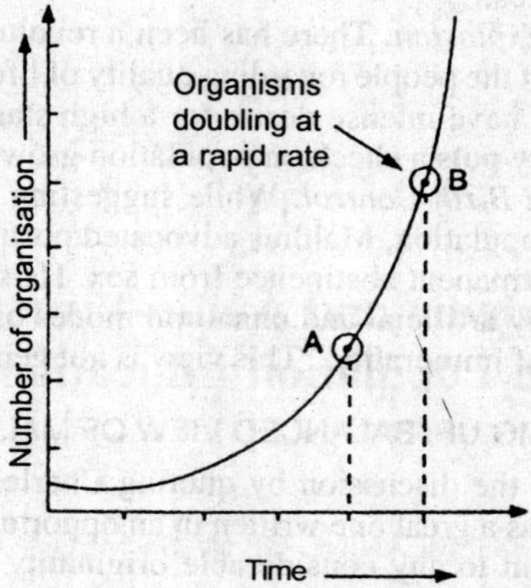

Fig. 32.1 J-shaped curve or the exponential growth curve

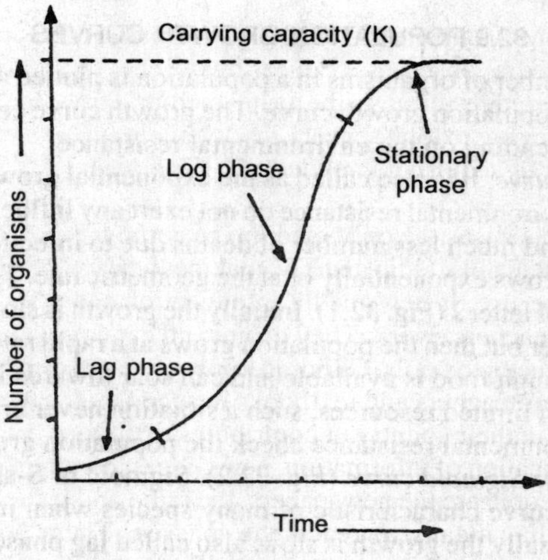

Fig. 32.2 S-shaped or Sigmoid population growth curve, K-carrying capacity

33

Mass Media and Audio-Visual Aids in Population Education

33.1 MEANING OF MASS MEDIA

Mass media are means or instruments of communication that reach large number of people or pupils. The media may be printed like newspapers or may take the form of cinema, radio and T.V. Now new media like Internet and e-mail etc. are also increasingly being used. As observed by Erickson and others, "In recent years technology has swept through society from research laboratories into manufacturing communications, the space age and finally now, into education".

Prof. Marshall MC Luhan (1911-1980) who has written extensively on 'Understanding Media' observes, "Education will no longer depend entirely on obtaining knowledge through the print media. The visual approach to learning is fast changing to total sensory involvement (visual, auditory modes etc.) in the process of acquiring knowledge". His slogan was 'Medium is the message'.

Earlier, the teacher was the only medium of communication for children. Now we see new media like radio and T.V. making their inroads into education. A close look at the use of new media in education indicates that they are supplementary to teachers' work. They do not and cannot replace the teacher.

Everyone must need to know. Children know or learn from their parents at home and from their teachers and textbooks in schools. Adults need to know what is happening in their country. It contributes to the success of living. The means of communication of information, news, ideas, comments, pictures and the like to all the people are the newspapers, the radio and the television. They are the mass media, means to reach the masses. These media of mass communication have a deep impact on the life and culture of the people. Whatever the people read, hear or see at the same time or the same day, they think over it, analyse and generally discuss among themselves, exchange their views and judge or think what is good and what is wrong about a subject, to feel what should be or should not be and to form judgement. This is the way the public opinion is formed. This exercise of thinking independently, analysing facts and judging for oneself contributes to the success of democracy. Radio and TV also provide entertainment and knowledge about many things besides news.

33.2 IMPORTANCE OF MASS MEDIA IN EDUCATION

1. Mass media are very helpful in spreading literacy.
2. Mass media are very useful in social education.
3. Mass media provide very useful information on almost all matters of significance in life.
4. They can bring the entire world in to the classroom.
5. They send information to remote places and helps in distant learning.
6. They help in providing a simplified and vivid description even of complicated skills like performing of operations, experiments etc.
7. They help in the modification of attitudes and values of individuals.
8. They provide information very speedily.
9. They are useful in reinforcing group dynamics.
10. They appeal to various senses and this is helpful in developing motivation.

Sometimes it is felt that the mass media tend to diminish the importance of the teacher. It is also claimed in certain circles that the use of these media of education indicates that they are supplementary media. A lot of work by way of pre-telecast, during telecast and post telecast remains to be done by the teachers. Many gaps are to be filed up by them. In spite of the explosion of technological media in the developed countries, the teacher still occupies the place of importance. Fears about the replacement of teachers are unfounded.

Newspapers

With the spread of literacy within the country, the demand for newspapers has grown. For educated people reading the newspaper is an essential morning routine. Even in villages the craze of the illiterate populace for news is satisfied by somebody reading the newspaper to them.

During the freedom struggle, the newspapers played a very important role in spreading national consciousness. Many freedom fighters started printing and distributing newspapers of their own for boosting the courage and spirit of their countrymen by reporting the truth about their conditions under the British rule and preparing and exhorting them to make the freedom struggle a success. Many were arrested and deported and their newspapers were banned.

Newspapers have certain advantages over the radio and TV as they cover more news and in much greater details than the other media. News stories cover the latest developments in such fields as populations, government, politics, sports, science, business and the arts. The editorials offer critical comments on national problems, events and the performance of the government. Sometimes, the government, respecting the public opinion, makes changes in its policy.

33.3 RADIO AS AGENCY OF POPULATION EDUCATION

In the words of R.G. Reynolds, "Radio is the most significant medium of education in its broadest sense. As a supplement to classroom teaching its possibilities are almost unlimited". Frederic Wittis has observed, "I like to think of education by radio as a timely, vital and dramatic thing".

Of comparatively recent growth is the system of educational broadcast. These broadcasts can either be 'live' or 'transcribed' depending on the physical presence of the person broadcasting or his recorded speech. Broadcasting organisations throughout the world, including AIR, include in their output various school broadcasts. Such programmes are normally arranged in consultation with the heads of various institutions. This liaison between the radio and education helps in bringing out effective and useful programmes for the pupils. The planning of such talks is undertaken with great care and by persons of repute. The programmes are prepared termwise and copies are supplied to schools sufficiently in advance to enable the teachers to discuss the subject with the pupils.

A variety of broadcasting programmes on population education can be organised.

Deficiencies and Limitations of Radio Broadcasts

1. Broadcast exposition leaves some gaps.
2. Broadcast time may not be suitable.
3. Radio sets may develop defects and need immediate repairs.

Suggestions for the Improvement of School Broadcast Programmes

(i) The broadcasts should have a wider horizon of application in day-to-day life.
(ii) The school broadcasts should also be designed according to the needs of the syllabus.
(iii) Teachers should be actively involved in various dimensions of broadcasts meant for the students.
(iv) The radio programmes should be intended to give supplementary information on the various topics in the curriculum.
(v) Teachers should occasionally meet, discuss and plan the type of assistance required in producing effective broadcast programmes.
(vi) Students should be asked to give suitable suggestions to make further improvement in broadcasts.
(vii) Every school should have one teacher trained in the electronic media.
(viii) Proper follow-up may be taken up on school broadcasts.
(ix) Suitable listing facilities should be provided to the students in the school.
(x) Broadcasts should be made in a pleasing style.
(xi) Language used in broadcasts should be easy simple and forceful.

33.4 POPULATION AND TELEVISION AS AN EDUCATIONAL MEDIUM

Importance of Television. For a country like India which has vast and inaccessible areas, T.V. can serve as one of the important media of educating the masses. It can be used as formal, non-formal and informal agency of education. It attracts attention which is essential for learning. Following are the important merits of T.V.:

1. T.V. comes to the assistance of those persons who are unable to acquire education through the traditional system.
2. It promotes the goal of equalisation of educational opportunity by reaching the remote areas.
3. It provides technical advantages which normally are not readily available in normal classroom for demonstration or illustration.
4. It makes possible close-up magnification of small objects, components, intricate mechanisms, diagrams, etc. by providing students a 'front-row-seat automatically.
5. It makes quick and lasting visual and aural impressions.
6. It makes possible to bring large, scarce or new equipment into the classroom electronically.
7. It saves time, effort and cost of setting up classroom projection equipment.
8. It brings into the classroom demonstration, videotape or film presentations at the instant or immediately after they occur.
9. It allows relationship between two illustrations or time lapse between two stages of a process by dissolving one picture into another.
10. It directs the attention of the student to the exact details of an objet.
11. It permits inclusion of up-to-the-moment information, modifications, new equipment or techniques into classroom instruction.
12. It permits the use of the services of the best available teachers to teach a subject to a large member of viewer students.
13. It permits to preserve the expert teaching skills on video tape or film for later use.
14. It provides a uniform experience to all students when they see the basic ideas or techniques on television.
15. It provides classroom teachers the opportunity to observe the teaching process of the best teachers and to increase their skills of teaching.
16. It incorporates useful film sequences, slides, graphic art and makes teaching process of the best teachers and to increase their skills of teaching.
17. Educational telecasts can re-create the past through dramatisation, films or lectures.
18. Educational telecasts can explain several scientific phenomena which are too small, too slow, too fast or too dangerous to be observed first hand, by sound films.
19. Educational T.V. has both amusement and instruction value.
20. Educational T.V. reduces dependence on the classroom teachers.
21. It bridges the gap between the private school and public school to some extent by making the best teachers available to all students.
22. Educational T.V. helps in the in-service training of teachers.
23. In case of distance learning, television reduces cost of instruction.
24. On account of the combination of audio and video components, T.V. has greater appeal than radio and print media.

Limitations of T.V. Instruction

1. There is one-way communication from teacher to students.
2. It does not provide opportunity for question-answer, discussion and interaction of the viewers with the T.V. teacher at the time of telecast.
3. Educational T.V. expects thousands of students who view telecasts to be of the same educational standard.
4. T.V. teachers cannot cater to the individual differences of the students.
5. Teaching through T.V. is a costly affair. It is not within the reach of every school.
6. All schools do not have the proper viewing facilities.
7. T.V. lessons to large number of students in the hall may create disciplinary problems.

Suggestion for Making T.V. Instruction More Effective

1. Effective arrangement for pre-telecast and post-telecast should be made.
2. There should be interaction among the students, subject teachers and the teachers who telecast, irrespective of the fact whether teachers who telecast are practising teachers or not.
3. There should be proper seating arrangements so that all the students have a proper view of the lesson.
4. Provision for T.V. repairs should be made suitably.

Software Approach

This uses the principles of psychology for building in the learner a complex repertory of knowledge modifying his behaviour. It has originated from the pioneering work of Skinner and other behaviourists. The programmes which such a technology produces, are often called 'software'. Software approach is characterised by task analysis, writing precise objectives, selection of appropriate learning strategies, immediate reinforcement of responses and constant evaluation. Newspapers, books, magazines, educational games, flash cards may also form part of software.

33.5 AUDIO-VISUAL AIDS IN POPULATION EDUCATION

Meaning, Significance and Merits of Audio-visual Aids

Audio-visual aids or devices or technological media or learning devices are added devices that help the teacher to clarify, establish, corelate and co-ordinate accurate concepts, interpretations and appreciations and enable him to make learning more concrete, effective, interesting, inspirational, meaningful and vivid. They help in completing the triangular process of learning, viz., motivation-clarification-stimulation. The aim of teaching with technological media is 'clearing the channel between the learner and the things that are worth learning'. The basic assumption underlying Audio-visual Aids is that learning—clear understanding—stems from sense experience. *The teachers must 'show' as well as 'tell'*. Audio-visual aids provide significant gains in informational learning, retention and recall, thinking and reasoning, activity, interest, imagination, better assimilation and personal growth and development. The aids are the stimuli for learning 'why', 'how', 'when' and 'where'. The 'hard to understand principles' are usually made clear by the intelligent use of skilfully designed instructional aids.

Following are the main merits of the instructional aids:

1. They are potent motivators.
2. They lend reality to the classroom teaching and link instruction with real life.
3. They supply a concrete basis for conceptful thinking and hence reduce meaningless word responses of students.
4. They have a high degree of interest for the students as they are interested in things they can see, hear, touch, taste, plan, make, do and try.
5. They supply the necessary basis for developmental learning and hence make learning more permanent.
6. They offer a reality of experience which stimulates self-activity on the part of the students.
7. They develop a continuity of thought; this is especially true of motion pictures.
8. They contribute to increase retentivity as they stimulate the maximum response of the whole organism to the situation in which the learning is done.
9. They help in making right types of images which facilitate learning.

Projected and Non-Projected Aids

Projected Aids	*Non-Projected Aids*				
	Graphic Aids	*Display Boards*	*3-Dimensional Aids*	*Audio Aids*	*Activity Aids*
Films Filmstrips Opaque Projection Overhead Projection Slides	Cartons Charts Comics Diagrams Flash Cards Graphs Maps Photographs Pictures Posters	Black-board Bulletin Flannel Board Magnetic Board Peg Board	Diagrams Models Mock-ups Objects Puppets Specimens	Radio Recordings Television	Computer-Assisted Instruction Demonstrations Dramatics Experimentation Field Trips Programmed Instruction Teaching Machines

Types of Audio-Visual Aids

Audio Materials	*Visual Materials*	*Audio-visual Materials*
(1) Language laboratories	(1) Bulletin boards	(1) Demonstrations
(2) Radio	(2) Chalk boards	(2) Films
(3) Sound distribution system sets	(3) Charts	(3) Printed materials with recorded sound
(4) Tape and disco recordings	(4) Drawings etc.	(4) Sound filmstrips
	(5) Exhibits	(5) Study trips
	(6) Filmstrips	(6) Television
	(7) Flash cards	(7) Videotapes
	(8) Flannel boards	
	(9) Flip books	
	(10) Illustrated books	
	(11) Magnetic boards	
	(12) Maps	
	(13) Models	
	(14) Pictures	
	(15) Posters	
	(16) Photographs	
	(17) Self-instructional	
	(18) Silent films	
	(19) Slides	

Main Advantages of the Audio-visual Aids

1. *Best motivators.* They are the best motivators. The students work with more interest and zeal. They are more attentive.
2. *Fundamental to verbal instruction.* They help to reduce verbalism which is a major wear school. They convey the same meaning as words mean. They give clear concepts and thus help to bring accuracy in learning.
3. *Clear images.* Clear images are formed when we see, hear, touch, taste and smell as our experiences are direct, concrete and more or less permanent. Learning through the senses becomes the most natural and consequently the easiest.
4. *Vicarious experience.* It is beyond doubt that the first-hand experience is the best type of educative experience. But it is neither practicable nor desirable to provide such experience to pupils. Substituted experiences may be provided under such conditions. There are many inaccessible objects and phenomena. For example, it is not possible for the pupils living in India to see the person of Eskimoe. Similarly, it is not possible for an average man to climb the Mount Everest. There are innumerable such things to which it is not possible to have direct access. So, in all such cases, these aids help us.
5. *Variety.* Mere chalking and talking do not help. Audio-visual aids give variety and provide different tools in the hands of the teacher.
6. *Freedom.* When audio-visual aids are employed, there is great scope for children to move about, talk, laugh and comment upon. Under such

an atmosphere the students work because they want to work and not because the teacher wants them to work.

7. *Opportunities to handle and manipulate*. Many visual aids offer opportunities to students to handle and manipulate things.

Problems in the Use of Teaching Aids

While all these aids are becoming more and more popular day by day, there are still some problems to be faced and solved. These are:

(i) *Apathy of the teachers*. The teachers are yet to be convinced that teaching with words alone is very tedious, wasteful and ineffective.

(ii) *Indifference of students*. The judicious use of aids arouses interest but when used without a definite purpose they lose their significance and importance.

(iii) *Ineffectiveness of the aids*. Due to the absence of proper planning and the lethargy of the teacher and without proper preparation, correct presentation, appropriate application and discussion and the essential follow-up work, the aids have not proved their full usefulness. A film like a good lesson has various steps—Preparation, Presentation, Application and Discussion.

(iv) *Financial hurdles*. The Central and State Governments have set up Boards of Audio-Visual Education and have chalked out interesting programmes for the popularisation of teaching aids but the lack of finances is not enabling them to do their best.

(v) *Absence of electricity*. Most of the Projectors cannot work without the electric current.

(vi) *Lack of facilities for training*. More and more training colleges or specialised agencies should be opened to train teachers and workers in the use and usefulness of the these aids.

(vii) *Co-ordination between Centre and States*. Good film libraries, museums of Audio-visual education, fixed and mobile exhibitions and educational 'melas' should be organised both by Centre and the States.

(viii) *Language difficulty*. Most films are in English. We should have these in Hindi and other important Indian languages.

(ix) *Not catering for local needs*. No attention is paid in the production of Audio-visual aids to the sociological, psychological and pedagogical factors.

(x) *Improper selection of films*. Films are not selected according to the classroom needs.

Future. Today, the problem is not whether visual aids should have a place in education. Their place has been recognised long ago. The problem, now, is that of extending the benefits of these aids to all teachers and all children. The future can be bright if there is proper planning on the part of the Government and co-ordination between producers, teachers and students. Useful and effective aids can be produced after getting the reaction of the audience and

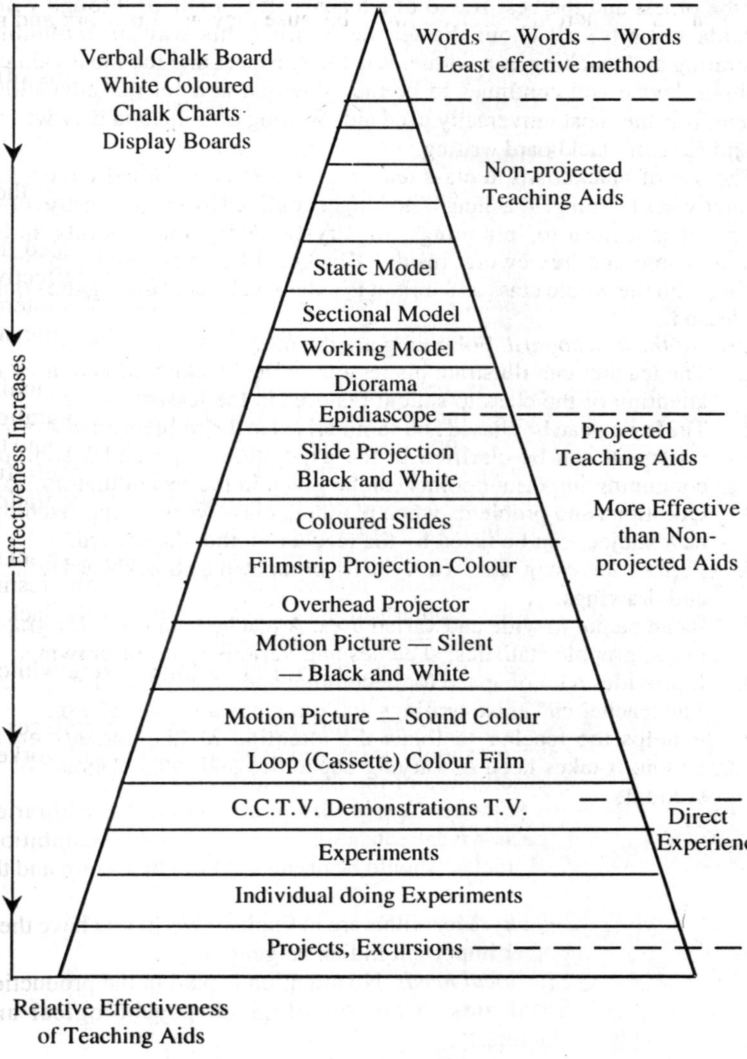

Fig. 33.1Cone of Experience illustrating the relative impact of audio-visual aids on population education instruction

Blackboard

Significance of backboard. Blackboard is a unique device which in spite of newer and better devices in vogue, is irreplacable as well as indispensable.

It is the oldest and the best friend of a teacher. It is a mirror through which students visualise all about the teacher's mind, his way of explaining, illustrating and teaching as a whole. It is the cheapest and the most valuable teaching device and continues to be the 'sine qua non' of our educational system. It is the most universally used aid. Writing on sand and clay was the ancient form of blackboard writing.

The use of blackboard in class teaching creates an informal atmosphere and motivates learning. Teaching is no longer confined to any one instructional device. It is a help to 'planning', to 'crystallising' main points and to 'summarising' and 'reviewing' results. Blackboard being a simple means of dealing with the whole class as a unit, it is extensively used during the course of a lesson.

Uses of the blackboard. Following are the uses:

1. The teacher can illustrate his lesson on the blackboard and draw the attention of the class to salient features in the lesson.
2. The lesson can be phased and summarised in the right manner. Abstract statement can be clarified in the exposition stage and a summary containing important points can be given in the recapitulatory stage.
3. Questions and problems when planning class work or approaching a new subject can be listed by the teacher on the blackboard.
4. Pupils' interest in class work can be stimulated by blackboard writings and drawings.
5. It can be put to wide and varied uses. A teacher can use it for graphs, maps, graphic statistics, sketches and various types of drawings.
6. It provides a lot of space for decorative and creative work.
7. The teacher can erase writings and drawings and start afresh.
8. It helps the teacher to focus the attention of his students on the lesson. It takes heed of varying capacities and rates of grasp of the students.

34

Main Features of World Population

WORLD POPULATION PROSPECTS: THE 2006 REVISION:
CHIEF DEMOGRAPHICS CHARACTERISTICS

The Population Division of the Department of Economic and Social Affairs has prepared the official United Nations estimates and projections of the world's population since 1951. The *2006 Revision* of the *World Population Prospects* is the twentieth round of such revisions. Population estimates and projections are an important input for the estimation of several of the indicators used to assess the progress made in achieving the internationally agreed development goals, including the Millennium Development Goals (MDGs).

34.1 Population of the World (2007)

According to the *2006 Revision,* the world population will likely increase by 2.5 billion over the next 43 years, passing from 6.7 billion in 2007 to 9.2 billion in 2050. This increase is equivalent to the size that the world population had in 1950 and it will be absorbed mostly by the less developed regions, whose population is projected to rise from 5.4 billion in 2007 to 7.9 billion in 2050. In contrast, the population of the more developed regions is expected to remain largely unchanged at 1.2 billion and would have declined were it not for the projected net migration from developing to developed countries, which is expected to average 2.3 million persons a year after 2010.

34.2 Ageing Population

As a result of declining fertility and increasing longevity, the populations of a growing number of countries are ageing rapidly. Between 2005 and 2050, half of the increase in the world population will be accounted for by a rise in the population aged 60 years or over, whereas the number of children (persons under age 15) will decline slightly. Furthermore, in the more developed regions, the population aged 60 or over is expected nearly to double (from 245 million in 2005 to 406 million in 2050) whereas that of persons under age 60 will likely decline (from 971 million in 2005 to 839 million in 2050).

34.3 Diversity of Demographic Dynamics

The 2006 Revision confirms the diversity of demographic dynamics among the different world regions. While the population at the global level is on track to surpass 9 billion by 2050 and hence continues to increase, that of the more developed regions is hardly changing and will age markedly. As already noted, virtually all population growth is occurring in the less developed regions and especially in the group of the 50 least developed countries, many of which still have relatively youthful populations that are expected to age only moderately over the foreseeable future. Among the rest of the developing countries, rapid population ageing is expected.

34.4 Distinct Trends on Fertility and Mortality

Underlying these varied patterns of growth and changes in the age structure are distinct trends in fertility and mortality. Below-replacement fertility prevails in the more developed regions and is expected to continue to 2050. Fertility is still high in most of the least developed countries and, although it is expected to decline, it will remain higher than in the rest of the world. In the rest of the developing countries, fertility has declined markedly since the late 1960s and is expected to reach below-replacement levels by 2050 in the majority of them.

Between 2005 and 2050, half of the increase in the world population will be accounted for by a rise in the population aged 60 years or over, whereas the number of children (persons under age 15) will decline slightly.

Mortality in the established market economies of the developed world is low and continues to decline, but it has been stagnant or has even increased in a number of countries with economies in transition, largely as a result of deteriorating social and economic conditions and, in some cases, because of the spread of HIV. Mortality is also decreasing in the majority of developing countries, but in those highly affected by the HIV/AIDS epidemic, mortality has been increasing.

34.5 HIV/AIDS

The HIV/AIDS epidemic continues to spread. The number of countries with a significant number of infected people in the 2006 Revision is 62, up from 60 in the 2004 Revision and 53 in the 2002 Revision. Although HIV prevalence in some countries has been revised downward since 2004 on the basis of newly available nationally representative data, the toll of the disease continues to be high and is expected to remain so, despite projected reductions in the prevalence of HIV/AIDS.

Lower projected levels of HIV prevalence depend on the realization of the commitments made by Governments in the 2000 Millennium Declaration[1] and the 2001 United Nations Declaration of Commitment on HIV/AIDS[2]. In particular, the projected population trends depend on achieving a major increase in the proportion of AIDS patients who get antiretroviral therapy to treat the disease and on the success of efforts to control the further spread of HIV. In the 2006 Revision, the 62 countries considered to be highly affected by the HIV/AIDS epidemic include 40 located in Africa. In projecting the effect of the disease, it is assumed that by 2015, 31 of the most affected countries will manage to provide antiretroviral treatment to 70 per cent or more of the persons suffering from AIDS. In the rest of the affected countries, treatment levels are expected to be lower, reaching between 40 per cent and 50 per cent by 2015. It is further assumed that persons receiving treatment survive, on average, 17.5 years instead of the 10 years expected in the absence of treatment. Mainly as a result of these assumptions and owing to the downward revision of the prevalence of HIV/AIDS in countries where nationally representative data on the epidemic have become available, an estimated 32 million fewer deaths are projected to occur during 2005-2020 in the 62 countries most affected by the epidemic according to the 2006 Revision than would have occurred if death rates were the same as in the 2004 Revision. These changes also contribute to make the population projected to 2050 larger according to the 2006 Revision than according to the 2004 Revision (9.2 billion vs. 9.1 billion).

The urgency of realizing the reductions of fertility projected is brought into focus by considering that, if fertility were to remain constant at the levels estimated for 2000-2005, the population of the less developed regions would increase to 10.6 billion instead of the 7.9 billion projected by assuming that fertility declines.

Realization of the medium variant projections contained in the 2006 Revision is also contingent on ensuring that fertility continues to decline in developing countries. According to the 2006 Revision, fertility in the less developed countries as a whole is expected to drop from 2.75 children per woman in 2005-2010 to 2.05 in 2045-2050. The reduction expected in the group of 50 least developed countries is even sharper: from 4.63 children per woman to 2.50 children per woman. To achieve such reductions, it is essential that access to family planning expands in the poorest countries of the world. The urgency of realizing the reductions of fertility projected is brought into focus by considering that, if fertility were to remain constant at the levels estimated for 2000-2005, the population of the less developed regions would increase to 10.6 billion instead of the 7.9 billion projected by assuming that fertility declines. That is, without further reductions of fertility, the world population could increase by twice as many people as those who were alive in 1950.

34.6 Miscellaneous Key Findings

Other key findings resulting from the comprehensive review of past worldwide demographic trends and future prospects presented in the 2006 Revision are summarized below.

1. In July 2007, the world population will reach 6.7 billion, 547 million more than in 2000 or a gain of 78 million persons annually. Assuming that fertility levels continue to decline, the world population is expected to reach 9.2 billion in 2050 and to be increasing by about 30 million persons annually at that time, according to the medium variant.

2. Future population growth is highly dependent on the path that future fertility takes (figure 34.1). In the medium variant, the total fertility of the world declines from 2.55 children per woman today to slightly over 2 children per woman in 2050. If fertility were to remain about half a child above the levels projected in the medium variant, world population would reach 10.8 billion by 2050. A fertility path half a child below the medium variant would lead to a population of 7.8 billion by mid-century. That is, at the world level, continued population growth until 2050 is inevitable even if the decline in fertility accelerates.

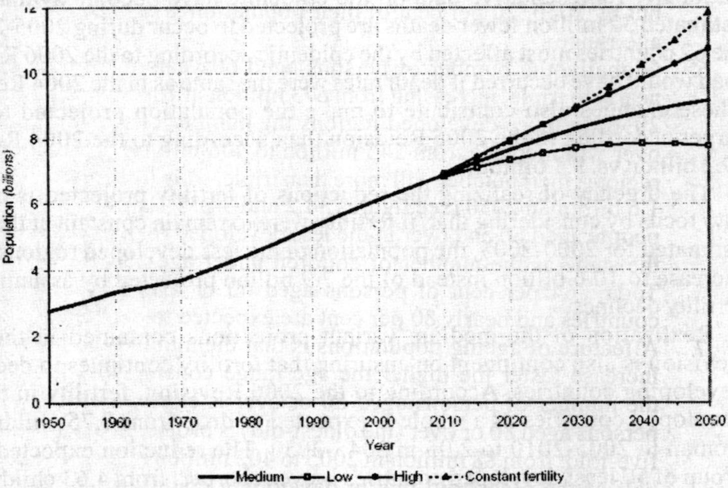

Fig. 34.1: Population of the world, estimates and projection variants, 1950-2050

3. Because of its low and declining rate of population growth, the population of developed countries as a whole is expected to remain virtually unchanged between 2007 and 2050, at about 1.2 billion, according to the medium variant. In contrast, the population of the 50 least developed countries will likely more than double, passing from 0.8 billion in 2007 to 1.7 billion in 2050. Growth in the rest of the developing world is also projected to be robust, though less rapid, with its population rising from 4.6 billion to 6.2 billion between 2007 and 2050 according to the medium variant.
   The population of the 50 least developed countries will likely more than double, passing from 0.8 billion in 2007 to 1.7 billion in 2030.
4. Slow population growth brought about by reductions in fertility leads to population ageing, that is, it produces populations where the proportion of older persons increases while that of younger persons decreases. In the more developed regions, 20 per cent of the population is already aged 60 years or over and that proportion

is projected to reach 33 per cent in 2050. In developed countries as a whole, the number of older persons (persons aged 60 or over) has already surpassed the number of children (persons under age 15) and by 2050 the number of older persons is expected to be more than double the number of children in developed countries (see figure 34.2).

5. Population ageing is less advanced in developing countries. Nevertheless, the populations of a majority of them are posed to enter a period of rapid population ageing. In developing countries as a whole, just 8 per cent of the population is today aged 60 years or over but by 2050, 20 per cent of their population is expected to be in that age range.
6. Globally, the number of persons aged 60 years or over is expected nearly to triple, increasing from 673 million in 2005 to over 2 billion by 2050. In more developed regions the number of persons aged 60 or over will increase from 245 million to 406 million; in less developed regions, their number will more than triple, from 428 million in 2005 to 1.6 billion in 2050 (see figures 34.2 and 34.3). By then, the number of people aged 60 and over in the less developed regions will be roughly the same as the number of children under age 15 (see figure 34.3). Today, 64 per cent of persons aged 60 or over live in developing countries and nearly 80 per cent are expected to do so in 2050.
7. A feature of ageing populations is that the numbers of older persons increase faster the higher the age range considered. Thus, whereas the number of persons aged 60 or over is expected to triple, that of persons aged 80 or over (the oldest-old) is projected to increase nearly five-fold, from 88 million in 2005 to 402 million in 2050. Today, about half of the oldest-old live in developing countries and that share is expected to reach 71 per cent in 2050.
8. Although the populations of all countries are expected to age over the foreseeable future, the populations of countries where fertility is still high will remain relatively young and will increase rapidly. High population growth rates prevail in a number of developing countries, the majority of which are least developed. Between 2005 and 2050, the populations of Afghanistan, Burundi, the Democratic Republic of the Congo, Guinea-Bissau, Liberia, Niger, Timor-Leste and Uganda are projected to increase at least threefold.
   The pervasiveness of population ageing is reflected by the fact that 93 countries are projected to have median ages above 40 years in 2050, 48 of which are developing countries.
9. In sharp contrast, the populations of 46 countries or areas, including Germany, Italy, Japan, the Republic of Korea, most of the successor States of the former USSR and several small island States are expected to be smaller in 2050 than in 2005.
10 Population growth remains concentrated in the populous countries. During 2005-2050, eight countries are expected to account for half of the world's projected population increase: India, Nigeria, Pakistan, the

Democratic Republic of the Congo, Ethiopia, the United States of America, Bangladesh and China, listed according to the size of their contribution to global population growth.

11. The median age, that is, the age that divides the population in two equal halves, is an indicator of population ageing. At the world level, the median age is projected to increase from 28 to 38 years between 2005 and 2050. Europe has today the oldest population, with a median age of nearly 39 years that is expected to reach 47 years in 2050.
12. The median age is higher in countries having low fertility for long periods. In 2005, the median age in 13 developed countries or areas was higher than 40 years. The pervasiveness of population ageing is reflected by the fact that 93 countries are projected to have median ages above 40 years in 2050, 48 of which are developing countries.

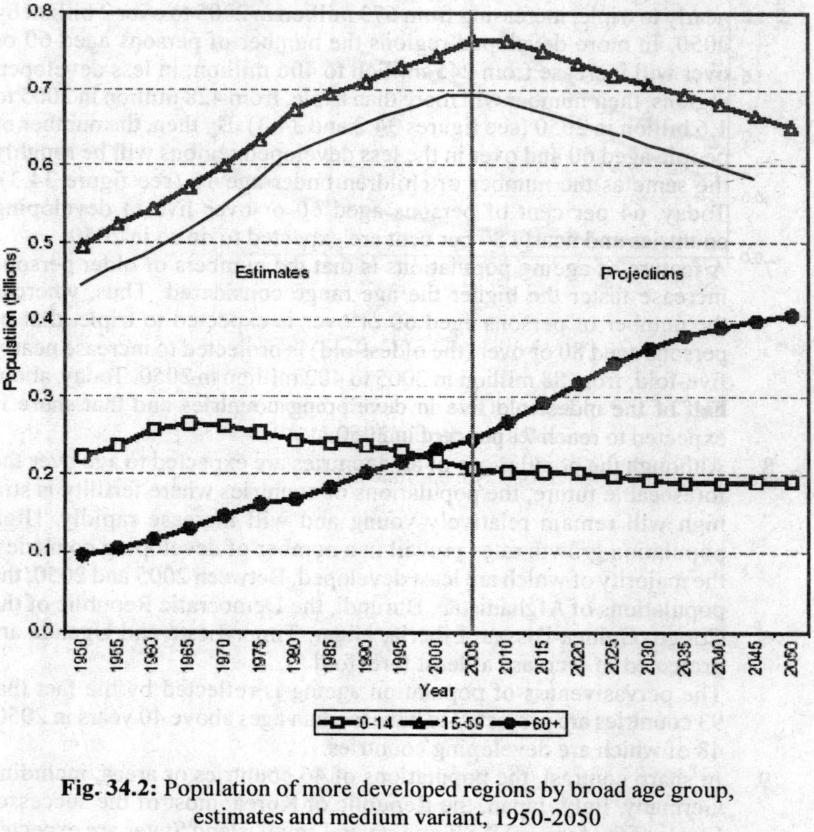

Fig. 34.2: Population of more developed regions by broad age group, estimates and medium variant, 1950-2050

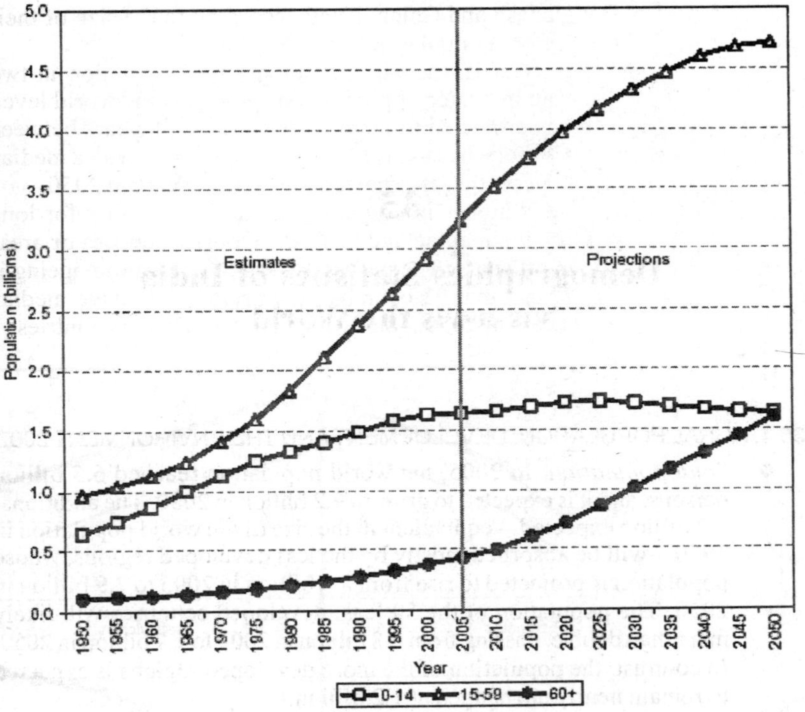

Fig. 34.3: Population of less developed regions by broad age group, estimates and medium variant, 1950-2050

Source: *Population Newsletter*, No. 83, June 2007

35

Demographics Statistics of India vis-a-vis the World

35.1. RURAL POPULATION, DEVELOPMENT AND THE ENVIRONMENT 2007

- *Total population*: In 2005, the world population reached 6.5 billion persons, and it is expected to grow to 9.2 billion in 2050. The additional 2.7 billion expected—equivalent to the size of the world population in 1950—will be absorbed mostly by the less developed regions, whose population is projected to rise from 5.3 billion in 2005 to 7.9 billion in 2050. The population of the 50 least developed countries will likely more than double, passing from 0.8 billion in 2005 to 1.7 billion in 2050. In contrast, the population of the more developed regions is expected to remain nearly unchanged at 1.2 billion.
- *Cropland*: Rapid population growth during the twentieth century resulted in large-scale conversion of wild land to agriculture, the largest single use of land. Currently, 12 per cent of the global land area is occupied by cropland and an additional 26 per cent by permanent pastures. On average, the share of cropland differs only slightly between the more and the less developed regions, while in the least developed countries the average share (8 per cent) is lower. Although farmers have traditionally satisfied increasing demand by ploughing new land, in many countries opportunities for expanding cropland are limited because most of the land remaining is unsuitable for agriculture or is reserved for other uses. Boosting productivity is therefore crucial to ensure increasing food production. However, agricultural intensification needs to be sustainable. Unsustainable agricultural practices can disrupt local ecosystems and eventually destroy the land's productive potential.
- *Forest area*: Forests provide vital resources and services, including wood products, habitat for wildlife, water and soil conservation, and a filter for pollutants. Today, forests cover nearly one third of the Earth's land surface. During 2000-2005, deforestation, caused mainly by the conversion of forests into agricultural land, has continued at a rapid pace, with some 130 km^2 of forested land cleared every year— an area

about the size of Bangladesh. However, as a result of replanting and natural forest growth in some areas, the net loss has been less: about 73 km^2 annually. The pace of net forest loss is estimated to have decreased slightly since the 1990s and in some regions it has stabilized (Asia) or there has been a net gain in forested land (Europe and Northern America). The regions experiencing the greatest recent losses of forest area are Africa and Latin America and the Caribbean.

- *Irrigated area*: Irrigated agricultural land comprises less than one fifth of the total cropped area of the world but produces about two fifths of the world's food. Irrigation also accounts for about 70 per cent of global water withdrawals. The proportion of cropland equipped for irrigation is particularly high in Asia, especially Eastern Asia, where almost half of cropland is irrigated. Excessive and poorly managed irrigation can degrade soils through erosion and salinization. According to the United Nations Environment Programme, over 10 per cent of the world's irrigated lands are severely degraded.
- *Rural population*: The world's rural population stood at about 3.4 billion persons in 2005, slightly over half of the global population. Over 90 per cent of the world's rural residents (3.0 billion) live in the less developed regions. Between 2000 and 2005, the average annual growth rate of the world's rural population was 0.5 per cent, compared to 2.1 per cent for urban areas. Most of the future growth in the world's rural population will occur in Africa, where the rural population is still increasing. During 2000-2005 it grew at 1.7 per cent per year. Globally, the growth rate of the rural population has been declining since 1970 and, in the more developed regions, the number of rural-dwellers has been decreasing slowly for many years. The rural population of the less developed regions is projected to reach a maximum of 3.2 billion by 2020 and then start a slow and prolonged decline.
- *Access to improved water source and sanitation in rural areas*: Access to safe drinking water and adequate sanitation improves health, well-being and economic and social productivity. Access to safe water and access to sanitation are also among the indicators that the international community uses to monitor progress towards environmental sustainability, since surface and groundwater sources are increasingly at risk of pollution by pesticides, industry effluents and untreated household wastewater. The overextraction of water for agriculture and manufacturing has threatened the sustainability of water resources in many parts of the world. About 85 per cent of persons who lack access to improved water sources live in rural areas, as do approximately 75 per cent of those without access to adequate sanitation. Globally, about 900 million rural-dwellers (28 per cent) lack access to an improved water supply and 2 billion (62 per cent) lack adequate sanitation services. In the least developed countries, half of the rural population lack access to an improved water supply and more than two thirds lack adequate sanitation.

- *Agricultural labour intensity*: The number of agricultural workers per unit of cultivated land is markedly higher in the less developed regions than in the more developed regions. Agricultural labour intensity responds to changes in the structure of national economies and in agricultural technology. In recent decades, agricultural labour intensity has been declining in most middle-income and highincome countries but has risen substantially in many low-income countries.
- *Gross domestic product (GDP) per capita*: Between 1995 and 2005, per capita GDP growth accelerated in low-income and middle-income countries. Growth in GDP per capita was more rapid in developing countries than in high-income countries during 2000-2005. However, these favourable recent trends have produced only a small narrowing of the wide income gap that still exists between the developed and the developing economies. Average GDP per capita in the developing regions, expressed in purchasing power parity terms, stands at $5,181 and is equivalent to 18 per cent of that in the more developed regions. In the least developed countries, the average GDP per capita is equivalent to 5 per cent of that in the more developed regions.
- *Value added by agriculture*: A fundamental aspect of economic development is the increasing concentration of activity in high value added sectors, including industry and services. In most countries, the economic share of agriculture has been declining in recent periods, while that of services has increased. The share of industry has changed less. Currently, agriculture contributes only 3 per cent of the GDP in the more developed regions and 12 per cent of the GDP in the less developed regions. In the least developed countries, the share of agriculture in GDP is higher, at 26 per cent. In some countries in Africa, agriculture accounts for over half of GDP.
- *Energy use*: Although access to energy is essential for development, its production and use as well as its by-products have heavy impacts on the environment. Energy generated by the combustion of fossil fuels and biomass often results in air pollution, with negative impacts on the health of both people and ecosystems. Aside from being major users of energy, agriculture and forestry are also major suppliers of energy. The increasing demand for biofuels derived from agricultural biomass is contributing to changes in land-use patterns. On average, per capita energy use in the more developed regions is five times greater than in the less developed regions and more than 15 times greater than in the least developed countries. Whereas energy consumption in developed countries has continued to increase and currently accounts for about 70 per cent of the world's energy demand, much of the future growth in energy demand is expected to occur in developing countries where a large proportion of the population still lacks access to modern, high-quality energy sources.
- *Fertilizer use*: Although fertilizer is an essential input for increasing agricultural production, heavy applications of fertilizer also put pressure on the environment. Fertilizer use contributes to soil acidification,

contamination of water supplies with nitrates, emission of nitrous oxide into the air and severe disruption of natural aquatic life, especially in lakes and coastal estuaries. The environmental effects of fertilizer use vary, depending on pollution abatement practices, soil and plant types, and meteorological conditions, among other factors. Better timing of fertilizer application, more accurate delivery and more precise calculation of doses can substantially reduce its damaging effects. Currently, the amount of fertilizer applied per unit of cropland differs little between the more developed regions and the less developed regions, but is considerably lower in the least developed countries.

Table 35.1: Rural Population, Development and the Environment, 2007

Country of area	*Land area (km^2)*	*Agricultural labour intensity (per km^2 of cropland)*	*GDP per capita (PPP) (international equivalent to US dollar)*	*Value added by agriculture (as percentage of GDP)*	*Energy use (kg of oil equivalent per capita)*	*Fertilizer use (kg per km^2 of cropland)*
	2005	2004	2005	2005	2004	2005
(1)	(2)	(3)	(4)	(5)	(6)	(7)
Afghanistan	652 090	83	—	36	—	—
Australia	7 682 300	1	34 024	3	5 765	3 155
Austria	82 450	11	33 299	2	4 021	19 311
Bangladesh	130 170	472	1 901	20	151	15 542
Bhutan	47 000	—	5 236	25	—	—
Brazil	8 459 420	18	8 567	8	1 111	6 125
Canada	9 093 510	1	33 400	—	8 420	19 434
China	9 326 410	452	6 716	13	1 233	37 934
Korea	120 410	109	—	—	866	9 179
Denmark	42 430	4	34 298	2	3 715	5 132
Egypt	995 450	247	4 391	15	795	63 340
Finland	304 590	5	32 467	3	7 282	11 850
France	550 100	4	31 846	2	4 539	12 777
Germany	348 770	7	29 913	1	4 212	42 076
India	**2 973 190**	**163**	**3 331**	**18**	**513**	**9 838**
Indonesia	1 811 570	138	3 753	13	780	7 709
Iran	1 636 200	37	7 837	10	2 124	6 180
Iraq	437 370	10	—	9	1 083	—
Mexico	1 908 690	31	10 689	4	1 601	4 330
Myanmar	657 550	172	—	—	297	19
Nepal	143 000	460	1 553	38	341	323
Nigeria	910 770	45	1 095	23	717	344
Pakistan	770 880	121	2 348	22	479	15 462
Republic of Korea	98 730	106	22 276	3	4 468	34 088
Russian Federation	16 381 390	6	10 783	6	4 434	7 944
Sri Lanka	64 630	206	4 754	17	496	10 118
Switzerland	40 000	33	35 954	1	3 671	11 814
United Finland Kingdom	241 930	8	33 125	1	3 897	32 665
United States of America	9 161 920	2	41 410	1	7 835	12 153
Zimbabwe	386 850	106	2 048	18	714	2 252

Summary Indicator

World	129 830 789	90	9 462	3	1 713	11 123
More developed regions	49 068 852	6	28 296	3	4 937	11 840
Less developed regions	80 761 937	143	5 181	12	981	10 656
Least developed countries	20 169 840	152	1 421	26	292	1 281

Carbon Dioxide Emissions, 2004 (metric tones per capita)

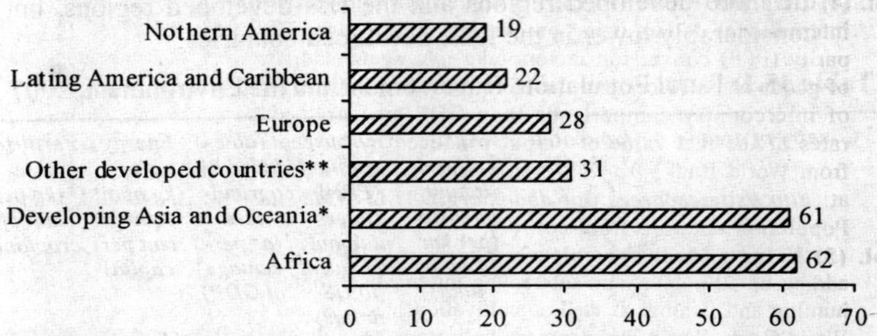

Value Added, Agriculture, 2005 (percentage of GDP)

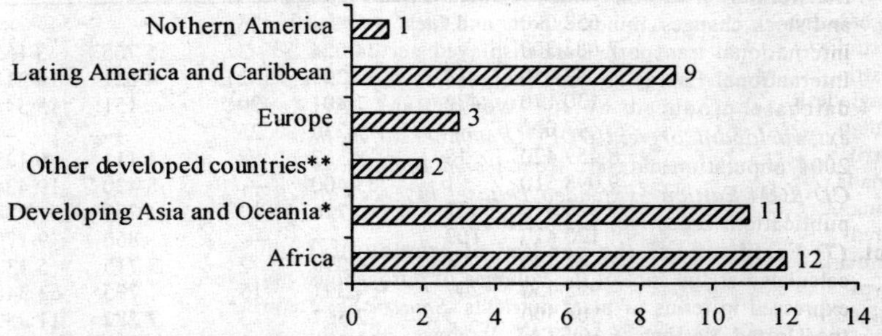

Value Added, Agriculture, 2005 (percentage of GDP)

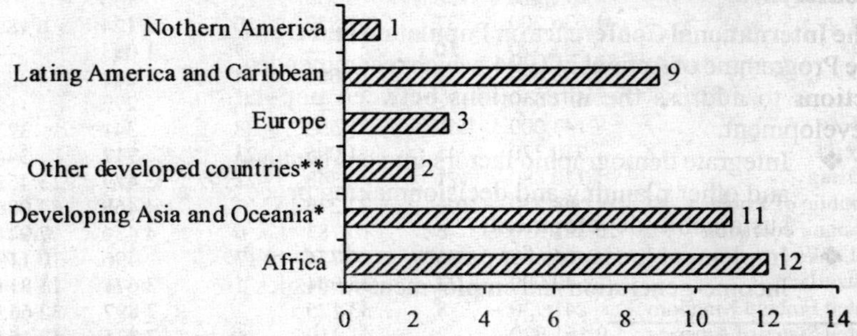

Note * Excluding Austrilia, New Zealand and Japan.
** Austrialia, New Zealand and Japan.

Note: **All URL addresses refer to sites accessed as of 16 November 2007**

Col. (2) Land area (km²): Total land area, excluding area under inland water bodies. *Source*: Food and Agriculture Organization of the United Nations, FAOSTAT database. Data available online at: *http://www.fao.org/es/ess/yearbook/vol_1_1/site_en.asp?page=resources*.

Col. (3) Agricultural labour intensity (per km² of cropland): Number of agricultural workers (agricultural labour force) per unit of arable and permanent cropland. *Source*: Food and Agriculture Organization of the United Nations, FAOSTAT database. Data available online at: *http://faostat.fao.org*.

Col. (4) GDP per capita (PPP): Per capita gross domestic product converted to current international dollars using purchasing power parity (PPP) rates. Purchasing power parity (PPP) conversion factors take into account differences in the relative prices of goods and services and therefore provide a better overall measure for the purposes of intercountry comparisons than GDP measured at currency-market exchange rates of the real value of output produced by an economy. *Source*: GDP data are from World Bank, *World Development Indicators 2007 database*, available online at: *http://siteresources.worldbank.org/DATASTATISTICS/Resources/GDP_PPP.pdf*. Population data are from col. (1).

Col. (5) Value added, agriculture (share of GDP): Net output of agriculture after adding up all outputs and subtracting intermediate inputs. Agriculture includes forestry, hunting and fishing, as well as cultivation of crops and livestock production. *Source*: World Bank, World Development Indicators 2007 database, available online at: *http://ddp-ext.worldbank.org/ext/DDPQQ/member.do?method=getMembers &userid=*.

Col. (6) Energy use (kg of oil equivalent per capita): Use of primary energy before transformation to other end-use fuels. Equals indigenous production plus imports and stock changes, minus exports and fuels supplied to ships and aircraft engaged in international transport. Data displayed per capita. *Source*: 2004 estimates by the International Energy Agency included in the *World Development Indicators 2007* database produced by the World Bank. Available online at: *http://ddp-ext.worldbank.org/ext/DDPQQ/member.do?method=getMembers&userid=*. The 2004 population data are from *World Population Prospects: The 2004 Revision, CD-ROM Edition—Extended Dataset in Excel and PDF formats* (United Nations publication, Sales No. E.05.XIII.12).

Col. (7) Fertilizer use (kg per km² of cropland): Total amount of fertilizers used calculated as the sum of the volumes of nitrogenous, phosphate and potash fertilizers expressed in terms of plant nutrients. *Source*: Food and Agriculture Organization of the United Nations, FAOSTAT database, available at: *http://www.fao.org/es/ess/yearbook/vol_1_1/site_en.asp?page=resources*

Conferences

The International Conference on Population and Development (ICPD) adopted the Programme of Action[1] in 1994, which recommended, inter alia, the following actions to address the interactions between population, environment and development:

- Integrate demographic factors into environmental impact assessments and other planning and decisionmaking processes aimed at achieving sustainable development;
- Implement measures for poverty eradication, with special attention to income-generation and employment strategies directed at the rural poor

1 Report of the International Conference on Population and Development, Cairo, 5-13 September 1994 *(United Nations Population Division, Sales No.* E.95.XIII.18).

and those living within or on the edge of fragile ecosystems;

- Utilize demographic data to promote sustainable resource management, especially of ecologically fragile systems;
- Modify unsustainable consumption and production patterns through economic, legislative and administrative measures, as appropriate, aimed at fostering sustainable resource use and preventing environmental degradation;
- Implement policies to address the ecological implications of future population increases, particularly in ecologically vulnerable areas and urban agglomerations.

The United Nations Conference on Environment and Development, which adopted Agenda 21[2] in 1992, identified a number of key objectives relative to population, including:

- To incorporate demographic trends in the global analysis of environment and development issues;
- To develop a better understanding of the relationships among demographic dynamics, technology, cultural behaviour, natural resources and life-support systems;
- To assess human vulnerability in ecologically sensitive areas and centres of population to determine the priorities for action at all levels;
- To implement population programmes along with national resource management and development programmes at the local level to ensure the sustainable use of natural resources, improve the quality of people's lives and enhance environmental quality.

The key actions for the further implementation of the ICPD Programme of Action,[3] the Programme for the Further Implementation of Agenda 21[4] and the Plan of Implementation of the World Summit on Sustainable Development,[5] adopted in Johannesburg in 2002, made further recommendations for changing unsustainable patterns of consumption and production as well as for promoting sustainable development. The recommendations contained in those documents set priorities for action to eradicate poverty, combat environmental threats to health and promote sustainable development in the rural and urban areas of the world.

Participation in Multilateral Treaties

To address global environmental issues, many Governments have signed and ratified[6] international treaties launched in the wake of the 1972 United Nations

---

2 Report of the United Nations Conference on Environment and Development, Rio de Janeiro, 3-14 June 1992, *vol. I,* Resolutions Adopted by the Conference *(United Nations publication, Sales No. E.93.XI.8).*

3 Resolution S-21/2.

4 Resolution S-19/2, annex.

5 Report of the World Summit on Sustainable Development, Johannesburg, South Africa, *26 August-4 September 2002 (United Nations publication,* Sales No. E.03.11.A.1 and corrigendum), chap. I, resolution 2, annex.

6 Ratification including acceptance, approval, accession or succession. Ratification is the act whereby a State indicates its consent to being bound to a treaty if the parties intend to show their consent by such an act.

Conference on the Human Environment and the 1992 United Nations Conference on Environment and Development. The following are some of the major multilateral environmental treaties currently in force:

The Vienna Convention for the Protection of the Ozone Layer (1985), ratified by 191 countries, aims to protect human health and the environment by promoting research on the effects of changes in the ozone layer and on alternative substances and technologies, monitoring the ozone level and taking measures to control the activities that produce adverse effects.

The Montreal Protocol on Substances that Deplete the Ozone Layer (1987), ratified by 191 countries, requires that countries help protect the Earth from excessive ultraviolet radiation by cutting chlorofluorocarbon consumption by specific amounts and target dates, with allowances for increases in consumption by developing countries. The Protocol contained flexible implementation schemes and evaluation procedures and recognized the principle of "common but differentiated" responsibilities for developed and developing countries. The Protocol has contributed to reducing levels of ozone-depleting substances.

The United Nations Framework Convention on Climate Change (1992), ratified by 192 countries, aims to stabilize atmospheric concentrations of greenhouse gases at levels that will prevent human activities from interfering dangerously with the global environment. The Convention was not binding and did not establish targets or deadlines.

The Kyoto Protocol to the United Nations Framework Convention on Climate Change (1997), ratified by 176 countries, entered into force in 2005. It commits 36 developed countries to reduce their greenhouse gas emissions by 2012 to at least 5 per cent below emission levels of 1990. In December 2007 in Bali, Indonesia, the United Nations Climate Change Conference adopted the Bali Road Map, which charts the course for a new negotiating process to be concluded by 2009 that will ultimately lead to a post-2012 international agreement on climate change.

The United Nations Convention on the Law of the Sea (1982), ratified by 155 countries, went into effect in 1994 and created a comprehensive legal regime for seas and oceans. Rules were established for environmental standards and enforcement provisions, while international rules and national legislation to prevent and control marine pollution were developed. The Convention afforded all countries the right to manage marine resources within their 200-nautical-mile Exclusive Economic Zone. For many developing countries, however, it is difficult to enforce regulations over such a vast expanse.

The Convention on Biological Diversity (1992), ratified by 190 countries, promotes conservation of biodiversity among nations through scientific and technological cooperation, access to financial and genetic resources and transfer of ecologically sound technologies. The major objectives are to conserve biodiversity, ensure its sustainable use and guarantee the fair and equitable sharing of its benefits.

35.2. URBAN POPULATION DEVELOPMENT AND THE ENVIRONMENT 2007

- *Total population*: In 2005, the world population reached 6.5 billion persons, and it is expected to reach 9.2billion in 2050. The additional 2.7 billion persons expected—equivalent to the total world population in 1950—will be absorbed mostly by the less developed regions, whose population is projected to rise from 5.3 billion in 2005 to 7.9 billion in 2050. The population of the 50 least developed countries will likely more than double, passing from 0.8 billion in 2005 to 1.7 billion in 2050. In contrast, the population of the more developed regions is expected to remain nearly unchanged at 1.2 billion.
- *Urban population*: The twentieth century witnessed the rapid urbanization of the world's population. In 1900, urban-dwellers made up only 13 per cent of the global population. The proportion urban grew to 29 per cent in 1950 and reached 49 per cent in 2005 (3.2 billion people). By 2030, 60 per cent of the global population, or 5.0 billion people, are expected to live in urban areas. The populations of Europe, Latin America and the Caribbean, Northern America and Oceania are already over 70 per cent urban. Africa and Asia are the least urbanized regions of the world (approximately 40 per cent urban), but by 2030 a majority of the population in these regions is projected to live in urban areas. Currently, the average annual growth rate of the urban population in the less developed regions (2.7 per cent) is almost over four times that of the more developed regions (0.6 per cent). Africa has the world's highest rates of urban population growth, averaging 3.4 per cent per year during 2000-2005. Growth in the urban areas of the less developed regions is projected to account for almost all of total world population growth between 2005 and 2030 (93 per cent). Although urban growth rates have been decreasing in most countries, every year a larger absolute number of persons is being added to the world's urban population. The number added annually was about 62 million during 2000-2005 and is projected to rise to 73 million in 2015-2020 and to reach 76 million in 2025-2030.
- *Urban density*: Although nearly half the world's population lived in urban areas in 2005, urban settlements were estimated to occupy just 2.7 per cent of the world's land area. At the world level, urban density averages 906 persons per km^2, but urban population density is considerably higher in the less developed regions (1,392 persons per km^2) and especially in the least developed countries (2,547 persons per km^2). In the more developed regions, rising affluence accompanied by improved transportation networks and increased access to motor vehicles has typically led to a lower density of urban settlement, averaging 482 persons per km^2. A few countries or areas, notably Macao

Special Administrative Region of China and the Maldives, exhibit exceptionally high urban densities.

- *Urban population in slums*: In 2005, 37 per cent of the urban population of the less developed regions were estimated to be living in slums. In the least developed countries, almost three quarters of the urban population were slum-dwellers. By region, Africa had the largest proportion of the urban population living in slums in 2005 (51 per cent), followed by Asia (35 per cent) and Latin America and the Caribbean (27 per cent).
- *Access to improved water sources and sanitation in urban areas*: Access to safe drinking water and adequate sanitation improves health, well-being and economic and social productivity. Access to safe water and sanitation are also among the indicators that the international community uses to monitor progress towards environmental sustainability, since surface and groundwater sources are increasingly at risk of pollution by pesticides, industry effluents and untreated household wastewater. The overextraction of water for agriculture and manufacturing has threatened the sustainability of water resources in many parts of the world. Globally, 170 million urban-dwellers (5 per cent) lack access to an improved water supply and over 600 million (20 per cent) lack adequate sanitation services. Most of these people live in informal, overcrowded urban settlements in developing countries, particularly in Africa and Asia. In Africa, 16 per cent of the population lack access to an improved water supply and 38 per cent lack adequate sanitation.
- *Gross domestic product (GDP) per capita*: Between 1995 and 2005, per capita GDP growth accelerated in low-income and middle-income countries. Growth in GDP per capita was more rapid in developing countries than in high-income countries during 2000-2005. However, these favourable recent trends have produced only a small narrowing of the wide income gap that still exists between the developed and the developing economies. Average GDP per capita in the developing regions, expressed in purchasing power parity terms, stands at $5,181 and is equivalent to 18 per cent of that in the more developed regions. In the least developed countries, the average GDP per capita is equivalent to 5 per cent of that in the more developed regions.
- *Value added by industry and services*: A fundamental aspect of economic development is the increasing concentration of activity in high value added sectors, including industry and services, which in turn are mostly concentrated in urban areas. In most countries, the share of services has been rising in recent periods, while that of agriculture has declined. The share of industry has changed less. Currently, industry and services account for 95 per cent of the GDP in the more developed regions and 89 per cent of that in the less developed

regions. In the least developed countries, the share of industry and services in GDP is lower, at 74 per cent.

- *Energy use*: Although access to energy is essential for development, its production and use as well as its by-products have heavy impacts on the environment. Energy generated by the combustion of fossil fuels and biomass often results in air pollution, with negative impacts on the health of both people and ecosystems. On average, per capita energy use in the more developed regions is five times greater than in the less developed regions and more than 15 times greater than in the least developed countries. Whereas energy consumption in developed countries has continued to increase and currently accounts for about 70 per cent of the world energy demand, much of the future growth in energy demand is expected to occur in developing countries where a large proportion of the population still lacks access to modern, high-quality energy sources.
- *Carbon dioxide* (CO_2) *emissions*: Atmospheric concentrations of carbon dioxide, the main gas linked with global warming, have increased substantially in the course of economic and industrial development. CO_2 emissions are largely determined by a country's energy use and production systems, its industrial structure, its transportation system, its agricultural and forestry sectors, and the consumption patterns of the population. In addition to the impact of CO_2 and other greenhouse gases on the global climate, the use of carbon-based energy also affects human health through local air pollution. Currently, CO_2 emissions per person are markedly higher in the more developed regions (11.9 metric tons per capita) than in the less developed regions (2.5 metric tons per capita) and are lowest in the least developed countries (0.2 metric tons per capita).
- *Motor vehicles in use*: In recent years, ownership of passenger cars has increased considerably worldwide and the transportation of goods and services by road has intensified. Rising demand for roads and vehicles is associated with economic growth but also contributes to urban congestion, air and noise pollution, increasing health hazards, traffic accidents and injuries. Motor vehicle use also places pressure on the environment, since transportation now accounts for about one quarter of world energy use and half of the world's oil consumption and is a major contributor to greenhouse gas emissions. The number of motor vehicles per capita in the less developed regions remains markedly lower than in the more developed regions, but is now increasing more rapidly than in the more developed regions.

Table 35.2: Urban Population, Development and the Environment, 2007

Country of area	*Total Population (thousands)*	*Land area (km^2)*	*Urban settlements (percentage of land area)*	*GDP per capita (PPP) (international equivalent to)*	*Energy use (kg of oil equivalent per capita)*	*Carbon dioxide emissions (metric tons per capita)*	*Motor vehicles in use (per 1,000 population)*
	2005	2005	2000	2005	2004	2004	2000-05
	(1)	(2)	(3)	(4)	(5)	(6)	(7)
Zimbabwe	13 120	386 850	1.3	2 048	714	0.8	54
Egypt	72 850	995 450	2.4	4 391	795	2.2	39
Nigeria	141 356	910 770	1.6	1 095	717	0.8	—
China	1 312 979	9 326 410	2.9	6 716	1 233	4.0	24
Dem. People's Rep. of Korea	23 616	120 410	0.9	—	866	3.4	—
Republic of Korea	47 870	98 730	19.9	22 276	4 468	9.8	312
Afghanistan	25 067	652 090	0.3	—	—	0.0	6
Bangladesh	153 281	130 170	7.8	1 901	151	0.2	—
Bhutan	637	47 000	0.4	5 236	—	0.7	—
India	**1 134 403**	**2 973 190**	**6.9**	**3 331**	**513**	**1.2**	**18**
Iran (Islamic Republic of)	69 421	1 636 200	3.7	7 837	2 124	6.3	—
Nepal	27 094	143 000	1.9	1 553	341	0.1	5
Pakistan	158 081	770 880	3.4	2 348	479	0.8	13
Sri Lanka	19 121	64 630	5.3	4 754	496	0.6	41
Indonesia	226 063	1 811 570	1.8	3 753	780	1.7	42
Myanmar	47 967	657 550	0.7	—	297	0.2	7
Iraq	27 996	437 370	2.3	—	1 083	3.0	43
Russian Federation	143 953	16 381 390	1.1	10 783	4 434	10.5	209
Denmark	5 417	42 430	22.6	34 298	3 715	9.8	452
Finland	5 246	304 590	6.4	32 467	7 282	12.6	535
United Kingdom	60 245	241 930	22.9	33 125	3 897	9.8	537
Austria	8 292	82 450	13.4	33 299	4 021	8.5	546
France	60 991	550 100	13.7	31 846	4 539	6.2	490
Germany	82 652	348 770	17.3	29 913	4 212	9.8	591
Mexico	104 266	1 908 690	5.3	10 689	1 601	4.2	211
Brazil	186 831	8 459 420	2.2	8 567	1 111	1.8	—
Canada	32 271	9 093 510	1.4	33 400	8 420	20.0	584
United States of America	299 846	9 161 920	8.2	41 410	7 835	20.4	787
Australia	20 310	7 682 300	0.5	34 024	5 765	16.3	663

Table Summary

World	6 514 751	129 830 789	2.7	9 462	1 713	4.5	153
More developed regions	1 215 636	49 068 852	3.8	28 296	4 937	11.9	536
Less developed regions	5 299 115	80 761 937	2.0	5 181	981	2.5	43
Least developed countries	766 816	20 169 840	0.4	1 421	292	0.2	8

Note: All URL addresses refer to sites aaccessed as of 16 November 2007.

Col. (1) Total population (thousands): Midyear de facto population. *Source*: *World Population Prospects: The 2006 Revision, CD-ROM Edition*—Extended Dataset in Excel and ASCII formats (United Nations publication, Sales No. E.07.XIII.7). Data also available online at: *http://esa.un.org/unpp/*.

Col. (2) Land area (km²): Total land area, excluding area under inland water bodies. *Source*: Food and Agriculture Organization of the United Nations, FAOSTAT database. Data available online at: *http://www.fao.org/es/ess/yearbook/vol_1_1/site_en.asp?page=resources*.

Col. (3) Land area occupied by urban settlements: Share of total land area that corresponds to the geographical units classified as urban according to the criteria used by each country or area. *Source*: Global Rural-Urban Mapping Project (GRUMP), Alpha version. Data available at: *http://sedac.ciesin.org/gateway/guides/grump.html*.

Col. (4) GDP per capita (PPP): Per capita gross domestic product converted to current international dollars using purchasing power parity (PPP) rates. Purchasing power parity (PPP) conversion factors take into account differences in the relative prices of goods and services and therefore provide a better overall measure for the purposes of intercountry comparisons than GDP measured at currency-market exchange rates of the real value of output produced by an economy. *Source*: GDP data are from The World Bank, World Development Indicators 2007 database, available online at: *http://siteresources.worldbank.org/DATASTATISTICS/Resources/GDP_PPP.pdf*. Population data are from col. (1).

Col. (5) Energy use (kg of oil equivalent per capita): Use of primary energy before transformation to other end-use fuels. Equals indigenous production plus imports and stock changes, minus exports and fuels supplied to ships and aircraft engaged in international transport. Data displayed per capita. *Source*: 2004 estimates by the International Energy Agency included in the World Development Indicators 2007 database of the World Bank. Available online at: *http://ddp-ext.worldbank.org/ext/DDPQQ/member.do?method=getMembers&userid=1&queryId=135*. The 2004 population data are from *World Population Prospects: The 2006 Revision, CD-ROM Edition—Extended Dataset in Excel and ASCII formats* (United Nations publication, Sales No. E.07.XIII.7). Data also available online at: *http://esa.un.org/unpp/*.

Col. (6) Carbon dioxide emissions (metric tons per capita): Emissions stemming from the burning of fossil fuels and the manufacture of cement, including carbon dioxide produced during consumption of solid, liquid and gas fuels and gas flaring. Data displayed per capita. *Sources*: G. Marland, T. A. Boden and R. J. Andres (2007), "Global, regional, and national CO2 emissions", in *Trends: A Compendium of Data on Global Change* (Oak Ridge, Tenn., USA, Carbon Dioxide Information Analysis Center, U.S. Department of Energy). Data available online at: *http://cdiac.ornl.gov/trends/emis/tre_coun.htm*. The 2004 population data are from *World Population Prospects: The 2006 Revision, CD-ROM Edition—Extended Dataset in Excel and ASCII formats* (United Nations publication, Sales No. E.07.XIII.7). Data also available online at: *http://esa.un.org/unpp/*.

Col. (7) Motor vehicles in use (per 1000 population): Includes motor cars and buses, passenger motor vehicles for unusual terrain such as snowmobiles and golf carts, motor vehicles for the transport of goods and special-purpose trucks, such as fire engines and mobile clinics. The reference year varies by country and ranges between 2000 and 2004. Data are displayed per thousand persons. Sources: Transport Statistics Database, *UN Statistical Yearbook*, Statistics Division, Department of Economic and Social Affairs. Data available online at: *http://unstats.un.org/unsd/cdb/cdb_advanced_data_extract.asp*. The population data are from *World Population Prospects: The 2006 Revision, CD-ROM Edition—Extended Dataset in Excel and ASCII formats* (United Nations publication, Sales No. E.07.XIII.7).

Urban Population as Percentage of the Total Population, 2005

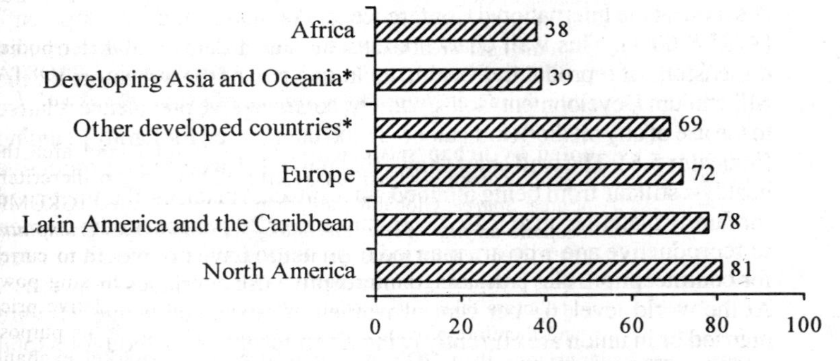

GDP Per Capita, 2005 (thousands of International equivalents to US dollars)

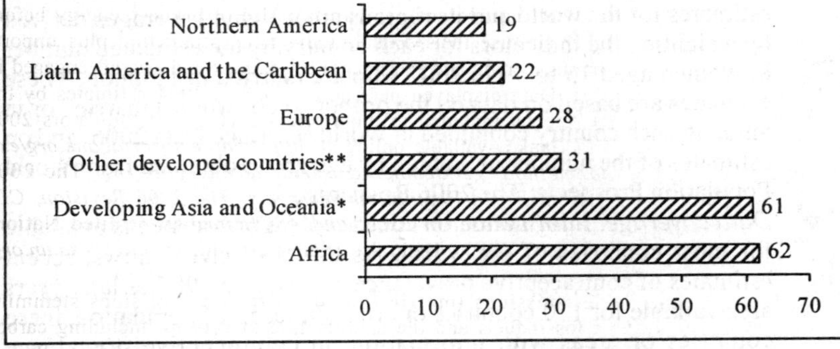

Carbon Dioxide Emissions, 2004 (metric tones per capita)

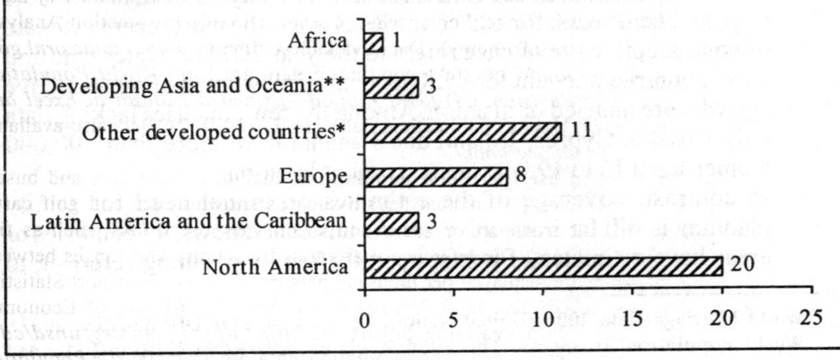

Note: * Austrialia, New Zealand and Japan.

** Excluding Austrilia, New Zealand and Japan.

35.3. WORLD CONTRACEPTIVE USE 2007

❖ *Introduction:* At the 2005 World Summit, Governments committed themselves to "achieving universal access to reproductive health by 2015, as set out at the International Conference on Population and Development" (A/RES/60/1). This wall chart presents the latest data available on key dimensions of reproductive health, including two of the indicators for the Millennium Development Goals, namely, contraceptive prevalence relative to the use of any method (indicator 5.3) and unmet need for family planning (indicator 5.6). The wall chart shows that universal access to reproductive health is still far from being attained since, at least in terms of unmet need for family planning, in at least 43 countries over 20 per cent of the women of reproductive age who are married or in union have not met their need for contraception. Nevertheless, contraceptive use continues to increase. At the world level, 63 per cent of women of reproductive age who are married or in union are currently using a contraceptive method for a total of 716 million worldwide.

❖ *Data sources*: Data on contraceptive prevalence and unmet need for family planning at the country level were obtained from surveys of nationally representative samples of women of reproductive age. The estimates for the world and its regions are weighted averages derived by weighting the indicators for each country by the estimated number of women aged 15 to 49 in 2007 who are married or in union. These estimates are based on data on the proportion of women married or in union in each country contained in World Marriage Data 2006[1] and on estimates of the number of women by age group obtained from World Population Prospects: The 2006 Revision[2].

❖ *Data coverage*: Information on contraceptive prevalence is available for most countries of the world. As this wall chart shows, recent estimates of contraceptive prevalence referring to 1985 or later years are available for 170 countries or areas. In terms of population, these countries or areas with information on contraceptive prevalence account for 99.7 per cent of all women of reproductive age who were married or in union in 2007. Moreover, a majority of the data available refer to recent years: for 109 countries or areas the most recent estimate of contraceptive prevalence refers to the year 2000 or a later date and these countries account for 85.8 per cent of all women of reproductive age who are married or in union. Among the few countries lacking data only Croatia, Cyprus, Ireland and Panama have more than 100,000 women aged 15 to 49 who are married or in union.

In contrast, coverage of the estimates on unmet need for family planning is still far from universal. As this chart shows, 97 countries or areas have estimates of unmet need for family planning referring to

1. World Marriage Data 2006 (United Nations Publication, POP/DB/Mar/Rev. 2007).
2. World Population Prospects: The 2006 Revision. CD-ROM Edition-Extended Dataset in Excel and ASCII format (United Nations Populations, Sales No. E. 07.XIII.7).

1985 or later years. Those countries account for only 59.5 per cent of all women of reproductive age who are married or in union. Countries lacking the data necessary to estimate the unmet need for family planning are located mainly in the more developed regions (several countries in Europe as well as Australia, Canada, Japan, New Zealand and the United States lack data) and in Western Asia, the Caribbean, South America and Oceania. In addition, there are no data on unmet need for family planning in China.

❖ *Contraceptive prevalence*: According to the most recent data available, contraceptive prevalence among women of reproductive age who are married or in union varies between 3 per cent in Chad and 90 per cent in China, with a world average of 63 per cent. The level of contraceptive use is somewhat higher in the more developed regions (67 per cent) than in the less developed regions (62 per cent), but the similarity of the two figures has to be underscored. In the majority of the less developed regions, contraceptive prevalence has reached levels of at least 60 per cent. The major exceptions are Sub-Saharan Africa, Melanesia, Micronesia and Polynesia where the levels of contraceptive prevalence are still below 30 per cent. As a region, sub-Saharan Africa has the lowest level of contraceptive prevalence, with only 22 per cent of women of reproductive age who are married or in union using contraception. About half of the 47 countries with data in sub-Saharan Africa had a contraceptive prevalence level lower than 20 per cent and they are located mainly in Western Africa and in the Horn of Africa.

❖ In all other regions of the developing world, contraceptive prevalence is high: 60 per cent in Northern Africa (excluding Sudan), 68 per cent on average in Asia, and 71 per cent on average in Latin America and the Caribbean. Asia as whole had a level of contraceptive prevalence comparable to that of Europe. Only six out of the 47 countries of Asia with data available had levels of contraceptive prevalence below 30 per cent: Afghanistan, Pakistan, Oman, Timor-Leste, the United Arab Emirates and Yemen. As already noted, China, the most populous country of the world, had the highest level of contraceptive prevalence not only in Asia but in the world, at 90 per cent.

In Latin America and the Caribbean, the level of contraceptive prevalence was comparable to that in Northern America. No country in that major area had a level of contraceptive prevalence lower than 30 per cent, and only seven of the 32 countries with data available in that major area had contraceptive prevalence levels ranging between 30 per cent and 50 per cent. Those countries are located mainly in the Caribbean and they are: Dominica, Haiti, Guatemala, Guyana, Saint Lucia, Suriname, and Trinidad and Tobago.

Trends in contraceptive prevalence exhibit contrasts among development groups and regions. In developed countries, contraceptive prevalence has been high for many decades and its level has changed little since 1997. In the less developed regions, contraceptive prevalence has increased substantially in the past decade. Among 44 per cent of the developing countries with data, contraceptive prevalence has increased by more than one percentage point per year since 1997 and in 8 per cent of the developing countries, the increase has averaged at least two percentage points per year. However, in 32 per cent of developing countries the increase in contraceptive prevalence was below half a percentage point per year. This last group includes several of the countries with contraceptive prevalence levels below 20 per cent, such as Benin, Burkina Faso, Chad, Eritrea, Guinea, Mali, Niger, Nigeria, Rwanda, Senegal, Sierra Leona or Sudan.

❖ *Main methods of contraception used:* Nine out of every 10 contraceptive users in the world rely on modern methods. Short-acting and reversible methods are more commonly used than other methods in developed countries whereas longer-acting and highly effective clinical methods are used more frequently in the developing countries. Thus, in developed countries as a whole, contraceptive prevalence was highest for the pill (16 per cent) and the male condom (14 per cent). Those two methods accounted for almost half of overall contraceptive use in the developed countries, while only two out of every 10 users relied on female sterilization or the IUD. By contrast, in developing countries the methods with the highest prevalence were female sterilization (22 per cent) and the IUD (17 per cent), accounting for 60 per cent of overall contraceptive use.

For the world as a whole, female sterilization is the most commonly used method of contraception, used by 20 per cent of women aged 15 to 49 who are married or in union. Female sterilization is most prevalent in the countries of Latin America and the Caribbean. The prevalence levels of female sterilization are highest—over 40 per cent—in Brazil, the Dominican Republic and Puerto Rico. They ranged between 30 per cent and 39 per cent in Colombia, El Salvador and Mexico. The prevalence of female sterilization is also high in a few countries in other regions, including Canada, China and India. In some countries, such as Argentina and Poland, sterilization for contraceptive reasons is not legal.

The IUD, used by 16 per cent of women of reproductive age who are married or in union, is the second most widely used contraceptive method in the world. The IUD is most commonly used in Asia and its prevalence levels are highest—over 40 per cent—in China, the Democratic People's Republic of Korea, Kazakhstan and Uzbekistan. In addition, levels of IUD use ranged between 30 per cent and 39 per cent in Israel, Kyrgyzstan, Mongolia, Turkmenistan and Viet Nam.

The pill is the third most widely used contraceptive method in the world, with 9 per cent of women aged 15 to 49 who are married or in union relying on it. Use of the contraceptive pill has the widest geographic distribution of any method. Pill prevalence is relatively high, ranging from 20 per cent to 55 per cent, in four countries in Africa, four in Asia, 13 in Europe, 11 in Latin America and the Caribbean, and three in Oceania. Countries with the highest prevalence of pill use (over 40 per cent) include Algeria, Belgium, France, Germany, Morocco, the Netherlands, Réunion and Zimbabwe. Regarding the share of the pill in overall contraceptive use, there are more countries where at least 30 per cent of contraceptive users rely on the pill than there are countries where a similar share is accounted for by either female sterilization or the IUD. That is, in many countries, the pill is more popular among contraceptive users than female sterilization or the IUD even if the global prevalence of the pill is lower than that of female sterilization or the IUD.

The male condom ranked fourth among modern contraceptive methods in terms of global prevalence of use, with 6 per cent of women aged 15 to 49 who are married or in union relying on this method. The prevalence of condom use is highest in Japan—41 per cent. Most of the other countries with high levels of condom use are located in Europe though there are also a few in Asia and in Latin America and the Caribbean. Thus, condom prevalence levels range from 20 per cent to 35 per cent in Argentina, Denmark, Finland, Greece, Grenada, Hong Kong SAR of China, Jamaica, Singapore, Slovakia, Spain, United Kingdom and Uruguay.

Other modern contraceptive methods are also popular in certain regions. In Eastern Africa and Southern Africa, for instance, injectables and implants are the most popular methods, accounting for over 40 per cent of overall contraceptive use.

Traditional methods, generally not recommended as contraceptives because of their lower effectiveness in preventing pregnancy, are still commonly used in Middle Africa, Western Africa and Eastern Europe, where 76 per cent, 37 per cent and 35 per cent, respectively, of female contraceptive users rely on a traditional method. In Albania, for instance, 89 per cent of contraceptive users rely on withdrawal.

❖ *Unmet Need for Family Planning*: The level of unmet need for family planning varies from 1 per cent in Albania to 51 per cent in Yemen. In Africa, almost half of the 42 countries with data have unmet need levels ranging from 20 per cent to 30 per cent and a quarter have unmet need levels of at least 30 per cent. In Asia, Europe and Latin America and the Caribbean, by contrast, the majority of countries with data have unmet need levels below 20 per cent. Thus, half of the 26 countries in Asia, a third of the 12 in Europe, and over a third of the 17 in Latin America and the Caribbean have levels of unmet need for family planning ranging between 10 per cent and 20 per cent. In addition, a quarter of the countries in Asia, three-quarters of those in Europe and over a third of those in Latin America and the Caribbean have unmet need levels below 10 per cent. In general, unmet need for family planning is lowest in countries where contraceptive prevalence is already high (above 60 per cent). The indicator of unmet need for family planning considered here should be interpreted in conjunction with other information on contraceptive use. Albania, for instance, has a very low level of unmet need for family planning while at the same time a large majority of women of reproductive age who are married or in union still rely on a traditional method of contraception.

Table 35.3: Contraceptive Prevalence

Country or Area	Year(s)	Total	Sterilization Female	Sterilization Male	Pill	IUD	Condom
Afghanistan	2003	8.5	0.7	0.0	5.0	0.0	0.6
Australia	1995	63.9	12.8	9.7	26.7	2.0	11.7
Australia/New Zealand	1995	65.5	13.1	11.8	25.4	2.3	11.6
Austria	1995/96	46.8	0.0	0.5	30.8	7.3	7.2
Bangladesh	2004	47.3	5.2	0.6	26.2	0.6	4.2
Bhutan	2000	30.7	3.1	13.6	3.4	3.4	1 2
Brazil	1996	70.3	40.1	2.6	20.7	1.1	4.4
Canada	1995	73.3	30.6	15.2	14.4	2.9	9.4
China	2004	90.0	31.2	6.7	1.5	44.9	5.2
China, Hong Kong SAR	1992	79.7	18.9	0.9	17.1	5.1	34.5
Democratic People's Republic of Korea	2002	58.4	4.4	0.8	3.7	42.8	5.8
Denmark	1988	72.0	5.0	5.0	26.0	11.0	22.0
Egypt	2005	56.5	1.3	0.0	9.9	36.5	1.0
Finland	1989	75.4	14.9	1.1	11.3	25.8	20.1
France	2000	76.5	←5.5→		43.8	21.9	4.7
Germany	1992	65.6	5.5	0.5	52.6	5.3	1.1
India	**2005/06**	**48.5**	**37.3**	**1.0**	**3.1**	**1.7**	**5.2**
Indonesia	2002/03	56.7	3.7	0.4	13.2	6.2	0.9
Iran	2000	55.9	17.3	2.8	18.4	8.4	5.6
Iraq	2006[j]	32.9	2.6	0.0	14.6	12.2	1.1
Mexico	2006	66.5	←38.4→		4.7	11.6	6.4
Myanmar	2001	32.8	4.6	1.5	9.8	1.8	0.3
Nepal	2006	44.2	18.0	6.3	3.5	0.7	4.8
Nigeria	2003	8.2	0.2	0.0	1.8	0.7	1.9
Pakistan	2000/01	20.2	6.9	0.0	1.9	3.5	5.5
Republic of Korea	1997	66.9	24.1	12.7	1.8	13.2	15.1
Russian Federation	1996	47.1	←12.1→		5.3	29.7	—
Sri Lanka	2000	49.6	21.0	2.1	6.7	5.1	3.7
United Kingdom	2005/06	82.0	14.0	20.0	26.0	7.0	25.0
United States of America	2002	68.1	21.2	9.7	18.3	1.8	12.2
Zimbabwe	2005/06	58.4	2.0	0.1	43.0	0.3	1.4

Table Summary

WORLD	2003	56.1	19.7	2.7	8.5	15.5	5.7	—
More developed regions	1999	56.1	8.6	4.5	16.5	9.4	13.9	—
Less developed regions	2004	56.1	21.5	2.5	7.2	16.5	4.4	—

Contraceptive Prevalence by Method for Each of the World Regions

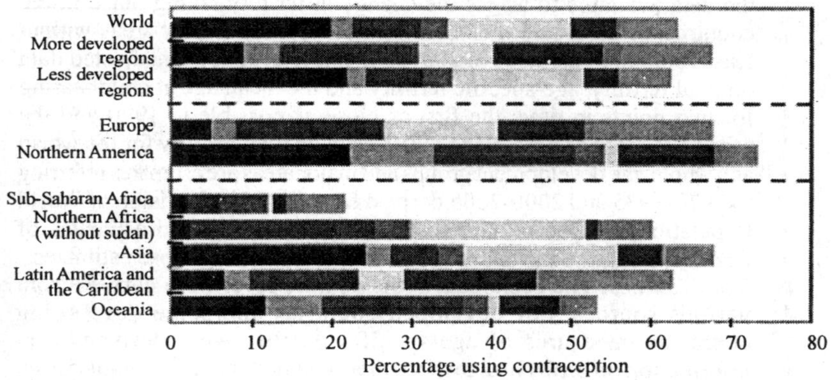

Percentage Distribution of Contraceptive Users by Method for Each of the World Regions

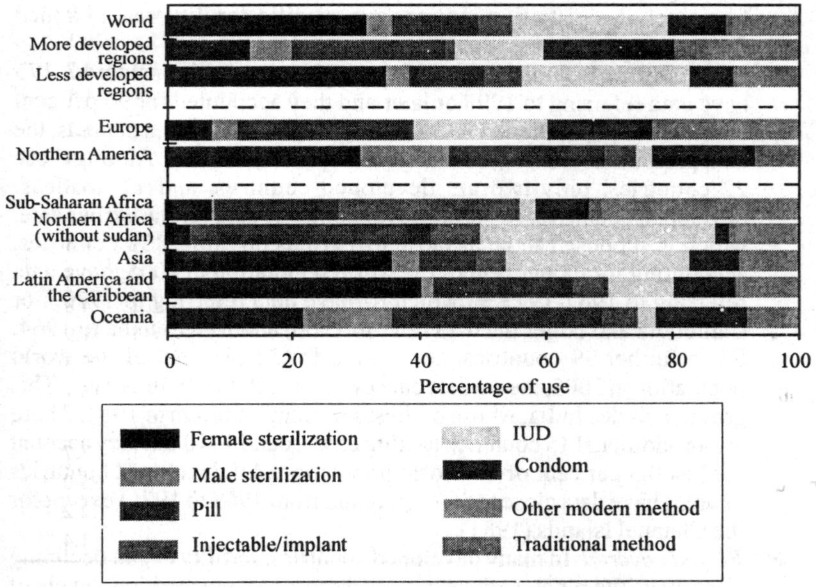

35.4. WORLD FERTILITY PATTERNS 2007

❖ *Introduction*: The last decades of the twentieth century witnessed a major transformation in world fertility: total fertility fell from an average of 4.5 children per woman in 1970-1975 to 2.6 children per woman in 2000-2005. This change was driven mostly by developing countries whose fertility dropped by nearly half (from 5.4 to 2.9 children per woman) with the decline being less marked among the least developed countries where fertility remains high (their average fertility declined from 6.6 children per woman in 1970-1975 to 5.0 in 2000-2005). This chart presents some of the data available to assess the change in fertility taking place in the countries of the world. For each of the 195 countries or areas with at least 100,000 inhabitants in 2007, it displays available unadjusted data on total fertility, age-specific fertility and the mean age at childbearing for two points in time: the first as close as possible to 1970 and the second as close as possible to 2005. Data on total fertility for the world as a whole, the development groups and major areas are estimates referring to 1970-1975 and 2000-2005 derived from the 2006 Revision of World Population Prospects.[1] The chart thus presents regional estimates of fertility change and part of the basic data underlying those estimates.

❖ *Data sources*: The basic data at the country level were derived from various sources. For developed countries and some developing countries, measures of age-specific fertility were derived from information on births by age of mother obtained from civil registration systems achieving a level of coverage of at least 90 per cent. For developing countries whose civil registration systems achieved a coverage of births lower than 90 per cent or where there were no data from a civil registration system, age-specific fertility was obtained from surveys or censuses.

❖ *Data coverage*: Among the 195 countries or areas considered, 173 have data referring to 1998 or later and they accounted for 96 per cent of the world population in 2005. For the other 22 countries or areas, the data presented refer to years ranging from 1991 to 1997. Among those 22 countries, only two are developed countries and 11 are least developed countries. Regarding availability of data for the earlier date, which is supposed to be as close to 1970 as possible, 138 countries, accounting for 68 per cent of the world population in 2005, have data referring to 1967-1975, of which 87 have data referring to 1970. For Cambodia and Niger the data refer to 1960, and for Grenada to 1964. For a further 39 countries, accounting for 31 per cent of the world population in 2005, the earliest data available refer to 1976 or later. This group includes India, whose earliest information refers to 1981. There are an additional 15 countries lacking data around 1970 but they account for just 0.8 per cent of the world population. All developed countries or areas have data close to 1970 (ranging from 1969 to 1975) except for the Channel Islands (1981).

❖ *Period covered*: In many developed countries, fertility began declining as early as the nineteenth century and most had reached low levels of fertility by 1950. Indeed, fertility rose in many developed countries during parts of the period 1945-1965, as it recovered from the low levels reached during the Second World War. By the 1970s, however, fertility in developed countries was falling again. In the developing world, fertility levels remained high until the 1960s and began falling in

---

1 World Population Prospects: The 2006 Revision, Vol. 1, Comprehensive Tables (United Nations Publication, Sales No. 07.XIII.2).

most countries of Latin America and the Caribbean and some in Asia during in the late 1960s. By the 1970s and early 1980s declining fertility was common in most developing countries outside of sub-Saharan Africa. In the latter, fertility started declining later, mostly in the late 1980s or the 1990s. The data presented in this chart are intended to bracket the period of decline for most developing countries. However, the periods actually spanned by the earliest and latest data sets for each country or area vary considerably. Among the 195 countries or areas covered, 97 have data spanning intervals ranging from 30 to 35 years. This group includes all developed countries or areas except Belgium, Bosnia and Herzegovina, the Channel Islands and Malta, as well as 23 countries and areas in Asia including China, 24 in Latin America and the Caribbean, and 9 in Africa. For a further 66 countries, the data span intervals ranging from 19 to 29 years, and in another 12, the data span intervals ranging from 10 to 18 years. Namibia exhibits a particularly short interval of 10 years with the most recent observation referring to 1988 and for Niger the interval is 44 years long. There are 15 countries or areas lacking data for two points in time.

- *Total fertility*: Focusing on the 171 countries or areas with two observations and whose most recent data refer to a year between 1995 and 2006, total fertility varies between 0.85 children per woman in Macao, Special Administrative Region of China, in 2004 and 7.3 children per woman in the Democratic Republic of Congo in 1995. Among the 45 developed countries in the group, total fertility varies between 1.2 and 2.0 children per woman, with only two countries having fertility levels outside that range: New Zealand with 2.1 children per woman in 2004 and Albania with 2.6 in 2001. Except for Albania, Belgium, Bosnia and Herzegovina, and the Channel Islands, all developed countries have data for years ranging from 2002 and 2005. In 27 developed countries, fertility declined by between 0.2 and 0.4 children per decade since around 1970. The fastest decline among developed countries occurred in Albania, at 0.8 children per decade. In the 126 developing countries considered, all but 15 experienced a reduction of fertility averaging 0.4 children per decade or more. However, in Guinea-Bissau, Equatorial Guinea and Uganda, fertility hardly changed. According to the unadjusted data presented in this chart, 41 developing countries achieved reductions of fertility averaging one child per decade or more. As a result of rapid fertility declines, total fertility in 66 of the developing countries considered was at or below 3 children per woman in the most recent date considered. Yet 30 countries in sub-Saharan Africa still exhibit a total fertility equal or higher than 5 children per woman for the most recent date available.
- *The mean age at childbearing*: The process of fertility decline brings about changes in the age distribution of childbearing. Usually fertility starts declining when women limit the size of their families by stopping childbearing earlier than their mothers did. Hence, fertility drops at older ages making the mean age at childbearing decrease. When

fertility is already moderately low, a different process may be observed: women postpone childbearing thus reducing fertility at young ages and increasing the mean age at childbearing. Among the 42 developed countries whose recent data refer to 2000 or later years, eight show a decreasing mean age at childbearing and all are countries in transition. Among the rest, 22 exhibit an increase averaging at least half a year per decade. The mean age at childbearing is particularly high in the OECD developed countries. It has surpassed 30 years in eight of them: Denmark, France, Ireland, Italy, the Netherlands, Spain, Sweden and Switzerland. In the 112 developing countries with two observations and recent data dating from 1995 to 2006, the mean age at childbearing has declined in 80 but in just 30 of them has the decline amounted to at least half a year per decade. Armenia has the lowest mean age at childbearing at 25.2 years and the Libyan Arab Jamahiriya the highest, at 33.3 years. Among the 20 developing countries with a mean age at childbearing higher than 30 years, 11 have experienced increases. Overall, the median value of the mean age at childbearing among the developing countries considered has decreased from 29.3 to 28.7 years. For developed countries the median values rose from 27.0 to 28.8 years.

❖ *Adolescent birth rate*: Fertility levels among women aged 15-19 are an important indicator of the status of women, since women who bear children early in life often forego the opportunity to study or find employment away from home. Reducing the adolescent birth rate is one of the objectives included in the drive to achieve the Millennium Development Goals. Among developed countries, the adolescent birth rate is generally low but it varies between 4.9 and 43.0 births per 1000 women aged 15-19. Only three developed countries have an adolescent birth rate above 30: Bulgaria, Romania and the United States of America. In developing countries the range of variation of the adolescent birth rate is considerably larger: from 2.2 in the Republic of Korea to 200.1 in Gambia. The adolescent birth rate is particularly high (above 90 births per 1000 women aged 15-19) in at least 55 developing countries, 33 of which are in Africa, 15 in Latin America and the Caribbean, and 7 in Asia. In 32 developing countries, the adolescent birth rate is already below 30 births per 1000 women aged 15-19. Among the 122 developing countries with data for two points in time, the adolescent birth rate fell in 103. In 31 of them, the adolescent birth rate declined by at least 20 points per decade and in all but two of them the initial level of the adolescent birth rate had been above 90 births per 1000 women aged 15-19.

1. *World Population Prospects: The 2006 Revision, Vol. 1, Comprehensive Tables* (United Nations publication, Sales No. 07.XIII.2).

Table 35.4: Trends in Total Fertility, Age Patterns of Fertility and Timing of Childbearing

Country or area	*Year*	*Total fertility per woman*	*15-19*	*30-34*	*45-49*	*Mean age at child bearing*
	(1)	(2)	(3)	(4)	(5)	(6)
Afghanistan	2001	6.8	151	..	..	..
Australia	2003	1.8	16	113	0	29.9
Australia/New Zealand	2000-2005	1.8	19	112	0	29.7
Austria	2004	1.4	14	77	0	28.8
Bangladesh	2003	3.0	135	83	3	25.5
Bhutan	2000	4.7	62	162	24	29.4
Brazil	2000	2.1	71	71	0	26.1
Canada	2003	1.5	14	94	0	29.3
China	2002	1.4	3	43	0	26.6
China, Hong Kong Special Administrative Region	2005	1.0	4	62	0	29.8
China, Macao Special Administrative Region	2004	0.8	4	54	0	29.7
Democratic People's Republic of Korea	1993	2.2	0	101	1	28.7
Denmark	2004	1.8	6	126	0	30.1
Egypt	2003	3.2	48	129	3	27.9
Finland	2004	1.8	11	111	1	29.9
France	2003	1.9	8	119	1	30.0
Germany	2004	1.4	11	81	0	29.3
India	**2004**	**2.8**	**97**	**66**	**3**	**25.2**
Indonesia	2001	2.6	54	101	5	28.2
Iran	2000	2.2	35	90	4	28.3
Iraq	2000	2.8	17	147	13	30.3
Mexico	2000	3.3	94	119	6	27.3
Myanmar	1999	2.6	29	117	12	30.3
Nepal	2004	3.3	106	92	3	26.3
Nigeria	2002	5.7	126	237	25	29.2
Pakistan	2003	4.0	24	190	19	30.3
Republic of Korea	2004	1.2	2	90	0	29.8
Russian Federation	2004	1.3	28	46	0	26.4
Sri Lanka	1996	2.3	29	111	2	29.6
United Kingdom	2002	1.6	27	90	1	28.7
United States of America	2002	2.0	43	92	0	27.6
Zimbabwe	2004	3.9	101	143	12	28.2

Table Summary

WORLD	2000-2005	2.6	55	95	4	27.4
More developed regions	2000-2005	1.6	24	81	0	28.2
Less developed regions	2000-2005	2.6	47	87	4	27.2
Least developed countries	2000-2005	5.0	130	184	22	28.5

Notes

The data presented in this chart are for countries and areas whose population in 2007 was greater than 100,000. The term **country** refers also to territories or areas, irrespective to their legal status or the delimitation of their frontiers or boundaries.

Countries and areas are grouped geographically into six major areas: Africa; Asia; Europe; Latin America and the Caribbean; Northern America; and Oceania. These major areas are further divided into 21 geographical regions. In addition, for statistical convenience, the regions are classified as belonging to either of two categories: more developed or less developed. The less developed regions include all the regions of Africa, Asia (excluding Japan), and Latin America and the Caribbean, as well as Melanesia, Micronesia and Polynesia. The more developed regions comprise Australia/New Zealand, Europe, Northern America and Japan. Countries in the more developed regions are denominated developed countries and those in the less developed regions are denominated developing countries.

The group of least developed countries currently comprises 50 countries: Afghanistan, Angola, Bangladesh, Benin, Bhutan, Burkina Faso, Burundi, Cambodia, Cape Verde, Central African Republic, Chad, Comoros, Democratic Republic of the Congo, Djibouti, Equatorial Guinea, Eritrea, Ethiopia, Gambia, Guinea, Guinea-Bissau, Haiti, Kiribati, Lao People's Democratic Republic, Lesotho, Liberia, Madagascar, Malawi, Maldives, Mali, Mauritania, Mozambique, Myanmar, Nepal, Niger, Rwanda, Samoa, Sao Tome and Principe, Senegal, Sierra Leone, Solomon Islands, Somalia, Sudan, Timor-Leste, Togo, Tuvalu, Uganda, United Republic of Tanzania, Vanuatu, Yemen and Zambia.

Two dots (..) indicate that data are not available.

An age-specific fertility rate is defined as the annual number of births to women in a particular age group divided by the number of years lived by the women in that age group. It is expressed as number of births per 1000 women in the age group considered.

Adolescent birth rate is the age-specific fertility rate for women aged 15 to 19.

Mean age at childbearing is the average age mothers would have at the birth of their children if women were subject throughout their lives to the age-specific fertility rates observed in a given year.

Total fertility is the average number of live births a woman would have by age 50ifsheweresub-50 if she were subject, throughout her life, to the age-specific fertility rates observed in a given year. Its calculation assumes that there is no mortality or migration. Total fertility is expressed as number of children per woman.

More developed Regions

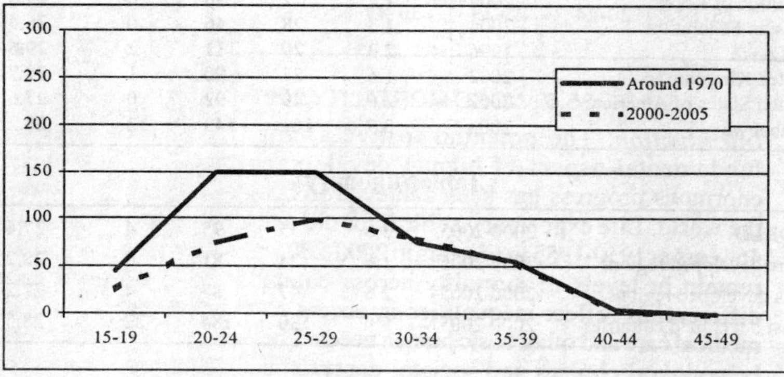

Less Developed Regions
(excluding least developed contries)

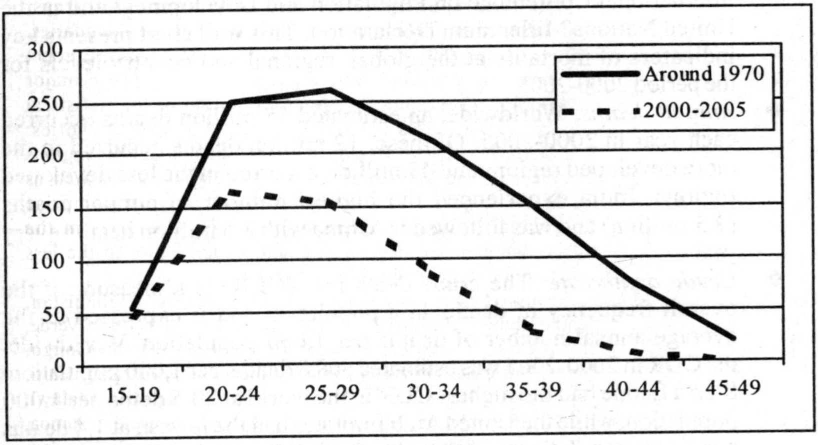

Least Developed Regions

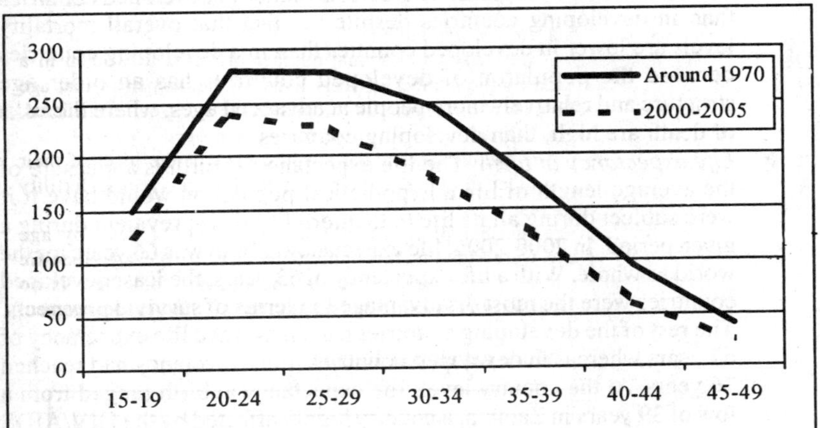

35.5. WORD MORTALITY 2007

❖ *Introduction*: The potential to live a long and healthy life is a fundamental aspect of human development. In recent decades, enormous progress has been achieved in health and survival around the world. Life expectancy at birth for the world population rose from 46 years in 1950-1955 to 66 years in 2000-2005. However, wide disparities remain in levels of mortality across countries and regions. These differentials reflect inequalities in access to food, water, sanitation, medical care and other basic human needs. They also reflect risk factors, behavioural choices and societal contexts that affect the survival of individuals. the reduction of mortality, particularly child and maternal mortality, is a core target in the internationally agreed development goals, such as those contained in the Programme of Action of the International Conference on Population and Development and in the United Nations Millennium Declaration. This wall chart presents key indicators of mortality at the global, regional and country levels for the period 2000-2005.

- *Annual deaths*: Worldwide, an estimated 55 million deaths occurred each year in 2000-2005. Of these, 12 million deaths occurred in the more developed regions and 43 million occurred in the less developed regions. India experienced the highest number of annual deaths (9.5 million) and was followed by China with 8.6 million deaths every year.
- *Crude death rate*: The crude death rate (CDR) is a measure of the overall frequency of deaths in a population and is expressed as the average annual number of deaths per 1,000 population. Worldwide, the CDR in 2000-2005 was estimated at 8.8 deaths per 1,000 population. Sierra Leone had the highest CDR in the world at 23.5 deths per 1,000 population, while the United Arab Emirates had the lowest, at 1.4 deaths per 1,000 population, compared to 8.4 deaths per 1,000 population in the less developed regions. The CDR is higher in developed countries than in developing countries despite the fact that overall mortality levels are lower in developed counties than in a developing countries because the populaton of developed countries has an older age structure and relatively more people at advanced ages, where the risks of death are high, than developing countries.
- *Life expectancy at birth*: The life expectancy at birth is a measure of the average length of life a hypothetical population would have it if were subject during all its life to themortality risks prevalent during a given period. In 2000-2005, life expectancy at birth was 66 years for the world as whole. With a life expectancy of 53 years, the least developed countries were the most disadvantaged in terms of survival prospects. The rest of the developing countries had an average life expectancy of 67 years whereas in developed countries, life expectancy had reached 76 years. At the country level, life expectancy at birth ranged from a low of 39 years in Zambia, a country highly affected by the HIV/AIDS epidemic, to a high of 82 years in Japan. In most countries, women have higher life expectancy at birth than men. At the world level, average female life expectancy was 68 years compared to 64 years compared to 64 years for males in 2000-2005.
- *Infant and under-five mortality*: The United Nations Millennium Declaration identified the reduction of child mortality as a critical challenge for the twenty-first century. Every year millions of young children die of preventable causes. Mortality in childhood is highest in the least developed countries, where infant mortality averaged 95 deaths per 1,000 live births in 2000-2005. In the least developed countries, 153 children out of every 1,000 born alive were expected to die before age five over that period. Among the world's major areas,

Africa had the highest level of under-five mortality in 2000-2005, 154 deaths per 1,000 births, and has experienced a slower decline in child mortality than other developing regions. The survival chances of young children reflect major inequalities among countries in terms of health and development. Under-five mortality was highest in Sierra Leone, Where 290 children out of every 1,000 born alive died before age 5 in 2000-2005. In sharp contrast, in countries with lowest under-five mortality-Japan, Iceland, Sweden and Singapore–only 4 children out of every 1,000 born alive died before their fifth birthday.

- *Survival probabilities*: Mortality across different parts of the age range can be characterized by the probability of survival between selected ages, expressed per 1,000 individuals alive at the first age. The probability of survival from birth to age 15 expresses the likelihood of surviving through the vulnerable period of childhood. In Western Europe, 993 children out of every 1,000 born alive would survive to age 15 to age 60 reflects the level of mortality among adults of working age. In the Russian Federation, the probability of surviving from birth to age 15 is relatively high (974 per 1,000) while that of surviving from age 15 to age 60 is remarkably low (694 per 1,000). For developed countries as a whole, the probability of surviving from age 15 to 60 was 863 per 1,000 in 2000-2005, while that for developing countries was 797 per 1,000. The probability of surviving through adulthood was particularly low in countries highly affected by the HIV/AIDS epidemic because the disease afflicts adults disproportionately. In Zimbabwe, for instane, the probability of surviving from age 15 to 60 in 2000-2005 was 230 per 1,000. The probability of survival from birth to age 60 reflects the cumulative impact of the risks of death from birth to age 60. In countries with low mortality, the great majority of people survive to their sixtieth birthday In Iceland, where the probability of survival to age 60 was highest, 941 out of every 1,000 children born alive would reach age 60 given the mortality risks prevalent during 2000-2005. In contrast, in Sub-Saharan Africa the probability of survival to age 60 was a low 460 per 1,000.
- *Distribution of deaths by cause*: As countries undergo the transition from high to low mortality, they experience a shift in the major causes of death. When mortality is high, large proportions of deaths are caused by communicable diseases, as well as by maternal, perinatal and nutritional causes (collectively called Group I causes), while lower percentages of deaths are caused by non-communicable diseases, which include cardiovascular diseases and cancers (collectively called Group II causes). In countries where mortality has fallen to low levels, the majority of deaths occur because of Group II causes. The change in the distribution of causes of death is striking when comparing the least developed countries with the developed countries. In the least developed countries, where mortality remains high, 67 per cent of deaths were the result of Group I cases in 2002, while 26 per cent were from Group II causes. In contrast, in developed countries, 6 per cent of

deaths were due to Group I causes and 86 per cent to Group II causes. A third major group of causes includes injuries from accidents, homicide or suicide. This group caused 9 per cent of deaths worldwide, with its share ranging from 2 per cent to 24 per cent among countries.

- *HIV prevalence*: The Millennium Declaration called for halting and reversing the spread of HIV by 2015. Despite recent downward revisions of HIV prevalence estimates in a number of countries, the number of people living with HIV continues to increase in all regions of the world. In 2007, over 33 million people around the world were living with HIV, including nearly 31 million people aged 15 or over and more than two million children under age 15. Adult HIV prevalence, measured s the percentage of HIV-Positive persons among those aged 15 to 49, varied widely across regions and countries. At the end of 2005, Southern Africa had the highest HIV prevalence of any world region, with 22 per cent of adults infected. Sub-Saharan Africa as a whole had an adult HIV prevalence of 6 per cent. Out side of Africa, the region with the highest HIV prevalence was the Caribbean (1.6 per cent.).
- *AIDS deaths*: The annual of deaths caused by AIDS increased steadily throughout the 1990s and until 2005. The most recent estimates from UNAIDS indicate that AIDS caused 2.1 million deaths in 2007, a slight decline since 2005 that is partly attributable to the scaling up of antiretroviral treatment services. More than three-quarters of AIDS deaths in 2007 occurred in sub-Saharan Africa. AIDS remains a major cause of death worldwide and is the leading cause of death in sub-Saharan Africa, where the provision of treatment services will remain an immense challenge in coming years.
- *Maternal mortality*: The Millenium Declaration urged the international community to strive for a dramatic reduction in maternal mortality. The World Health Organization defines maternal death as "the death of a woman while pregnant or within 42 days of termination of pregnancy, irrespective of the duration and site of the pregnancy, from any cause related to or aggravated by the pregnancy or its management but not from accidental or incidental causes" (WHO and others, 2007; see the source of column (16) for a full reference). The level of maternal mortality is usually expressed using the maternal mortality ratio MMR, defined as the number of maternal deaths per 100,000 live births. In 2005, an estimated 536 thousand women worldwide died of maternal causes, resulting in a MMR of 400 maternal deaths per 100, 000 live births. In developing countries as a whole, the MMR was estimated at 450 maternal deaths per 100, 000 live births, while in developed countries it averaged 11 maternal deaths per 100, 000 live births. Mothers in the least developed countries faced the highest risk of death, with 870 maternal deaths occurring for every 100,000 live births. Efforts to reduce maternal mortality must be targeted to these most disadvantaged populations.

Table 35.5: World Mortality 2007

Country of area	*Annual number of deaths (thousands)*	*Crude death rate (per 1,000)*	*Infant mortality (deaths per 1,000 live births)*	*HIV prevalence (among adults aged 15-49 as percentage)*	*AIDS deaths (thousands)*	*Maternal mortality ratio (maternal deaths per 100,000 live births)*
	2000-2005			2005		
(1)	(2)	(3)	(4)	(5)	(6)	(7)
Afghanistan	496	21.6	168	<0.1	<0.1	1 800
Australia	135	6.8	51	0.1	<0.5	4
Austria	78	9.5	5	0.3	<0.1	4
Bangladesh	1 200	8.2	61	<0.1	<0.5	570
Bhutan	5	7.8	53	<0.1	<0.1	440
Brazil	1 143	6.3	27	0.5	14	110
Canada	227	7.2	5	0.3	<1	7
China	8 586	6.6	26	0.1	31	45
Korea	217	9.3	50	—	—	370
Denmark	57	10.7	5	0.2	<0.1	3
Egypt	409	5.9	36	<0.1	<0.5	130
Finland	50	9.5	4	0.1	<0.1	7
France	551	9.2	4	0.4	2	8
Germany	846	10.3	4	0.1	<1	4
India	**9 5.5**	**8.7**	62	**0.4**	**270**	**450**
Indonesia	1 449	6.6	34	0.1	6	420
Iran	376	5.5	37	0.2	2	140
Iraq	280	10.6	94	—	—	300
Mexico	481	4.7	21	0.3	6	60
Myanmar	480	10.2	75	1.3	37	380
Nepal	224	8.7	64	0.5	5	830
Nigeria	2 327	17.5	116	3.9	220	1100
Pakistan	1 161	7.7	75	0.1	3	320
Republic of Korea	258	5.4	5	<0.1	<0.5	14
Russian Federation	2 318	15.9	17	101	—	28
Sri Lanka	139	7.3	12	<0.1	<0.5	58
Switzerland	60	8.1	4	0.4	<0.1	5
United Arab Emirates	5	1.4	9	—	—	37
United States of America	2 425	8.3	7	0.6	16	11
Zimbabwe	265	20.5	64	20.1	180	880

Table Summary

World	55 368	8.8	54	0.8	2 100	400
More developed regions	12 330	10.2	8	0.6	55	11
Less developed regions	43 038	8.4	59	1.1	2 540	450
Least developed countries	9 636	13.3	95	2.9	1 044	870
Other less developed countries	33 401	7.6	49	0.8	1 496	310

- *A note on the data*: The quality of data available for estimating mortality varies widely from country to country. Data for countries with high-quality vital registration systems are the most reliable. For other countries, estimates of overall mortality are most often based on data gathered via special questions on mortality included in sample surveys or populaton censuses. Such sources can produce robust estimates of child mortality but are less successful in producing adequate estimates of adult mortality. Therefore, estimates for these countries are frequently based on model mortality schedules that permit extrapolating the estimate including HIV/AIDS and maternal causes, are less commonly available than data on overall morality and reported causes of death re more prone to error than reports on the occurrence of deaths even in counties with good vital registration coverage. Readers are encouraged to consult the references for the data in columns (11) to (16) for detailed documentation on data quality and the uncertainty associated with the estimates of deaths by causes, prevalence of HIV, deaths causes by AIDS, and maternal mortality presented in this chart.

Definitions and Sources

Annual number of deaths: *Source:* World Population Prospects: The 2006 Revision, CD-ROM Edition-Extended Dataset in Excel and ASCII formats, *United Nations publication, Sales No. E.07.XIII.7, 2007.*

Crude death rate: *Number of death over a given period divided by the person-years lived by the population over that period. It is expressed as number of deaths per 1,000 population. Source:* World Population Prospects: The 2006 Revision, CD-ROM Edition-Extended Dataset in Excel and ASCII formats, United Nations Publications, Sales No. E.07.XIII. 7, 2007.

Life expectancy at birth: *The average number of years of life expected by a hypothetical cohort of individuals who would be subject during all their lives to the mortality rates of a given period. It is expressed in years. Source:* World Population Prospects: The 2006 Revision. CD-ROM Edition-Extended Dataset in Excel and ASCII formats. *United Nations publication, Sales No. E.07.XIII.7,2007.*

Infant mortality: *Probability of dying between birth and exact age 1. It is expressed as deaths per 1,000 live births. Source:* World Population Prospects: The 2006 Revision, CD-ROM Edition-Extended Dataset in Excel and ASCII formats, United Nations publication, *Sales No. E.07.XIII.7, 2007.*

Under-five morality: *Probability of dying between birth and exact age 5. It is expressed as deaths per 1,000 live birth. Source:* World Population Prospects: The 2006 Revision. CD-ROM Edition-Extended Dataset in Excel and ASCII formats, *United Nations publication, Sales No. E.07.XIII, 2007.*

Survival probability: *The probability that, given the morality conditions of the given year of period, an individual alive at exact age x would survive to age x+n; here, the probability of survival from birth to exact age 15 (column 8), from exact age 15 to exact age 60 (column 9), and from birth to exact age 60 (column 10). It is expressed as deaths per 1,000 persons living at exact age 15 (column 9). Source:* World Population Prospects: The 2006 Revision. *CD-ROM Edition-Extended* Dataset in Excel and ASCII formats, *Unites Nations publication, Sales No. E.07.XIII.7,2007.*

Percentage of deaths by cause: *Group I refers to deaths from communicable, maternal, perinatal and nutritional conditions; Group II refers to deaths from no communicable diseases; and Group III refers to deaths from injuries. Aggregate values for proportion of deaths by cause exclude areas that are not Member States of the WHO. Source:* Death and DALY Estimates for 2002 by Cause for WHO Member States. World Health Organization, *2004. Data available online at* http:/ www.who.int/entity/healthinfo/statistics/bodgbddeathdalyestimates.xls.

HIV prevalence: The percentage of adults aged 15 to 49 who were living with HIV at the end of 2005. Source for the aggregate values for prevalence: numerators are obtained from UNAIDS estimates referring to the end of 2005; denominators are obtained from World Population Prospects: The *2004 Revision,* United Nations Publication, Sales No.E.05.XIII.6. Source for HIV prevalence data by country: obtained from *2006 Report on the Global HIV/AIDS Epidemic,* UNAIDS publication, Sales No. UNAIDS/06.13E, 2006. Data available online at *http://www.unaids.org/en/HIV_data/ 2006GlobalReport/defalut.asp.* Estimates for the world total and India are from 2007 AIDS Epidemic Update, UNAIDS publication, Sales No. UNAIDS/07.27E.

Maternal mortality ratio: The number of maternal deaths during a given time period per 100,000 live births during the same time-period. A maternal death is defined as the death of a woman while pregnant or within 42 days of termination of pregnancy, irrespective of the duration and site of the pregnancy, from any cause related to or aggravated by the pregnancy or its management but not from accidental or incidental causes. Source: *Maternal morality in 2005,* World Health Organization, UNICEF, UNFPA and The World Bank, 2007, Geneva: WHO. Data available online at *http:/ /www.who.int/reproductive health/publications/materanl_mortality_2005/ index.html.*

Source: '*Wall Charts 2007*'. Department of Economic and Social Affairs, United Nations, 2008.

36

Practical Work

Charts, Curves, Graphs and Maps Related to Population Education

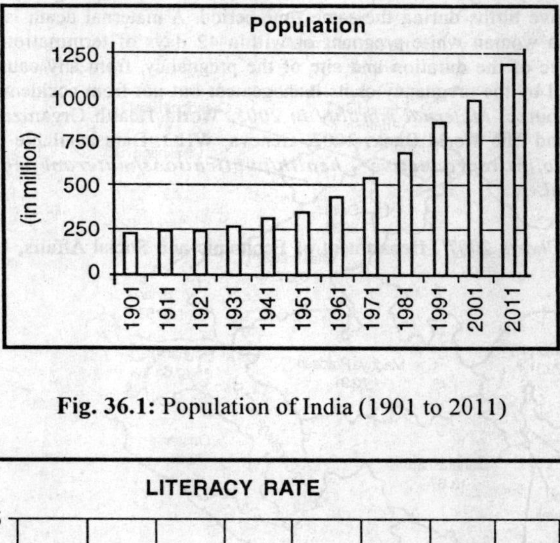

Fig. 36.1: Population of India (1901 to 2011)

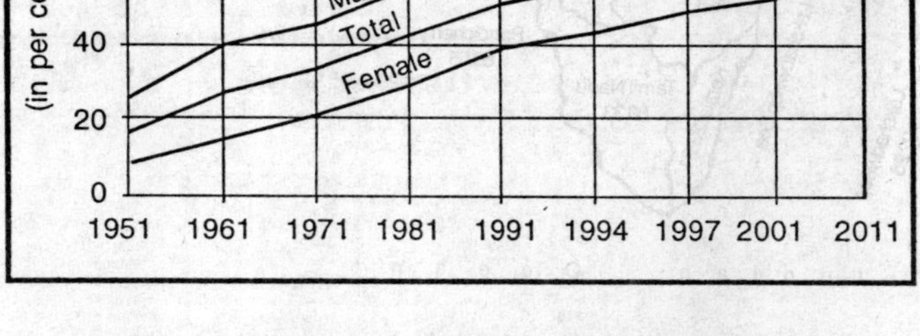

Fig. 36.2: Literate Population in India (1951 to 2011)

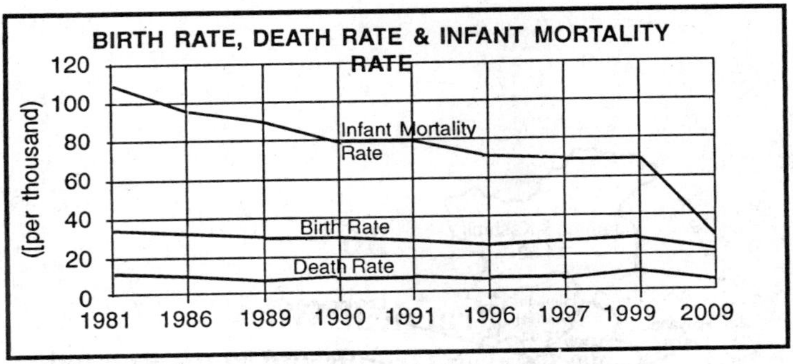

Fig. 36.3: Birth Rate, Death Rate and Infant Mortality Rate in India

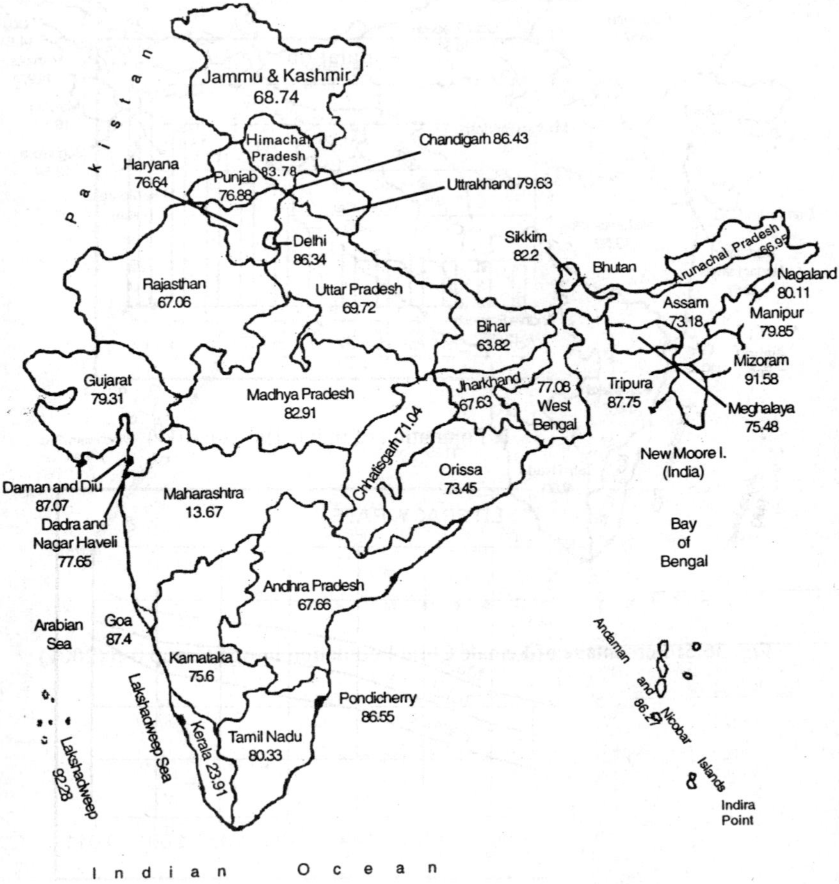

Fig. 36.4: State and UT-wiseLiteracy Rate – 2001-2011

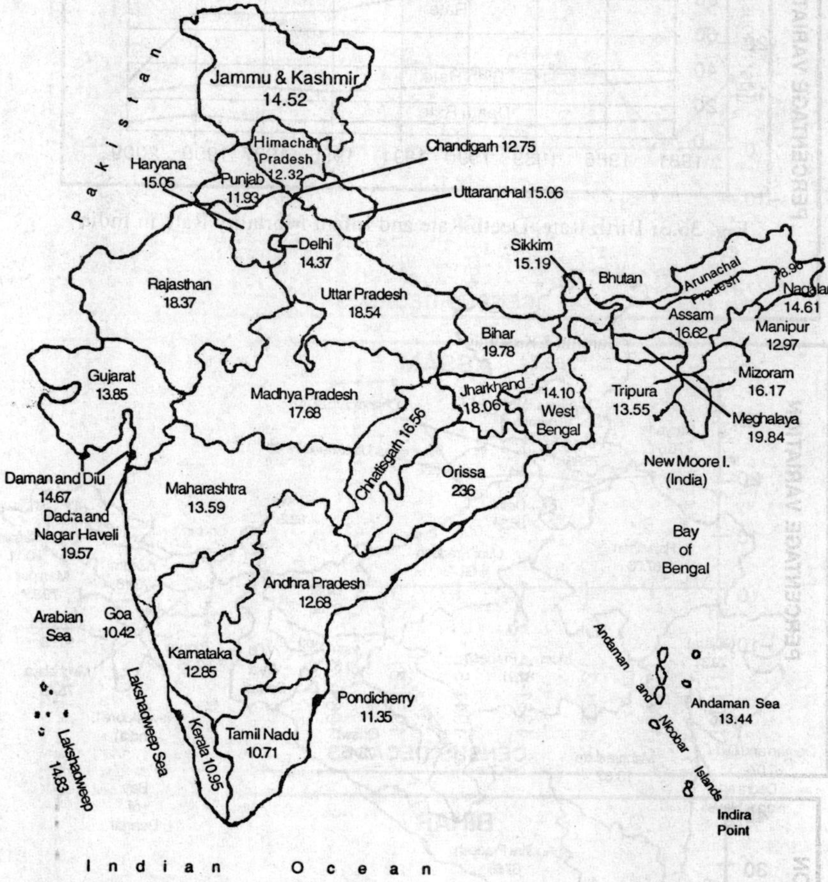

Fig. 36.5: Percentage of Female Child Population in Age Group 0-6 (2001)

TRENDS IN DECADAL GROWTH RATE OF POPULATION

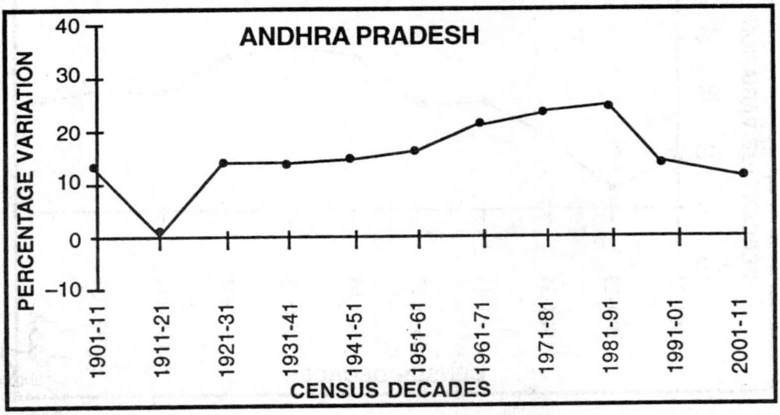

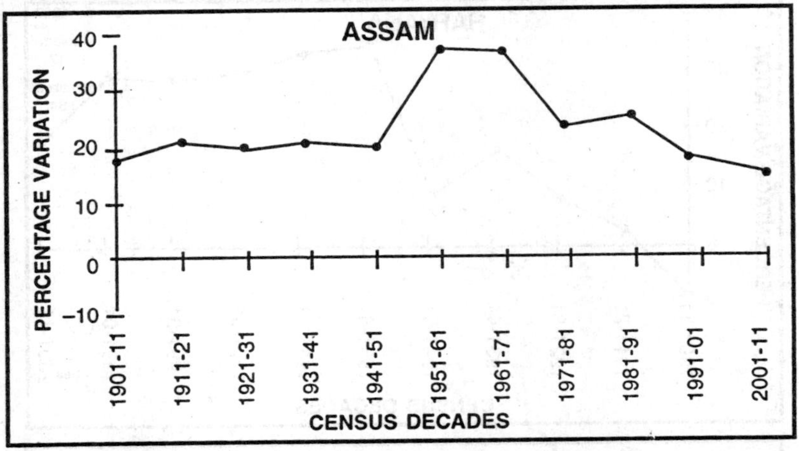

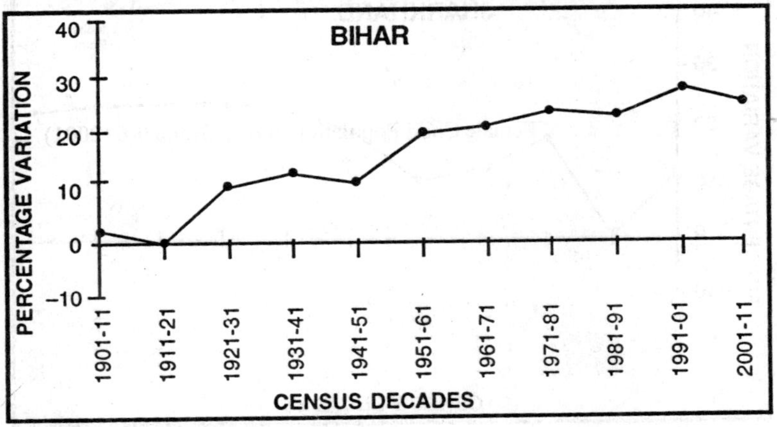

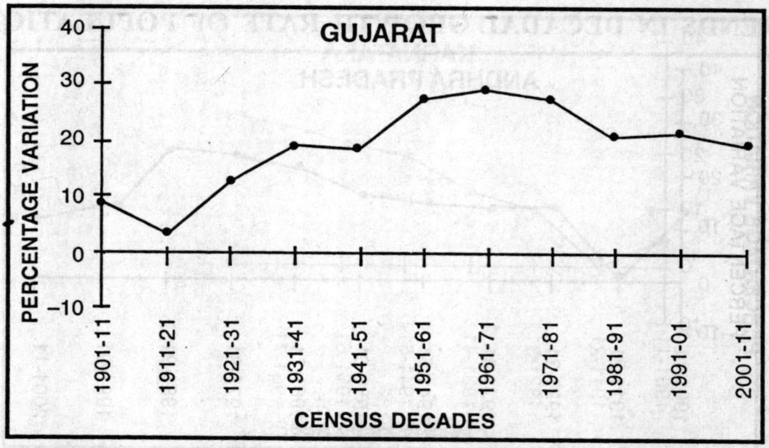
GUJARAT
PERCENTAGE VARIATION
40
30
20
10
0
–10
1901-11
1911-21
1921-31
1931-41
1941-51
1951-61
1961-71
1971-81
1981-91
1991-01
2001-11
CENSUS DECADES

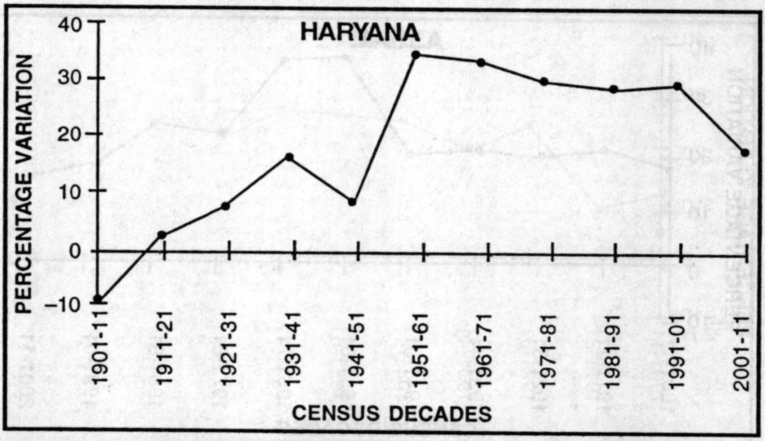
HARYANA
PERCENTAGE VARIATION
40
30
20
10
0
–10
1901-11
1911-21
1921-31
1931-41
1941-51
1951-61
1961-71
1971-81
1981-91
1991-01
2001-11
CENSUS DECADES

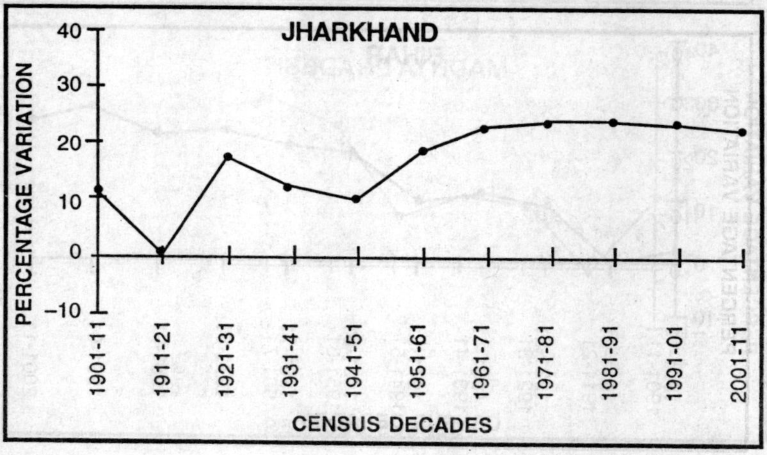
JHARKHAND
PERCENTAGE VARIATION
40
30
20
10
0
–10
1901-11
1911-21
1921-31
1931-41
1941-51
1951-61
1961-71
1971-81
1981-91
1991-01
2001-11
CENSUS DECADES

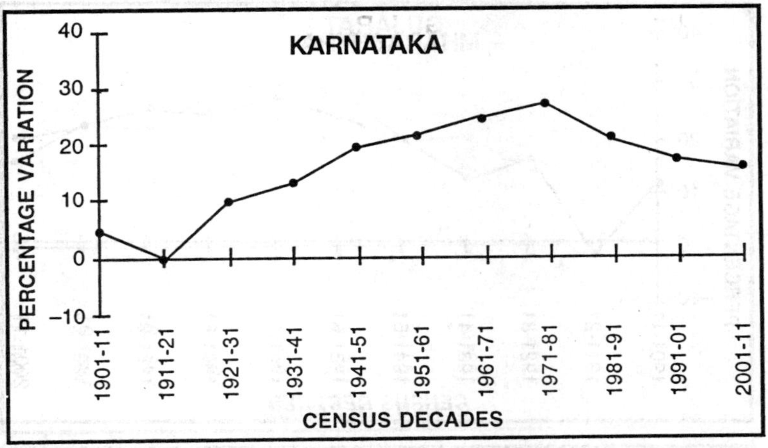
KARNATAKA
PERCENTAGE VARIATION
40
30
20
10
0
-10
1901-11
1911-21
1921-31
1931-41
1941-51
1951-61
1961-71
1971-81
1981-91
1991-01
2001-11
CENSUS DECADES

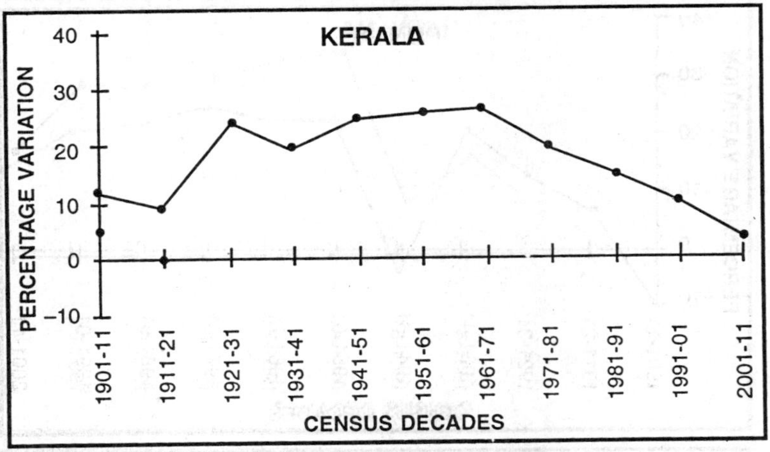
KERALA
PERCENTAGE VARIATION
40
30
20
10
0
-10
1901-11
1911-21
1921-31
1931-41
1941-51
1951-61
1961-71
1971-81
1981-91
1991-01
2001-11
CENSUS DECADES

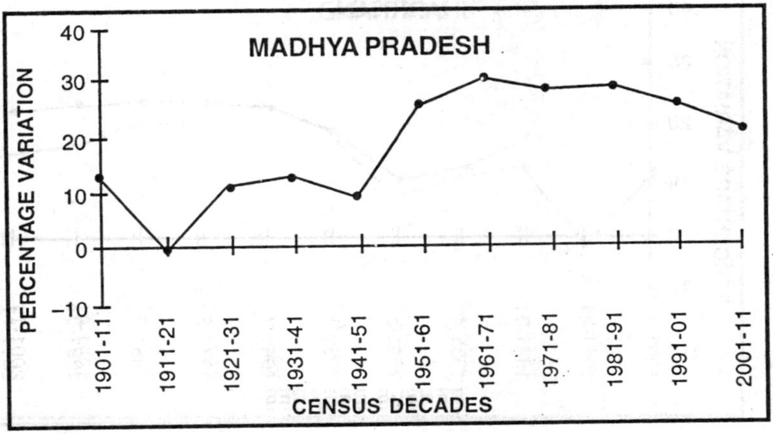
MADHYA PRADESH
PERCENTAGE VARIATION
40
30
20
10
0
-10
1901-11
1911-21
1921-31
1931-41
1941-51
1951-61
1961-71
1971-81
1981-91
1991-01
2001-11
CENSUS DECADES

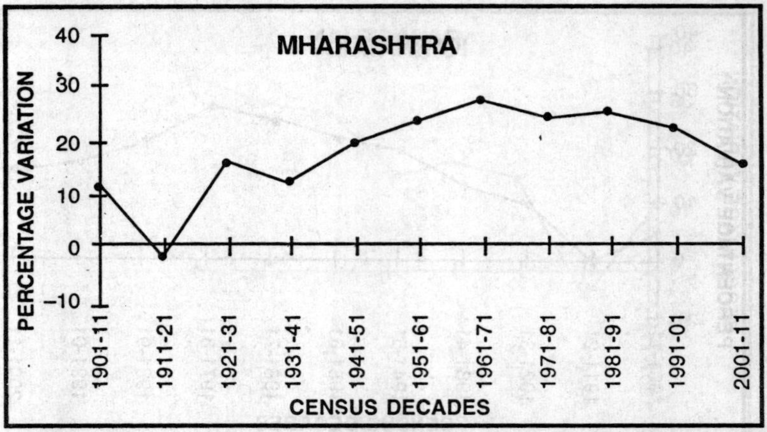
MHARASHTRA
PERCENTAGE VARIATION
40
30
20
10
0
−10
1901-11
1911-21
1921-31
1931-41
1941-51
1951-61
1961-71
1971-81
1981-91
1991-01
2001-11
CENSUS DECADES

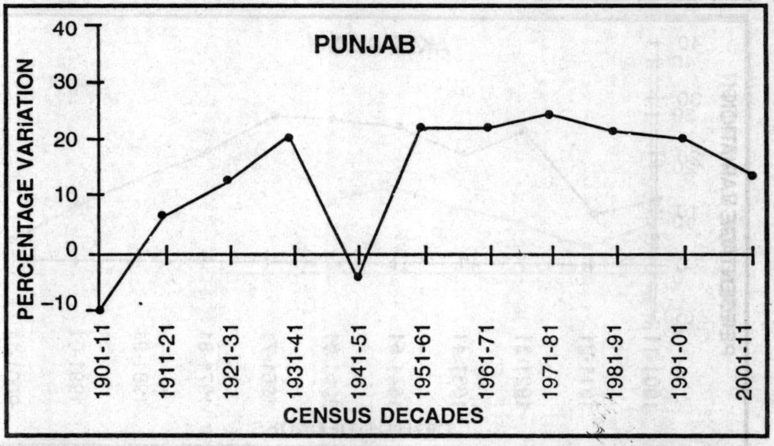
PUNJAB
PERCENTAGE VARIATION
40
30
20
10
0
−10
1901-11
1911-21
1921-31
1931-41
1941-51
1951-61
1961-71
1971-81
1981-91
1991-01
2001-11
CENSUS DECADES

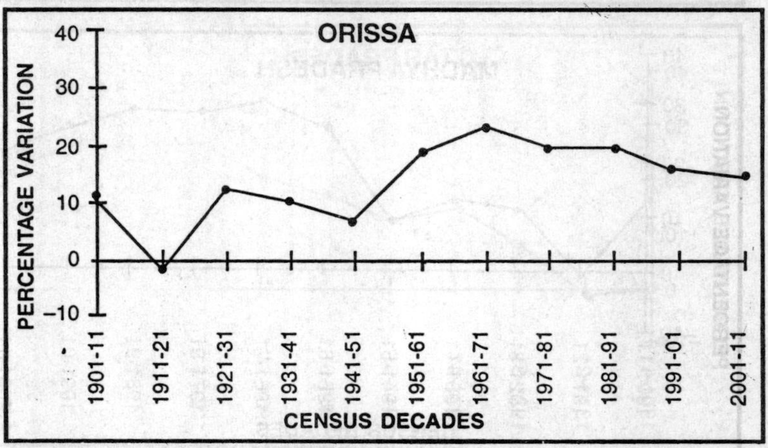
ORISSA
PERCENTAGE VARIATION
40
30
20
10
0
−10
1901-11
1911-21
1921-31
1931-41
1941-51
1951-61
1961-71
1971-81
1981-91
1991-01
2001-11
CENSUS DECADES

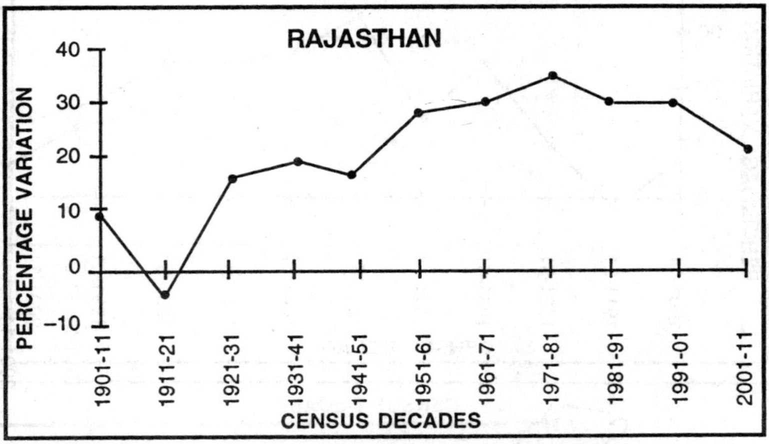
RAJASTHAN
PERCENTAGE VARIATION
40
30
20
10
0
–10
1901-11
1911-21
1921-31
1931-41
1941-51
1951-61
1961-71
1971-81
1981-91
1991-01
2001-11
CENSUS DECADES

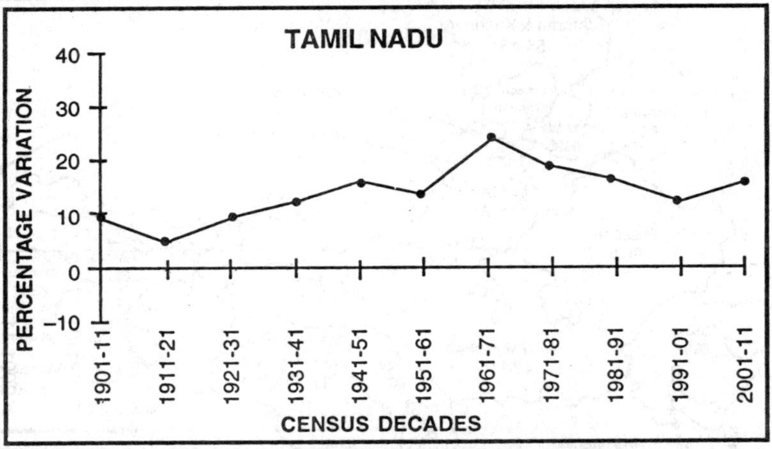
TAMIL NADU
PERCENTAGE VARIATION
40
30
20
10
0
–10
1901-11
1911-21
1921-31
1931-41
1941-51
1951-61
1961-71
1971-81
1981-91
1991-01
2001-11
CENSUS DECADES

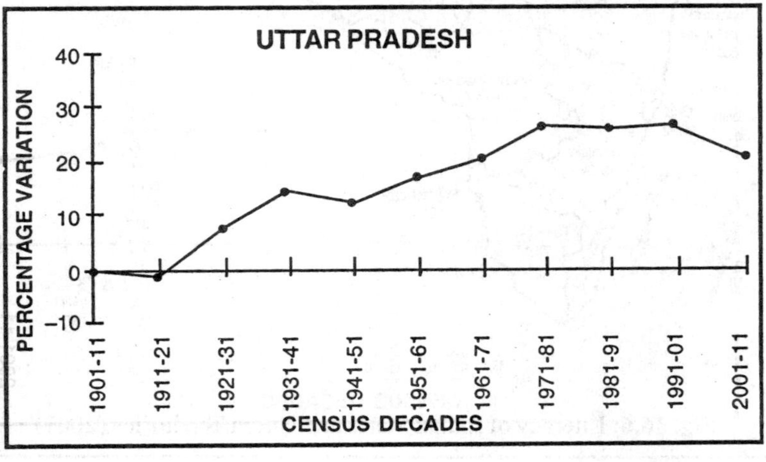
UTTAR PRADESH
PERCENTAGE VARIATION
40
30
20
10
0
–10
1901-11
1911-21
1921-31
1931-41
1941-51
1951-61
1961-71
1971-81
1981-91
1991-01
2001-11
CENSUS DECADES

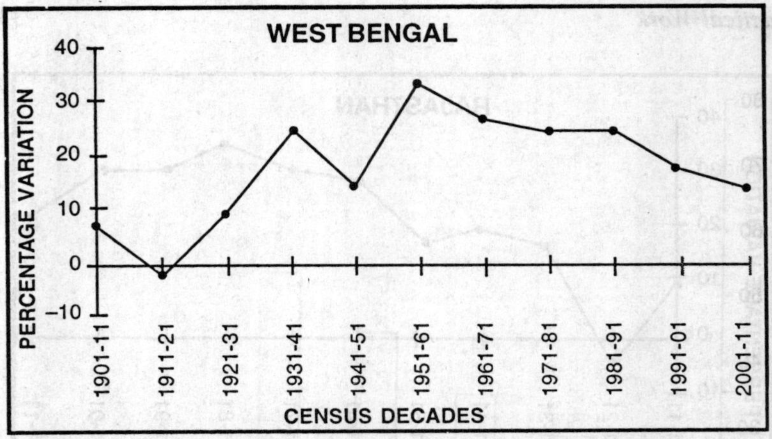

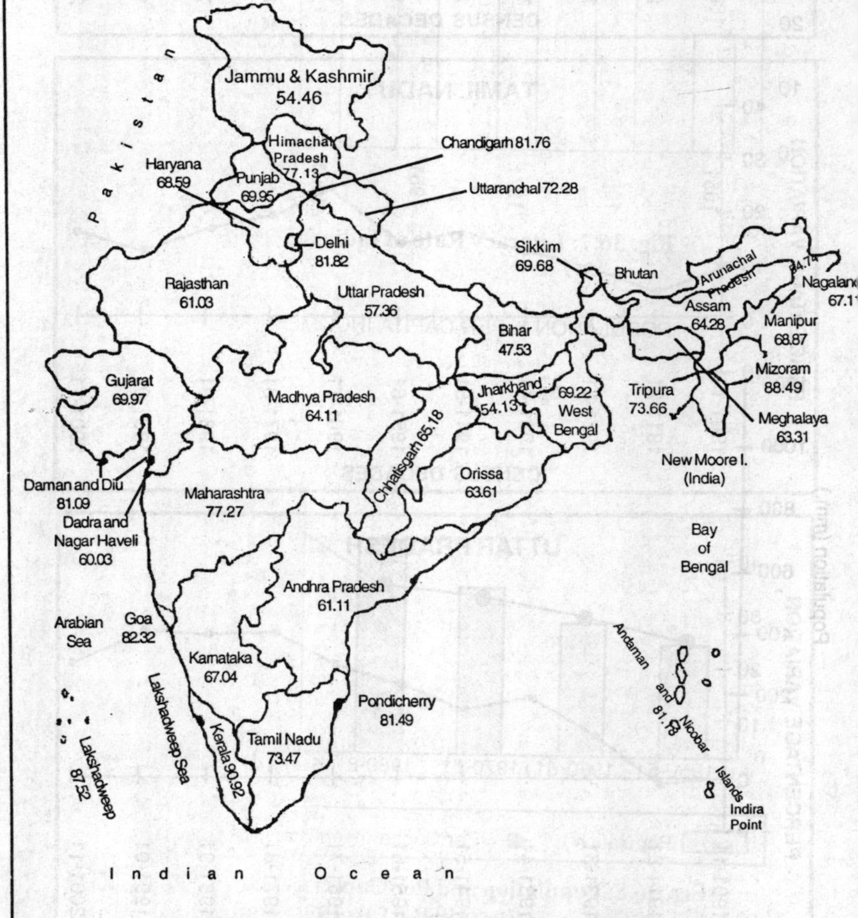

Fig. 36.6: Literacy of Indian States and Union Territories (2001)

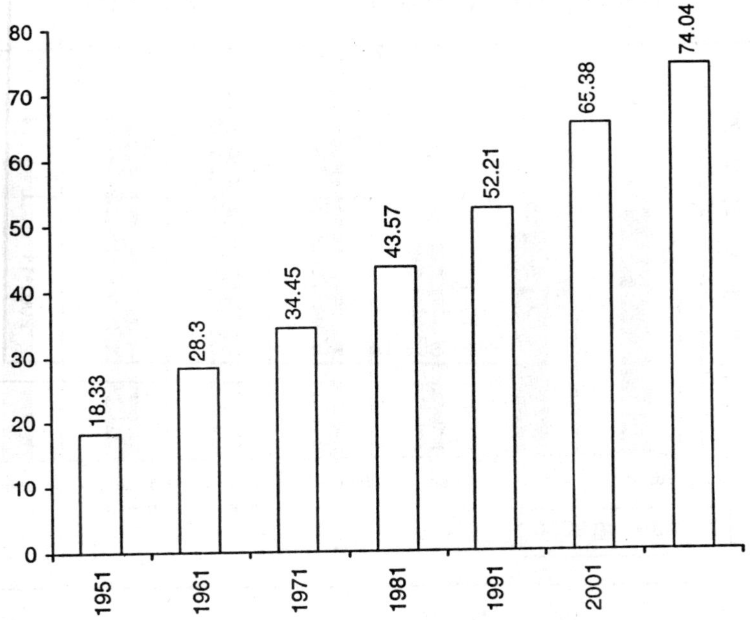

Fig. 36.7: Literacy Rate of India (1951-2011)

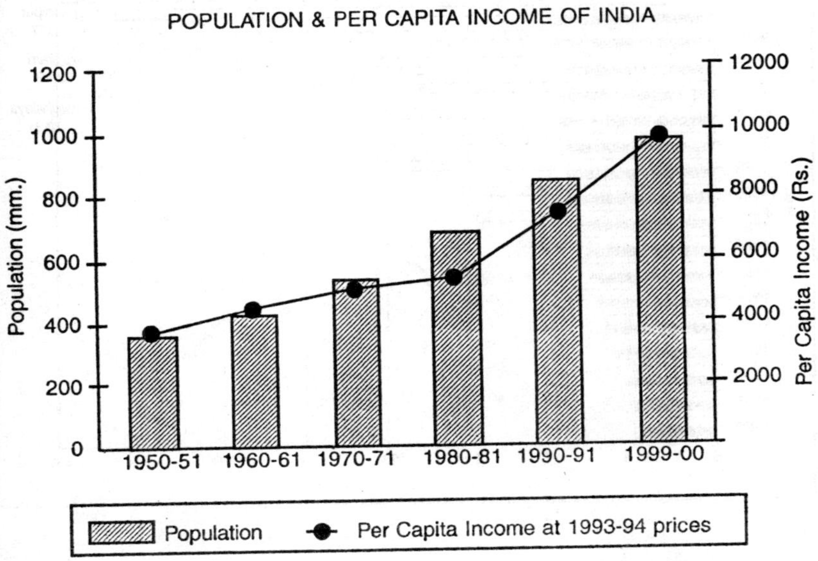

Fig. 36.8: Population and Per Capita Income of India (1950-51 to 1999-2000)

Percentage of Population Living Areas, 1999 and 2030

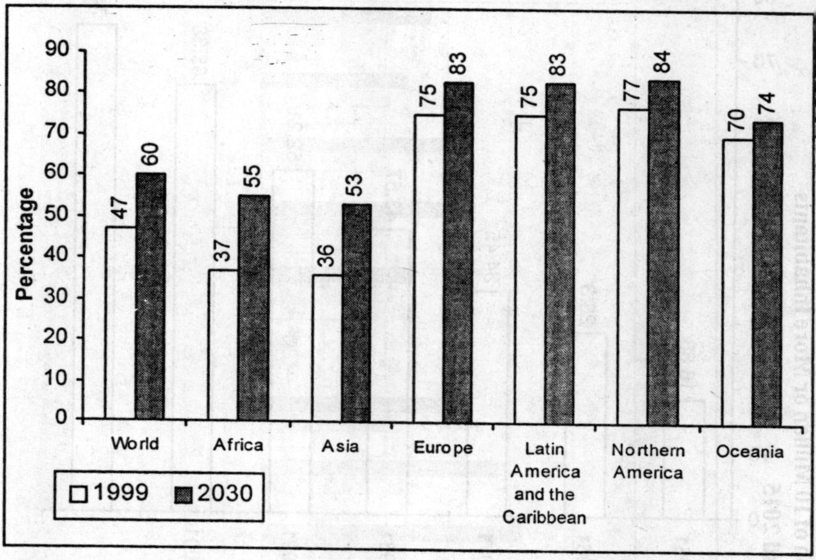

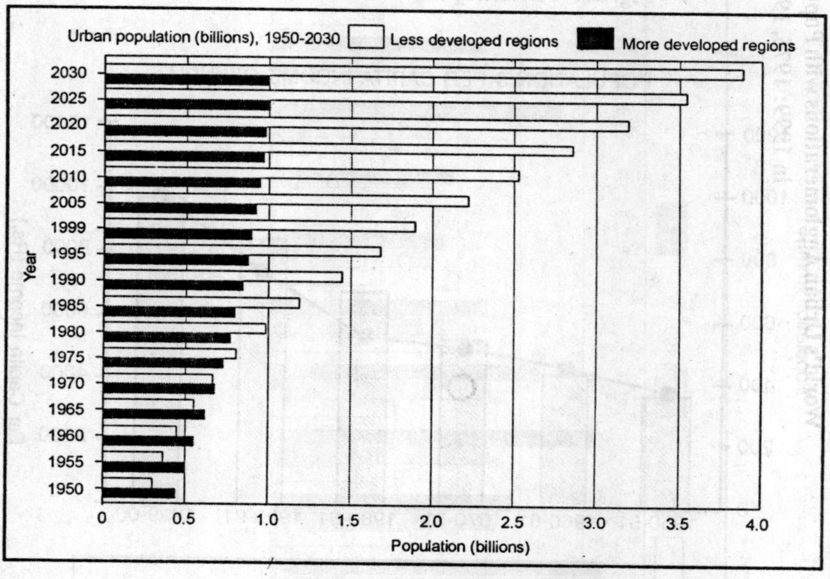

World's Urban Agglomerations with Population of 10 Million or More Inhabitants in 1999: 1975, 1999 and 2015

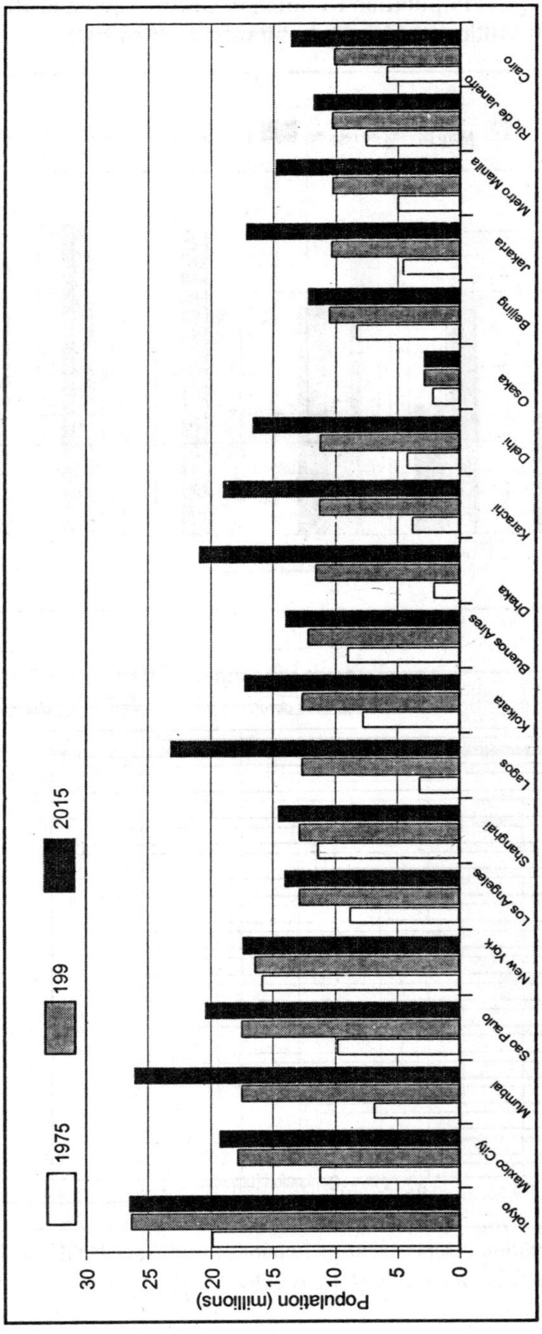

Percentage of Population Residing in Urban Agglomerations of 10 Million or More Inhabitants: 1975 to 2015

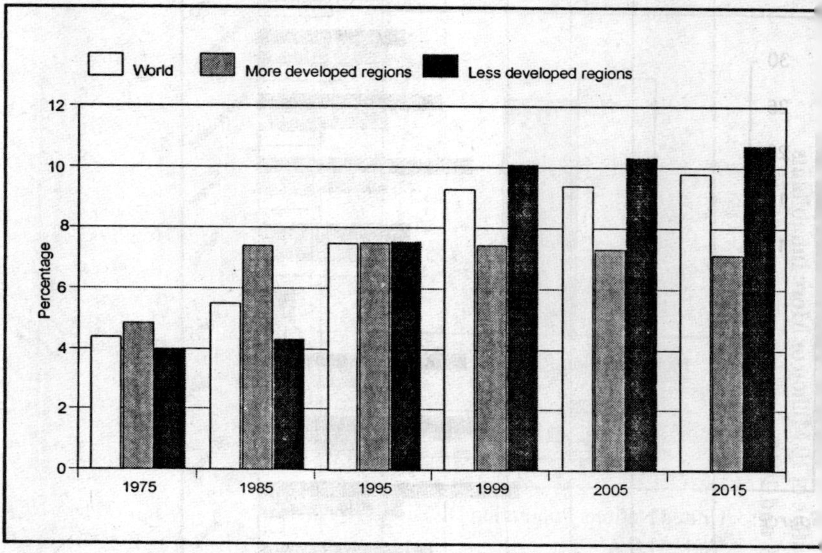

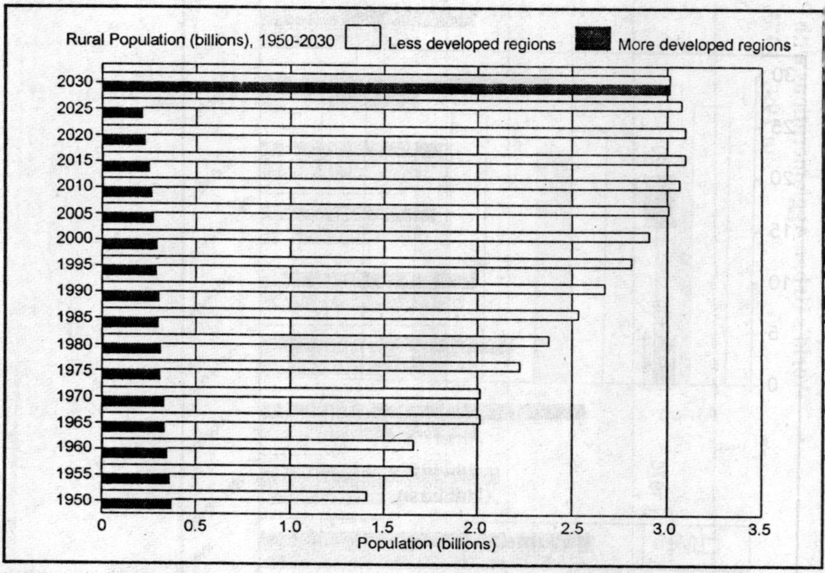

Source: United Nations Department of Economic and Social Affairs: Population Division. '*Urban and Rural Areas 1999*'.

Average Mean Age at Marriage (SMAM), More Developed and Less Developed Regions

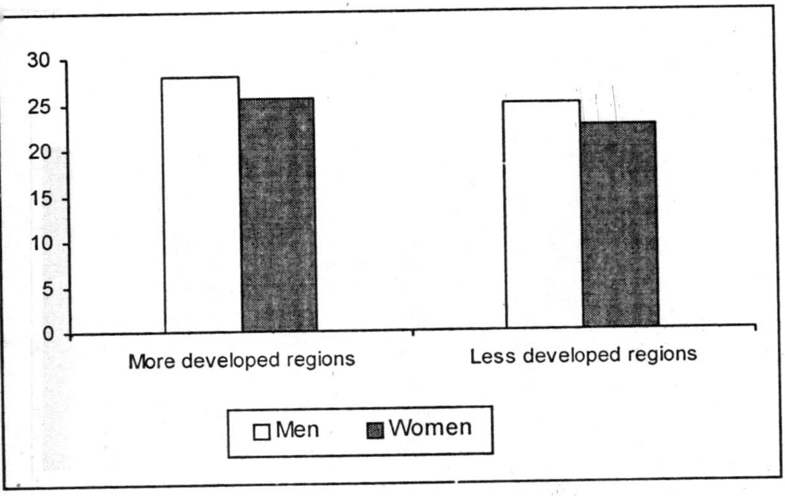

Source: United Nations Population Division. '*World Marriage Patterns 2000*'. New York, U.S.A.

Average Mean Age at Marriage (SMAM), Major Areas

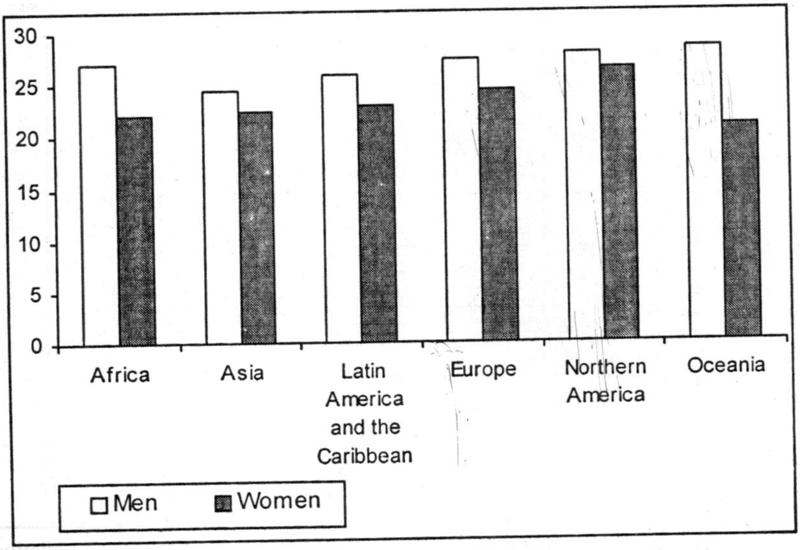

SMAM: Singulated Mean Age at Marriage or Average Age at the First Marriage.